Protest, Property Rights, and the Law in British Columbia

LAW AND SOCIETY
Law and Society Series
W. Wesley Pue, Founding Editor

We pay tribute to the late Wes Pue, under whose broad vision, extraordinary leadership, and unwavering commitment to socio-legal studies our Law and Society Series was established and rose to prominence.

The Law and Society Series explores law as a socially embedded phenomenon. It is premised on the understanding that the conventional division of law from society creates false dichotomies in thinking, scholarship, educational practice, and social life. Books in the series treat law and society as mutually constitutive and seek to bridge scholarship emerging from interdisciplinary engagement of law with disciplines such as politics, social theory, history, political economy, and gender studies.

Recent books in the series:

Alan Hanna, *Indigenous Law in Context: Tŝilhqot'in Dechen Ts'edilhtan in the Governance of Water* (2026)

Eric M. Adams and Jordan Stranger-Ross, *Challenging Exile: Japanese Canadians and the Wartime Constitution* (2025)

Qiaoling He, *Greyscale Legality: The Diverse Landscape of Intellectual Property Law Enforcement in China* (2025)

Laszlo Sarkany, *The Independence of the Prosecutor: Controversy in the Creation of the International Criminal Court* (2024)

Adam Dodek, *Heenan Blaikie: The Making and Unmaking of a Great Canadian Law Firm* (2024)

John W. Burchill, Richard Jochelson, Akwasi Owusu-Bempah, and Terry Skolnik, *Ancillary Police Powers in Canada: A Critical Reassessment* (2024)

James B. Kelly, *Constraining the Court: Judicial Power and Policy Implementation in the Charter Era* (2024)

Howard Kislowicz, Richard J. Moon, and Kerri Anne Froc, eds., *Canada's Surprising Constitution: Unexpected Interpretations of the* Constitution Act, 1982 (2024)

Mandi Gray, *Suing for Silence: Sexual Violence and Defamation Law* (2024)

Azar Masoumi, *Refugees Are (Not) Welcome Here: The Paradox of Protection in Canada* (2023)

Jonathan Swainger, *The Notorious Georges: Crime and Community in British Columbia's Northern Interior, 1909–25* (2023)

For a complete list of the titles in the series, see the UBC Press website, www.ubcpress.ca.

PROTEST, PROPERTY RIGHTS, AND THE LAW IN BRITISH COLUMBIA

Benjamin Isitt

UBCPress · Vancouver

Printed in Canada, this book is made of FSC-certified and recycled (forest-based) material. The FSC-certified materials meet FSC's standards for responsible forestry, and recycled materials are used instead of virgin forest materials. www.fsc.org.

UBC Press is an eBOUND Digital Certified publisher. The epub version of this book meets stringent accessibility standards, ensuring it is available to people with diverse needs.

Library and Archives Canada Cataloguing in Publication

Title: Protest, property rights, and the law in British Columbia / Benjamin Isitt.

Names: Isitt, Benjamin, 1978- author

Series: Law and society series (Vancouver, B.C.)

Description: Series statement: Law and society series | Includes bibliographical references and index.

Identifiers: Canadiana (print) 20260188093 | Canadiana (ebook) 20260188107 | ISBN 9780774868754 (hardcover) | ISBN 9780774868778 (PDF) | ISBN 9780774868785 (EPUB)

Subjects: LCSH: Demonstrations—Law and legislation—British Columbia—Case studies. | LCSH: Assembly, Right of—British Columbia—Case studies. | LCSH: Right of property—British Columbia—Case studies. | LCSH: Protest movements—British Columbia—Case studies. | LCGFT: Case studies.

Classification: LCC KE4425 .I85 2026 | LCC KF4483.A8 I85 2026 kfmod | DDC 342.71108/54—dc23

Canada Council for the Arts Conseil des arts du Canada

Canada

BRITISH COLUMBIA ARTS COUNCIL

BRITISH COLUMBIA

UBC Press gratefully acknowledges the financial support for our publishing program of the Government of Canada, the Canada Council for the Arts, and the British Columbia Arts Council.

This book has been published with the help of a grant from the Canadian Federation for the Humanities and Social Sciences, through the Scholarly Book Awards, using funds provided by the Social Sciences and Humanities Research Council of Canada.

UBC Press is situated on the traditional, ancestral, and unceded territory of the xʷməθkʷəy̓əm (Musqueam) people. This land has always been a place of learning for the xʷməθkʷəy̓əm, who have passed on their culture, history, and traditions for millennia, from one generation to the next.

UBC Press
The University of British Columbia
www.ubcpress.ca

For Linda, Julian, and Aviva

CONTENTS

ILLUSTRATIONS

ABBREVIATIONS

AAC	Annual Allowable Cut
AFN	Assembly of First Nations
AIM	American Indian Movement
BCCA	British Columbia Court of Appeal
BCCLA	British Columbia Civil Liberties Association
BCFL	British Columbia Federation of Labour
BCGEU	British Columbia Government Employees' Union
BCSC	British Columbia Supreme Court
BCTF	British Columbia Teachers' Federation
CCF	Co-operative Commonwealth Federation
CFI	Council of Forest Industries
CGL	Coastal GasLink
CHN	Council of the Haida Nation
C-IRG	Community-Industry Response Group (RCMP)
CLC	Canadian Labour Congress
CMA	Canadian Manufacturers Association
CPC	Communist Party of Canada
HTG	Hul'qumi'num Treaty Group
IBEW	International Brotherhood of Electrical Workers
IPS	Islands Protection Society

ITU	International Typographical Union
IWA	International Woodworkers of America
IWW	Industrial Workers of the World
LRB	Labour Relations Board
LSBC	Law Society of British Columbia
MLA	Member of the Legislative Assembly
MLL	Miners' Liberation League
NBBC	Native Brotherhood of British Columbia
NDP	New Democratic Party
RCMP	Royal Canadian Mounted Police
RFS	Rainforest Flying Squad
SC	Social Credit Party
SCC	Supreme Court of Canada
SPC	Socialist Party of Canada
SPEC	Society Promoting Environmental Conservation
TAPS	Together Against Poverty Society
TFL	Tree Farm Licence
TMX	Trans Mountain Pipeline ULC
UBCIC	Union of British Columbia Indian Chiefs
UFAWU	United Fishermen and Allied Workers' Union
UMWA	United Mine Workers of America
VBT	Vancouver Board of Trade
VDLC	Vancouver and District Labour Council
VOW	Voice of Women
VSE	Vancouver Stock Exchange
VWC	Vancouver Women's Caucus
WCWC	Western Canada Wilderness Committee
WFM	Western Federation of Miners
WFP	Western Forest Products

PREFACE

THERE IS A BIOGRAPHICAL element to this story, particularly in connection with protests that occurred in recent decades of British Columbia's legal history. I will therefore disclose at the outset that I am not a neutral observer: my values and political commitments align with most of the social movement protagonists in the case studies that follow (with the notable exception of the anti-abortionists in Chapter 3). My personal location as a socially engaged citizen, as a former elected official, and as a relatively new member of the legal profession has shaped this book – providing first-hand experience of the interactions between property, social movements, and the law in British Columbia. My privilege, as a male white settler of Ashkenazi Jewish and English heritage, living as an uninvited guest in the territory of the Lekwungen Coast Salish peoples, is also integral to this work – opening doors to formal education, financial support for research and writing, and relative security from harm when challenging vested interests. I am mindful of the ways in which this privilege has empowered me to tell this story, and of how ongoing structural, systemic, and cultural factors impede the voice and power of Indigenous peoples and other equity-seeking individuals and groups in academia, law, and other institutions of the settler society.

My research has its genesis in a doctoral dissertation in law that I defended at the University of Victoria in 2018, with substantial revisions in the intervening period. I wish to thank Rebecca Johnson and Eric Tucker for supervising my research with a blend of critical insight, mentorship, and good humour. I would also like to thank Judy Fudge for her encouragement of my graduate studies in law, beginning with a generous fellowship followed by useful advice that ingrained in me the importance of locating technical legal rules within the wider social relations of law. I appreciate the assistance of colleagues in the University of Victoria Faculty of Law, particularly John McLaren, Hester Lessard, Hamar Foster, Jeremy Webber, Michael M'Gonigle, Lorinda Fraser, Dalyce Barrs, and Abby Winograd. William Carroll introduced me to the method of network analysis, helping shape the analytical approach. Jim Phillips provided useful comments as the external examiner to the doctoral dissertation, while James Muir provided guidance as the external examiner to the candidacy examination. Don Mitchell and Andy Herod provided a valuable introduction into the world of labour geography and critical geography. Librarians, archivists, and kindred scholars at several institutions contributed to the book in important ways, sharing sources and theoretical insights. The University of Victoria and its Faculty of Law materially supported this research through a doctoral fellowship and the Howard E. Petch Graduate Research Award. A number of participants, from Haida leader Guujaaw to fisherman's union organizer George Hewison to myriad members of the Rainforest Flying Squad, shared insights into how law has operated in response to clashes between private property and social movements. Finally, I wish to thank family and friends, particularly Linda, Julian, and Aviva, for ongoing encouragement and support.

Protest, Property Rights, and the Law in British Columbia

INTRODUCTION: The Social Relations of Property, Protest, and the Law

IN 1959, BRITISH COLUMBIA Supreme Court Justice Norman Whitaker, a former Liberal speaker of the provincial legislature, sentenced labour journalist George North to thirty days in jail for publishing an editorial that lamented the "closeness of the companies and the courts." North's writings in the Communist-aligned *Fisherman* newspaper, particularly his editorial "Injunctions Won't Build Bridges or Catch Fish," were found to incite "defiance of the court's authority," thereby interfering with the administration of justice in British Columbia.[1] The case occurred against the backdrop of a fractious labour dispute between the Dominion Bridge Company and the Ironworkers' union, which had halted construction of the Second Narrows Bridge over Burrard Inlet in Vancouver. The George North case illuminates a larger phenomenon in the legal history of British Columbia and Canada – a pattern where judges and other members of the legal community have been called upon to intervene in response to protest, often in the form of *ex parte* and interlocutory injunctions that sought to curb the agency of social movements attempting to assert customary rights in the face of competing private property rights. Often, these legal clashes between competing property claims occasioned crises of legal legitimacy, a fundamental questioning of the fairness of judges, courts, police, and the rule of law generally.

More than half a century after the George North case, in 2021, BC Supreme Court Justice Douglas Thompson expressed concerns similar to those that had landed North in jail. During a hearing at the Nanaimo Courthouse – on an application from logging company Teal Cedar Products Ltd. to extend an injunction against environmental protesters at Fairy Creek on Vancouver Island, more than 1,100 of whom had already been arrested – Thompson questioned the wisdom of deploying injunctions in response to protests, rather than allowing police and prosecutors to enforce the ordinary criminal law. "It inserts the court into a difficult situation," Thompson said during submissions from counsel for the plaintiff logging company. "Where does the court's reputation get weighed in this balance?" he asked Teal Cedar's lawyer, referring to the balance-of-convenience test upon which many injunction applications hinge. "The court gets dragged into these situations."[2] Two weeks later, Thompson provided his reasons for judgment, denying the logging company's application to renew the injunction (a decision that was later reversed by the BC Court of Appeal). Thus, he sought to "get the Court out from the middle of this dispute."[3]

Embracing a spatial and historical lens and the insights of critical legal theory, this book maps the patterns of property, protest, and the law in modern British Columbia – the social relations of adjudication – and the changing ways in which conflict between private property rights and customary rights invoked by social movement actors has been contested and adjudicated in public spaces and legal arenas. What is a social movement? For the purposes of this study, I define a social movement as an aggregation of people subscribing to a common ideology who work collectively to achieve shared goals, often embracing a common critique and pursuing a common challenge to the prevailing normative order. From labour strikes in the Vancouver Island coal mines more than a century ago, to more recent protests by Indigenous peoples, environmentalists, pro- and anti-abortion activists, and urban "poor people's" movements, social movement actors have asserted customary rights to property through the control or appropriation of space. Owners and managers of property have responded by enlisting an array of legal remedies and an army of legal actors – lawyers, judges, police, parliaments, and soldiers – to restore control over space and uphold private property rights. For most of the past century, conventional private property claims trumped the customary claims of social movements in the legal arena, provoking crises of legitimacy where social movement actors questioned the impartiality of judges and the fairness of adjudicative procedures. Remedies and legal technologies asserted by company lawyers, awarded by judges, and enforced by police and soldiers were often severe – from *Criminal Code* proscriptions against riotous assembly and deployment of military force, to the equitable remedy of the injunction and lengthy prison sentences following contempt of court proceedings.

But this pattern appears to be loosening to a limited extent in recent years, driven by three major trends in British Columbian and Canadian law: (1) the effective assertion of Indigenous customary rights; (2) growing recognition of the importance of human rights in democratic societies, particularly in the context of the *Canadian Charter of Rights and Freedoms*; and (3) changes in the composition of the legal profession and judiciary, reflecting changing societal attitudes and representation of more diverse social, cultural, and ideological constituencies. These trends have given rise to a new and evolving legal space (albeit in an uneven and incomplete way), where property is increasingly treated as contingent rather than absolute, and where the rights of one party are balanced by customary rights, interests, and aspirations of others. Consequently, we may be witnessing a shift toward the dilution of legal remedies traditionally available to the powerful, creating space for the assertion of nonconventional property claims and the emergence of new patterns of power relations.

Property Claims, Public Spaces, and Crises of Legal Legitimacy

While completing the research for this book, I personally became engaged in a battle between customary and private claims to property when I was named in a notice of civil claim relating to protests over a Coast Salish burial ground at a place called Grace Islet in the Salish Sea. The private owner, who held title in fee simple to the rocky islet off Salt Spring Island, sought to build a private vacation home on the identified cultural heritage site, which included two dozen burial cairns. The registered owner alleged trespass by Indigenous and non-Indigenous people who were protesting at the site and disrupting the construction process. Upon being served by counsel for the plaintiff property owner, I worked with pro bono legal counsel, other named defendants, and lawyers retained by the chief councillor of the Tsartlip First Nation to defeat an interlocutory injunction application that aimed to restrain further protests. As BC Supreme Court Justice Douglas Thompson ruled in postponing the hearing on the plaintiff's application: "The matter may be as simple as the plaintiff says it is, [or] it may not be that simple."[4] Two weeks later, the plaintiff discontinued the civil action and agreed to pay costs, shortly after receiving robust responses to the claim and affidavits outlining how the Tsartlip and other Coast Salish people were asserting customary rights by attending at the burial ground, and how non-Indigenous supporters (myself included) were rendering assistance in the exercise of these customary rights. Justice Thompson's preliminary ruling on the adjournment application, and the plaintiff's response in abandoning the lawsuit, demonstrated a growing contingency in the jurisprudence of customary and conventional claims to property – an increasingly liminal legal space where judges and other legal actors appear more reluctant to unilaterally grant interlocutory orders to enforce private rights and dismiss customary rights asserted by parties aligned with social movements.

This liminality is not confined to assertions of Indigenous customary rights, as I have observed in legal proceedings since the Grace Islet case. It can also be found in emerging jurisprudence relating to rights recognized in the *Canadian Charter of Rights and Freedoms*, including courts' interpretations of freedom of association that support assertions of workers' rights, and interpretations of the right to security of the person, which translate into a growing recognition of the right of people who are homeless to shelter themselves in public spaces. As my research continued, I submitted a nine-hundred-page affidavit (inclusive of twenty-six exhibits of evidence) relating to "the right to sleep" in the city of Victoria and a homeless encampment that had taken shape on the Victoria Courthouse grounds. In denying an application from the Province of British Columbia for an injunction ordering the removal of the encampment, Chief Justice Christopher Hinkson declared:

> Ultimately, in determining whether or not to grant an interim injunction at this time, I find that the balance of convenience is overwhelmingly in favour of the defendants, who simply have nowhere to move to, if the injunction were to issue, other than shelters that are incapable of meeting the needs of some of them, or will result in their constant disruption and a perpetuation of a relentless series of daily moves to the streets, doorways, and parks of the City of Victoria.[5]

Demonstrating the phenomenon at the heart of my argument in this book, the courts of British Columbia appear to be increasingly reluctant to act with haste in enforcing conventional private property claims in response to protest, at least at the interlocutory injunction stage, particularly when such claims clash with robust assertions of customary and constitutional rights.

In 2021, as this book moved closer to publication, Justice Thompson issued another unorthodox ruling that departed from the predominant jurisprudence regarding private property rights, social movement protest, and equitable injunctive relief. This decision followed more than a year of protests obstructing logging of old-growth rainforests at Fairy Creek and Caycuse River on southern Vancouver Island. Under the banner of the "Rainforest Flying Squad," an eclectic, decentralized band of forest defenders mounted a dozen encampments and blockades amid widening societal concern over the impacts of climate change and biodiversity loss. Teal Cedar Products Ltd., which held Tree Farm Licence 46 and permits authorizing logging and road building in the area, had obtained an earlier injunction; during four months of enforcement operations, RCMP officers arrested more than 1,100 people for contempt of court and obstruction of justice. The Fairy Creek protests surpassed the Clayoquot Sound "hot summer" of 1993 as the largest act of mass civil disobedience in Canadian history, amid allegations of police misconduct and civil liberties violations at checkpoints and "exclusion zones" throughout the injunction area. Faced with these circumstances, and following four days of hearings at the Nanaimo Courthouse (in which I acted as a legal assistant for counsel opposing the logging company's application), Thompson exercised his discretion and refused to extend the injunction.

In his reasons for judgment, Thompson found that the public interest in preserving the court's reputation outweighed potential harm to the logging company – seeking to avert a crisis of legitimacy arising from further enforcement of the court order. Emphasizing "the strong public interest in keeping the Court away from the front line of this dispute," and "serious and substantial infringement of civil liberties ... in the name of enforcing this Court's order," Thompson chose to "get the Court out from the middle of this dispute, and let the government and police do what they will with the tools at their disposal," endorsing ordinary criminal law remedies over the equitable remedy of an injunction.[6]

Stirrings of this more contingent approach to property rights could be discerned in the 1980s, for example, in the Meares Island case relating to logging of old-growth rainforest in Clayoquot Sound, *MacMillan Bloedel Ltd v Mullin* (1985). In that case, the BC Court of Appeal ruled in a landmark three-to-two decision that the balance of inconvenience favoured the granting of an injunction to the Nuu-chah-nulth leaders to restrain logging operations by the company, MacMillan Bloedel Ltd., pending the determination of an Aboriginal title claim. The court made this decision despite the fact that the logging company held all necessary permits and licences to harvest the trees on the Crown land. Writing for the majority of judges in the appellate division, Justice Peter Seaton succinctly described the rationale for granting the injunction: "If logging proceeds and it turns out that the Indians have the right to the area with the trees standing, it will no longer be possible to give them that right." Seaton also acknowledged the limits of appropriate judicial intervention, suggesting that the real issue at the heart of the dispute was a political one between the

Indigenous peoples and the Crown, which would be resolved through negotiation and a reasonable exchange. "There is a problem about tenure that has not been attended to in the past," he declared, and he was not prepared to ignore it, even if the province chose to ignore the problem and even if industry had undertaken substantial capital investments based on assumptions about tenure over the land.[7]

For most of British Columbia's post-contact legal history, however, judges and other members of the legal community have sided squarely with established owners and managers of property, and against social movement actors who challenged those property claims by asserting customary rights through the control or appropriation of space. This pattern is apparent in the case law relating to labour disputes, particularly until the 1970s, when the legislature responded to public concern by narrowing the courts' jurisdiction in this area. The case law of environmental disputes also displays an overwhelming pattern of judges and other legal actors intervening in favour of private property claims to natural resources, rather than ecological claims asserted by members of the public aligned with environmental organizations. "There is an almost unlimited supply of cases dealing with interlocutory injunctions," Justice Seaton noted in the Meares Island case. "Each of the decisions represents an attempt on the part of the court to see that justice is done. Often it is an attempt to preserve property so that a claimant will not find at the end of a successful trial that the subject matter is gone, and always there is an attempt not to impede others unnecessarily."[8]

Legal scholar Basil Alexander examines this "prior status quo focus" of injunction law in a recent study on demonstrations and the law, noting how "specific 'rights' (such as property rights or regulated public property use) usually prevail over more general aspirational 'privileges' (such as freedom of expression and freedom of peaceful assembly)." He posits that law "takes a cautious, limited, and conservative approach to interim decisions that are generally close to the legal status quo," and, as a result, "usually tends to be an instrument used against demonstrations ... instead of protecting them. However, rare circumstances can also arise where demonstrators' interests are more consonant with status quo and societal perspectives so that injunctions can be more helpful."[9] Irina Ceric has noted that injunction applications relating to natural resource disputes often turn on how the courts define the "status quo": "what is to be maintained, the unimpeded progress of the extractive project or the pre-development status of the lands and waters?"[10] The Supreme Court of Canada recognized this pattern of judicial prioritization of corporate and government interests in *Haida Nation v British Columbia* (2004), noting how "the balance of convenience test tips the scales in favour of protecting jobs and government revenues" over Indigenous interest.[11]

The case studies in this book highlight the changing pattern of protest and the law in British Columbia – the changing social relations of adjudication – centred on crises of legal legitimacy where private property interests and social movement interests clashed, and intervention by the legal community prompted a questioning of law's legitimacy.

Crises of legal legitimacy strike at the root of the functioning of law in society.[12] They highlight the sometimes tense relationship between the judiciary and social movement actors while raising challenging questions over the ability of the state and its network of judges, lawyers, legislators, police, and other officials to make and enforce rules in a manner consistent with the norms of a free and democratic society. As Eric Tucker notes, law does not operate in a vacuum, and it often lacks internal consistency, reflecting "legal and social zones of toleration," a system of formal rules and informal social attitudes of legal actors that vary based on particular social contexts.[13] Crises of legal legitimacy expose the liminal legal spaces created within and between these zones of toleration. They also cast critical light on the appointment procedures, composition, and impartiality of the judiciary, illuminating the socio-political background of judges and their relationships to corporations, political parties, and private individuals and groups. A core tenet of natural justice is the maxim that justice not only must be done but must be seen to be done. At diverse moments in British Columbia's history, social movement actors arrived at the conclusion that justice was being denied in both appearance and in fact, that judges and the courts, by deploying the state's monopoly on coercive violence in service of vested property interests, were serving as agents of injustice rather than justice. Such crises of legal legitimacy therefore provide a potent lens through which to examine broader questions of the relationship between law and society and the social relations within which law and adjudication operate.

By "customary" rights (and "customary" interests and property claims), I mean rights and interests arising from traditional sources of law (such as Indigenous legal orders) or from popular conceptions of justice, such as those described by historian E.P. Thompson and others with reference to battles over the "commons" in early modern England.[14] This category of rights and interests draws heavily from popular understandings of what is "right" or "just," which have at times been sharply counterposed to formal legal rights recognized under the English common law or under statutes enacted by legislatures. In *Customs in Common* (1991), Thompson notes how "custom had close affinities with the common law" and that "plebeian culture is rebellious, but rebellious in defence of custom."[15] Examining popular resistance to enclosure of commonly held agrarian land, he described the operation of customary law and the "common right" as "a subtle and sometimes complex vocabulary of usages, of claims to property, or hierarchy and of preferential access to resources ... Alternative assertions of right could be fiercely divisive."[16] While important distinctions can be discerned between this "plebeian" conception of rights and motivations of the social movement actors in this book, a common thread can be traced, rooted in popular conceptions of "right," which gave rise to at times fierce expressions of popular power.

One of my core arguments – that growing legal recognition of customary claims to property by social movement actors has moderated legal interventions on behalf of conventional private property interests – cuts against a body of literature on neoliberalism and the erosion of democratic rights. Influential studies, such as Leo Panitch and Donald Swartz's *From Consent to Coercion* (1983, revised 2003), identify a general retrenchment of workers' rights and other democratic rights in the face of neoliberalism, the erosion of a "postwar compromise" between capital and labour that shaped social relations in western societies in the decades following the Second World War.[17] I do not discount the destructive impacts of neoliberalism on social rights, including harms caused by a retreat from redistributive social programs, progressive taxation policies, and statutory protections that provided a measure of economic security for working people and other equity-seeking individuals and groups in capitalist societies. I argue, however, that in the judicial arena at least, the decades since the passage of the *Constitution Act, 1982* have witnessed a growing if limited recognition of customary and constitutional claims to property by social movement actors, and a corresponding weakening of legal interventions on behalf of private property interests. This interpretation builds upon concepts in Dominique Clément's *Canada's Rights Revolution* (2008) and *Equality Deferred* (2014) on the development of the "human rights state" in British Columbia and Canada in tandem with social movement mobilization.[18] It also suggests a widening ambit for the "legal and social zones of toleration" described by Tucker.[19]

Many of the cases I examine relate to contempt of court proceedings, arising from defiance of court injunctions by social movement actors challenging private property rights. It is therefore worthwhile at this stage to briefly describe the basic contours of the law in this area, to provide context for subsequent chapters. In the leading case of *Poje* (1953), a British Columbia labour case discussed in Chapter 2, the Supreme Court of Canada drew a distinction between *criminal contempt of court* – a public challenge to the court's authority that brings the administration of justice into disrepute, and thereby rises beyond a dispute between private parties – and lesser forms of *civil contempt of court*, where the defendant has disobeyed a civil injunction in less public ways, and which can be addressed by ordinary civil (rather than criminal) procedures and sanctions.[20]

Contempt of court is a controversial area of law, the only nonstatutory criminal offence remaining in Canadian law; judges' inherent jurisdiction to initiate criminal proceedings against those who defy their authority is preserved under section 9 of the *Criminal Code*, with an ensuing "lack of clarity of definition of procedure and the elements of the offence."[21] While the Supreme Court of Canada clarified the elements of criminal contempt in *United Nurses of Alberta v Alberta (Attorney General)* (1992), stating that wilful knowledge that breach of a court order would be public provides sufficient *mens rea* of bringing the court's authority into contempt, ambiguity remains.[22] This ambiguity contributes to allegations of abuse of process and has fuelled calls for reform. As the Law Reform Commission of Canada noted in 1977, the law of contempt is "unnecessarily complicated," it "lacks organizing principles," and "the continuing use of common law contempt offences is an unnecessary anomaly."[23] Nearly half a century later, the law of contempt remains unreformed and these criticisms continue to resonate among social movement actors and others who find themselves facing contempt proceedings.

The law of injunctions is similarly ambiguous, deriving from equity rather than statute with a corresponding lack of definition. However, some clarification of rules has emerged over time, and the authority of private parties to seek judicial relief in the form of injunctions is provided for in section 39 of British Columbia's *Law and Equity Act*, which states that an injunction may be granted "in all cases in which it appears to the court to be just or convenient that the order should be made."[24] This wide discretion is tempered to an extent by the leading Canadian authority, *RJR-MacDonald* (1994) (a case arising from restrictions on tobacco advertising, which largely superseded the earlier BC case of *Wale*). *RJR-MacDonald* established a three-part test to determine whether an injunction should be granted: (1) Is there a serious question to be tried? (2) Will the party seeking the injunction suffer irreparable harm if relief is not granted (meaning harm that cannot be quantified in monetary terms or compensated through an award of monetary damages)? (3) Does the balance of inconvenience favour the granting of the injunction?[25] Many cases hinge on the final stage of this test, including cases involving social movement challenges to private property rights. The courts assess which party would be more significantly impacted if the injunction were granted or denied. The emerging jurisprudence suggests a growing (though still limited) openness on the part of judges to recognizing the balance of inconvenience as favouring customary claims to property, and novel expressions of the public interest, and a growing reluctance to automatically issue injunctions to enforce private rights.

Critical Approaches to Property, Social Movements, and the Law

In this book, I examine patterns of protest and social relations of adjudication through the interdisciplinary lenses of space and time, engaging the fields of critical geography and social history. The case studies illuminate moments when social movement actors asserted customary and constitutional claims to property through the control or appropriation of space, prompting owners and managers of property to tap a changing arsenal of legal tools to contain or defeat these challenges. With judges often at the apex of the legal order, the study is informed by the sociological method of social network analysis, treating the judiciary as a distinct social group, with its own traditions, practices, interests, values, and associations. The study also engages recent and older literature on the legal history of British Columbia and Canada, including biographical treatments of particular judges, lawyers, and courts, as well as broader analyses of development of legal institutions, statutes, and the common law. By examining diverse social movements, the study intersects with several areas of law. It begins with the law of employment and labour, where the operation of modern injunctions developed in British Columbia, then moves to more recent arenas of social and legal contestation: feminist law, environmental law, Indigenous law, and poverty law. In the process, I explore common-law concepts, including property, contempt of court, tort, and the equitable remedy of the injunction. The study fills a lacuna in these areas of legal scholarship, while contributing to the fields of labour and working-class history, political economy, critical geography, and historical and sociological studies of social movements and the state in British Columbia and other Canadian and international jurisdictions.

Space – and conceptions of property – are socially constructed, and therefore contingent and open to contestation and divergent understandings. This contingency in the conceptualization of space and property is reflected in changing legal responses to social movement challenges to private property rights. Doreen Massey, a pioneer in the field of legal geography, suggested that "we need to conceptualize space as constructed out of interrelations, as the simultaneous coexistence of social interrelations and interactions at all spatial scales, from the most local level to the most global."[26] Overlapping, concurrent, and competing property claims are at the heart of the case studies in this book, with social movement actors asserting customary claims to space and property, and "legitimate" owners and managers of property invoking legal powers to re-establish control over space and assert competing claims. Nicholas Blomley has stated that "legal spaces are embedded in broader social and political claims," constituted "by often competing visions of space and political life under law."[27] Violence (and the threat or exercise of law's coercive force) plays an important role in this legal delineation of space, according to Blomley: "Physical violence, whether realized or implied, is important to the legitimation, foundation, and operation of a Western property regime."[28]

Often, social movement actors viewed the spaces they were occupying as "public," while property managers and owners sought to define them as extensions of the "private" business domain. In this regard, studies in critical geography[29] and "the right to the city"[30] are instructive, highlighting processes of marginalization, displacement, and resistance in the context of neoliberal restructuring of the economy, state, and society (themes that figure prominently in the final case study). As Lynn Staeheli and Don Mitchell have noted, "understanding public space as a set of property relationships is foundational."[31] Sarah Hamill has examined the concept of "common property" with reference to Canadian jurisprudence.[32] Melinda Benson demonstrates how legal *procedures*, which are often treated as neutral in legal scholarship, can have a decisive impact on the outcome of legal proceedings. Law "reflects a dynamic relationship between spatial forms and social discourses with corresponding productions of control, authority, and power."[33]

Alongside a spatial lens, I employ the historical method in the structuring and interpretation of material, examining the social relations of adjudication with an emphasis on how judicial reasoning and the broader social relations of law change over time. I define social relations of adjudication as the social context within which law and adjudicative processes operate. This includes the ways in which class interests, socio-economic power relations, and other forms of social relations and tensions are manifested within courtrooms, in adjudicative procedures and outcomes, and in dynamics among legal actors – including parties to disputes, lawyers, judges, police, soldiers, state officials, and legislators. What historical patterns can we discern in these social relations of adjudication and in the approach of legal actors to social movement protest? How have legal procedures, judges' attitudes, and lines of judicial reasoning changed over time? What elements of injunction law and other legal technologies have remained constant as the locus of judicial intervention has shifted from unorganized workers to union members to anti-abortionists to environmentalists to Indigenous sovereigntists to anti-poverty activists? Eric Tucker highlights the complex relationship between history and law, distinguishing "the nuance and complexity that is the hallmark of good historical work" from "law-office" history, fodder for legal briefs where advocates and judges invoke history for merely instrumental purposes.[34] Alfred Kelly pejoratively describes this process as creating history by "judicial fiat."[35] In contrast, I endeavour to take both the historical process and the evolution of courts' jurisprudence seriously, revealing the social relations of adjudication through attention to the changing legal technology deployed in response to protest in modern British Columbia.[36]

Theoretically, this book is located in the critical school of legal scholarship, viewing the operation of law, struggles over rights, and behaviour of legal actors in a socio-political context of economic power and contested class relationships. My approach aligns with Joseph Singer's "social relations" model of property, which Blomley locates among "progressive property critiques" of the "ownership model":

> Property is much more diverse than the ownership model allows. Breaking the "confines" of the ownership model would appear to be a powerful move, opening property up to diverse possibilities. While property can, indeed, be individualized, paranoid and antisocial, it can also be collective, inclusive and indelibly human.[37]

This critical approach to property runs through diverse works in far-flung temporal and geographical contexts: Janice Neeson's *Commoners* (1993), examining extinguishment of the legal concept of the "common right" with the enclosure movement in early modern England; international research such as Minoti Chakravarty-Kaul's work on common land and customary law in India; and studies of the legal regulation of economic power in modern times, such as Joel Bakan's *The Corporation* (2004).[38]

Critical approaches to property align with a historical materialist conception of law's role in society. While I reject a crude "base-superstructure" schema, which dismisses law as a blunt instrument of class rule, I seek to locate judicial reasoning in the context of contested social relations and competing social constructions of space, examining ways in which class relationships and economic power influence adjudicative processes and the responses of legal actors.

My approach is informed by, yet departs from, strict structuralist approaches that coloured the work of political economists from Adam Smith to Karl Marx to more recent theorists. Smith declared in a 1762 lecture:

> Laws and governments may be considered ... as a combination of the rich to oppress the poor, and preserve to themselves the inequality of goods which would otherwise be soon destroyed by the attacks of the poor, who if not hindered by the government would soon reduce the others to an equality with themselves by open violence.[39]

According to Marx, "a legal and political superstructure" rested on a foundation of the social relations of production.[40] In the *Communist Manifesto* (1848), Marx and Friedrich Engels proposed that jurisprudence was "but the will of [the ruling] class made into a law for all ... determined by the economical conditions of the existence of [that] class."[41]

Marx himself, as well as later generations of scholars, moved away from this crudely instrumentalist approach, preserving a critique of structural inequality and the economic purposes to which law was deployed, while retreating from economic determinism, which conflated all legal acts and institutions into manifestations of class behaviour. This refined structuralist approach located the law and state actions within a framework of capital accumulation and contested social relations, while allowing a wide degree of autonomy for how law operated in specific contexts.[42] Neo-Marxists have suggested that crude economic determinism risks obscuring the explanatory potential of more nuanced approaches. According to Andrew Vincent, orthodox Marxism's wholesale rejection of the legitimacy of law prevented a more meaningful discussion of the ways in which class shapes the nature of the law, its reform, and its future.[43]

This critique echoed British historian E.P. Thompson, who rejected the view that "the revolutionary can have no interest in law, unless as a phenomenon of ruling-class power and hypocrisy."[44] A pioneer of the "cultural turn" in labour and working-class history, Thompson sought to root Marxism's high-level political economy, with its emphasis on states, epochs, and historic conflict between the classes, in a ground-level view of the lived experiences of ordinary people. This required a more nuanced appreciation of law's operation. Occupying a "narrow theoretical ledge," Thompson called for separating law conceptually from the superstructure, analyzing its operation as an institution, as an ideology, as well as its own internal logic, rules, and procedures.[45] Departing from a "highly schematic Marxism," Thompson defended the ideal of the rule of law as "a cultural achievement of universal significance" and "an unqualified human good."[46] The legacy of successive struggles against autocracy, law imposes "inhibitions upon power," according to Thompson. To effectively mediate and legitimize class relations, law must "seem to be just" by upholding "its own logic and criteria of equity" and, "on occasion, by actually *being just*."[47] Law as a logic of equity "must always seek to transcend the inequalities of class power which, instrumentally, it is harnessed to serve."[48] To discard the rule of law as a sham of class rule is a "desperate error of intellectual abstraction," Thompson argued, "a self-fulfilling error, which encourages us to give up the struggle against bad laws and class-bound procedures, and to disarm ourselves before power." Moreover, such an approach throws away "a whole inheritance of struggle *about* law."[49] Law may fall short of its rhetoric, and it may serve to mediate, legitimate, and reinforce unequal class relations, but this does not mean that the rule of law itself should be viewed as analogous to the exercise of unmediated force.

Historical and Legal Contexts

My historical method aligns with critical approaches to labour law, conceptualizing worker rights as historically contingent and contested, rather than evolving in a straightforward natural progression, as the "industrial pluralist" school claimed.[50] Commenting on the recognition of collective bargaining as a Charter-protected right, Tucker described the Supreme Court of Canada's historical claims in *Health Services and Support v British Columbia* (2007) as "flawed," arguing (like Judy Fudge) that collective bargaining is a deeply rooted *social practice* rather than a long-standing *procedural right*.[51] Struggles of working people and their organizations spurred the enactment of statutes and development of a corresponding statutory regime, translating the social practice into a recognized legal right. Reflecting complex jural relations (as W.N. Hohfeld described them), recognition of workers' legal rights necessarily placed restrictions on the freedom of employers.[52]

In British Columbia, like other Canadian jurisdictions, collective bargaining has been rigorously contested, both before and since the advent of modern labour law, in workplaces, legislatures, and courtrooms. Judges (and, more recently, labour relations boards and arbitrators) have been called upon to intervene in disputes between workers and employers, as conflict over the balance of power in industrial relations – motivated by a basic antagonism of economic interests – erupted into work stoppages and demands by employers and legislators for judges and police (at times even soldiers) to intervene to resume production.[53] In the era of "labour before the law," courts intervened to enforce laws against breaches of contract and criminal conspiracy, informed by the premodern law of master and servant.[54] As Randall Echlin points out, "the para-military code of discipline of the Hudson's Bay Company" shaped relations between workers and employees as much as the English common law in colonial-era British Columbia.[55] Indeed, it was a strike of coal miners at Fort Rupert on northern Vancouver Island that prompted the appointment of the colony's first justice of the peace.[56] Absenteeism, desertion, and similar infractions, whether by individual workers or combinations thereof, resulted in fines and prison sentences for the industrializing workforce in late nineteenth- and early twentieth-century British Columbia. The case study of the Vancouver Island "war" (1912–19) in Chapter 1, which saw more than eight hundred coal miners arrested (and more than two hundred jailed) as military forces occupied the Vancouver Island coalfields during a bitter labour dispute, highlights contested legal relations in this era of "labour before the law." Criminal sedition charges were also deployed at tense moments during the twentieth century to curb radical protest movements, as Dennis Molinaro and others have demonstrated – against socialist union organizer William Pritchard and other leaders of the One Big Union (OBU) during the wave of general strikes following the First World War, and again in the 1930s against Arthur "Slim" Evans and Communist organizers who were making major organizational advances among sections of the working class.[57]

With the advent of modern "free collective bargaining" after the Second World War, courts and judges continued to play a central role in determining the balance of power in labour relations and shaping the outcome of specific disputes. From deciding the law of picketing to levying injunctions, fines, contempt convictions, and prison sentences against working-class leaders and unions, the role of the courts was a matter of heated public and scholarly controversy during North American capitalism's long boom in the 1950s and 1960s, prompting institutional change. However, even after most authority to grant injunctions was moved from BC courts to the administrative framework of the Labour Relations Board in the 1970s, judges continued to play an important role in labour relations, providing judicial oversight to tribunal decisions, levying financial and other penalties against offending unions, and even granting injunctions from time to time.[58]

The broad contours of the legal regulation of collective bargaining in twentieth-century Canada are traced in Judy Fudge and Eric Tucker's *Labour Before the Law* (2001) and Peter McInnis's *Harnessing Labour Confrontation* (2002), enhanced by a diverse literature on judicial intervention in labour disputes in British Columbia and other jurisdictions.[59] It was in the labour context that the law of injunctions matured in British Columbia, moving beyond an obscure equitable remedy to become a frequently wielded device to curb the agency of workers who acted collectively during bargaining disputes and challenged employers' property rights. BC courts entertained applications for no fewer than 224 *ex parte* injunctions in response to labour disputes between 1956 and 1965 and denied only 2, establishing procedures and principles that would be applied in later legal responses to anti-abortion, environmental, Indigenous, and anti-poverty protests.[60] Reflecting the origins of modern injunction law in the labour context, this book is grounded in the literature of the law of employment and labour, mapping the social relations, jurisprudence, and forms of state intervention that shaped disputes between workers and employers.

Moving thematically to examine how the law of injunctions was applied in response to later protest movements, this book engages the rich and varied international scholarship on social movements.[61] My definition of social movements – an aggregation of people subscribing to a common ideology who work collectively to achieve shared goals, often embracing a common critique and pursuing a common challenge to the prevailing normative order – draws from the work of Manuel Castells.[62] It acknowledges a space for non-class-based movements, such as the feminist movement and poor peoples' movements, and even reactionary social movements, such as fascist movements or (as in the case study in Chapter 3) anti-abortionists. To understand the connection between social movements and protests, I examine the shift in the *consciousness* and the *behaviour* of social movement actors, a useful distinction drawn by Frances Fox Piven and Richard Cloward: the former hinges on individuals' loss of faith in the legitimacy of the system and their conception of their own "rights" and capacity to effect change, whereas the latter signals a shift in the behaviour of individuals, from quiescence to defiance, which is then acted out collectively.[63] Hegemony and counter-hegemony also shape the ideological and strategic landscape within which social movement actors operate, concepts running from Antonio Gramsci's writings a century ago to the work of William Carroll and other contemporary scholars, "a protracted 'war of position' in which a coalition of oppositional movements wins space and constructs mutual solidarities."[64]

The relationship between social movements and the law engages distinct fields of legal research. This includes the dynamic and growing literature on Indigenous legal orders as well as historical studies of conflicts over law, property, authority, land, and Indigenous rights.[65] As John Borrows notes, "colonization is not a strong place to rest the foundation of Canada's laws. It creates a fiction that continues to erase Indigenous legal systems as a source of law in Canada."[66] Studies of specific Indigenous land struggles and Indigenous legal orders, such as Jisgang Nika Collison's recent collaborative work with the Council of the Haida Nation on the Athlii Gwaii stand, illuminate my topic in important ways, noting that "the boldness was not that of defiance, or blatantly breaking Canadian law. Rather the boldness was upholding Haida laws."[67] The environmental movement and its clashes with authority have also spawned a valuable body of work, including studies on the Clayoquot Sound protests of 1993.[68] The connection between the women's movement and the legal politics of abortion is examined by Christabelle Sethna and Steve Hewitt and others, though no previous studies have focused on the relationship between protests, injunctions, and British Columbia's "bubble law."[69] There is also a body of literature on "alter-globalization" protests and policing, including a case study of the Group of 20 (G20) global leaders' summit in Toronto in 2010, *Putting the State on Trial* (2015).[70]

Politics of the Judiciary

This book engages and builds upon studies on the legal history of British Columbia and Canada, including studies of the judiciary and recent works on specific judges and the BC Court of Appeal and other Canadian courts.[71] As Fudge and Tucker note with respect to the law of picketing, "a large majority" of Court of Appeal judges believed "that the privilege to trade was of significantly greater social value than the privilege of workers to act collectively."[72] Fudge and Tucker consider both the *internal* and *external* explanations for judicial reasoning in labour cases, finding that the internal impulses of the "taught tradition of the common law" and judicial precedent – favouring individual rights, freedom of contract, and the supremacy of private property – cannot provide a complete explanation. Rather, they argue that the social background of judges and institutional processes such as recruitment must also be considered in order to understand judges' behaviour in labour cases.

The sociological method of *social network analysis* is particularly useful in this regard, providing a means for assessing judicial reasoning through the analysis of judges as a distinct social group, with their own norms, institutions, interests, cultural practices, and associations. While I do not purport to provide a social network analysis of the British Columbia judiciary, this book is informed by William Carroll's methodology in examining corporate networks in Canada and beyond.[73] Michael Tigar and Madeleine Levy's influential book

Law and the Rise of Capitalism (1977) demonstrated how the close connection between lawyers and the ascendant bourgeoisie contributed to the development of the modern legal system and its particular legal ideology and approaches toward property rights, contract rights, and individual rights.[74] A recent contribution in the field of labour history, Reinhold Kramer and Tom Mitchell's *When the State Trembled* (2010), similarly provides insight on mapping the often invisible associations and allegiances that contribute to state and nonstate responses to social movement protest.[75] Michel Foucault's work on power relations provides additional insight into the functioning of legal processes, actors, and institutions. According to Foucault, "one must analyze institutions from the standpoint of power relations ... [T]he fundamental point of anchorage of the relationships, even if they are embodied and crystallized in an institution, is to be found outside the institution."[76] Drawing from Canadian and transnational material, processes of judicial appointment are relevant to understanding the composition and functioning of the judiciary.[77]

The question of possible bias of judges and the politics of the judiciary is often treated as a taboo subject, striking at the root of common-law ideals of fair and independent hearings between the parties. An allegation of bias on the part of judges casts doubt on the whole legitimacy of legal reasoning and the rule of law. Public commentary in recent decades (at least until the recent rightward turn of the American judiciary) often seemed to focus on an allegedly "liberal" bias of judges and criticism of "judicial activism" in advancing equality claims of minority groups. In contrast, traditional Marxist critiques of structural inequality and bias in class societies have coloured legal scholarship in this area. John Griffith's work *The Politics of the Judiciary* (1977) examined judicial bias in the British context, suggesting that the "Oxbridge" background of judges and their high incomes prior to appointment to the bench influenced their handling of cases relating to labour and public order, giving rise to a distinct group identity:

> These judges have by their education and training and the pursuit of their profession as barristers acquired a strikingly homogenous collection of attitudes, beliefs, and principles which to them represents the public interest ... The judges define the public interest, inevitably, from the viewpoint of their own class.[78]

This class background of judges shaped their approach to judicial reasoning and created a bias in favour of property interests and stability, according to Griffiths:

> It is demonstrable that on every major social issue which has come before the courts during the last 30 years – concerning industrial relations, political protest, race relations, government secrecy, police powers, moral behaviour – the judges have supported the conventional, established, and settled interests.[79]

Griffiths concluded, however, that judicial bias operated on an institutional level, with reform requiring more than a mere change of personnel: "There are those who believe that if more grammar or comprehensive schoolboys, graduating at red brick or new glass universities, became barristers and then judges, the judiciary would be that much less conservative. This is extremely doubtful."[80] A similar line of reform proposals speculates on whether the appointment of more women to the bench has had the effect of making the exercise of law less patriarchal or partial.[81]

The theme of judicial bias is explored in the Canadian context, and through diverse interpretive lenses, in works by F.L Morton and others.[82] As Morton notes in *Law, Politics and the Judicial Process in Canada* (2002), "the authority of contemporary Canadian courts still rests on the ancient requirement of impartiality ... In order to insure impartiality, we expect a judge to be independent of our adversary."[83] While offering a more muted criticism than Griffiths, Morton raises important questions over the role of judges in the public arena as exemplified by controversies involving Justices Berger, McLachlin, Bienvenue, L'Heureux-Dubé, and Bastarache. Former BC Chief Justice Nathan Nemetz, who had represented unions prior to his appointment to the bench, suggested that Griffiths's criticism "cannot be overlooked," and that "judicial attitudes towards political and social questions lack an understanding of the views of labour unions, minorities and the underprivileged."[84] James Walker's research on the Supreme Court of Canada has illuminated the influence that the religious background of judges can have in shaping judicial reasoning.[85]

Moving to the American context, there are studies that challenge suggestions of judicial bias. Drawing on statistical analysis of civil rights cases, Orley Ashenfelter, Theodore Eisenberg, and Stewart Schwab conclude that there is no clear evidence linking the partisan allegiances of judges to their decisions: "Individual judge characteristics cannot be assumed to influence substantially the mass of cases."[86] Duncan Kennedy, meanwhile, sees a fundamental arbitrariness in judicial reasoning – a decisive choice in every case notwithstanding the common claim that judges "find" (rather than "make") the law.[87] Kennedy's views on the radical contingency of the law can be tempered by a more structural analysis, which acknowledges the degree of discretion enjoyed by judges (shaped by particular backgrounds and interests), while tracing enduring patterns in lines of judicial reasoning and action.[88]

The literature on bias and the British Columbia judiciary is slim, particularly with respect to labour and social movements. In his recent history of the BC Court of Appeal, Christopher Moore quotes former Court of Appeal Justice Ian Donald, who practised labour law with the firm Rankin and Company before his call to the bench, and recalled that early BC judges were

> unsympathetic to trade unions, administering a regime that was not particularly friendly to labour or employees in general. They understood managers and industrialists and owners, they worked with those people, met them at the Vancouver Club.
>
> It changed during my years in practice [1970s and 1980s], with judges who had more knowledge of modern trends, more tolerance of differences. You began to have some judges who had dealt in labour matters. You could lose at trial and actually win at the Court of Appeal.[89]

Hamar Foster and John McLaren discuss this change, from a body with the corporate mindset of "a small group of economically successful, middle-class white men whose politics were acceptable to the federal government of the day" and who had worked in private practice for clients with the financial resources to retain them, toward a more diverse body that "demonstrates some sensitivity to changes in the composition of Canadian and BC society, and to the changing social values and mores."[90]

We can also turn to nonscholarly works, such as memoirs of labour lawyers John Stanton and Harry Rankin, who served as counsel in many of the cases examined in Chapter 2. Though hardly lacking bias themselves, Stanton and Rankin offer rich detail on these heated events and provide analyses that are atypical of the practising legal profession. Writing about the George North case, Rankin pulls no punches: "[The attorney general] made the courts an instrument for the bosses! Under the Social Credit government there were *more* injunctions issued here than in any other province, or in any other country using our system of justice."[91] He also describes the political screening process for access to the BC Bar (and, by extension, the judiciary), tense hearings before the Benchers of the Law Society in 1950 where he was questioned about his attitudes on the Korean War and his affiliation with the Communist Party. Rankin narrowly passed the Benchers' screening process that year (and again in 1972, when he faced disciplinary hearings for alleging a two-tier justice system with respect to Indigenous peoples). He is unequivocal about the political purposes of the Benchers' procedure: "This was simple political intimidation, the Law Society letting a whole generation of law students know that it was unacceptable to do any real thinking about change."[92]

However, the Law Society's actions are placed in a more measured historical context in an article by Wesley Pue examining the case of Gordon Martin. A war veteran, UBC law school graduate, and former candidate of the Labor-Progressive Party (as the Communist Party was then called), Martin was denied admission to the Bar after completing his articles on grounds that he lacked an ill-defined "good repute." When Martin filed a petition for judicial review, Justice Coady of the BC Supreme Court and a five-judge division of the BC Court of Appeal refused to overrule the Benchers' decision, emphasizing Martin's ties to Communism. Challenging contemporary and scholarly criticism, Pue locates the decisions of the Benchers, Justice Coady, and the Court of Appeal judges in differing notions of "character" and administrative law that prevailed in mid-twentieth-century British Columbia: the Benchers may have lacked evidence in a strict legal sense, but their decision, and those of the courts, were informed by the context of the palpable fear of Communism that existed in North America at the time.[93]

Case Studies and Thematic Structure

Each case study in this book provides a powerful window into the social relations of adjudication and how the legal community has responded to conflict between private property rights and social movements. As Robert Sharpe noted, "legal historians have adopted a method developed by social historians and turned to the study of ordinary cases that have faded from modern memory."[94] I selected the case studies based on their contemporary significance as sites of social and legal contestation, and for their effectiveness in highlighting major themes in the social and legal history of the province – labour relations, reproductive choice, environmental protection, Indigenous rights, and the legal politics of poverty and homelessness. The attitudes, actions, pronouncements, and procedures of legal actors are examined through interviews and detailed reading of reasons for judgment and published decisions, alongside public debates inside and outside the Legislative Assembly as recorded in Hansard and the daily press. These case studies provide a framework for understanding the behaviour of the legal community as a distinct social group. The voices of social movement actors, accessed through interviews and archival records, reveal contested notions of the rule of law, competing customary claims to space and property, and questioning of the impartiality of legal actors and wider questions of law's legitimacy. Records of corporations, government departments, and other interested parties further illuminate legal responses to conflict between private property interests and social movements.

The book is organized thematically and chronologically around seven chapters. This introductory chapter has explored the social relations of adjudication and connected the work with a diverse interdisciplinary literature. Chapter 1 examines legal responses during the "Vancouver Island War," the tense coal miners' strike of 1912–14 when miners challenged the rights of Canadian Collieries (Dunsmuir) Ltd. and the state responded with military force in the era of "labour before the law." Chapter 2 explores conflict between private property and workers' rights in the period following the Second World War, the heyday of collective bargaining, when workers achieved a larger share of wealth through increased union density and militant strikes, prompting the development of modern injunction law and bitter controversies over the imprisonment of labour leaders. Chapter 3 moves toward the close of the twentieth century, exploring how the law of injunctions was adapted from the labour context during battles over reproductive choice, as anti-abortionists invoked a customary and constitutional right to freedom of expression and the BC legislature responded with the "Bubble Law," a statute aimed at restraining protest around abortion clinics and protecting the right of women to access health services. Chapter 4 engages environmental law, looking at the crisis of legitimacy when nine hundred people defied injunctions and were arrested for contempt of court in a challenge to the property rights of logging corporations in the old-growth rainforests of Vancouver Island's Clayoquot Sound. Chapter 5 examines Indigenous assertions of customary rights to space and property, manifested in road blockades and other challenges to the property law of the settler society, and a corresponding weakening and mellowing of judicial and state responses to social movement protest. Finally, Chapter 6 moves the study into the twenty-first century and up to the present, examining the phenomenon of urban "tent cities," the Occupy movement, and successful efforts by poor people and their advocates to assert a Charter-protected "right to sleep" and "right to shelter" in public spaces, revealing conflict between the common law of trespass and growing legal recognition of human rights in the Charter era.

* * *

The pattern of property, protest, and the law in British Columbia demonstrates continuity and change. Social movement actors have consistently asserted customary and constitutional claims to property through the appropriation or control of space, challenging prevailing private property rights and provoking sharp responses by members of the legal community: judges, lawyers, police, soldiers, legislators, and other state officials. This pattern has prevailed even as the locus of social contestation has shifted – from labour strikes in the early twentieth century to protests over Indigenous rights, reproductive choice, environmental protection, and poor people's rights by the twenty-first century. The legal technology and attitude of legal actors has also changed over time, from the rough-and-tumble response of military intervention during the Vancouver Island War over a century ago, to the indiscriminate granting of labour injunctions in the postwar period, toward an (at times) more measured approach in recent years in response to Indigenous and poor peoples' assertions of power. Despite this apparent shift, crises of legal legitimacy continue to surface – as graphically demonstrated in recent controversies over the Coastal GasLink and Trans Mountain pipelines and logging of old-growth rainforests at Fairy Creek. Social movement actors continue to question the legal community's response to conflict between customary and private property rights (and the fairness of adjudicative procedures), even as property itself becomes more contingent and less certain in the face of competing claims.

Chapter 1

MASTERS, SERVANTS, AND JUDGES DURING THE "VANCOUVER ISLAND WAR"

In August 1913, 213 coal miners were jailed at Nanaimo and nearby mining towns for their role in an event that British Columbia's labour movement described at the time as "the Vancouver Island war."[1] Against the backdrop of a deep economic recession, declining global prices for coal, and the growing drumbeat of world war, workers paralyzed the operations of Canadian Collieries (Dunsmuir) Ltd. and other mine operators for nearly two years, in a bid for union recognition that grew from a walkout in a single mine in protest against the dismissal of a union-appointed gas inspector. As the "war" deteriorated, with violent clashes between strikers, replacement workers, and mine managers – including the burning down of mine managers' homes and the barricading of replacement workers in mine shafts – the BC government responded firmly, deploying the militia in "Aid to the Civil Power" to occupy the island coalfields (the third time soldiers intervened in a labour dispute in the island coal mines, and the longest deployment of the militia in a Canadian labour dispute up to that point).[2]

Local magistrates and Supreme Court judges played a key role in the province's response to the Vancouver Island war, informed by the premodern law of master and servant and criminal conspiracy, which governed the employment relationship prior to the era of collective bargaining. Magistrates and judges also intervened to enforce laws against unlawful assembly, intimidation, and rioting, imposing penalties that had the effect of curbing miners' collective power and aiding Canadian Collieries and other employers to resume production in the island pits. "The State is a class institution functioning in the interest of the ruling class," wrote Vancouver trade unionist and Socialist Party member Jack Kavanagh in a pamphlet issued during the strike.[3] Kavanagh's claim reveals the deep chasm that emerged between sections of British Columbia's working class and the province's legal, political, and economic elite, a crisis of legal legitimacy where labour fundamentally questioned the fairness of state institutions, the independence of the judiciary, and the legitimacy of adjudicative processes. This crisis of legal legitimacy was rooted in conflicting visions of the employment relationship and the unwillingness of workers to occupy the subordinate space reinforced by the law of master and servant, breaking the law to assert customary claims to employers' property – and exposing the contested social relations of adjudication at this tense moment in British Columbia's legal history.

The Vancouver Island war provides fertile ground for a dialogue between an older labour historiography and newer works in critical legal scholarship.[4] As legal historian John Orth noted, the law of employment and labour incorporates elements of property, contract, tort, and the criminal law – "the instinctual resort of elites confronted with new and unsettling realities."[5] Local histories of Nanaimo and Vancouver Island described important aspects of the strike and the island's working-class tradition, while earlier scholarly studies highlighted themes including the role of the militia, organizational aspects of the dispute, and the contribution of women to the miners' cause.[6] However, treatment of legal aspects of the dispute and the arrested miners' stories has been peripheral at best. Even the experience of twenty-one-year-old Joseph Mairs of Ladysmith, who died in state custody at Burnaby's notorious Oakalla prison while incarcerated for the *Criminal Code* offence of rioting, remains shrouded in unanswered questions. Kavanagh's 1913 pamphlet and John Hinde's larger study of coal mining in Ladysmith provide the most thorough treatment, with Hinde suggesting that "the arrival of the militia was seen as a declaration of war against the striking miners and politicized the dispute, as the state, rather than just the mining companies, became the focus of working-class agitation throughout the province."[7]

This chapter fills a scholarly lacuna, providing a detailed examination of legal issues surrounding the Vancouver Island war. It maps the social relations of adjudication in early twentieth-century British Columbia, highlighting the ways in which conflicting conceptions of property shaped the responses of

FIGURE 1 Joseph Mairs, a coal miner from the town of Ladysmith, who died in state custody at Oakalla prison at the age of twenty-one in January 1914, while incarcerated after pleading guilty to the *Criminal Code* offence of rioting in connection with the Vancouver Island miners' strike. The cause of death was tuberculosis relating to a bowel infection. | MsC 47, box 2, Hawthornthwaite fonds, Simon Fraser University Special Collections and Rare Books

workers, companies, and members of the legal community during the dispute.[8] As with Alan Grove and Ross Lambertson's study of the Union Colliery case, this chapter connects lawyers' arguments and judges' decisions in the courtroom to the changing statutory regime and the broader socio-political context or extra-legal values that inform judicial reasoning.[9] It therefore illuminates technical aspects of how the employment relationship was conceived and regulated in early twentieth-century British Columbia, as well as broader social and political questions relating to patterns of protest and the legitimacy of adjudicative procedures.

Early Legal Regulation of the Employment Relationship in British Columbia

At the dawn of the twentieth century, employment relations in British Columbia were characterized by sharp antagonism between the interests of workers and of employers. Robber barons such as coal mine owner Robert Dunsmuir had coloured the industrial relations landscape a decisively anti-union hue, even as militant organizations such as the Western Federation of Miners (WFM), the Industrial Workers of the World (IWW), and the United Mine Workers of America (UMWA) sought to extend the benefits of union protection to Anglo-Canadian workers in BC's resource frontier (while excluding Indigenous workers and workers from Japan, China, and India from their ranks).[10] As several political economists have demonstrated, conditions of life and work for itinerant workers in this "corporate industrial frontier" imbued industrial relations and politics with a militant, radical edge.[11] Alongside burgeoning unions of railway workers, miners, construction workers, and various trades in the province's emerging towns and cities, radical politics were pursued through the Socialist Party of Canada (SPC) and other groups advocating for an "end to the wages system" and "production for use rather than profit."[12]

This was long before the era of "free collective bargaining" – a period described in Judy Fudge and Eric Tucker's *Labour Before the Law* – when legal actors and institutions approached industrial conflict through the lens of "the common law's traditional bias in favour of employers' private rights."[13] However, as Douglas Hay and Paul Craven point out, the law of master and servant was "in its essentials statute law," existing as a separate body of law that had remarkably little contact "with the high legal regimes in which it was everywhere nestled." The law of master and servant rested on three principal assumptions:

> The first was the idea that the employment relation was a matter of *private contract* ... between an employer who thereby acquired the right to command and an employee who undertook to obey. The second was the provision for *summary enforcement* of these private agreements by lay justices of the peace and other magistrates, largely unsupervised by the senior courts. The third was *punishment* of the uncooperative worker: not damages to remedy the breach of contract, but whipping, imprisonment, forced labor, fines, the forfeit of all wages earned.[14]

In the Canadian context, the statutory criminal law governing conspiracy, unlawful assembly, rioting, intimidation, and breach of contract augmented the operation of contract, tort, and property at common law – providing sufficiently robust responses when workers' collective actions disrupted the public order and threatened private rights, engaging an array of state actors in the legal regulation of the employment relationship: police, soldiers, politicians, lawyers, lay magistrates, and judges.

Describing this era of labour before the law, Fudge and Tucker note that employers "could refuse to hire union members and could fire those who became union members after taking up employment. Moreover, to protect the property and contract rights of employers and of workers who were not members of the union, the criminal law narrowly defined the scope of permissible tactics that workers acting collectively could use to advance their interests."[15] When the tools of police, judges, and lawyers seemed inadequate to curb militant collective action, the militia was deployed to occupy the Vancouver Island coalfields in response to strikes by Dunsmuir's workers (a pattern mirrored in Atlantic Canada in the state's response to the militant agency of Cape Breton miners).[16] That Dunsmuir's son, James, served first as British Columbia's premier and then as lieutenant governor seemed to confirm in the eyes of workers that the state was no neutral body, that the executive function had been hijacked by a narrow class interest, and that the law was therefore serving as a vehicle for the exploitation of the working class rather than as a means for achieving its equality, dignity, and emancipation.[17] As an editorial in the *Western Socialist* newspaper noted in 1903, in the midst of bitter strikes on the Canadian Pacific Railway (CPR) and in the Dunsmuirs' island coal mines:

> When courts become contemptible, contempt of court becomes both logical and virtuous ...
>
> Carlyle said the whole moral law was contained in the words, "Thou shalt not steal." Prof. Frank Parsons says, nothing during the last century of wonderful achievements has improved so much as the art of stealing. We are inclined

> to believe all this when we read of the B.C. government backing out of a huge conspiracy to steal public lands of the value of millions and under cover of the word "blunder." Petty larceny is still punished with the old-time severity, but as crime rises in magnitude, the punishment declines until its [sic] reaches a point where stealing becomes that paragon of modern virtues – "good business methods."[18]

A clash between a customary conception of justice and the actual, often brutal exercise of state power ingrained a deep-seated distrust and contempt for the law within British Columbia's emerging industrial working class.

Tentative steps toward the legal protection and regulation of the collective rights of employees had been taken before the dawn of the twentieth century, as workers carved out "narrow exemptions from prosecution for criminal conspiracy," rendering that offence largely obsolete.[19] Statutory protections for workers were further expanded as the locus of legal remedies shifted from the criminal law toward civil actions against unions, influenced by a tense strike of hard-rock miners at the interior city of Rossland and the landmark British House of Lords' decision in *Taff Vale* (1901), which held unions liable in tort for loss-of-profits damages incurred by employers during strikes. In October 1901, the LeRoi Mining Company had obtained an injunction restraining members and officers of the Western Federation of Miners at Rossland (as well as smaller unions) from "watching or besetting" various locations (including local railway stations and strikebreakers' homes) "for the purpose of persuading or otherwise preventing persons from working for the plaintiffs" or procuring persons "to commit a breach of ... contracts" entered into with the company.[20] The injunction, combined with the use of replacement workers from the United States (employed in violation of the *Alien Labour Act*), resulted in the defeat of the strike. In early 1902, as a civil suit for damages against the union went to trial, Smith Curtis, the local labour-backed Member of the Legislative Assembly (MLA) for Rossland, introduced a bill protecting unions from injunctions and civil liability for damages for "any threat or act of intimidation or conspiracy"; the legislation included a clause providing for retroactive effect of the indemnity provisions.[21] A substitute bill, lacking retroactivity as well as the proscription against injunctions, received majority support in the politically unstable legislature, despite opposition from the governing laissez-faire Liberals (at a time when the province's party system was at its inception and the Socialist MLA for Nanaimo, former mining clerk James Hawthornthwaite, had recently won election). Notwithstanding its ambiguities, economist Paul Phillips described the *Trade-Unions Act, 1902* as "a major triumph for labour."[22]

The federal government also intervened during the Rossland strike, deploying the young labour relations expert William Lyon Mackenzie King to investigate. King arrived at Rossland in late 1901 and reported that "discrimination by the company against members of the union ... was probably the most important cause" of the strike.[23] King, who had been appointed as Canada's first deputy minister of labour a year earlier, served as secretary to the 1903 Royal Commission on Industrial Disputes in the Province of British Columbia, which responded to sympathetic strikes of coal miners and railroad workers by proposing legislative provisions for the conciliation and investigation of disputes.[24] Building on these recommendations, King was influential in Canada's selection of conciliation as its preferred means of settling industrial disputes, a decision embodied in the *Industrial Disputes Investigation Act, 1907* (the "Lemieux Act" or *IDI Act*), which was prompted by a strike of Prairie coal miners. However, as Jeremy Webber has argued, this legislation had only a limited impact on how labour relations were actually conducted in British Columbia and other Canadian jurisdictions.[25] Moreover, conciliation boards appointed under the legislation uncritically accepted the supremacy of capital and the subordination of labour in the employment relationship; this included the authority of employers to direct the work process, control wealth created through productivity gains, and negotiate individually with workers.[26] Indeed, when King was called upon to directly intervene in a strike of Fernie, BC, coal miners in 1907 – the first test of the new *IDI Act* – labour roundly criticized his capitulation to employers' demands for the open shop, perceiving a broader anti-union bias extending from the selection of investigative chairpersons under the act to delays that facilitated the use of strikebreakers.[27] From the outset, BC miners and their organizations condemned the federal labour law as favouring employers' interests and revealing the state's bias in relations between workers and employers; at other times, however, miners and other workers sought protection under the limited provisions of the *IDI Act*, most notably as vicissitudes in the labour market and business cycle curbed their bargaining power.

On the ground, residual elements of the law of master and servant informed the attitude of employers and the approach of judges as industrial disputes arose with greater frequency and intensity in the first decades of twentieth-century British Columbia. This legacy of the common law combined with emerging statutes to arm employers with an array of legal tools to curb working-class agency – from the coercive apparatus of the criminal law to enforce breaches in the employment contract; to injunctions issued in equity (often with workers and the organizations denied notice and hearing); to public-order proscriptions against unlawful assembly, rioting, and intimidation; to the ultimate tool at the disposal of states to assert their authority: military occupation.[28]

The Vancouver Island miners' strike of 1912–14 saw coal-mining employers appeal to magistrates, judges, police, politicians, and soldiers to tap this arsenal of legal tools in a coordinated and ultimately successful effort to curb the collective agency of the striking island coal miners. The exercise of law's coercive powers by legal actors and institutions during the strike fuelled a deep resentment among the island miners and a broader layer of organized workers in British Columbia. They saw a thoroughly unequal playing field and viewed the state and its apparatus as serving employers' interests to the detriment of the rights, interests, and aspirations of the working class. As Fudge and Tucker noted with reference to an earlier coal miners' strike that resulted in military occupation of the Cape Breton coalfield, "the law overwhelmingly favoured the employers."[29]

The "Big Strike," 1912–14

The Vancouver Island miners' strike began on September 16, 1912, in Cumberland, after the Canadian Collieries mine manager fired union activist Oscar Mottishaw and his fellow miners voted to take a mass "holiday" to protest the dismissal.[30] In this, they borrowed a tactic developed by British and American workers to evade legal proscriptions against criminal breach of contract. The immediate issue behind Mottishaw's dismissal was his role as a union-appointed gas inspector under the terms of the *Coal Mines Regulation Act, 1911* and his filing of a "true report" warning of dangerous gas levels at No. 2 mine in Extension (in the preceding three decades, nearly four hundred island miners had been killed in gas explosions). But the larger issue behind the strike was the employer's refusal to recognize the UMWA, which had organized locals in Cumberland, Nanaimo, Extension, and South Wellington and, in June 1912, sent a request to all companies on Vancouver Island to open negotiations on wages and other issues.[31] In 1910, two eastern Canadian railway promoters and capitalists, William Mackenzie and Donald Mann, had purchased the Dunsmuirs' island mining assets, creating the Canadian Collieries (Dunsmuir) Ltd., which, like the previous employer entity, was vehemently anti-union. Other coal operations on the island included the Pacific Coast Coal Mines in South Wellington, the Vancouver and Nanaimo Coal Company's Jingle Pot mine in Nanaimo, and the Nanaimo operations of the Western Fuel Company, an American-owned firm, which implemented a "system of espionage" to guard against unionization.[32]

The strike therefore erupted in the context of a concerted campaign by employers to keep the union out of the Vancouver Island coalfields and a sense of desperation among the miners that collective organization offered the only hope of achieving safety at work and a decent income for themselves and their families. When the Cumberland miners attempted to return to work the day after their "general holiday," they found notices posted at the entrances to the mines instructing them to collect their tools unless they were prepared to sign individual contracts agreeing to work under the existing conditions for a period of two years. When workers at the Extension mines near Nanaimo held their own "holiday" the following day to protest the action in Cumberland, they too were summarily dismissed by Canadian Collieries. As the Socialist trade unionist Jack Kavanagh wrote at the time: "Thus commenced the strike on Vancouver Island – by a lock-out at the hands of the mine owners."[33] From its origins in Cumberland and Extension in September 1912, the strike raged on through 1913 and 1914, spreading over the entire island coalfields, with UMWA district president Robert Foster declaring a district-wide strike on April 30, 1913, the eve of international workers' day (a decision affirmed at a mass meeting of Nanaimo miners the following day).[34] The Conservative premier of the province, Richard McBride (who also held the portfolio of minister of mines), refused repeated overtures from the union and the BC Federation of Labour (BCFL) to intervene to negotiate a settlement.[35]

By the summer of 1913, tensions had reached fever pitch. Work had largely stopped in the mines at Nanaimo and nearby South Wellington and Extension, and in Cumberland to the north. Work proceeded intermittently and contentiously when the company, aided by police, brought replacement workers into the pits. A month into the dispute, 120 special provincial police were hired to protect the strikebreakers.[36] Chinese and Japanese workers, who had originally refused to work, were physically segregated from the Anglo-European strikers by special police and pressured to return to work under threat of deportation. Other replacement workers, shipped from as far away as San Francisco and Britain, arrived in an attempt to break the strike.[37] When Canadian Collieries attempted to transport thirty strikebreakers from Vancouver to Cumberland aboard the steamer *Charmer* in July 1913, a group of miners accosted the workers when the ship stopped at the Nanaimo wharves, prompting police to intervene.[38]

The miners' strike illuminated widely divergent perceptions of the employment relationship and the rights and obligations of workers. A correspondent to the *Nanaimo Free Press* accused the UMWA of inducing "the employees ... to break their contract ... thus exposing them to the charge of being a body of

FIGURE 2 Vancouver Island coal miners, who worked in what were described at the time as the most dangerous mines in the world. Nearly four hundred boys and men died in gas explosions and other incidents in the decades preceding the 1912–14 strike. | Image B-03624, courtesy of the BC Archives

men without business honour, devoid of regard for business obligations." The writer advocated "a legal punishment for the violation of a Dominion statute" (presumably the *IDI Act*).[39] In contrast, UMWA official Frank Farrington, representing the international leadership, asked rhetorically: "Should the workers ... be compelled to accept without question the terms of employment offered by their employer? ... Crude experience is gradually forcing the workers to realize that without combination they are wretchedly helpless and utterly incapable of coping with the mighty powers of wealth."[40] The editor of the Victoria *Week* newspaper, meanwhile, suggested that the government should "not allow either employer or employee to ruin the country with their fractious disputes," and should therefore take over the operation of the island coal mines.[41]

In July 1913, Canada's Conservative minister of labour, Thomas Crothers, arrived on Vancouver Island to investigate the strike. He had met briefly with labour officials and Nanaimo MP Francis Shepherd in Vancouver before sailing to Victoria to meet with McBride and the provincial cabinet, and then boarded a train for a week-long tour of the strike zone. Prior to the minister's arrival, the general manager of Canadian Collieries had issued a public statement announcing that the company would decline any offer for the Department of Labour to serve as mediator. In contrast, UMWA officials insisted that they had "made application for the assistance of the Department of Labor at the beginning of the trouble," a view countered by the minister, who expressed disapproval of the miners' going on strike without invoking the aid of the *IDI Act*.[42] Embracing the language of master and servant, Crothers identified "two of the great causes of unrest" as "the selfish employer and, on the other hand, the indolent servant."[43] But despite this ostensibly balanced stance, labour was strongly critical of Crothers' schedule during the trip. As Kavanagh noted, "during his tour of the mining camps the most notable feature was the scarcity of time at his disposal when being interviewed by the strikers, and an apparent conviction that all men were liars, particularly if they happened to be miners on strike."[44] Kavanagh estimated that the minister devoted 20 percent of his time to speaking with strikers and the remainder with mine managers and strikebreakers; in South Wellington, he spent two hours at the Canadian Collieries offices, while the miners were allegedly refused a meeting (a claim contradicted by press reports).[45]

Crothers left the island on July 19 after giving a speech at a UMWA-sponsored concert, where he declared that industrial war was "indefensible except in the last resort," and that the issues in the present strike "were local and the settlement must be left to Nanaimo."[46] Premier McBride also waded into the fray, musing about summoning the companies and the union to a special conference in Victoria to settle the strike.[47] During his visit, Crothers had announced the appointment of Sam Price, his law partner and mining commissioner in Ontario (who joined Crothers on his island tour), as a Royal Commissioner to investigate the dispute and effect "an adjustment of the differences between the coal miners and the operators."[48] Price remained on Vancouver Island, "ready at all times to offer his mediation."[49] While he was not called upon due to the company's intransigence, his written report provided "a charter of legitimate employer and union behaviour," according to Fudge and Tucker, proposing an end to premature work "holidays" and use of the derogatory term "scab," while giving legal effect to collective agreements and outlawing discrimination against workers for belonging to, or being active in, a union.[50] Price's report was never acted upon, but this attempt at mediation by federal authorities can be distinguished from the more aggressive and openly partial intervention of the provincial government on behalf of mine operators during the strike.

Before the federal labour minister had left the island, the strike assumed more ominous tones. In Cumberland, a fight erupted on Dunsmuir Street on the night of July 18 between strikers and a group of strikebreakers led by a man named Cave. Police arrested several strikers while Cave was released, prompting an angry mob of strikers to drive the strikebreakers out of the town and onto company property. In the wake of the incident, the leader of the UMWA's Cumberland local, British-born socialist Joseph Naylor, was arrested along with several others for "unlawful assembly" and held without bail.[51] In Ladysmith, a striker was stabbed on August 9, culminating in a mass meeting at the Union Hall, where a resolution was passed stating "that if the police do not extend to our members the protection of the law, we will be compelled to take measures to protect ourselves."[52] The night of that meeting, August 11, strikers surrounded Ladysmith's Temperance Hotel, where a dozen strikebreakers were lodged, bombarding the building with stones amid catcalls from the second-storey rooms. An explosion erupted outside the hotel when someone threw a stick of dynamite. A second explosion that night, in one of the cottages lodging strikebreakers, ripped the hand off Alex Mackinnon, a striker who had returned to work, badly burning his face and body. In Nanaimo, a group of seven hundred miners and their families converged on the pithead of No. 1 mine on August 11 urging strikebreakers to quit work before following a group to a home, which they pelted with rocks as the head of household brandished a shotgun.[53] Reports circulated that other strikebreakers were carrying arms, fuelling speculation among the miners that the province was surreptitiously supplying the arms. According to Jack Kavanagh, the coal companies were feeling the financial strain of the strike from the loss of profits, and it appeared that "the executive of the BC Provincial legislature" was "conniving with the coal operators for the purpose of fomenting trouble in the mining camps."[54]

The situation was rapidly deteriorating. On August 12, Nanaimo miners again staged a mass picket at No. 1 mine, refusing to allow fire bosses to enter the mine despite the intervention of local Conservative MP Francis Shepherd, leading to flooding. At nearby South Wellington, a group of between six hundred and eight hundred miners surrounded company housing, beating strikebreakers and driving them and their families into the bush.[55] The following day, mass picketing prevented twenty-three special police constables from disembarking at the Nanaimo wharf; one of the officers was forcibly disarmed and beaten when he drew a gun, and the ship sailed back to Vancouver.[56] At the mining camp of Extension, miners set fire to strikebreakers' lodgings at a place called the "bullpen" and drove the strikebreakers and their families into the mine shaft. The strikebreakers responded with fusillades of bullets into the night; a bystander by the name of James Baxter was shot.[57] Women participated in these crowd actions, and their participation, according to historian John Hinde, "was not a spasmodic act but a deliberate response to months of provocation, frustration, and growing anger that built upon a general consensus in the mining community."[58] While none were arrested, these activists in the UMWA's women's auxiliary were among the most militant members of the mining community, with the *Nanaimo Free Press* reporting: "At Ladysmith and at Extension a great deal of the damage done was the work of women sympathizers."[59]

The miners had wired BC attorney general William Bowser, offering to preserve the peace if the special police were withdrawn. Bowser (who was serving as acting premier, with McBride away on business in Europe), responded with an unequivocal message in the daily press: "When day breaks there will be nearly a thousand men in the strike zone wearing the uniform of His Majesty. This is my answer to the proposition of the strikers that they will preserve the peace if they are left unmolested by the special police."[60] Invoking Military Aid to the Civil Power, the provincial cabinet met in special session to discuss the deployment, as Bowser strong-armed two prominent Nanaimo justices of the peace (one of whom was a former Dunsmuir employee, the other a former mayor) to sign the special requisition for military aid as required under the provisions of the *Militia Act*.[61] Before dawn on August 15, 1913, 250 "citizen-soldiers" from the 72nd Regiment, Seaforth Highlanders, landed at Union Bay from Vancouver, encamping in Cumberland. They were joined by approximately 700 other troops, who sailed from Victoria and Vancouver for Nanaimo, and militiamen from the 88th Regiment Victoria Fusiliers, who left Victoria by train on the Esquimalt and Nanaimo Railway to occupy Ladysmith, Extension, and other points. The "Civil Aid Force in Nanaimo" was headed by Lt.-Col. John A. Hall, a prominent Victoria businessman and founder of the Canadian Explosives Ltd. plant on James Island.[62] Like other militia forces deployed in response to civil disturbances in Canada in the decades prior to the First World War, the force consisted primarily of citizen-soldiers, ordinary civilians who worked at various occupations and volunteered their time as members of local militias, commanded by a smattering of officers with some military experience.[63]

The citizen-soldiers of the Civil Aid Force fanned out across the strike zone, liberating strikebreakers who had been trapped in the pits, detaining perceived ringleaders, and establishing control of ports, railroad stations, and government telegraph offices. On August 17, the district vice president of the UMWA, J.J. Taylor, was arrested in Duncan by plainclothes detectives on his way to a meeting of the BC Federation of Labour executive in Victoria. The following day, August 18, citizen-soldiers under the command of John Hall surrounded a mass meeting of nearly one thousand miners at the Nanaimo Athletic Club. A mounted machine gun was posted at the door, and the entire group was marched out of the hall in groups of ten and escorted at bayonet point to the local courthouse; a total of 773 miners were detained and searched, with 43 arrested and charged for "unlawful assembly" and other offences. Among those arrested was Jack Place, the Social Democratic Party's MLA for Nanaimo, accused of disarming the policeman on the Nanaimo wharf.[64] In an apparent case of overkill, the soldiers destroyed the Athletic Club's hardwood floors, removing the planks under the pretence of searching for a cache of firearms.[65]

Hardware stores throughout the strike zone had their supplies of ammunition confiscated by military authorities, ostensibly to keep them out of the

FIGURE 3 Members of the militia in Duncan, en route to the strike zone, following invocation of Military Aid to the Civil Power during the Vancouver Island miners' strike, August 1913. | Image A-00979, courtesy of the BC Archives

FIGURE 4 Miners under arrest in Ladysmith following the military occupation of the island coalfields, August 1913. | Image E-01194, courtesy of the BC Archives

strikers' hands. In Ladysmith, special police and militia raided private homes in the early hours of August 19, arresting a number of miners, including the president of the UMWA local, Sam Guthrie, whom Kavanagh described as "one of the greatest factors in keeping the peace in Ladysmith."[66] Kavanagh elaborated on the military operation of August 1913:

> Martial law had not been proclaimed, yet Russia was never more militarized than was Vancouver Island. Soldiers armed with rifles and bayonets searched the trains, looked under all the seats, (presumably for machine guns) and subjected all passengers to an inquisition as to their business, etc. All persons travelling to Nanaimo by boat, had to pass an examination at the hand of special police, reinforced by a file of soldiers. It was impossible to send telephone or telegraph messages out of the city without the military knowing the text of such messages.[67]

While a military official claimed in the *Nanaimo Free Press* that no censorship was exercised, Capt. William Rae, adjutant of the 72nd Seaforths, recalled that an officer was posted at the Government Telegraph Office, "inspecting all messages sent and received."[68]

In total, 213 miners were arrested and held without bail pending preliminary hearings. The vast majority were charged with "rioting" in connection with the incidents at Nanaimo, Extension, South Wellington, and Ladysmith, while a smaller number faced charges of intimidation, unlawful assembly, vagrancy, being in possession of stolen property, assault, attempted murder, and other offences against the person; 166 would ultimately be tried and 50 would serve prison sentences.[69] In contrast, two strikebreakers, Bill Rafter of Ladysmith and Cave of Cumberland, were charged with unlawful assembly.[70] With Nanaimo's jail filled beyond capacity, groups of prisoners were transported by train and ship to Victoria and New Westminster to await trial.[71] The UMWA hired the law firms of Bird, Darling and Leighton and Killam and Farris to defend the miners, with prominent Vancouver lawyers Clarence Darling and John Wallace de Beque Farris (who would later serve as British Columbia's first labour minister, then attorney general and senator) representing the accused. Nanaimo citizens formed their own Miners' Defence Fund, bolstered by a $2,000 contribution from a Mrs. Fiddicks of South Wellington, and hired Vancouver lawyer Israel Rubinowitz.[72]

The Trials

Toward the end of August 1913, the arrested miners faced police magistrates James Henry Simpson in Nanaimo and John Stewart in Ladysmith. For years, Magistrate Simpson had been a contentious figure in the local community, with Nanaimo City Council going so far as to petition (unsuccessfully) the premier and the attorney general to abolish the position of police magistrate in 1898; Simpson was removed from the office the following year but was later reappointed.[73] The principal case against the strikers rested on sections 78 to 82 of the *Criminal Code*, which defined the offences of "unlawful assembly" and "rioting" and specified sentences of one and two years' imprisonment, respectively.[74] Notwithstanding this statutory basis, however, the older common law of master and servant could be discerned in the language and reasoning of Magistrates Simpson and Stewart, Judge Frederic William Howay, and the Crown-appointed attorneys who prosecuted the cases. Jack Kavanagh later opined that "the visitors in the court were treated to the edifying spectacle of Magistrate Simpson retiring to the judges [sic] room in company with Prosecuting Attorney Shoebottom, any time he happened to be in doubt as to what course to pursue."[75]

Beginning on August 26, more than one hundred Nanaimo and Extension miners appeared before Simpson for preliminary hearings. Following a formal complaint by defence counsel Clarence Darling that the prosecution had introduced new charges (substituting the more severe offence of "rioting" for "unlawful assembly"), the court heard witnesses who outlined the tumultuous events of the previous weeks. Police officers, bystanders, strikebreakers, and miners gave detailed evidence, which was reported prominently in the local press. Reflecting his views toward workers' collective action, Crown prosecutor T.B. Shoebottom declared that it was a "disgrace" to think that people would take to the streets "to molest people going about their lawful employment, and no sympathy was deserving for those violating the law."[76] Demonstrating a lack of compassion toward the accused, Simpson refused to allow age to be a factor in the cases against a half-dozen youth, suggesting the "unseemly time" in which a disturbance occurred – around midnight – undermined the claim that they acted with a peaceful purpose.[77] All but two dozen of the accused miners had their charges remitted for trial, with bail denied in the interim.[78]

In Ladysmith, Magistrate John Stewart presided over "a strenuous session" in the cases of sixty-four miners accused of rioting. The preliminary hearings opened at the end of August in the unlikely setting of a "moving picture theatre without windows and with a very low ceiling," with a "want of light and air" in the sweltering summer heat. W.H. Bullock-Webster prosecuted the case for the Crown, while local lawyers T.P. Elder and C.K. Kearns defended the miners, with the exception of David Williams, who was defended by his father, Parker Williams, Socialist MLA for Newcastle (who narrowly escaped arrest himself on account of looking after his six children while his wife was in hospital).[79] Midway through the Ladysmith hearings, the wife of Charles Axelton was called as a witness by the Crown prosecutor and asked whether she was the ringleader of the unlawful assembly. Mrs. Axelton, whom the press described as "a veritable amazon, both in build, vigor and strength," denied this but admitted she had joined in the singing of the "Strikers' Rally," the battle song of the Ladysmith miners. "Would you oblige us with a verse or two of the song the strikers were singing?" the Crown attorney asked, and Mrs. Axelton proceeded to lead the courtroom in song. According to a contemporary observer:

> She had a lovely trained voice and in a short time the whole large audience wholeheartedly joined in. The judge tried in every way to stop them and had great difficulty in restoring order to court. There were laughs and boos and the

> whole proceeding was turned into an empty farce. Prisoners, witnesses and spectators burst forth in round after round of applause.[80]

The press reported that even the "threatening bayonet" of the soldier in the courtroom failed to quell the disturbance, and it was "many minutes" before Magistrate Stewart resumed the "dismal, tedious proceedings" in the hot, dark movie theatre.[81] After a week of hearings, Stewart ordered fifty-two of the sixty-four men to stand trial.[82]

The preliminary hearings concluded in mid-September as the militia force in the strike zone was reduced from 1,000 to about 250 men. With the alleged ringleaders behind bars, the military presence in the coalfields was pared down, with Crown prosecutor Shoebottom believing that the remaining soldiers could be removed "without the slightest risk" (at the same time that work began to extend the Esquimalt and Nanaimo Railway to the Comox Valley, perhaps reflecting strategic considerations arising from the crisis, e.g., the need to establish a reliable line of communication for future emergencies).[83] The wives and family members sought to aid the imprisoned miners in material ways. When a group of miners was transported by train from Victoria to Nanaimo for preliminary hearings, their wives and daughters arrived at the train station and attempted to hand them tobacco, food, and clean clothing. Soldiers prevented them from passing the packages, culminating in a tense confrontation at the courthouse and back at the station as the prisoners entrained for the return journey to Victoria.[84] Earlier, Shoebottom had informed the court that prisoners were receiving "goods from their friends" in violation of the law, prompting Simpson to warn that future offenders would be dealt with summarily.[85] When defence counsel Darling asked that the miners be permitted to communicate with their wives to obtain clean linens, with some of the men not having had a change of clothes since their arrest, Shoebottom insisted the matter be left to jail wardens, so as to avoid turning the courthouse into "a washhouse."[86]

On October 9, the trial of the Ladysmith miners opened in Nanaimo. County Court Judge Howay had been brought over from New Westminster to replace the local magistrate, which caused concern among counsel for the accused miners.[87] The circumstances surrounding Howay's appointment to preside at the Nanaimo trials are murky. The County Court judge and historian had graduated from Dalhousie law school with Premier McBride and Attorney General Bowser, had run unsuccessfully for the Liberal Party in the 1907 provincial election, and, following his appointment to the County Court shortly after that election, hobnobbed with the local elite as a member of Vancouver's Terminal City Club, Victoria's Pacific Club, and the Freemasons' lodge.[88] Thirty-nine of the accused had agreed to an expedited trial without jury. On the advice of their lawyers, who intimated that a plea deal was in the works (and that they could therefore expect light sentences), the miners pleaded guilty to charges of unlawful assembly and rioting. A lawyer named Taylor served as Crown prosecutor, and was described in the press as standing "for fair play," reflecting "the best traditions of the English bar."[89] However, Howay's conduct during the trial and sentencing soon revealed that no such agreement existed. In an unusual statement prior to sentencing, the judge accused the miners of "terrorism" and described the disturbance at Extension as "no ordinary riot" but rather the product of "deliberate scheming and planning."[90]

Howay imposed sentences of between three months' and two years' imprisonment with hard labour (the maximum sentence for rioting in the *Criminal Code*); those receiving less than two years were fined on top of the prison sentences.[91] The convicted Ladysmith miners included Sam Guthrie, president of the UMWA's Ladysmith local, local vice president Joseph Taylor (who also served as vice president of the BC Federation of Labour), former alderman William Bauld, and twenty-one-year-old Joseph Mairs, who would die in prison a few months later. (Interestingly, Mairs's father, who had also been arrested, was the one Ladysmith miner who refused the expedited trial, seeking a hearing before a jury of his peers). The decision of the Ladysmith miners to plead guilty in the hope of reduced sentences was likely influenced by economic considerations. Production was slated to resume at Nanaimo's Jingle Pot mine (where, according to the *Nanaimo Free Press*, an agreement had been reached between the company and the strikers, demonstrating "harmony" between "employer and employee" that "all operators having the good will of their employees at heart might do well to study and emulate").[92] In his statement prior to sentencing, Howay described how the conduct of the miners' wives influenced his decision in sentencing: "I was appealed to on behalf of your wives and children but what do I find here? I find your women singing 'Drive the Scabs Away' and throwing rocks themselves and these actions take away very much of the strength of the appeal for mercy on your behalf, because of your women."[93] The Crown prosecutor ended the proceedings expressing the hope that the harsh sentences would have a deterrent effect, leading to a "dissolution of the forces of agitation."[94] The opposite may have in fact ensued, however, with Howay's attempt to make an example of the miners strengthening their solidarity. As an undercover police agent reported to the government: "It is almost certain that not over two dozen men have quitted the ranks of the union, to resume work since the critical period which followed the passing of sentence here by Judge Howay ... The men are far from giving up the battle."[95]

The trials of the other miners moved from Nanaimo to New Westminster on the mainland and resulted in very different outcomes. In contrast to the thirty-eight convictions handed down by Howay in Nanaimo in the absence of a jury, only 12 of the 127 miners tried by jury in New Westminster would receive prison sentences.[96] In the intervening period, Howay was replaced by Justice Aulay Morrison as the presiding judge, after Howay made a statement to the press vilifying the imprisoned miners.[97] In Kavanagh's view, Howay's statement was "calculated to influence the jury before whom the remainder of the prisoners would be tried ... ranchers ... men whose minds were first biased by the lying reports in the newspapers of Vancouver and the lower mainland, and secondly by the interview given to the press by Judge Howay."[98] Howay also attracted controversy for visiting Ladysmith to personally look into the evidence against the accused miners, crossing a line between the prosecutorial and adjudicative functions.[99] The one case decided by Howay in New Westminster, that of miner Richard Goodwin for the disturbance in Cumberland on July 19, 1913, resulted in a sentence of nine months in prison for assaulting a police officer. The remaining trials of the Cumberland miners were delayed owing to a remark by one of the jurors (overheard by a reporter from the *Vancouver World* newspaper) indicating prejudice against the accused before any evidence had been adduced.[100] Justice Morrison, a former Liberal MP (and future chief justice of the BC Supreme Court), was promptly appointed to replace Howay as the presiding judge.[101] While counsel for the miners had opposed the change of trial venue, fearing that a jury composed of farmers would negate the miners' right to a fair trial before a jury "of their peers" (fellow workers), the judge who heard the procedural application refused to recognize "a principle of the law that men are to be tried by their own class," asserting that "no fairer class of men can be found for jury duty than the farming class."[102]

As the special assizes ("the Strikers' Assizes") opened in New Westminster in November 1913, organized labour intensified its campaign in support of the miners and amplified its critique of the judiciary, forming the Miners' Liberation League (MLL) with representation from the BC Federation of Labour, the Vancouver Trades and Labor Council, the IWW, the Socialist Party of Canada, the Social Democratic Party of Canada, and the UMWA. The MLL organized large protest meetings in Vancouver's Dominion Hall and in Victoria,

Edmonton, and other centres demanding the miners' release. The league also raised funds for the miners' legal defence and for their families through "tag days," soliciting money from the public on downtown street corners.[103] In Nanaimo, canvassers sold red MLL buttons and window display posters "depicting a prisoner in stripes, in a cell while his wife and two children stand outside the bars looking at him."[104] Perhaps reflecting agitation from the MLL, Justice Morrison granted bail to all but three of the miners awaiting trial, a demand that had previously been refused.[105]

In the first trial before the Strikers' Assizes in New Westminster on November 14, miners accused of rioting in Cumberland were found not guilty by the jury. The same verdict was delivered in the trial of Thomas Cowler and other miners accused of rioting and assaulting police officer Harry Taylor at the Nanaimo wharf. Cowler's defence had relied on "plain perjury," an undercover Pinkerton agent alleged, after overhearing associates of Cowler in Nanaimo recounting "with glee" details of the assault. Due to the acquittals, the strikers felt that no jury would "believe the word of policemen as against that of a civilian," resulting in acquittals "as fast as the trials are held."[106] Cowler and the other acquitted strikers returned to a heroes' welcome in Nanaimo, greeted by hundreds of cheering strikers on the wharves, hoisted "high on the shoulders of their fellows and carried up to the union headquarters, the hundreds of marchers singing the Marseillaise."[107] The third trial in New Westminster, involving fourteen miners accused of rioting in Ladysmith, was coloured by the earlier guilty pleas of thirty-eight accused in Nanaimo (including Guthrie, Taylor, and Mairs) and sharp instructions from Justice Morrison. The jury found eleven of the accused guilty. The final trial, which began on December 15 and extended into March, related to charges of rioting and property destruction in South Wellington, with the thirty-three accused strikers pleading guilty as part of an amnesty agreement that saw them sentenced to time already served and released.[108]

There appears to have been only one reported appeal against the convictions of the arrested miners: over the admissibility of evidence given by a provincial police constable, George Hanney, who testified against a miner named Angelo and others in their preliminary hearing, but then failed to appear at the trial. The BC Court of Appeal upheld Morrison's conviction of Angelo and the other miners on charges of rioting and unlawful assembly at Extension in August 1913, finding that Morrison had reasonable grounds to believe that the police officer had absconded and was absent from Canada during the trial (and therefore could admit Hanney's disposition from the preliminary hearing as evidence for consideration by the jury).[109]

Aftermath

Organized labour railed against the military occupation of the island coalfields and the judicial proceedings against the strikers. They pointed out that while a number of the miners were arrested, charged, and jailed for relatively minor infractions, not a single strikebreaker had been arrested for the gunplay in Extension in August 1913.[110]

Shortly after the mass arrests, a group of "miners and other citizens" had petitioned Acting Premier Bowser, demanding

> British fair play in the present crisis ... The law should be no respecter of persons; that if miners are to be lodged in jail for breaking the law, then inspectors, mine owners [who started] the present serious trouble and all persons responsible, who have broken the law should also be put in jail, they having set the example of lawlessness. Failing this, we demand the release of the imprisoned miners, in other words we demand British fair play.[111]

Like other social movement actors, the strikers appealed for the protection of the law, invoking the language of natural justice and "Britishness" as rhetorical tools in their battle for public opinion. The BC Federation of Labour contemplated a province-wide general strike in sympathy with the striking coal miners, but, following a referendum vote of its affiliated members and protracted debate, no action was taken.[112]

Reflecting strong labour feeling against the deployment of the militia, the Seaforth Highlanders had faced "a good deal of hostility" while marching to the Vancouver wharf en route to the strike zone in August 1913.[113] Later, the BC Federation of Labour and several unions would amend their constitutions to bar militiamen from their membership ranks.[114] Fissures within the armed forces were celebrated in the labour press, with the *Federationist* recounting the experience of a soldier who left the militia after being deployed on strike duty in Nanaimo, serving time in military prison for having the "moral courage to revolt."[115] The UMWA's BC representative, Frank Farrington, was a lonely voice when he publicly condemned the imprisoned miners as "fools who had not sense enough to keep their mouths shut."[116]

Sympathy for the miners and questioning of legal legitimacy extended to other quarters. The Reverend John Hedley, who ministered at a Methodist church in the south end of Nanaimo, where many miners lived, said: "As far as the miner can see the law and the administration of law exists solely for the protection and help of the mining companies. All loyalty to the state must

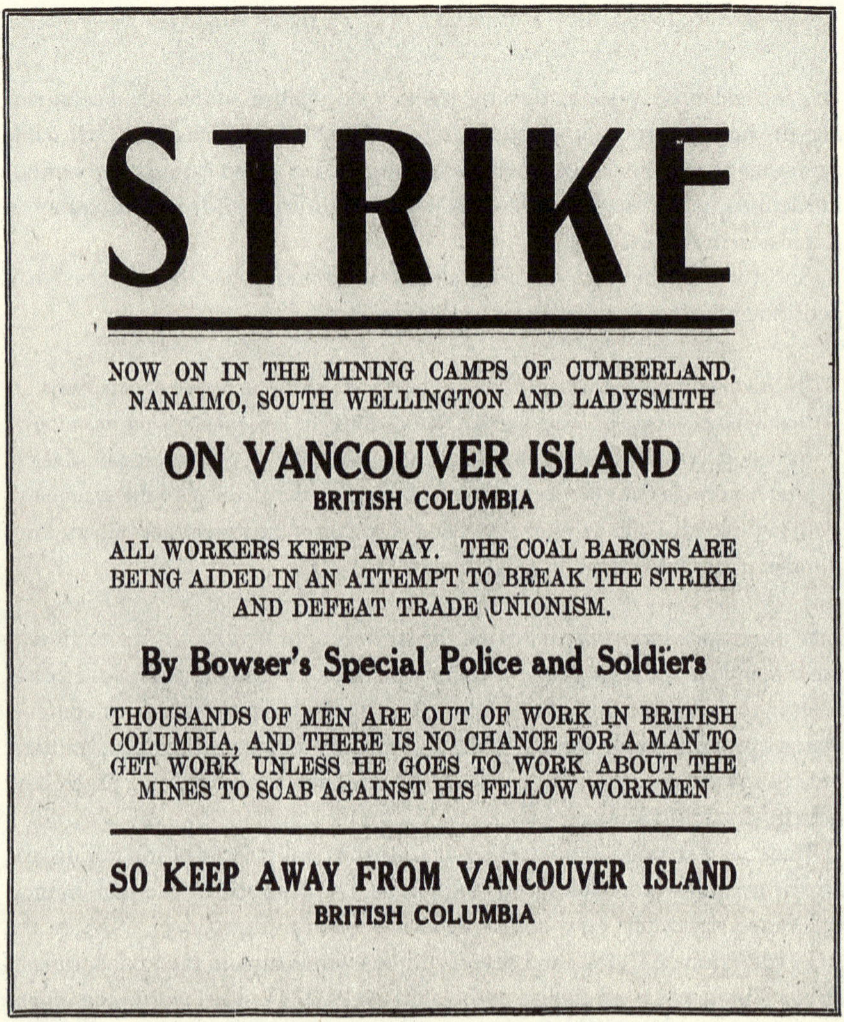
STRIKE

NOW ON IN THE MINING CAMPS OF CUMBERLAND, NANAIMO, SOUTH WELLINGTON AND LADYSMITH

ON VANCOUVER ISLAND

BRITISH COLUMBIA

ALL WORKERS KEEP AWAY. THE COAL BARONS ARE BEING AIDED IN AN ATTEMPT TO BREAK THE STRIKE AND DEFEAT TRADE UNIONISM.

By Bowser's Special Police and Soldiers

THOUSANDS OF MEN ARE OUT OF WORK IN BRITISH COLUMBIA, AND THERE IS NO CHANCE FOR A MAN TO GET WORK UNLESS HE GOES TO WORK ABOUT THE MINES TO SCAB AGAINST HIS FELLOW WORKMEN

SO KEEP AWAY FROM VANCOUVER ISLAND

BRITISH COLUMBIA

FIGURE 5 Strike notice urging workers to keep away during the Vancouver Island miners' strike, 1914. | *British Columbia Federationist* (Vancouver), February 13, 1914, 2

vanish when it is recognized that the state does not stand for justice and fair play."[117] The mayor of Cumberland, meanwhile, expressed the "sympathy of the constituted authorities in this city" with the miners, who had been subjected to the "most extreme provocation and insult" by the coal companies; the mayor, Alexander Campbell, described the "invasion" of Cumberland by special police, followed by more than three hundred militiamen, as "instances of imbecility not to say insanity that would be difficult to find paralleled in the history of the British Empire."[118] This mirrored the pattern in other localities where elected officials, dependent on working-class votes and amenable to local sympathies, deplored the militia call. However, an anticipated breakthrough for Socialist candidates in the municipal election in Nanaimo in early 1914 failed to materialize, in part due to a protest held the same day in Victoria, which many strikers and strikers' wives attended by train.[119] At the end of January 1914, the BC Provincial Police discontinued the contract with the private Pinkerton's National Detective Agency for an undercover agent in Nanaimo, "as matters seem to be settling down."[120]

Another prominent figure, Vancouver lawyer and well-connected Liberal John Wallace de Beque Farris (who had acted for the UMWA), commented on the violent turn of the strike in a 1915 address at the Vancouver Labour Temple Forum: "Human endurance could stand it no longer and they got mad." A "bond of sympathy" between the coal companies and the provincial government constituted "a menace to the interests of labour, and a crime against the coal miners and their families."[121] Increasingly, sections of the Canadian elite were recognizing the benefits of a more regulated approach to labour disputes, with the postwar Royal Commission on Industrial Relations (the Mathers Commission) advocating for the recognition of unions, workers' right to organize, and collective bargaining.[122] Demonstrating a more immediate response to the social unrest on Vancouver Island, the provincial government appointed a commission of inquiry headed by BC Supreme Court Justice Francis Brooke Gregory, and later advanced legislation to provide compensation for damages sustained by property owners during the riots.[123]

Fifty Vancouver Island miners spent the winter of 1913–14 at the Oakalla prison and other penal facilities, including twenty-one-year-old Joseph Mairs of Ladysmith, who died of tuberculosis relating to a bowel infection on January 20, 1914. Parker Williams, Socialist MLA for Newcastle, expressed the indignation of labour when he rose in the legislature to accuse the premier, Judge Howay, and the province's prison system of Mairs's death.[124] Controversy was also generated when figures leaked out of Oakalla showed that the provincial government spent thirteen cents per prisoner per day as the total cost of feeding the inmates.[125] That spring, the provincial government granted a general amnesty to most of the imprisoned miners as discussions proceeded on ways to end the nearly two-year-long strike.[126] They sailed home aboard the SS *Cowichan* to a heroes' welcome at the Nanaimo wharves, as the crowd sang the French revolutionary anthem "La Marseillaise."[127] In July 1914, as war loomed in Europe, the UMWA (from its North American headquarters in Indianapolis) suspended strike pay to the island miners, claiming that $1 million had already been spent.[128] Miners began drifting back to work on terms proposed in a letter from the premier: the companies agreed to a no-discrimination clause against the strikers but refused to recognize the UMWA. As Fudge and Tucker conclude in *Labour Before the Law*, "Vancouver Island coal operators could thank the provincial government and the courts for their help in driving another union off the Island."[129]

Working-class criticism of the role of the judiciary and other state actors was rampant in the wake of the strike. Albert "Ginger" Goodwin, an island coal miner who was blacklisted from the industry for his role in the strike (and who would be killed by a special federal policeman's bullet in 1918 while evading the *Military Service Act, 1917*), suggested that "the forces of government had been used to beat the miners into subjection" and that the "inhuman sentences" handed down by the courts would provide "invaluable material as propaganda for the workers' movement."[130] Goodwin offered a far-reaching critique of the role of the courts during the strike and of workers' perceptions of justice:

> When we find the workers howling about "not getting justice" and that it is "not right" – that is proof that they do not understand the class nature of society. It has been in evidence during the coal strike that this sentiment is nothing but a sham, for those that have [been] brought up before the court and are strikers are given the maximum penalty, while those that are helping the masters to defeat the strikers are let off with the minimum penalty – showing conclusively that the courts are at the disposal of the master class.[131]

This view, that the courts were "at the disposal of the master class," would be sustained in criticisms from labour and other social movement actors in the century that followed.

The response of an array of legal actors and institutions to working-class protests during the Vancouver Island miners' strike of 1912–19 occasioned a deep crisis of law's legitimacy – a fundamental criticism of the law and judiciary among a substantial layer of BC workers – as the coal miners and their families asserted customary claims to challenge employers' property rights, and the legal community responded with coercive violence to restore employer and state control over space, including military occupation, criminal charges, and imprisonment. According to this view, the courts, like the broader legal system and the state itself, was a class institution, with judges serving the narrow class interests of the economic elite, safeguarding private property rights to the detriment of the legitimate interests, aspirations, and customary rights of the working class. Statements from Judge Howay conveyed in his reasons for sentencing and in comments to the press appeared to confirm this view, disclosing attitudes and a bias that were favourable to employers and detrimental to working people. This mirrored legal historian John Orth's findings on the development of labour's approach to the law in Britain: "New legal doctrines ... struck practical workmen as betrayals of traditional fair play. Surpassing parliament as the chief threat to labour, the courts had to be sidelined if not defeated. The lesson labour learned from its history was to see the common law as inherently hostile to its organizational aspirations."[132] Far from being neutral arbiters called upon to fairly adjudicate disputes in the employment relationship, judges such as Howay and Simpson drew from the common law of master and servant and from tort, contract, and the criminal law to re-establish workers' subordinate economic position and restore the authority and spatial control of employers in the mining communities.

The crisis of legal legitimacy occasioned by the Vancouver Island war had far-reaching effects – shaping the politics of protest and BC workers' attitudes and approach to the judiciary and the state far into the twentieth century. These social relations of adjudication also helped lay the groundwork for the more regulated – if fractious – system of labour relations that emerged in British Columbia after the Second World War.

Chapter 2

"THE CLOSENESS OF THE COMPANIES AND THE COURTS"

Crafting Injunction Law in the Era of Industrial Legality

> The judiciary, by its readiness to grant injunctions, aligns itself on the side of employers ... such judicial action inevitably leads to a loss of respect for the judiciary, and is bound just as inevitably to lead to defiance of the law.
>
> – RESOLUTION ADOPTED BY THE CANADIAN LABOUR CONGRESS, JUNE 1966[1]

IN 1966, LABOUR LAWYER Tom Berger, citing jurist Bora Laskin, declared that injunctions "place the judiciary, as far as the labourer is concerned, in the ranks of the employers."[2] The future BC Supreme Court judge and social democratic politician made this observation in a brief presented to a special conference on injunctions organized by the BC Federation of Labour, for which he served as counsel. The wider context for Berger's report and the conference was a heightening of working-class anger against the use of injunctions in labour disputes, provoked by a tense strike involving 250 workers at the Lenkurt Electric Company plant in the Vancouver suburb of Burnaby in 1966. This action culminated in the arrests of 30 trade unionists, including the leaders of the Vancouver and District Labour Council (VDLC) and locals of the International Woodworkers of America, the Marine Workers and Boilermakers, and the striking International Brotherhood of Electrical Workers (IBEW). "Lenkurt sparked an all-out campaign by the labour movement against the use of injunctions, the jailing of labour leaders, and restrictive labour legislation," historian Elaine Bernard noted.[3]

In the decade preceding the Lenkurt strike, BC judges had received 224 applications for *ex parte* injunctions against picketing and had denied only 2.[4] Compared with the previous decade, this marked a threefold increase in the number of applications for injunctive relief received and granted by the courts, to uphold employers' property rights in the face of customary working-class challenges.[5] In a tangible way, the judiciary intervened to legally delineate the spaces around workplaces as employers' property – demonstrating the contestation of space in relation to protest. In the 1950s and 1960s, employers turned from the *Criminal Code* proscriptions discussed in the previous chapter to the law of tort to "minimize risk" arising from labour disputes, combining civil claims against workers and unions for economic losses suffered in relation to "unlawful" picketing with applications for the equitable remedy of the injunction to restrain the picketing, prevent the losses, and restore production. This shift from the criminal law to civil tort remedies continued to rely on the one nonstatutory criminal offence that endured in Canada from the common law – the offence of criminal contempt of court, arising from the inherent jurisdiction of the judiciary to uphold its own authority. In the leading labour case of *Poje* (discussed later in this chapter), the Supreme Court of Canada defined this offence as a contempt that was sufficiently public as to bring the administration of justice into disrepute.[6]

By their very nature, *ex parte* ("for one party") injunctions were lopsided and blunt legal tools, approved by judges on application of company lawyers, with workers and their organizations denied notice and hearing. Critics viewed such injunctions as evidence of an unhealthy relationship between companies and courts, issued by the proverbial judge in a nightgown, awakened in the dead of night by a company lawyer to hastily scrawl a signature on a court order. "The closeness of the companies and the courts" was how labour journalist George North described the relationship in his 1959 newspaper editorial titled "Injunctions Won't Build Bridges or Catch Fish," which got him a month in prison for contempt.[7] Such *ex parte* injunctions placed the full weight of the criminal law – authorized by judges and enforced by police – at the disposal of employers to restrain workers from acting collectively, by removing pickets and restoring production, before the substantive issues behind the dispute had ever been heard. Indeed, with picket lines gone, the actual issues behind the underlying tort action often never returned to the courtroom. It was this lack of due process – and the lopsided way in which the coercive power of the law was deployed – that inflamed organized workers, just as it would inflame social movement actors in later decades when companies and governments initiated injunction proceedings to curb Indigenous, anti-abortion, environmental, and poor peoples' protests. This feeling of outrage was reflected in the resolution adopted by the Canadian Labour Congress in the wake of the Lenkurt strike.[8]

This chapter explores the contested social relations of adjudication and crises of legal legitimacy surrounding the proliferation of injunctions granted by BC judges in response to working-class incursions on employers' private property rights in the decades that followed the Second World War. The law of injunctions and contempt was hotly contested during this era, and many of the practices, procedures, and precedents emerged at this time – establishing a line of jurisprudence that would be deployed in diverse social contexts in later decades as the locus of extra-legal protest shifted from organized workers to other social movement actors. Focusing on key cases, including *Poje, North, Lenkurt*, and *United Fishermen and Allied Workers' Union* (UFAWU), I examine the technical procedures deployed by companies, lawyers, and judges and the broader pattern of judicial reasoning that developed in response to labour disputes in the 1950s and 1960s. I also demonstrate how the crises of legal legitimacy occasioned by judicial interventions against labour protests – specifically, working-class political mobilization against "the closeness of the companies and the courts" – prompted intervention by the provincial legislature, with the enactment of statutory law to sharply curb the power of the judiciary to intervene in labour disputes.

Injunctions in the Era of "Free" Collective Bargaining

If the period before the Second World War can be described as the era of "labour before the law," then the years that followed represented the heyday of collective bargaining, a high-water mark in the collective power of workers to shape conditions of work and capture a larger share of wealth. However, even in this period of postwar "industrial legality," which coincided with the "long boom" of North American capitalism in the 1950s and 1960s, sharp constraints were imposed on the freedom of workers to act collectively, particularly to picket and to withdraw their labour. Challenging the image of a steady progression of worker rights, as envisioned by the "industrial pluralist" school, and the myth of a hands-off, benevolent liberal democratic state, evidence from postwar British Columbia points to a consistently high degree of state intervention. Intervention extended from giving shape and form to the statutory context within which collective bargaining occurred, to frequent legal intervention by judges who imposed injunctions, fines, and prison sentences to curb the collective power of workers when they threatened the property rights of employers. Rather than the state and judiciary stepping back to allow "free" collective bargaining to proceed, worker rights were constantly contested, shaped, and defined, with the law of injunctions and contempt standing out as a crucial site of social and legal contestation.

The law of injunctions had preceded the advent of twentieth-century collective bargaining. Indeed, it owed its origins to premodern times, as an ancient equitable remedy evolving from the Roman *interdict* and writs issued by the Court of Chancery in English law.[9] However, it was in the twentieth century that injunctions moved from a fairly narrow application in commercial and other areas of law to become a central legal device wielded by employers to curb the collective power of unionized workers. As Eric Tucker and Judy Fudge demonstrate, the labour injunction first emerged in Canada in industrial Ontario prior to the First World War, as employers responded to metalworkers' strikes by turning to a line of jurisprudence that had developed in England and the United States in the 1890s. In those countries, judges fashioned new economic torts to protect employers against harm caused by labour disputes. Moving beyond the criminal law, Canadian employers sought to exploit the "more directly coercive possibilities" of the common law, especially the law of tort.[10] With the "active support of judges," they brought actions for damages against unions and their officers, aimed to prohibit workers from inducing others to quit work or boycott products, and sought injunctions to "stop immediately the workers' offending behaviour." According to Tucker and Fudge, interlocutory injunctions could be obtained "whenever a *prima facie* case of illegality was made out and grave damage to the employer was threatened," resulting in expedited proceedings and contempt charges against offending workers.[11] Unlike most areas of criminal law, defendants facing contempt proceedings for breaching injunctions were denied the right to a trial by jury – as the judiciary had jealously guarded its inherent jurisdiction to protect its own authority since the *Almon* case in Britain in 1765.[12]

In the era of labour before the law, the procedural unfairness of the labour injunction drew the ire of critical lawyers and legal scholars, including Felix Frankfurter, a Harvard professor and future US Supreme Court judge. Frankfurter co-authored (with Nathan Greene) the 1930 book *The Labor Injunction*, documenting "beyond any reasonable doubt that the labour injunction was deployed abusively by an anti-union judiciary to shore up the prerogatives of capital."[13] Frankfurter was instrumental in persuading American legislators to sharply curb the powers of superior courts with respect to labour injunctions with the passage of the *Norris–La Guardia Act* (1932).[14] No similar law reform occurred in Canada. However, the American experience coloured the perspective of some Canadian legal practitioners and academics, including Bora Laskin, the labour lawyer and teacher turned Supreme Court judge, who had studied under Frankfurter at Harvard. In a 1937 article, Laskin noted that the labour injunction had been used only infrequently in Canada, but feared that a recent decision at the Ontario Court of Appeal (the *Bassel's Lunch* case, where striking restaurant workers were jailed for ten days for defying a court injunction against picketing) indicated a widening ambit for this legal mechanism. Laskin warned that "Canadian courts will find themselves similarly circumscribed by legislative enactments if they fail to infuse their equitable jurisdiction in labour injunction decrees and contempt, with a spirit of social understanding."[15] Prior to 1948, only three picketing cases had reached the BC Court of Appeal, all of them in response to picketing in front of movie theatres, where strikers "targeted consumers as much as owners" and where the prerogatives of twentieth-century mass consumerism "required the creation of common orderly spaces where middle-class patrons could safely mix with working-class viewers." During that era, employers' preferred legal remedy to quash working-class protest was the criminal law; earlier, it was the common law of master and servant.[16]

The BC model of postwar industrial legality was marked by the ascendency of the labour injunction, undermining the promise of legislative recognition of worker rights.[17] Prior to the Second World War, the provincial Liberal government of Thomas "Duff" Pattullo had enacted the *Industrial Conciliation and Arbitration Act* (*ICA Act*) in 1937, responding to working-class demands for recognition of bargaining rights amid legislative changes in the United States and raucous disputes in British Columbia, such as a 1935 longshore workers' strike. However, Pattullo's legislation recognized only committees of employees, rather than unions, a move that favoured "company unions," aimed at blocking the spread of the militant International Woodworkers of America (IWA) along the coast.[18] Following a violent and protracted strike at Blubber Bay in 1938, and a concerted campaign by the province's union movement, the *ICA Act* was amended to recognize unions, but the legislation fell short of more far-reaching recognition of workers' rights embodied in the US *Wagner Act*.[19] In 1941, the labour-aligned Co-operative Commonwealth Federation (CCF) won a plurality of votes in the BC general election, forcing the two establishment parties into a coalition government. Faced with this political threat as well as wartime labour pressures, the Liberal-Conservative coalition introduced more expansive protections for workers in a 1943 amendment to the *ICA Act*, which, among other provisions, outlawed discriminatory conduct by employers toward union members.[20] British Columbia's amended

ICA Act had an important role in shaping federal Privy Council Order 1003, adopted in 1944, which provided the framework for postwar collective bargaining in Canada.[21]

In 1947, the Liberal-Conservative coalition government substantially amended the *ICA Act* again, with Bill 39, incorporating the collective bargaining provisions of the wartime Privy Council Order 1003 while imposing stiff penalties for illegal strikes and walkouts. These legislative changes were consistent with developments in the United States, where the *Taft-Hartley Act* of 1947 substantially amended the Wagner model by restricting workers' rights, tipping the balance in labour relations back in employers' favour. The passage of Bill 39 "signified the defeat of reform liberalism in British Columbia."[22] A year later, the province went further in response to employer lobbying and unsuccessful prosecutions of strikers, further amending the *ICA Act* to wrap unions "in a straitjacket of legality – any violation of the multitude of restrictions on collective action both threatened a union's legal status to insist on recognition and left it open to costly civil actions."[23] Though less draconian than anti-Communist legislation adopted in Quebec, British Columbia's amended *ICA Act* of 1948 placed much stronger restrictions on workers and unions than the more permissive legislation in place in Ontario and Saskatchewan.[24] Section 72 prohibited workers from going on strike "contrary to any of the provisions of this Act," under threat of union decertification, while sections 57, 62, 70, and 76 expanded the ambit for civil litigation against unions and reduced protections against unfair labour practices.[25]

The legal constraints of this emerging era of industrial "legality" were demonstrated and contested in a strike of printers at the *Vancouver Daily Province* that began in 1946 and dragged on for nearly three years. Early in the strike, the employer attempted to resume production with the aid of strikebreakers, but "the pickets chased these men away," according to an RCMP Security Service officer.[26] As members of other unions, including the Communist-led Canadian Seamen's Union and International Union of Mine, Mill and Smelter Workers (Mine-Mill), joined the picket lines of the striking International Typographical Union (ITU), the employer obtained an injunction to prevent picketing. This was the "first major postwar injunction case in Canada."[27] Union officials were fined a total of $10,000 in civil damages, while twelve picketers were convicted of the *Criminal Code* offence of "watching and besetting."[28] The printers' strike was coloured by technological changes in the industry, toward more machine-intensive processes that reduced labour requirements and weakened workers' bargaining power, reflecting the wider challenge posed by automation in the postwar era.[29] The *Vancouver Daily*

Province strike also marked the decline of that publication as the pre-eminent daily newspaper in British Columbia.

The anti-labour tone of postwar labour legislation and judicial pronouncements led a growing number of workers to question the legitimacy of the law and to openly defy the *ICA Act* provisions that restricted picketing and the timing of strikes. John Stanton, a labour lawyer who served as counsel for many BC unions in postwar injunction and contempt proceedings, raised a fundamental question underpinning the law of injunctions and contempt: "Should judges, like anyone else in society, have to earn and keep the respect of their fellow citizens and not try to impose it by harsh methods? Hadn't some judges created their own dilemma by allowing 'closeness,' real or perceived, to develop between themselves and employers?"[30] Examining working-class responses to injunctions in an earlier period, Tucker and Fudge suggest that judicial intervention encouraged workers to view themselves as "victims of a system that systematically favoured employers," rather than engendering greater respect for the law.[31] Focusing on the postwar period in Ontario, labour historian Joan Sangster emphasized the labour movement's "deeply ambivalent attitudes towards the state," with the pattern of strikes and judicial intervention disrupting "prevailing faith in industrial legality." Lenkurt resembled the Tilco strike the same year; as Sangster opined with respect to the latter, it "exposed the extent to which the 'free' in collective bargaining was an ideological legitimization of capitalism rather than a reality of class relations, showing how injunctions could still be used ... to buttress the raw power of employers determined to bar unions from the workplace."[32]

"Injunctions Won't Build Bridges or Catch Fish": From Poje *to Lenkurt*

In the summer of 1952, in the midst of a major strike of woodworkers against employers in the coastal forest products sector, Tony Poje, vice president of the IWA local in Duncan on Vancouver Island, led a group of picketers to the Nanaimo wharves, where lumber was being loaded onto the MS *Vedby*. Work halted when longshore workers refused to cross the woodworkers' picket line. The owner of the ship, Canadian Transport (U.K.) Ltd., applied for and received an injunction from BC Supreme Court Justice (and future MacMillan Bloedel Ltd. executive) John Clyne enjoining Poje and others from "watching and besetting" the ship and preventing or interfering with loading or access. When Poje persisted with the picketing, mobilizing 150 woodworkers to fortify the picket line at the wharf until a settlement was reached a week later, he was charged and convicted of criminal contempt of court at the initiative of the chief justice of the BC Supreme Court, Wendell Farris (brother of John Wallace de Beque Farris). Although Canadian Transport applied to the court, after the settlement had been reached, to discontinue the civil action, dissolve the injunction, and withdraw the motion for contempt, Farris felt that the contempt was sufficiently serious that it was necessary to proceed. Describing Poje's "reprehensive conduct" as "ringleader" as "a particularly brazen and contumacious contempt," Farris sentenced him to three months in prison and a $3,000 fine (or an additional nine months in prison in default of payment). Fourteen other picketers, who offered a complete apology to the court, received lesser sentences of a $300 fine or one month in prison.[33]

The BC Court of Appeal and the Supreme Court of Canada upheld this ruling, finding that "the large numbers of men involved and the public nature of the defiance of the order" rendered the conduct criminal contempt of court.[34] The *Poje* case rested on a vital question in injunction and contempt law – whether any rules apply in contempt proceedings initiated by the court itself. Court of Appeal Justice Sidney Smith, writing for the majority of the three-member division, had no hesitation accepting Chief Justice Farris's decision, stating that "when a judge acts on his own motion, no rules apply." However, in strong dissenting reasons, Justice Cornelius O'Halloran found that Poje and the other picketers were improperly charged and tried, and that the injunction itself should never have been issued *ex parte*. "If something did occur beyond legal picketing it has not emerged as anything serious. The surrounding atmosphere pictured in the evidence points more to maintenance and upholding of civil rights, viz., the legal right to picket," O'Halloran stated.[35] The Supreme Court of Canada wavered on this question, finding that the contempt was of sufficient magnitude to make it criminal, rendering "the rules of court ... inapplicable as they apply only in civil proceedings."[36] The law remained unsettled on this question, due to ambiguities in the Supreme Court's decision, creating uncertainty in future labour cases. Nonetheless, *Poje* would emerge as the leading case of criminal contempt in British Columbia, establishing legal procedures and principles that were followed in subsequent decades. From its origins in the labour injunction, the principles and technology established in *Poje* would be applied by judges and other members of the legal community later in the twentieth century and into the twenty-first century in response to protests by anti-abortionists, environmentalists, Indigenous activists, and homeless people and their allies.[37]

In 1959, the labour injunction and legal principles contested in *Poje* were again brought into the spotlight, during a periodic upturn in labour militancy that saw major strikes of fishers, woodworkers, and civil servants. This militancy influenced – and was influenced by – legislative changes introduced by British Columbia's conservative Social Credit government, which further restricted labour rights and magnified divisions between organized workers and the state. Bill 43, which amended the *Labour Relations Act, 1954*, restricted picketing and strikes and gave the Labour Relations Board (LRB) and government the power to issue injunctions. The legislation "allowed companies to obtain injunctions practically at will against striking unions," according to labour lawyer Harry Rankin. The right to freely disseminate information during labour disputes, a hallmark of Supreme Court of Canada Justice Ivan Rand's famous 1946 arbitration decision in the Ford Windsor strike, was set aside. Bill 43 also weakened workers' bargaining power by prohibiting secondary picketing and confirmed the status of unions as legal entities that could be sued for damages. A second piece of legislation, Bill 128, outlawed civil service strikes, amending the province's *Constitution Act* to ensure "the continuation without interference or interruption of public services."[38]

In the wake of these legislative changes, labour opposition to injunctions was brought into sharp relief in 1959 during a strike of ironworkers employed in the construction of the new bridge crossing over the Second Narrows of Burrard Inlet in Vancouver. A year earlier, the half-built bridge had collapsed, taking the lives of eighteen ironworkers. When the contract came up for negotiation and ironworkers walked off the job, BC Supreme Court Justice Alex Manson granted an *ex parte* injunction to Dominion Bridge ordering the workers back to work. The leadership of ironworkers Local 97 complied with the letter of Manson's ruling, but noted that they did so under compulsion and included legal advice (from Tom Berger) to the effect that the decision was bad and was under appeal. When the workers remained off the job, ignoring the union's meek direction to end the strike, Manson promptly summoned twenty-one union members and officers into his courtroom and, following heated questioning, fined them $19,000 (equivalent to the union's total liquid assets).[39] Although Berger succeeded in overturning Manson's ruling on appeal, with the higher court noting the resentment felt by workers when "the person regarded as prosecutor acts as judge" and finding that no contempt existed (since the union had complied with the order), that was not the end of the story.[40]

Before the appeal had been heard, George North, editor of the *Fisherman* newspaper, had lambasted Manson's ruling in an editorial titled "Injunctions Won't Build Bridges or Catch Fish."[41] The editorial quoted favourably an ironworkers official to the effect that "a court order instructing men to return to work constitutes slavery," and suggested that "the answer given by the strikers" (in defying Manson's injunction) was providing "sensible leadership" to the rest of the labour movement. Referring to pending disputes of woodworkers and fishers, the editorial (presumably written by North, though this was never proved in court) declared that "united action by all labor" could win these strikes "despite the opposition of employers, government, and courts. Injunctions can't catch fish, cut logs, nor in the case of the Ironworkers' strike, can they build bridges."[42] Manson was outraged and responded by taking notice of the editorial in open court, claiming that it brought the court into contempt and interfered with the administration of justice: "It has been held that the courts should not be above criticism in the press, but to suggest partiality and prejudice is quite another matter."[43] He appointed J.A. Clark to act as prosecutor.[44]

In July 1959, the North case came before Justice Norman Whitaker (a former Liberal speaker of the provincial legislature). North and the Fisherman's Publishing Society were represented by two lawyers, John Stanton and Harry Rankin. Stanton focused on procedural matters, pointing out that if the case had evolved from the original civil lawsuit (brought by Dominion Bridge against the union) into a criminal proceeding, then North should be entitled to the ordinary protections afforded to anyone charged with a criminal offence, including the right to have the prosecution prove its case beyond a reasonable doubt and the right to be provided with particulars of any charges. The judge and prosecutor dodged both issues, guided by the view in *Poje* (which the appeal court had affirmed but on which the Supreme Court of Canada had wavered) that in contempt proceedings brought by a judge, no rules apply.[45] Turning to the substantive issues, Rankin read a statement from North into the record, emphasizing North's long-standing opposition to repressive labour laws, and noted that "behind and above all this legislation stands that court injunction ... Instead of the strike being the 'court of last resort,' the injunction has assumed that status." North suggested that courts, by "allowing themselves to become involved in industrial disputes," brought themselves into disrepute.[46] He repeated UBC law professor Fred Carrothers's caution against using the injunction as a "sword of collective bargaining rather than a shield of legal rights." Rankin, in a submission for the defence, suggested that "respect ... cannot be compelled."[47] Whitaker advised Rankin that "if Mr. North had written all that in his paper I don't think he would be here today," to which Rankin quipped: "He probably would not be editor of the Fisherman either. Editors have to be brief, pungent and to the point."[48] Not persuaded by Rankin's arguments, Whitaker did not call on Clark for argument on behalf of the prosecution, and instead promptly found North guilty of criminal contempt of court. In his reasons for judgment, Whitaker stated that "the effect of the article is to undermine public confidence in the courts," describing North's conduct as "a particularly flagrant contempt of court."[49] Whitaker sentenced North to thirty days in prison and fined his employer, the Fisherman's Publishing Society, $3,000, a considerable sum for a nonprofit organization (approximately $33,000 in 2026 dollars).[50]

North appealed the conviction and was released on $1,000 bail after spending twenty-four hours at Oakalla.[51] At the appeal hearing in Vancouver on October 9, 1959, Stanton appeared with Rankin on behalf of North, telling the three-judge division of the Court of Appeal that North should have been entitled to the same protections afforded to other individuals accused of indictable criminal offences, including being provided with full particulars of the criminal charge so that the accused could answer the charge. Citing precedent, Stanton suggested that "the liberty of the subject was at stake and the charge must be proved step by step."[52] Crown prosecutor Clark challenged this assertion, stating that *Criminal Code* rules did not apply in contempt proceedings. He cited contempt proceedings against the *Province* newspaper and journalist Eric Nicol for comment in relation to a murder conviction, in which case the *Criminal Code* had not applied and the newspaper and journalist were acquitted after apologizing in open court. Clark pointed out that North had offered no similar apology, and suggested that the courts were merely enforcing the law, and if the unions objected to the law, they should challenge Bill 43 through proper political channels, rather than by bringing the administration of justice into disrepute.[53] The Court of Appeal pronounced judgment on October 20, denying the appeal and upholding North's conviction. North was remanded into RCMP custody to rigorous handshakes from union members who had packed the courtroom, and proceeded to serve the remainder of his sentence at Oakalla.[54]

In the wake of North's conviction, unions representing Vancouver painters and BC pulp mill workers adopted resolutions calling on the Government of Canada and the BC attorney general to remove Manson as a judge for his conduct toward the ironworkers and North.[55] (No action appears to have been taken on this request.) After North's conviction was upheld on appeal and while he was serving his sentence at Oakalla, the United Fishermen and Allied Workers' Union organized a picket line at the ruling BC Social Credit League's annual convention at the Pacific National Exhibition in Vancouver, seeking to ramp up pressure on the province.[56] The UFAWU also sent a petition to Attorney General Robert Bonner, asking whether the cabinet could exercise

FIGURE 6 George North, editor of *The Fisherman* newspaper, receives a hero's welcome after being released from Burnaby's Oakalla prison on November 14, 1959, after serving a thirty-day jail sentence for criminal contempt of court for publishing an editorial titled "Injunctions Won't Build Bridges or Catch Fish." | BC 1532/2/1, Fisherman Publishing Society Collection, University of British Columbia Rare Books and Special Collections

executive clemency and grant North a pardon from the contempt conviction. Bonner responded that the power to grant a pardon resided solely with the federal government, and advised the eighty-four petitioners to take up the matter with Ottawa.[57] Federal Justice Minister E. Davie Fulton promised to look into the matter, but delayed making a decision until after North had served the remainder of his thirty-day sentence, whereupon he announced that the federal government would not intervene in North's case (nor would it quash the $3,000 fine against the Fisherman's Publishing Society).[58] In the intervening period, North was released to a hero's welcome, as a crowd of eighty fishers congregated at the gates of Oakalla, hoisting North onto their shoulders and singing "Solidarity Forever."[59] North also received a thirty-day paid holiday from the UFAWU executive, in recognition of his time served in prison.[60] "His challenge to the system of free-wheeling injunctions had made a considerable impression," Stanton commented in his memoirs.[61]

The Lenkurt Strike

Controversy over labour injunctions continued in the 1960s, as working-class militancy intensified against the backdrop of a wider current of social protest that enveloped British Columbia, North America, and the world. This rebellious mood set the stage for the spring 1966 confrontation at the Lenkurt Electric Company plant in the Vancouver suburb of Burnaby. In the middle of contract negotiations, the parent International Brotherhood of Electrical Workers (IBEW) had agreed to allow management to increase the use of overtime. Workers at the plant, members of a renegade union local with a long history of dissent against the parent union, walked out in protest at the end of April. The company responded by firing 257 workers.[62] When other unions joined the dismissed workers' picket line, the company successfully applied for an *ex parte* injunction, which the court granted at the beginning of May.[63]

Vancouver's labour movement responded with the tactic of mass picketing under the aegis of a committee spearheaded by the BCFL, the VDLC, and IBEW Local 213. Three hundred workers converged on the Lenkurt line at 7 a.m. on May 12, 1966, breaking through a cordon of three dozen RCMP officers to block a road leading into the plant. In the ensuing clashes between strikers, sympathizers, RCMP officers, and replacement workers – and amid the singing of "Solidarity Forever" and "We Shall Overcome" – several picketers were hit by moving vehicles, police officers were allegedly assaulted, and nine people were arrested, including one woman, the *Globe and Mail* noted.[64] The violence prompted Attorney General Bonner to appoint Vancouver lawyer George Murray to investigate the dispute.[65] Thirty picketers were jailed or fined during the Lenkurt strike, including VDLC secretary Paddy Neale, Marine Workers and Boilermakers president Jeff Power, IWA Local 1-217 vice president Tom Clarke, and IBEW Local 213 business agent Art O'Keeffe – who received prison sentences of between three and six months. Another twenty-six activists were fined a total of $3,100. Neale, who spent four and a half months in prison, declared defiantly: "We would act in the same manner if it became necessary."[66]

The jailing of BC labour leaders in the Lenkurt strike focused attention on the labour injunction as never before, not only in British Columbia but also across Canada, where a similar case involving injunctions and mass arrests centred on women workers at the Tilco Paint plant in Peterborough, Ontario. In June 1966, delegates at the Canadian Labour Congress convention approved a resolution instructing officers to urge affiliated unions to "engage in a strong and militant campaign to eliminate the use of the injunction in labour disputes," to "challenge injunctions wherever and whenever they are granted," to materially support unions and workers affected by injunctions, and to take this campaign into the legislative and political fields. The readiness of the judiciary to grant injunctions aligned judges "on the side of employers," the resolution declared, leading to a "loss of respect" for the judiciary and "defiance of the law" (see Appendix 3).[67] Provincially, the BCFL organized a special conference on injunctions in October 1966, distributed 100,000 copies of a pamphlet titled *Guilty Until Proven Innocent*, raised funds for the families of the jailed labour leaders, and commissioned lawyer Tom Berger to prepare a report on the exercise of injunctions in labour disputes.[68] Political organizations of the left declared their sympathies with labour and called for reform of the law to remove judges' power to issue injunctions during labour disputes. The social democratic New Democratic Party (NDP), which counted Berger among its legislative caucus after the September 1966 provincial election (and which he would briefly lead in 1969), insisted that injunctions "must be completely eliminated."[69] The more radical Communist Party of Canada, meanwhile, located the controversy surrounding injunctions in the context of the balance of class forces and social and political fault lines in the province: "Our labour leaders are willing to go to jail to defend their principles. On the other side the Socred government is pressing charges against the strikers and issuing injunctions to the monopolies." According to the Communists, 1966 put "a stop to a lot of apathy."[70]

Contemptuous Fishers

These fault lines were exposed a year later, in the spring of 1967, when trawl fishers at Prince Rupert on British Columbia's north coast went on strike and shoreworkers refused to handle "hot" fish. Four days into the strike (which was coloured by a dispute among rival unions over jurisdiction in the industry), BC Supreme Court Justice Kirke Smith granted an *ex parte* injunction requested by several vessel owners, ordering the shoreworkers to handle the fish to prevent it from spoiling.[71] Reflecting the defiant spirit of British Columbia's labour movement and the distinctly militant and democratic tradition of the United Fishermen and Allied Workers' Union, which represented most fishers and shoreworkers, union leaders Homer Stevens, Steve Stavenes, and Jack Nichol refused to communicate Smith's order to the membership. A day later, Smith issued a second injunction, spelling out the specific action required of the union officers: to send a telegram informing "all members ... concerned in the landing and processing of ground-fish" to carry out such operations "forthwith."[72]

Rather than comply, the UFAWU executive put the question of whether to send the telegram to a membership vote, receiving an 89 percent mandate to ignore the court order.[73] Half a million pounds of fish rotted in the holds of five vessels as a result of UFAWU members' refusal to handle the "hot" fish.[74]

Smith's second injunction order was distinct from many court orders issued against striking unions around this time, due to its *mandatory* rather than *prohibitive* provisions, requiring the union to undertake a specific action rather than merely restraining it from interfering with employers' operations or property. On April 28, 1967, another BC Supreme Court judge, Thomas Dohm (who would soon leave the bench to preside over the Vancouver Stock Exchange),[75] took notice in open court of the UFAWU's apparent defiance of the court's authority. Dohm invited Stevens, Stavenes, and Nichol to "show cause" why they should not be found in contempt, and invited the attorney general to assume conduct of the prosecutions. In issuing the order, Dohm acted *ex meru motu*, by way of his own motion.[76] The union responded by appealing Dohm's order, which it described as "bad" on several grounds, including depriving the union of its right to a fair hearing as provided for in the *Canadian Bill of Rights* and at common law, and being contrary to public policy by relying on procedures that were discriminatory, directed primarily "against a certain class of persons, namely, Trade Unions and their officers."[77] However, the BC Court of Appeal refused to hear the appeal, accepting the submission of counsel for the attorney general that it had no jurisdiction because Dohm's ruling was not an order but rather a process for bringing alleged contemnors before the court.[78] On May 11, 1967, Justice Smith issued a third injunction, prohibiting the UFAWU from declaring the Prince Rupert halibut fleet to be "hot" and from interfering with the lawful business of the vessel owners.[79]

The UFAWU's defiance of the court orders led to the stiffest criminal contempt sentences in British Columbia's legal history, with Stevens and Stavenes ultimately serving nine months of one-year prison sentences at Oakalla and other correctional facilities, and the union fined $25,000 for defying the judge's orders (equivalent to approximately $230,000 in 2026 dollars).[80] In the midst of the strike, the UFAWU's Central Council of Women's Auxiliaries defended the leadership and the rationale for the strike: "Our Union is a democratically run organization – it works only for the benefit of its many members. Its members vote for strike action only after all other means of settling differences have been exhausted."[81]

Earlier in the year, prior to the strike and the injunction and contempt proceedings, Stevens, Stavenes, and Nichol had jointly written in their annual officers' report to the UFAWU convention that the preceding year had witnessed "an unprecedented use of court procedures to strengthen the employer's hand in negotiations." They cited the jailed longshore workers and the leaders of several unions who remained in prison "for walking on a peaceful picket line" during the Lenkurt dispute, and the twenty-six imprisoned Tilco strikers in Ontario. Presciently, the UFAWU officers warned:

> Our Union will undoubtedly face the same kind of challenge in event the operators choose to force a strike in 1967. We have faced injunctions before on the basis that "injunctions cannot catch fish." We cannot permit the courts to destroy our fundamental rights without rendering ourselves helpless before the attacks of the employers.[82]

On May 14, 1967, the UFAWU's general executive board convened a marathon thirteen-hour joint meeting with the various negotiating committees involved in the dispute. The union's lawyer, John Stanton, walked the union leaders through the court order line by line and summarized its effect: "The union is ordered to do nothing that will interfere with the normal operations of the vessels engaged in the longline fishery or any other fishery."[83] In effect, Justice Smith and the BC Supreme Court had restrained the union from legally engaging in any actions that would strengthen its bargaining hand in the dispute with the vessel owners. The UFAWU leaders discussed their response to Smith's order, concluding with a motion – adopted with one opposing vote – endorsing the statement of the Prince Rupert bargaining committee to the effect that '"all members should live by trade union principles and be guided by their conscience' in the matter of the court order of May 11th, 1967."[84]

In early June 1967, the state intervened in response to the UFAWU's defiant stance, with RCMP officers arresting Nichol twice in a single day (at his Prince Rupert hotel and later near a shoreworkers' picket line), as well as union secretary Stevens and union organizers George Hewison and Joseph Verde prior to a union meeting. The police were armed with arrest warrants prepared by the BC attorney general's department, charging the union officers with failing to obey a lawful court order, in contravention of section 108 of the *Criminal Code.*[85] In an emergency meeting convened the day following the arrests, available members of the UFAWU's general executive board received a report from Stanton on the nature of the contempt proceedings and possible remedies. Stanton warned that the arrests of the union's leaders could be a precursor for the state to "move against the rank and file," a "tactic never before used in [the] history of BC," which should be of "deep concern to [the] whole labour movement."[86] The board voted unanimously that "the balance of the emergency fund be thrown into the battle," and approved a subsequent motion to assist Rose Nichol (wife of Jack Nichol) with travel arrangements to Prince Rupert if she so desired.[87] Two weeks later, on June 19, 1967, Dohm convicted Stevens, Stavenes, and Nichol of criminal contempt of court, imposing one-year prison sentences and fining the union $25,000 for its "planned flouting of the Court's authority" (Nichol would later be acquitted on appeal).[88]

To help cover legal costs, the union initiated a special levy of $10 per member, while demanding that the imprisoned trade unionists be released on bail pending their appeal. "We were seized right in the court room and spent the next ten days in Oakalla," Stevens recalled.[89] The three union leaders were released on bail at the end of June 1967, pending the disposition of their appeals. In September, Stevens informed UFAWU members that the Court of Appeal hearing on the convictions would take place in Victoria. "The effect is to make it difficult for members of our Union to attend," he wrote, encouraging locals in Vancouver, the Fraser Valley, and Vancouver Island to send representatives.[90] During a three-day hearing in mid-September, the Court of Appeal heard submissions from counsel for the accused and for the ministry of attorney general. In a decision pronounced on November 9, the three-judge division sustained the convictions and sentences against Stevens and Stavenes, while acquitting Nichol on a split two-to-one decision. Stevens and Stavenes returned to custody, serving the remainder of their sentences at the Oakalla Prison Farm, the Oakalla Vancouver Island Unit (Wilkinson Road Jail) in Saanich (including stints in solitary confinement), and the Mount Thurston prison camp near Chilliwack.[91]

Disunity within the ranks of labour (centring on the ideological divide between Communist-aligned and anti-Communist unions) undermined an appeal against the convictions to the Supreme Court of Canada, when prominent labour leaders bowed to anti-Communist pressure and refused to swear affidavits in support of Stevens's and Stavenes's appeals. While VDLC secretary Paddy Neale had sworn an affidavit, the UFAWU was informed by BC Federation of Labour secretary Ray Haynes that he had been instructed by the Canadian Labour Congress not to provide the document.[92] This reflected deeply rooted anti-Communist antipathy among sections of the Canadian labour movement toward the red-tinged UFAWU – notwithstanding the dangerous legal precedent established for all Canadian trade unionists if the jailing of Stevens and Stavenes and the fine against the union were allowed to stand.[93]

FIGURE 7 United Fishermen and Allied Workers' Union (UFAWU) secretary Homer Stevens and business agent Jack Nichol. Stevens, along with union president Steve Stavenes, spent nine months in jail for contempt of court for defying an injunction during the 1967 Prince Rupert trawlers' strike. Nichol's conviction was overturned on appeal. | BC 1532/978/2, Fisherman Publishing Society Collection, University of British Columbia Rare Books and Special Collections

Ultimately, the Supreme Court of Canada declined to the hear the appeals, finding that the grounds of appeal against the convictions had already been canvassed and rejected by the BC Court of Appeal, and that it was settled law that the Supreme Court lacked competence to consider appeals against sentences in criminal matters.[94]

As the appeals stalled, the imprisoned labour leaders, backed by the UFAWU, requested a Christmas amnesty, a request that British Columbia's Social Credit solicitor general refused. Meanwhile, the prisoners successfully defeated an attempt to relocate them to the remote Snowdon Forest Camp near Campbell River on Vancouver Island, with the UFAWU placing itself on record against the transfer.[95] Reflecting the extraordinary situation in which the union found itself, the executive board drafted amendments to the UFAWU constitution to allow it to name temporary officers to perform the duties of properly titled officers who were indisposed on account of illness or imprisonment.[96] At the same time, the board pledged to "keep in close contact" with Stevens and Stavenes, supplying them with meeting minutes and labour publications, and keeping the membership informed of their well-being and location through the pages of *The Fisherman*.[97] From prison, Homer Stevens maintained a voluminous correspondence with union officers, members, and allies in the labour movement, and received visitors, including Coquitlam MLA (and future premier) Dave Barrett.[98]

With its president and secretary detained at the Mount Thurston prison camp outside Chilliwack, the UFAWU ramped up its campaign against the labour injunction, holding a mass meeting at Vancouver's Pender Auditorium in conjunction with its annual convention in January 1968. More than 600 workers, 130 of whom were convention delegates, attended the meeting, the Vancouver local reported, and those in attendance "unanimously supported our Union in respect of injunctions and pledged support in the legal costs to get our jailed officers free."[99] Delegates from up and down the coast, as well as one delegate from Atlantic Canada, attended the convention, endorsing a report from the Fishermen's Defence Committee and re-electing Stevens as secretary and Stavenes as president.[100] The next month, several hundred fishers converged on the provincial legislature in Victoria to lobby against injunctions. This followed a long-standing labour tradition of bringing concerns directly to government, but the 1968 lobby was imbued with a sense of urgency as the

FIGURE 8 United Fishermen and Allied Workers' Union demonstration against injunctions at the BC legislature, February 15, 1968. | BC 1532/20/18, Fisherman Publishing Society Collection, University of British Columbia Rare Books and Special Collections

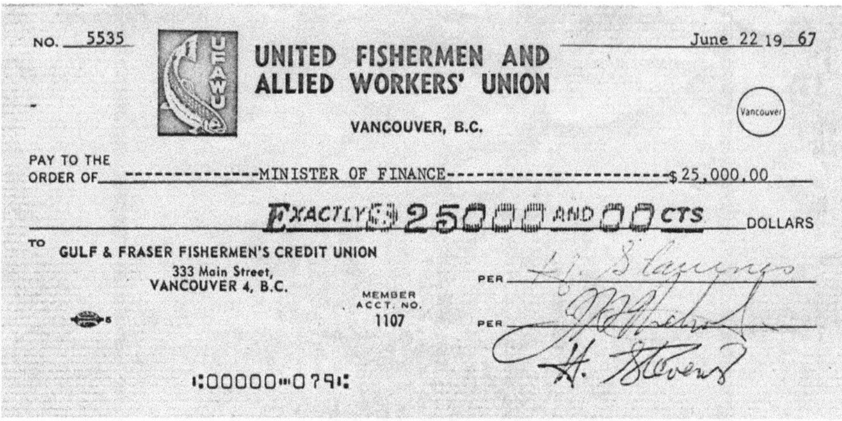
NO. 5535

UNITED FISHERMEN AND ALLIED WORKERS' UNION

VANCOUVER, B.C.

June 22 19 67

PAY TO THE ORDER OF --------------MINISTER OF FINANCE----------------------$25,000.00

EXACTLY $25000 AND 00 CTS DOLLARS

TO GULF & FRASER FISHERMEN'S CREDIT UNION
333 Main Street,
VANCOUVER 4, B.C.

MEMBER ACCT. NO. 1107

PER

PER

⑆00000⑈079⑆

FIGURE 9 Copy of a cheque issued by the United Fishermen and Allied Workers' Union to pay the fine levied against the union by BC Supreme Court Justice Thomas Dohm for breaching an injunction during the 1967 Prince Rupert trawlers' strike. | Neish Family Collection, Victoria, BC

UFAWU officers languished at Mount Thurston. On February 15, 1968, the fishers and their allies marched on the provincial legislature.[101] In June, Stevens and Stavenes applied for parole as a delegation of labour officials travelled to Ottawa to lobby Solicitor General John Turner for executive clemency, but the request was not granted.[102] They were released in September 1968, with remission of the final three months of the sentences; however, Stevens served an additional sixteen days at Mount Thurston, losing two weeks of his remission for arguing with prison guards while advocating on behalf of another prisoner, and an additional two days for having a pocket watch in contravention of prison rules.[103]

From the Courts to the Labour Relations Board in the 1970s and Beyond

In the 1970s, opposition by BC workers and their organizations to judicial intervention in labour disputes bore legislative fruit. Criticism of injunctions was not confined to labour circles. Indeed, Vancouver lawyer and future BC Supreme Court and Court of Appeal Justice Mary Southin – a pioneering female member of the legal profession who had run for public office under the Progressive Conservative banner in two federal elections in the 1960s – discussed the functioning of injunctions in a 1970 article in the Vancouver Bar Association's journal *The Advocate,* which is worth quoting at length:

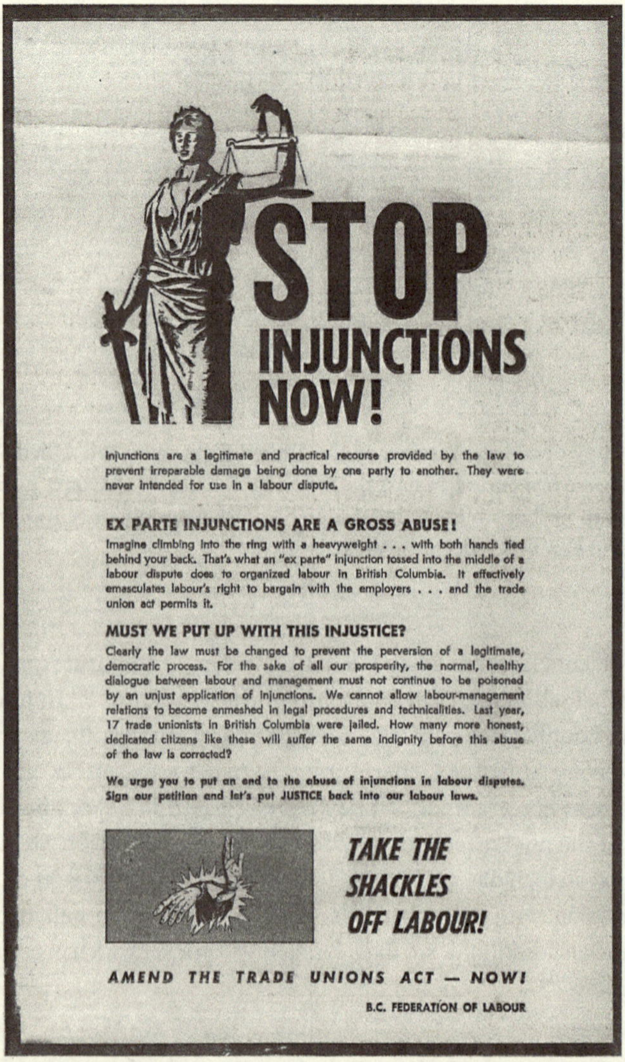

FIGURE 10 Advertisement published by the BC Federation of Labour as part of its campaign against injunctions, 1967. These advocacy efforts bore fruit in 1973, when the labour-aligned New Democratic Party government of Dave Barrett introduced major amendments to the province's labour laws that substantially curbed the jurisdiction of the courts in labour disputes. | Box 15, file 15-35, "Labour Injunction Publicity Campaign," British Columbia Federation of Labour fonds, University of British Columbia Rare Books and Special Collections

> There are some aspects of this whole problem which to my mind deserve some comment.
>
> *Ex parte* injunctions or injunctions on such short notice that they are in reality *ex parte* injunctions are still being granted. If somebody is served at midnight to be in Court at 10.00 a.m. the next morning what real opportunity has his Counsel to prepare? Short notice where there is evidence of violence or apprehended violence or damage to property is one thing; short notice where the employer simply says he is losing money, even a lot of money, is another.
>
> It should not be overlooked that when an injunction is granted on no notice or notice so short as to be derisory the men do not think they had a fair hearing and that reinforces their feelings of being victims of judicial bias ...
>
> Nor in my view should any *ex parte* injunction or injunction on short notice be granted with liberty to apply to set aside. All *ex parte* injunctions and if counsel requests, those granted on short notice should be to a day certain with liberty to the Plaintiff to move to continue. That puts the burden where it belongs: on the Plaintiff to show upon a full hearing that it is entitled to what it seeks.[104]

Southin's comments reflected growing concern within the legal community that the indiscriminate use of injunctions against labour in British Columbia was undermining the rule of law, and that some corrective measures were overdue. This reinforced a message that labour had conveyed throughout the postwar period.

Following the 1972 provincial general election, the NDP government led by social worker Dave Barrett (who had himself been fired as a civil servant for political activity) embarked on far-reaching changes to BC's labour laws, including a provision in the *Labour Code of British Columbia Act* (1973) that transferred most of the power to grant injunctions from judges to a reformed Labour Relations Board. The legislation recognized the board's "exclusive jurisdiction" to consider

> any application for the restraint or prohibition of any person or group of persons from:
>
> (i) ceasing or refusing to perform work ...
> (ii) picketing, striking, or locking out; or
> (iii) communicating information or opinion in a labour dispute by speech, writing, or any other means of communication.

The legislation specifically stated that "no court has or shall exercise any jurisdiction" in respect of any of the act's prohibitions against illegal strikes or picketing, while allowing a narrow exemption for judicial intervention where necessary to avoid "an immediate and serious danger to life or health" (but even that power could not be exercised by way of an *ex parte* injunction).[105]

Conflict between workers and employers continued, however, including bitter strikes between public sector workers and Barrett's labour-aligned government, while the Court of Appeal sought to "whittle away" at the LRB's statutory authority over picketing.[106] In 1974, the BC Civil Liberties Association (BCCLA) lambasted courts' interpretations of the *Trade-Unions Act, 1959,* which substantially expanded "the power of management to obtain interim and ex parte injunctions against illegal picketing or illegal forms of picketing [sic.] illegal strikes," provoking "the kind of confrontation which occurred in cases like the Lenkurt Electric strike."[107] Legal scholar Harry Arthurs noted shortly after the passage of the reformed labour legislation that despite the intentions of the drafters, the 1973 *Labour Code*'s reliance on the device of depriving the courts of jurisdiction, rather than removing causes of action available to employers or immunizing parties to their application, likely preserved a substantial residual role for the courts and the common law in labour disputes.[108]

In the 1980s, major battles erupted between BC unions and the Social Credit governments of Bill Bennett and Bill Vander Zalm, giving rise to protest strikes and attempts by the provincial state to deploy the labour injunction in its bid to roll back welfare state entitlements and curb the rights of public sector workers.[109] When court employees represented by the BC Government Employees' Union (BCGEU) picketed the Vancouver Law Courts and other courthouses around the province on November 1, 1983, during a contract strike tied to the government's "restraint" agenda and labour's Operation Solidarity mobilization, BC Supreme Court Chief Justice Allan McEachern ordered by way of his own motion and *ex parte* an injunction restraining all picketing in the vicinity of courthouses. McEachern's ruling was upheld by the Court of Appeal and, in the 1988 decision *BCGEU v BC (Attorney General),* by the Supreme Court of Canada. Justice Brian Dickson wrote for the majority of the latter:

> While the Labour Relations Board has jurisdiction in relation to what might be described as the labour relations aspect of picketing, the courts retain full authority to deal with violations of civil and criminal law arising from picketing. The order was issued in relation to a criminal contempt and therefore fell within the federal criminal law power and the inherent (or common law) jurisdiction of the courts to punish for contempt. Striking court employees must obey the

> law in relation to criminal contempt. The legality of all aspects of picketing was not put beyond the reach of the criminal law or criminal contempt simply because the strike was lawful and the Labour Code permitted picketing in the course of a lawful strike.[110]

The Supreme Court of Canada accepted the union's claim that McEachern's ruling violated the section 2(b) Charter right of the BCGEU picketers to freedom of expression, but held that this ruling was saved by section 1, allowing for "reasonable limits ... demonstrably justified in a free and democratic society," and was therefore constitutional. Applying the reasoning in *Poje,* the court agreed with McEachern that "the picketing of the court houses of British Columbia constituted a criminal contempt": "Conduct designed to interfere with the proper administration of justice constitutes contempt of court which is said to be 'criminal' in that it transcends the limits of any dispute between particular litigants and constitutes an affront to the administration of justice as a whole."[111]

The legality of picketing was again considered by the courts in 1987 during a renewed round of labour mobilization against provincial government restraint. On June 1, 1987, an estimated 250,000 workers participated in a one-day general strike against the Social Credit government, hoping to force a repeal of Bills 19 and 20, labour laws restricting the bargaining rights of teachers and other workers.[112] Attorney General Brian Smith responded by filing a writ for temporary and permanent injunctions prohibiting unions from using "force" (defined to include illegal work stoppages, picketing, and intimidation) to change the government or its policies.[113] With fiery rhetoric, the writ alluded to seditious libel and the use of intimidation by force or violence against the government. Labour hired as counsel an old stalwart, Tom Berger, a veteran of the 1960s battles who had served as leader of the official opposition and as a (controversial) provincial Supreme Court judge before returning to private practice. In his submission to Justice Kenneth Meredith on behalf of the Hospital Employees' Union, Berger described the government's injunction application as "an offence to free people and free institutions," invading the "jurisdiction of Parliament to define high crimes against the state." If granted, it would subject citizens to "arbitrary and erratic arrests, and no citizen would know where he stood with the law."[114] Justice Meredith appears to have been persuaded by Berger's arguments. In a demonstration of judicial restraint, he denied the government's application, suggesting that civil law was the wrong venue for deterring offences of the magnitude of sedition and intimidation by force against the government. He ordered the government to pay a $14,000 settlement as well as the unions' legal costs for frivolous litigation.[115]

Conclusion

Commenting on the Lenkurt dispute in his memoirs, labour lawyer and left-wing Vancouver alderman Harry Rankin suggested that until the right to strike and picket were recognized as inalienable, "the workers' battles will continue on the street *and in the courts,* if necessary."[116] This chapter has examined the social relations of adjudication surrounding the use of the labour injunction in postwar British Columbia – challenging the notion of an era of "free" collective bargaining where the state assumed a hands-off role in relations between workers and employers. On the contrary, the historical evidence indicates that state intervention was the norm rather than the exception, from legislative action regulating picketing and strikes, to judicial intervention in the form of injunctions, contempt convictions, fines, and prison sentences against working-class leaders and their organizations, who engaged in militant occupations of space to challenge employers' property interests and assert customary and working-class claims to property. The frequency and lopsided nature of this judicial intervention – from *Poje* through *North* to *Lenkurt, UFAWU,* and other cases – provoked crises of legal legitimacy involving a broad spectrum of working people who perceived an unhealthy and close relationship between companies and the courts. These crises of legal legitimacy occasioned contempt for the rule of law and a widespread belief that it was ethically sound to defy the courts' authority.

The judiciary, for its part, insisted that firm action was necessary to maintain the legal fabric of society, uphold the rule of law, and prevent anarchy. Chief Justice Wendell Farris, who had developed close affinities with employers' interests while practising as a corporate lawyer and serving as a corporate director prior to his appointment to the bench, provided a robust defence of the role of the courts as guardians of freedom, democracy, and public order in the 1952 BC Supreme Court decision in *Canadian Transport Co (UK) Ltd v Alsbury (Poje):*

> Once our laws are flouted and orders of our courts treated with contempt the whole fabric of our freedom is destroyed. We can then only revert to conditions of the dark ages when the only law recognized was that of might. One law broken and the breach thereof ignored is but an invitation to ignore further laws and

> this, if continued, can only result in the breakdown of the freedom under the law which we so greatly prize.[117]

This formulation, of the courts as the last line of defence for social order, would be invoked regularly by judges in other high-profile injunction and contempt proceedings in the decades that followed.

These social relations of adjudication and the legal technology of coercion developed in response to working-class challenges to private property interests in the postwar collective bargaining context – notably, procedures governing injunctions and contempt proceedings – would be carried into other social contexts later in the twentieth century, as the locus of political protest shifted from labour to other social movements. This line of jurisprudence was acknowledged in 1994, in the BC Court of Appeal's judgment in *MacMillan Bloedel v Brown*, an environmental case where the court noted the origins of modern contempt law in the labour case of *Poje* – "one of the leading authorities" establishing the principle that "the courts, particularly the judges of the Supreme Court of British Columbia, have the original responsibility to maintain the Rule of Law." After citing *Lenkurt*, Chief Justice McEachern stated that "more recently ... most protests have related to differences between citizens and between citizens and government on social, environmental and aboriginal issues."[118] The corresponding social critique of law's legitimacy, arising in the 1960s in response to criminalization of working-class protest by the courts, and reflected in legislative reforms that sharply curbed the courts' jurisdiction to issue injunctions during labour disputes, would be sustained by other social movement actors as conflicts between private and customary property claims persisted into the twenty-first century.

Chapter 3

BREACHING THE BUBBLE LAW
Spatial and Legal Battles over Reproductive Choice

On June 27, 1995, the Legislative Assembly of British Columbia voted 49 to 9 to approve the *Access to Abortion Services Act*. Its passage followed a week of vigorous debate in which the governing New Democratic Party (NDP) had hoped to exploit divisions within the opposition BC Liberal caucus over the controversial issue of reproductive choice. Sidestepping this political strategy, most Liberals backed the government bill, distancing themselves from socially conservative caucus members while reaching out to moderate and centrist elements of public opinion.[1] This legislation was the first of its kind in Canada. The bill included among its provisions a restriction on a range of activities in the vicinity of "access zones." These included engaging in a "sidewalk interference," protesting, besetting, and physically interfering with or intimidating medical practitioners or patients. The legislation also included a restriction on photographing, videotaping, sketching, or otherwise graphically recording medical practitioners or patients for the purpose of dissuading them from providing or accessing abortion services.[2] "Access zones," also known as "bubble zones," were defined as including the parcel of land on which medical facilities providing abortion services were located, as well as an area extending up to 50 metres from the boundary of the parcel. Reflecting the physical threat of violence to doctors and other service providers, "access zones" were defined as including doctors' offices and homes and an area extending 160 metres from these private residences. The legislation provided for "quasi-criminal" sanctions of up to six months' imprisonment and fines of up to $5,000.[3]

Legal protection for the bubble zones in the form of a permanent "legislative injunction" reflected the contested social relations of adjudication that had emerged in British Columbia over the issue of reproductive choice – as control over women's bodies and the spaces surrounding abortion clinics and doctors' homes and offices stood out (spatially and temporally) as "a moment in the intersection of configured social relations," to deploy Doreen Massey's terminology, "as a kind of 'power-geometry.'"[4] The legislation was viewed as a major victory by feminists, abortion service providers, and other progressive forces in British Columbia and beyond, who had agitated for freedom of reproductive choice for decades. Harassment, intimidation, and outright violence against medical practitioners and patients had accompanied the legalization of abortion services in the United States and Canada in the 1970s and 1980s and into the 1990s. Abortion clinics that opened in Vancouver and other cities in the wake of the Supreme Court of Canada's 1988 *Morgentaler* decision, which struck down *Criminal Code* restrictions on abortion as unconstitutional for violating women's right to security of the person, were besieged by chronic (usually male) protesters aligned with Christian organizations, prompting a wave of injunctions and a declaration by BC Court of Appeal Justice Mary Southin that the legislature rather than the courts was the appropriate venue for determining the reasonable limits of protest.[5] The NDP-controlled legislature that was elected in 1991 was more receptive to the feminist perspective that the legislature that preceded it, and responded to Justice Southin's invitation and ongoing concern over anti-abortion protests and the health and safety of women and medical practitioners by introducing the *Access to Abortion Services Act* – imposing the permanent "legislative injunction" against protests in the vicinity of abortion clinics and doctors' offices and homes.

Conversely, the "Bubble Law" was viewed as a major defeat by opponents of legal abortion services, who described themselves as "pro-life" and whom feminists and abortion services providers labelled "anti-choice." The legislation was also lambasted by some civil liberties advocates, who viewed it as an unreasonable incursion on rights to freedom of expression, assembly, conscience, and religion protected in the *Canadian Charter of Rights and Freedoms*. Abortion was a hotly contested and controversial social and political issue, striking at the root of the personal health, autonomy, and well-being of individual women, while clashing with the spiritual values of some members of religious communities. British Columbia's Bubble Law explicitly embraced the pro-choice perspective and imposed a substantial legal barrier in the way of the pro-life movement, which had embraced the picketing of abortion clinics and the harassment of practitioners as core tactics in its campaign seeking to recriminalize abortion services, or, if this failed, to at least directly discourage women from accessing these services or to cut off the supply of practitioners willing and able to provide these services.

Beyond the particular issue of abortion services, the Bubble Law represented a far-reaching infringement on political freedoms of expression and assembly, restricting certain forms of speech and activity on public sidewalks and road rights-of-way in the vicinity of clinics, offices, and homes. In the view of a majority of Members of the Legislative Assembly, as well as their supporters among service providers and feminist groups, and judges on the BC Supreme Court and Court of Appeal who upheld the constitutionality of the law, this represented a reasonable infringement on civil liberties, one that was necessary to safeguard access to abortion services, protect the dignity of women at a potentially very vulnerable time in their lives, and ensure the safety and supply of health practitioners. In attempting to strike a balance over competing rights and competing claims to public property and public space, the Bubble Law and the wider legal technology deployed by lawyers, judges, police, and legislators demonstrated continuity with earlier responses to social movement protest in British Columbia, while also demonstrating a robust example of intervention by the legislature in the legal arena governing protest and uses of public property.

This chapter explores the legal politics of abortion in British Columbia, where the locus of social movement organizing and criminalization shifted from women accessing abortion services and doctors performing the service to citizens opposed to the right of women to terminate a pregnancy. Highlighting the contested politics of freedom of choice and control over women's bodies, as well as debates over the appropriate limits of lawful protest, it draws from court decisions, newspaper coverage, and institutional records of pro-choice and anti-abortion advocacy organizations, while building on previous research.[6] In the process, it provides an original window into an atypical social movement and its clashes with authority, highlighting wider themes of how legal legitimacy has been constructed and contested in modern British Columbia. This case study is distinct from others in this book with its focus on a conservative social movement and its emphasis on a non-economic arena of social movement mobilization and social contestation.

Mobilizing for Choice

The legal politics of abortion, and social movement organizing on issues of reproductive rights, underwent fundamental change in British Columbia and Canada in the closing decades of the twentieth century, shifting from criminalization of women who accessed the service and doctors who performed the procedure to the criminalization of protesters who interfered with access to this health service. This change occurred in British Columbia in a short time span of seven years – beginning with a robust judicial intervention when the Supreme Court of Canada struck down *Criminal Code* restrictions on abortion in the *R v Morgentaler* (1988) case, and culminating in the BC legislature's enactment of the *Access to Abortion Services Act* in 1995 (and subsequent court decisions upholding the constitutionality of the legislation).

In the 1970s, feminists associated with the Women's Liberation Movement were the most visible advocates for reproductive rights. At the time, a woman required the approval of a three-member hospital committee of doctors attesting that the procedure was necessary to safeguard her physical, mental, or emotional health. While this represented a more permissive approach than *Criminal Code* provisions in place prior to 1969, which had made all abortions criminal unless the woman's life was at risk, it fell far short of the aspiration of the Women's Liberation Movement for "free abortion on demand." Moreover, hospitals were left to decide whether to establish therapeutic abortion committees (TACs); only about one-third of hospitals in Canada did so, meaning that women in many parts of the country had no access to legal abortion services. Parliament and the Liberal government had instituted the 1969 *Criminal Code* reform, and accompanying legislation legalizing contraceptives, including condoms and the birth control pill, in the face of fierce opposition from the Catholic Church and other conservative forces in the country.[7] However, the emerging Women's Liberation Movement demanded that Parliament go further and remove the remaining legal barriers to a woman's right to choose.

In April 1970, a group of seventeen women affiliated with the Vancouver Women's Caucus, including Ellen Woodsworth (niece of parliamentarians J.S. Woodsworth and Grace MacInnis, and a future Vancouver city councillor), embarked on an "Abortion Caravan" to Ottawa. The caravan demanded the removal "of all mention of abortion from the Criminal Code," pardons for all persons charged with these criminal offences, and construction and funding of women's community-controlled health clinics providing free birth control, abortion on demand, and pre- and postnatal care.[8] The activists declared in a

FIGURE 11 In 1970, a group of women affiliated with the Vancouver Women's Caucus embarked on an "Abortion Caravan" to Ottawa, demanding removal "of all mention of abortion from the Criminal Code." They converged on Parliament Hill, where several women chained themselves to the rails of the visitors' gallery of the House of Commons, while others breached the grounds of the Prime Minister's residence at 24 Sussex Drive. | *Toronto Star*

strongly worded letter to Prime Minister Pierre Elliott Trudeau and his ministers of health and justice that "the government of Canada is in a state of war with the women of Canada."[9] The caravan gathered support as it travelled through cities across western Canada, led by a vehicle bearing a coffin full of coat hangers to symbolize the death of women from botched abortions, and converged on Parliament Hill on Mother's Day weekend. More than four hundred women and supporters marched on Parliament, packing into the Railway Committee Room, where they heard from speakers including Dr. Henry Morgentaler and MP Grace MacInnis (both of whom were booed, the former for being a man and the latter for being too politically moderate), followed by an impromptu march to the prime minister's residence, where protesters breached the grounds of 24 Sussex Drive. The following day, thirty-seven women chained themselves to the wooden rails in the visitors' gallery above the chamber of the House of Commons, forcing adjournment.[10] As Christabelle Sethna and Steve Hewitt have noted, the RCMP Security Service took a keen interest in the Abortion Caravan as it travelled eastward, with informants reporting on the composition of the audiences at local events and on the anti-capitalist tone of the speakers, reflecting the wider pattern of state surveillance of left-wing radicalism in Canada in the Cold War period.[11] Judy Rebick suggests that the battle for reproductive choice and the Abortion Caravan were integral to the emergence of the "second-wave" feminist movement in Canada.[12]

Back in Vancouver, the Vancouver Women's Caucus and other successor feminist groups continued to organize visible and vocal demonstrations throughout the 1970s in support of abortion providers and in pursuit of legal access to abortion services. Several Women's Caucus members had formed an Abortion Information Service (later renamed the Abortion Referral and Counselling Service) in December 1969, shortly after the *Criminal Code* reform came into effect, to provide women with confidential information on medical practitioners inside and outside Canada who would provide abortions without hospital committee approval. The Women's Caucus rallied around Dr. Robert Makaroff, a Vancouver doctor who was arrested by an undercover police officer in the spring of 1970 and criminally convicted for performing abortions without the approval of a hospital committee, and incarcerated for three months at Oakalla prison. When Makaroff faced disciplinary proceedings before the BC College of Physicians and Surgeons, the Women's Caucus organized a demonstration outside the building where the hearing was being conducted. When the group learned that women were experiencing bureaucratic roadblocks in having their cases considered by the therapeutic abortion committee at Vancouver General Hospital, which reviewed applications in accordance with the 1969 *Criminal Code* provisions, members occupied the psychiatrists' offices at the hospital, leading to improved TAC procedures and expedited scheduling of approved abortions.[13]

Pro-choice organizing gained momentum in Vancouver and other Canadian cities throughout the 1970s and 1980s, and increasingly focused on the defence of Dr. Henry Morgentaler, a Montreal-based physician and Holocaust survivor who, like Makaroff, provided abortion services without the approval of a hospital committee. Morgentaler was convicted under section 251 of the *Criminal Code* and incarcerated for ten months in a Quebec prison, emerging as the figurehead of the growing national pro-choice movement, which demanded repeal of the *Criminal Code* restrictions on access to abortion services. He had been acquitted in three separate jury trials, successfully pleading the defence of necessity, but, in an extraordinary move, the Quebec Court of Appeal had overturned one of the jury acquittals and substituted a conviction and eighteen-month prison sentence, a decision upheld by the Supreme Court of Canada in

1975. Following the election of the Parti Québécois provincial government in 1976, additional charges against Morgentaler were dropped, with the government describing the federal abortion law as "inapplicable" in Quebec in light of the refusal of juries to convict, and announcing that it would pursue no further prosecutions relating to clinic abortions performed by qualified medical practitioners. Charges against several other doctors and a nurse were also dropped. The federal minister of justice described Quebec's decision to abandon the prosecutions as fair, just, and properly within provincial jurisdiction, while refusing to comment on Quebec's request that the abortion law be reformed. Morgentaler reopened his Montreal-area clinic.[14]

Following the adoption of the *Canadian Charter of Rights of Freedoms* in the 1982 *Constitution Act*, and with changing public attitudes suggesting that over 70 percent of Canadians supported a woman's "right to choose" whether or not to have an abortion, Morgentaler announced in 1983 that he would expand his services and advocacy efforts to other parts of Canada and opened clinics in Toronto and Winnipeg.[15] Mirroring the earlier pattern in Quebec, police raided the Toronto clinic. Morgentaler and two colleagues were charged with providing illegal miscarriages, but were acquitted in a jury trial based on the defence of necessity. As in Quebec, the Ontario Court of Appeal overturned the acquittal and substituted a conviction, but when the case reached the Supreme Court of Canada, Morgentaler successful invoked the Charter argument that section 251 of the *Criminal Code* was unconstitutional, as it violated a women's right to life, liberty, and security of the person under section 7 of the Charter, and was not saved by section 1. The Supreme Court of Canada's five-to-two ruling in *R v. Morgentaler*, released on January 28, 1988, struck down the *Criminal Code* restrictions on abortions, with Chief Justice Brian Dickson and Justice Antonio Lamer writing for the majority that "forcing a woman, by threat of criminal sanction, to carry a fetus to term unless she meets certain criteria unrelated to her own priorities and aspirations, is a profound interference with a woman's body and thus a violation of her security of the person."[16] Since the 1988 *Morgentaler* decision, Canada has had no law governing the termination of pregnancy.

Legal Abortion and Anti-Abortion Protest at the Everywoman's Health Centre

The Supreme Court of Canada's *Morgentaler* decision introduced a whole new set of challenges and reoriented the legal landscape on the abortion issue. The pro-choice movement and practitioners moved from advocacy and grassroots mobilization to the operation and practice of providing this newly legalized health service, while opponents of abortion turned to social movement organizing and direct action in a bid to prevent women from accessing the service and to convince legislators to restore statutory restrictions on abortion services.

The Everywoman's Health Centre, founded on East 44th Avenue in East Vancouver in November 1988, shortly after the *Morgentaler* decision, emerged as a key site of social contestation. Abortion opponents, many of whom were aligned with Christian organizations affiliated with a US-based anti-abortion initiative known as Operation Rescue, embraced the old labour tactic of the picket line, brandishing picket signs and offering unsolicited "sidewalk counselling" and more intimidating forms of communication aimed at preventing women from accessing abortion services. The stirrings of this direct action campaign by anti-abortionists were apparent even prior to *Morgentaler*. In 1986, Jim Demers, a twenty-nine-year-old carpenter from Nelson, BC, had been convicted of theft, possession of stolen property, and mischief after stealing

B.C.'s clinic coalition sees an abortion clinic as an interim measure and plans to establish a comprehensive women's health centre in five to six months. Above (left to right) Ruth Hule, Hilda Thomas, Maggie Thompson and Janet Vesterback, coalition spokespeople announcing go ahead plans for the clinic.

FIGURE 12 Founding of the Everywoman's Health Centre in the wake of the Supreme Court of Canada's *Morgentaler* decision, aimed at providing free access to abortion services on demand, Vancouver, 1988. | Jane Altshool, *Kinesis*, courtesy of the University of British Columbia Library Digitization Centre and its generous donors

and damaging a vacuum aspirator used to perform abortions at the Kootenay Regional General Hospital (abortions at the hospital were authorized at the time by a three-member hospital committee pursuant to the 1969 *Criminal Code* provisions). Demers raised the defence of necessity, arguing that because the hospital committee rubber-stamped therapeutic abortions, his actions were justified to protect the life of the unborn child and prevent the commission of an offence, but the BC Court of Appeal rejected this argument and upheld Demers's conviction.[17]

The Everywoman's Health Centre emerged as the primary target of the anti-abortion movement in British Columbia in the aftermath of *Morgentaler*. The first stand-alone abortion clinic in the province, it would be followed in 1991 by the Elizabeth Bagshaw Clinic, also in Vancouver, and, over time, by other stand-alone clinics in communities including Victoria, Kelowna, Cranbrook, and Trail, as well as hospital units that extended access to abortion services to approximately forty communities. In the initial period following *Morgentaler*, the Everywoman's clinic operated on a shoestring budget of approximately $3,000 per month, relying on charitable donations and user fees from patients who could afford to pay, with the provincial Medical Services Plan (MSP) initially refusing to cover the costs of the medical service. The clinic performed approximately one hundred abortions in its first three months of operation and was a lightning rod for anti-abortion protest.[18] Within weeks of its opening, activists aligned with Operation Rescue, including Jim Demers, established a physical presence on the municipal sidewalks in front of the East Vancouver clinic in a bid to obstruct access and raise the public profile of their campaign against legal abortions. Besides picketing and sidewalk counseling, activists with Operation Rescue chained themselves to the doors of the clinic, forcing it to close on several occasions, and vandalized the building, damaging locks, defacing the exterior with graffiti, and breaking into the clinic and destroying equipment.[19] According to an affidavit filed in the subsequent litigation, picketing at the Everywoman's clinic began within three weeks of the clinic's opening, "on or about November 24, 1988," and "continued with increasing frequency and severity."[20] On December 15, approximately 150 protesters aligned with Christian organizations from across the Lower Mainland converged on the site, blocking access to the doors; 69 were physically removed by Vancouver Police and taken into custody but released without charge.[21] The leniency demonstrated by police and prosecutors toward the anti-abortion protesters in this early phase can be contrasted with more robust legal responses to labour, environmental, and Indigenous protests during this period, revealing partiality in the deployment of coercive legal power.

Faced with large, aggressive, and growing protests in front of the clinic, the Everywoman's Health Centre, supported by feminist organizations, turned to the old legal remedy of civil proceedings and a court injunction to protect the right of women to access abortion services by restraining the picketing. This litigation against the anti-abortion picketers represented a new twist in long-standing legal battles over competing claims to public space in British Columbia – in this instance, the municipal sidewalks in the front of the Everywoman's Health Centre (and, later, other abortion clinics that opened across the province). The litigation surrounding anti-abortion picketing at the clinic culminated in arrests and criminal contempt of court convictions (which were upheld by the BC Court of Appeal in *Everywoman's Health Centre Society v Bridges* [1990]), setting the stage for legislative action to protect the right of women to access abortion services by restricting anti-abortion protests.

On Saturday, January 21, 1989, two and a half months after the clinic opened, Operation Rescue organized another convergence to disrupt its operations. Approximately 150 protesters converged on the clinic at 7:00 a.m., blocking all entrances and denying access to patients and staff, preventing the clinic from operating for the next fourteen hours. Lawyers for the clinic responded with an emergency application in front of BC Supreme Court Justice Lloyd McKenzie, who issued an interlocutory injunction following an extraordinary three-hour Saturday morning hearing that restrained picketing, watching and besetting, obstructing operations, and intimidating forms of communication in the vicinity of the clinic.[22] The crowd disregarded the judge's order, however, and did not disperse until 8:45 p.m., when Vancouver Police arrived with a second court order from Justice McKenzie, issued following another brief hearing at the Vancouver Courthouse and mandating that named and unnamed protesters appear before the judge on possible contempt of court charges. Hilda Thomas, a Vancouver feminist and spokesperson for the Everywoman's Health Centre, speculated that if the disruption had continued without satisfactory police intervention, the clinic might have had to invite its supporters to physically prevent protesters from obstructing access. Vancouver mayor (and future premier) Gordon Campbell advised caution, expressing concern over the suggestion that the clinic would take the law into its own hands and counselling the clinic to talk to police and "deal with it positively."[23]

Protests and legal wrangling over access to the Everywoman's Health Centre continued throughout the early months of 1989, with the clinic expressing concern that the judge had refused to issue an enforcement order, which would have mandated that police remove any person who breached the initial order from obstructing the sidewalk.[24] Questions also arose over the response of the

BC government, particularly the ministry of attorney general, to the growing protest movement, in light of the stated sympathies of Social Credit premier Bill Vander Zalm and leading members of his cabinet with the anti-abortion cause and their strong ties to evangelical Christianity. As the *Vancouver Sun* noted in an editorial, Attorney General Bud Smith's "first duty is to the law, not to politics or religion or even government policy… Confronted with evidence of contempt of court on a large scale, the attorney-general has a clear obligation to take matters into his own hands to prevent the administration of justice from falling into disrepute."[25] Opposition leader Mike Harcourt called for the attorney general to "initiate criminal proceedings" against the picketers, and also called for the provincial government to fund the Everywoman's clinic.[26] On January 28, 1989, an estimated six hundred anti-abortion protesters gathered in front of the clinic, marching two to four abreast at a rally that coincided with national demonstrations on the first anniversary of the *Morgentaler* decision. In anticipation of the protest, and given the legal ambiguity over enforcement provisions of the court order, the clinic decided not to schedule any abortions on that day. "If we'd wanted to bring in a patient, she would have probably found it very stressful," Hilda Thomas said.[27]

Protests at the Everywoman's Health Centre peaked on February 7, when 105 people were arrested for picketing in front of the clinic, blocking all three entrances and preventing patients and staff from accessing the building. A spokesperson for the protesters, identified only as Baby Doe 240, stated: "We don't want to obstruct anything. We just want to prevent the killings."[28] The protest, which converged on the clinic before 8:00 a.m., coincided with hearings at the Vancouver Courthouse, where Justice McKenzie was considering submissions from defence counsel to amend or set aside the original injunction. Upon learning of the protest, the judge issued an order directing police to immediately arrest the protesters and bring them to the courthouse, describing their actions as "a blatant defiance of the injunction" and "apparent total defiance of the court."[29]

Deliberations on the procedural application were overshadowed by the contempt proceedings for the 105 arrested protesters. "You decided while the court was making its determination … to stage another demonstration and to display by your actions your apparent total defiance of the court," Justice McKenzie told the protesters and ordered them detained overnight.[30] The following day, 42 of them elected to remain in jail pending trial on the contempt charges, rather than sign an undertaking not to re-attend at the clinic. Pending trial, male protesters were detained at Oakalla, while the women were held at the nearby Lakeside correctional centre, where they allegedly received more favourable treatment than other detainees.[31] The week of legal proceedings culminated with pleas and sentencing for the original January 21 detainees. Justice McKenzie found 13 of the accused guilty of civil contempt, sentencing them to between fifteen and twenty-four days' imprisonment to be served on weekends, and ordering them to pay the health clinic's legal costs. The judge was not persuaded by defence counsel's arguments that the protesters "were compelled by the righteous motive of rescuing unborn babies from death ... according to the will of God, whose laws supersede the laws of man."[32]

Legal proceedings arising from the February 7 protest continued through February and March 1989, with Justice Josiah Wood ruling on February 23 that the contempt committed at the February 7 protest had been criminal rather than civil in nature, prompting the BC attorney general to assume responsibility for the conduct of the prosecutions. On February 28, defence counsel Paul Formby indicated that the accused would rely on the defence of necessity, asserting that they were justified in breaching the injunction to prevent the commission of an offence (the killing of unborn children), a line of argument vigorously opposed by Crown counsel Joseph Arvay.[33] In a procedural ruling, Justice Wood found that the defence of necessity was not available to the accused, since the alleged harm they sought to prevent was not a recognized offence in the *Criminal Code*, and because natural human instincts did not impel all reasonable people to defy the law as they had done (applying the *Perka* test, which limited the defence to wrongful acts committed under a pressure "which no one could withstand," as described further below).[34]

On March 6, Justice Wood convicted all 102 accused of criminal contempt of court (2 others were convicted the following day, while charges against of one of the accused, who suffered from Alzheimer's disease, had been dropped prior to the trial). Wood described the actions of the accused at the February 7 protest as a "classic example of organized lawlessness," part of "a detailed and premeditated strategy," with the public nature of the contempt leading members of the public to conclude "that the very existence of law and order in this community was at risk." Moreover, the scheduling of the mass picket line – at the moment the court was considering an application to have the injunction set aside – indicated that the defendants "had clearly abandoned any resort to legal process." The judge said that it was not the proper role of the court to decide on the morality of abortion, and that the court applied the law as established by the legislature and previous court decisions, rather than the law of God as the defendants proposed.[35]

In sentencing them, Justice Wood shocked the assembled 102 contemnors and their supporters by imposing sentences of three months' imprisonment, which he agreed to suspend for a period of twelve months, provided they abided by orders of the court and kept the peace. Wood described the court as "that institution which alone stands between the rule of law and anarchy," stating that sentencing decisions in contempt cases aimed at preserving the rule of law through deterrence, rather than "preserving judicial vanity." Among the 102 contemnors were the 42 protesters who had remained in jail after the original breach rather than sign the undertaking. Wood imposed no additional penalty on Demers and Kathryn Davies, whom the prosecution had identified as organizers of the protest. He stated that the case against them had not been established beyond a reasonable doubt, but made it clear that any person proven to be a leader would have been "singled out for special punishment."[36] When 3 of the convicted protesters – Vancouver businessman James Hanlon, his wife, Karen, a Catholic schoolteacher, and David Forsyth of Port Moody, a church worker – breached the terms of their suspended sentences by blockading the clinic the day after Wood imposed the sanctions – they were promptly arrested and brought back in front of the judge, who imposed sentences of three months' imprisonment. Their lawyer, Robert Culos, said outside the courtroom that his clients had "very strongly and sincerely held beliefs that the taking of preborn human life is wrong" and that they were "prepared to pay the price."[37] Additional arrests took place in the weeks and months that followed as protesters broke the terms of probation and received three-month jail terms. A man who locked himself to a cement block at the doors of the clinic in July 1989 was sentenced to six months in jail and a $1,500 fine (with four months of the sentence and the fine suspended on the condition that he keep the peace and stay away from the clinic for two years), in what Justice John Bouck described as "an escalation of the ordinary sit-in procedure."[38]

Contempt of court convictions against anti-abortion picketers slowed but did not end protests at the Everywoman's Health Centre, as counsel for the protesters applied for leave to appeal several injunction and contempt decisions to the BC Court of Appeal.[39] Pending those appeals, large-scale obstruction of the operations at the clinic ceased. As the legal politics of abortion played out on the streets of East Vancouver and at the Vancouver Courthouse, the Parliament of Canada weighed in on the abortion debate, with the House of Commons voting in favour of a *Criminal Code* amendment in May 1990 to prohibit abortions unless a doctor considered the pregnancy to be a threat to a woman's "physical, mental, or psychological health." When the Senate of Canada defeated the proposed amendment on a tied vote, Canada's statutory criminal law was left silent on abortion.[40]

Meanwhile, a vandal broke into the Everywoman's Health Centre in February 1990 and used a crowbar to destroy an ultrasound machine and an aspirator. An anti-abortion activist named Lane Walker, who had been convicted of criminal contempt and sentenced to three months in jail among the initial group of contemnors, turned himself in to Vancouver Police, pleading guilty and receiving a sentence of one day in jail and a $10,000 fine.[41] In October, veteran anti-abortionist Jim Demers sat in the doorway of the clinic and was arrested for obstructing access. At his initial court appearance, Demers challenged the authority of BC Supreme Court Justice Sherman Hood, refusing to stay away from the clinic until a bail hearing. When he attempted to walk out of the courtroom, he was physically restrained by sheriffs and incurred an additional contempt charge.[42] Demers's conviction was upheld by the BC Court of Appeal, with Chief Justice McEachern dismissing his claim that the Charter provided the right to a jury trial, citing favourably from the Ontario Court of Appeal decision in *R v Cohn* (1985).[43]

In December, the BC Court of Appeal upheld the convictions of 117 anti-abortion protesters for criminal contempt of court, in *Everywoman's Health Centre Society v Bridges*, but Justice Mary Southin (writing for the three-judge division) sought to shift the onus of decision-making from the courts to the legislature. Southin expressed concern over the ongoing reliance on court injunctions in response to social movement protest, providing a brief historical summary of the relationship between injunctions and protests, and questioning the appropriateness of restraining picketing through injunctions and contempt proceedings rather than through the ordinary operation of the criminal law:

> Today, the citizenry take to the streets over many social issues. Once upon a time, the citizenry rarely took to the streets save in labour disputes ...
>
> I think it is not unfair or unkind to say that by the 1950s, the courts of British Columbia were thought by some to be anti-labour because of the number of injunctions granted in labour disputes.
>
> Ultimately, to the relief of most, if not all, judges, the jurisdiction to deal with what is commonly called picketing was, in large measure, placed in the hands of what is now the Industrial Relations Council.
>
> There is today the grave question of whether public order should be maintained by the granting of an injunction, which often leads thereafter to an application to commit for contempt, or should be maintained by the Attorney General insisting that the police who are under his control do their duty by enforcing the relevant provisions of the Criminal Code.[44]

Southin and her fellow judges upheld the injunction and convictions against the anti-abortion protesters, since neither the protesters nor their legal counsel had mounted a "sustained attack" against the appropriateness of responding to protests through interlocutory injunctions. But Southin expressed concern that counsel for property owners and the courts adhered to a pattern established in labour disputes, rather than fashioning responses based on specific circumstances:

> It is obvious to me that the terms of this order were taken from precedents developed during the course of labour disputes. There is much to be said for the proposition that such precedents should be put permanently away and the court should give, in these cases where the citizens take to the streets and an injunction is sought, a fresh consideration to the extent to which the court should go. That consideration should, in every case, depend on the precise nature of the dispute, the precise conduct in issue and so on.[45]

The Bubble Law and the Balancing of Conflicting Rights

Litigation surrounding anti-abortion picketing at BC abortion clinics in the wake of *Morgentaler*, and growing violence against abortion providers in British Columbia and across North America, prompted action by the Government of British Columbia and the Legislative Assembly in the form of a permanent "legislative injunction" restraining anti-abortion picketing – the *Access to Abortion Services Act* (1995). In November 1994, Dr. Garson Romalis, a gynecologist who performed abortions at Vancouver's Elizabeth Bagshaw Clinic and an outspoken advocate for access to legal abortion services, was shot while eating breakfast in his Kerrisdale home. Romalis nearly bled to death when a bullet fired from a military-style assault rifle by an assailant outside his home shattered his femur and severed his femoral artery. The doctor saved his own life by slowing the bleeding with a makeshift tourniquet fashioned from his bathrobe (the lead suspect in the shooting would later be convicted for the murder of New York abortion doctor Barnett Slepian, though charges were never pursued in Canada for the Romalis shooting or attacks on two other Canadian doctors).[46] The Vancouver shooting was preceded by two high-profile killings of abortion doctors in Florida and was followed a month later by the killing of two women outside a Boston-area abortion clinic in December 1994. Hilda Thomas attributed the violence to "a very small, frantic but sad [and] pathetic minority wanting to prevent women from getting access to safe medical abortions [who] have resorted to violence because, in essence, they have lost." The spokesperson for the BC Coalition for Abortion Clinics called on the attorney general and law enforcement agencies to enforce civil injunctions against watching, besetting, or picketing abortion clinics.[47] In October 1994, anti-abortion protester Gordon Watson had been convicted of criminal contempt of court and sentenced to twenty-one days' jail for intimidating members of the public and interfering with access to, and the operations of, the Everywoman's Health Centre in contravention of Justice McKenzie's court order (the sentence was later reduced to ten day's jail on appeal).[48]

The shooting of Dr. Romalis and the intensification of violence against abortion providers and women accessing abortion services lent urgency to a process underway to provide legislative protection to abortion services.[49] The BC NDP government responded to the Court of Appeal decision in *Everywoman's Health Centre Society v Bridges* by establishing a Task Force on Contraceptive and Abortion Services in 1992. The task force released a report in 1994 titled *Realizing Choices,* which included among its recommendations proposed legislated protection for access zones around abortion clinics and doctors' offices and homes.[50] Following the Boston shootings, the government announced that it was considering a ban on protests in the vicinity of abortion clinics, as sixty anti-abortion activists gathered outside the Everywoman's clinic for a weekly "prayer meeting," with a spokesperson for Campaign Life Coalition BC suggesting that freedom of expression should not be curbed because of the actions of a "twisted lunatic."[51] By the spring of 1995, the government announced that legislation was being prepared to replace the current system, which placed the onus on abortion providers to obtain civil injunctions to prevent "harassment" of women and doctors. "I'm very concerned about the safety of health workers, of medical specialists, of women who are seeking services," Premier Mike Harcourt said, contrasting his party's official pro-choice stance with sharp debates over abortion policy in the opposition BC Liberal Party.[52]

The NDP government introduced the *Access to Abortion Services Bill* in the Legislative Assembly on June 19, 1995, and the bill was adopted less than two weeks later following vigorous debate inside and outside the legislature. In introducing the legislation, Health Minister Paul Ramsey stated:

> This bill ensures that women have access to reproductive health services in an atmosphere of privacy and dignity ... Abortion is a legal medical service, and access to medical services is one of the foundations of medicare. We do not

> tolerate disruption of access in any sphere of the health care system, and we will not tolerate it here ... Our intention is to protect access to this legal medical service and ensure that health care providers work and live in a respectful atmosphere.[53]

Social Services Minister Joy MacPhail said that the government was responding to "an orchestrated, organizational exercise in limiting access to health care" by anti-abortion groups. She elaborated on the government's reasons for proceeding with the legislation to restrain the picketing, highlighting the violent methods of the North American anti-abortion movement, whose publications "advocate violence and denigration of women. We're not doing this for some glib, high-profile reason. We're doing it because we need to stop the concerted impediment."[54] In an opinion article in the *Vancouver Sun*, University of British Columbia law professor Joel Bakan suggested that the legislation was likely constitutional and consistent with the Charter, since the Supreme Court of Canada had "strongly and consistently" found that governments and legislatures could limit expression so long as they did so in a "carefully tailored" way to serve some "pressing and substantial" objective.[55]

Despite vocal opposition from "pro-life" organizations and socially conservative members of the Legislative Assembly, the *Access to Abortion Services Bill* passed third reading on June 27, 1995, on a vote of forty-nine to nine, with both the government and official opposition caucuses officially supporting the legislation.[56] BC Reform Party leader Jack Weisgerber, who was among the MLAs who voted against it, sidestepped the abortion issue during debate on the bill, attacking the bill on the grounds that he was "fundamentally opposed to bubble-zone injunctions in any form," and suggesting that the court system provided sufficient opportunities for parties to seek injunctive relief. He also took aim at the NDP government's record with public protest (in the wake of the Clayoquot controversy, discussed in the next chapter), questioning why "a government beset with problems of protests, blockades and interference" would focus on the specific issue of access to abortion services.[57]

The law came into effect on September 18, 1995, initiating a period of uncertainty and legal contestation as anti-abortion groups challenged the constitutionality of the act for violating freedom of religious expression. Pursuant to the power to enact regulations, the minister of health immediately designated the first "access zone" or bubble zone around the Everywoman's Health Centre, which at that time was located on Victoria Drive in East Vancouver. Maurice Lewis, an anti-abortion activist who had regularly protested outside the clinic on previous occasions, intentionally breached the access zone on September

22, 1995, while wearing a sandwich board that included an image of the Christian icon Our Lady of Guadalupe and the statement "Stop Abortion." Lewis was arrested by Vancouver Police for breaching the provisions of the act prohibiting sidewalk interference and protest in the access zone, and jailed for three months for refusing to sign an undertaking not to re-attend at the clinic. Lewis admitted the facts at trial before Provincial Court Judge E.J. Cronin. The contested issue was the constitutional question of whether the new law violated the Charter rights of the accused, with Lewis claiming that he was offering "sidewalk counselling" to women in a peaceful manner.

In a decision rendered in January 1996, Judge Cronin declared that section 2(1)(a) and section 2(1)(b) of the act, which prohibited sidewalk interference and protesting within the access zone, were unconstitutional, in that they violated freedom of expression, freedom of association, and freedom of conscience and religion, and were not saved by section 1 of the Charter. He based this ruling on the grounds that the law did not allow any exception: "It eliminates all peaceful protests and any form of communication or attempted communication regarding abortion within the access zone."[58] The cabinet immediately met and Attorney General Ujjal Dosanjh announced the following day that the Crown would appeal the trial judge's decision. Organizations on both sides of the abortion debate made submissions as intervenors in the case. In a submission to the BC Supreme Court in support of the Crown's appeal, a coalition of five women's health organizations – including the Everywoman's Health Centre, other abortion services providers, and women's advocacy groups – asserted that "legislative action is especially appropriate where, as here, there is evidence to show that injunctive relief has not adequately addressed the problem." The intervening pro-choice coalition cited the Supreme Court of Canada's finding in the *Keegstra* case that the equality guarantee in section 15 of the Charter "is the broadest of all guarantees."[59] On the opposite side of the debate, counsel for the intervening pro-life coalition (which included the Archdiocese of Vancouver's Respect for Life Office and several other anti-abortion organizations) argued that the bubble zones infringed upon not only Lewis's freedom of conscience and religion but also the freedom of conscience and religion of those entering the clinic, who were deprived of the opportunity to communicate with protesters.[60]

In a decision pronounced in October 1996 (eight months after Judge Cronin's ruling had struck down the impugned sections of the act) BC Supreme Court Justice Mary Saunders allowed the Crown's appeal, reversing the trial judge's acquittal and convicting Lewis for breaching the bubble zone and violating the *Access to Abortion Services Act*.[61] Saunders conceded that Lewis's beliefs were sincerely held and motivated by his religion, and that the act infringed upon freedom of expression and freedom of conscience and religion under section 2 of the Charter. But she pointed to the Supreme Court of Canada's finding in *Morgentaler* that impediments to access to abortion infringed upon a woman's right to security of person under section 7 of the Charter, and concluded: "Health care has fundamental value in our society. A woman's right to access health care without unnecessary loss of privacy and dignity is no more than the right of every Canadian to access health care." The appeal was allowed "because the objective of the legislation outweighs the infringement of section 2 of the Charter ... and is demonstrably justified in a free and democratic society." The case was remitted to the trial judge for sentencing.[62]

Despite the BC Supreme Court judgment in *Lewis,* the constitutionality of the province's Bubble Law remained unsettled for more than a decade. This reflected an unfortunate turn of events, as Maurice Lewis, who had appealed his conviction, was found dead in a car north of Wawa, Ontario, in September 1997, before his appeal to the BC Court of Appeal was heard. The RCMP attributed his death to "natural causes."[63] This left the constitutional question outstanding, with two other cases involving three anti-abortion picketers winding their way through the courts in the decade that followed. In December 1996, Jim Demers had wilfully violated sections of the *Access to Abortion Services Act* restricting sidewalk interference, protesting, and besetting in an access zone. Like Lewis, he admitted the facts of the case. Unlike Lewis, however, Demers's central argument that was section 7 of the Charter included the right to life of the fetus, and that section 2(b) of the *Access to Abortion Services Act* was therefore unconstitutional. Following the Supreme Court of Canada's reasoning in *Morgentaler,* the BC Court of Appeal rejected Demers's argument, finding that "the current law of this country supports the position of the Crown ... that a foetus is not included in the word 'everyone' in s. 7 of the *Charter.*" As a result, Demers's appeal was dismissed and his conviction was upheld in 2003.[64]

As the Demers case unfolded, two other well-known anti-abortion protesters, Gordon Watson and Donald Spratt, publicly defied the *Access to Abortion Services Act* in December 1998, engaging in "sidewalk interference" in front of the Everywoman's Health Centre. They were convicted of the "quasi-criminal" charges following a lengthy trial in August 2000, and the convictions were upheld by the BC Supreme Court in 2002. In the intervening period, Dr. Romalis, who had recovered from the 1994 shooting to the point where he was able to continue performing abortions (though not live births), was stabbed in the back in July 2000 at the Seymour Medical Clinic in Vancouver. The assail-

FIGURE 13 A guard monitors the entrance of the Everywoman's Health Centre in Vancouver on the tenth anniversary of the opening of the not-for-profit abortion clinic in 1998. Repeated and rowdy protests by anti-abortion demonstrators in the preceding years resulted in hundreds of arrests and ultimately to the enactment of the *Access to Abortion Services Act* (the Bubble Law) in 1995. | Ward Perrin, published with permission of *Vancouver Sun*

ant escaped, and Romalis was treated for a non-life-threatening wound to his rib cage.[65] BC premier Ujjal Dosanjh responded by calling for a *Criminal Code* amendment to strengthen sentencing provisions against persons convicted of attacking abortion doctors (a suggestion that was not acted upon, reflecting wide variations in public opinion on the abortion issue in different parts of the country).[66] In the United States, Colorado adopted its own bubble law, informed by the BC legislation; it included a provision for an eight-foot buffer or "floating bubble" surrounding a person accessing an abortion facility, which could not be "pierced for the purposes of politically charged conversation, leafleting, 'education,' and so forth" (as geographer Don Mitchell described the legislation, in a study of the emerging legal "right to be left alone," which blurred lines between the "public" and "private" spheres).[67]

Meanwhile, the BC Court of Appeal heard Watson's and Spratt's appeals of their convictions in 2004, with coalitions on both sides of the abortion issue intervening as they had done in *Lewis.*[68] Counsel for the Access Coalition, representing the abortion clinics and women's groups, argued that the *Access to Abortion Services Act* had been "carefully tailored to address a pressing legislative objective" and that the impugned sections were therefore constitutional.[69] Counsel for the Canadian Religious Freedom Alliance, representing three Christian organizations, claimed that the legislated prohibition on picketing was not "rationally connected to the objective of reasonable and secure access," and that the impairment of expression was neither minimal nor proportional, and was therefore not saved by section 1 of the Charter.[70] In 2008, the BC Court of Appeal upheld the constitutionality of the Bubble Law. On the secondary issue raised by Watson and Spratt, of whether the size of the access zones was disproportionate and larger than necessary to satisfy the stated purpose of ensuring safe access, the court similarly found that the extent of the zone (thirty metres at its widest point) was reasonable and did not constitute a "constitutional impairment." Writing for the appellate division, Justice Catherine Ryan found that "the objective of the Act justifies the limited infringement of freedom of expression in the circumstances."[71]

Conclusion

The *Access to Abortion Services Act* remains on the statute books in British Columbia, prohibiting protest in the vicinity of abortion clinics and the homes and offices of abortion providers, while providing a legal basis for the quasi-criminal prosecution of anti-abortion protesters. This legislation has superseded the traditional legal remedy of a civil injunction in relation to anti-abortion protests; it provides a permanent "legislative injunction," relieving abortion providers of the burden of initiating civil proceedings and seeking a court order to defend their property interests against social movement challenges. With this legislation, the state has assumed responsibility for prosecution of anti-abortion protests on a permanent basis. Despite periodic challenges by the pro-life movement, including the cases of *R v Demers* (2003), *R v Spratt and Watson* (2007), and *R v Spratt* (2011), the courts have upheld the provisions of the act restraining freedom of expression and freedom of conscience and religion, suggesting that these infringements are reasonable and justified to safeguard conflicting Charter rights regarding security of the person and equality.[72]

Jurisprudence surrounding abortion rights and anti-abortion protests demonstrates the growing phenomenon of *rights litigation* in Canada, as parties have engaged in protracted campaigns inside and outside the legal arena to assert rights claims, particularly since enactment of the *Canadian Charter of Rights of Freedoms* as part of the *Constitution Act, 1982*. The cases examined in this chapter demonstrate the complexity of rights litigation, where competing rights claims come into conflict and judges and other members of the legal community are called upon to decide where the balance of rights should be drawn and which interests should prevail.[73] With adoption of the Bubble Law in 1995, the BC legislature inserted itself as the arbiter of these competing rights claims – intervening with legislation to regulate and restrict social movement protest relating to abortion services, restraining claims to public space, and infringing upon political expression and constitutionally protected rights in the interests of protecting access to another constitutionally protected right – a controversial health service that rival social movements had agitated and litigated for and against for decades.

This chapter has illuminated the history of access to abortion services in British Columbia and the contested social relations of adjudication and crises of legal legitimacy surrounding access to these services. It highlights shifting strength among the rival "pro-choice" and "pro-life" movements, as well as changing legal technologies deployed by judges, legislatures, and other legal actors in response to social movement protest over the control of women's bodies and spaces in the vicinity of abortion clinics.

The emergence of the Bubble Law and the legal politics of abortion in the period since *Morgentaler* highlight the activity of the atypical pro-life social movement, an outlier in the legal history of clashes between social movements, property interests, and members of the legal community in British Columbia. Usually, social movement actors have been of the left or aligned with it: picketing workers on strike and facing criminal charges, injunctions, and prison terms for challenging employers' power; environmental or Indigenous road blockaders impeding access to natural resources in defiance of licences held by private companies; and urban anti-poverty activists and poor people occupying public spaces with tent cities to assert a "right to sleep" and advocate for a rebalancing of power relations. The Bubble Law case study tells us a different story and highlights social tensions and political debates based on a distinct alignment of forces: a social movement rooted in the Christian right and conservative world view challenging the property interests of health service providers oriented toward the not-for-profit sector and feminist movement. Both the social movement protesters and the conventional property interests seeking recourse in the legal arena are outliers in this respect. The experiences of these rival social movements in challenging the status quo and asserting competing rights claims through the control and appropriation of space since the 1970s demonstrates continuity and change in the legal technology of coercion deployed in response to protest in British Columbia's legal history.

In 2021, the NDP government of British Columbia introduced legislation to enact another bubble law, in response to protests at hospitals and schools by citizens opposed to vaccination and mask requirements associated with the COVID-19 pandemic.[74] Like the anti-abortion protesters described in this chapter, many of the anti-vaccination "Freedom" protesters were aligned with the political right and conservative organizations. BC solicitor general Mike Farnworth described the protesters as "Covidiots," while the protesters justified their actions and opposed legislative intervention on civil liberties grounds, invoking freedom to consent to medical care and freedom of assembly and association.[75] Parliament also amended the *Criminal Code* to make it an offence to block access to buildings providing health care, expanding the definition of "intimidation" under section 423.[76] In February 2022, a major social conflagration erupted when the Government of Canada invoked the *Emergencies Act* in response to a "Freedom Convoy" that had paralyzed mobility in the nation's capital and on key highways and bridges, in a protest against government responses to COVID-19 (with Federal Court of Canada Justice Richard Mosley later concluding that the government's decision to declare a Public Order Emergency was unreasonable, a decision upheld on appeal).[77]

As this and subsequent chapters demonstrate, clashes of values and competing conceptions of rights and claims to public space continue to animate public debate and legal interventions by various members of the legal community, extending to the legislative branch.

Chapter 4

LEGAL WARS IN THE WOODS

The Making of a Thousand Criminals at Clayoquot Sound

IN THE SUMMER OF 1993, more than nine hundred people were arrested at Clayoquot Sound on Vancouver Island, charged with criminal contempt of court for defying BC Supreme Court injunctions prohibiting interference with licence holder MacMillan Bloedel Ltd.'s logging of old-growth rainforest on Crown land. This was the largest incidence of mass arrests arising from nonviolent civil disobedience in Canadian history to that point – "the current high-water mark for persistent disobedience of Court orders," as British Columbia's Chief Justice Allan McEachern described the phenomenon in upholding sentences of forty-five days or more of jail time imposed on three dozen protesters in the first Clayoquot trial.[1] Debates swirling around the province during the Clayoquot protests and mass trials underscored the contested social relations of the law and a renewed crisis of law's legitimacy – a questioning of the neutrality of the provincial state and judiciary, and the fairness of adjudicative procedures as they relate to environmental policy and social movement protest. This crisis also raised questions of jurisdiction – who has authority to define and authorize "legitimate" uses of public land (a theme I pursue in greater depth in the next chapter, on Indigenous blockades). Similar to the pattern arising in relation to labour protests earlier in the twentieth century, the crisis of legal legitimacy and social relations of adjudication at

FIGURE 14 Of the estimated twelve thousand people who converged on the Clayoquot Sound Peace Camp during the "hot summer" of 1993, more than nine hundred were arrested for defying court injunctions issued to logging company MacMillan Bloedel Ltd. | Mark Hobson

Clayoquot Sound were influenced by close economic relationships linking the provincial government, judges, and logging companies, fuelling claims of partiality against a government that simultaneously issued timber licences (and owned shares in the logging company) while pursuing criminal prosecutions against environmentalists who challenged those permits. Customary assertions of rights to protect ecological values on Crown forest lands propelled the environmentalists on a collision course with an economically, legally, and politically powerful coalition of interests – exposing the contested legal, social, and spatial construction of legitimate uses of Clayoquot Sound. What conditions impelled a wide spectrum of ordinarily law-abiding citizens to converge on a remote protest camp and defy judges' authority, attracting criminal liability for contempt?

Blockades

Divergent visions for the proper management of British Columbia's natural resource wealth can be traced back to the early twentieth century, prior to the advent of the modern environmental movement.[2] By the 1970s, the fault lines were becoming increasingly clearly drawn, with growing numbers of citizens embracing an ecological viewpoint and gravitating toward environmental campaigns and organizations that advocated for conservation of resources and protection of biological diversity. As Jeremy Wilson has argued, environmental politics in British Columbia came to increasingly focus on forest resources, particularly the old-growth rainforests of Vancouver Island. In part, this reflected the pattern of economic development in the province, which had sidestepped some of the controversies that were prevalent elsewhere (for example, over waste management and nuclear and coal power). The emerging environmental movement's focus on forest resources also reflected the emotional impact of images of mountainsides and valleys denuded by clear-cuts, the preferred method of industrial logging by the late twentieth century.[3] According to geographer Roger Hayter, globalization intensified conflict over the province's forest resources, as bottom-line considerations of global shareholders drove increased extraction for commodity exports and declining government regulation, notwithstanding mounting public concern for ecological conservation.[4] Unsustainable logging impacted both ecological and working-class claims to forest resources, as historian Henry John has demonstrated, leading to mill closured and job losses.[5]

Throughout the 1980s, environmental consciousness grew in British Columbia, fuelling direct action where protesters blocked logging roads and otherwise interfered with logging operations in order to protect remaining stands of old-growth rainforest. Public ownership of forest lands imbued these resource conflicts with strong symbolic value, providing rhetorical weight to environmentalists' arguments that the remaining stands should be protected for ecological and recreational purposes, rather than cut down to generate profits for corporate licence holders such as MacMillan Bloedel, Western Forest Products, and Fletcher Challenge. At Meares Island and Sulphur Passage in Clayoquot Sound and the Tsitika River on northeastern Vancouver Island, environmental activists aligned with Greenpeace, Friends of Clayoquot Sound, the Western Canada Wilderness Committee, and the Sierra Club of Western Canada joined forces with local Indigenous peoples and developed tactics that would later be deployed on a mass scale during the Clayoquot blockade in the summer of 1993.[6] Mirroring earlier clashes between social movement actors and private property interests, counsel for the logging companies obtained injunctions and enlisted judges, police, and other members of the legal community to restrain the protests and allow the companies to harvest timber from Crown forest lands that had never been ceded by Indigenous peoples through conquest or treaty.

The Clayoquot Sound defenders objected to what they considered an unhealthily close relationship between the judiciary, the provincial government, and the logging companies; at the time, the BC government owned over 3 percent of the shares in MacMillan Bloedel, the province's largest forestry corporation and the primary licence holder of Crown forest lands in Clayoquot Sound, and therefore the plaintiff in the civil litigation that gave rise to the injunction and criminal contempt proceedings.[7] Maurice Gibbons, a professor emeritus at Simon Fraser University who, along with his wife, pleaded guilty to criminal contempt of court and was fined $1,250, described the view of many of the defendants: "These are the strangest criminals I have ever met, committing a crime so strange it is difficult to distinguish from an act of citizenship or public service."[8]

In 1990, the BC government responded to mounting protests by environmentalists on Vancouver Island by issuing a policy directive on civil disobedience to Crown prosecutors that stated: "On occasion those involved in public demonstrations come into conflict with the law and obstruct or interfere with the rights of others. The use of criminal sanctions in these situations is generally not appropriate." The directive suggested that individuals and other parties whose interests were affected by civil disobedience "should generally be encouraged to apply for a civil injunction to stop the disobedience," and "proceed with civil contempt proceedings" should the civil disobedience continue after the injunction was issued.[9]

Conflict over the future of Clayoquot Sound intensified in the summer of 1991, when MacMillan Bloedel announced plans to log 2.5 million cubic metres of old-growth rainforest in the watershed. The company, with one-third of the total Allowable Annual Cut (AAC) within Tree Farm Licences (TFLs) in British Columbia, had held logging rights to public land in TFL 44 (originally, Timber Management Licences 20 and 21) on Vancouver Island since 1955.[10] However, growing numbers of environmentally conscious citizens disagreed with the premise of corporate control of public forest lands, particularly clear-cut logging of old-growth rainforest, and launched a protracted campaign of civil disobedience to prevent the company from pursuing its harvesting plans. Like the anti-abortion protesters a few years earlier, the environmentalists who blocked logging roads in Clayoquot Sound invoked allegiance to a higher law in rejecting the authority of harvesting permits issued by the provincial government.

In September 1991, this conflict between the company and environmental activists entered the legal arena, when lawyers representing MacMillan Bloedel obtained an injunction from BC Supreme Court Justice John Spencer against three named defendants and an unspecified number of Jane and John Does to prevent them from obstructing or impeding its logging operations in Clayoquot Sound.[11] Three days after the initial order, on September 21, 1991, Justice Spencer issued a subsequent enforcement order, authorizing peace officers to arrest any person who they believed on reasonable and probable grounds had disobeyed the injunction. These initial injunctions were followed by subsequent court orders, naming additional defendants as they became known to the court and expanding the geographic scope of the earlier orders: from Justices Bouck (on September 25, 1991), Hamilton (June 30, 1992), Holmes (July 13, 1992), Tysoe (July 17 and July 20, 1992), Esson (July 16, 1993), and Hall (August 26, 1993). The first convictions for civil contempt of court were pronounced on December 9, 1991, when Justice Dennis Sheppard found six Tofino residents guilty of breaching Justice Spencer's order of September by blocking the MacMillan Bloedel logging road leading into the Bolson Creek watershed; Sheppard imposed sentences ranging from $500 fines to six months in jail, which were suspended on the condition that the protesters maintained good behaviour and complied with the injunction by refraining from interfering with future logging operations. "In a democracy, there are ways and means of changing laws and procedures ... by changing the minds of government or changing the government," Justice Sheppard said.[12]

A change in the provincial government following the October 1991 election – from the corporate-aligned, right-of-centre Social Credit government led by Rita Johnson to the social movement–aligned, left-of-centre New Democratic Party (NDP) government led by public interest lawyer Mike Harcourt – failed to produce significant change in the province's forest policy. The new government sought to reconcile working-class and ecological claims to forest resources – responding to two integral constituencies of the party's political base – with legislation in 1992 that aimed to address land use and resource conflicts through interest-based negotiation. However, the government's instructions to its appointee under the *Commissioner on Resources and Environment Act* conspicuously excluded Clayoquot Sound from the work of the multi-stakeholder commission.[13]

The social and legal battle over Clayoquot Sound heated up in the summer of 1992, when Justice Ian Drost responded to the growing civil disobedience campaign by directing that, henceforth, "these contempt proceedings be continued as criminal contempt proceedings." Following the practice established in the *Everywoman's Health Centre* case, the court also requested that the attorney general assume responsibility for the conduct of the contempt prosecutions, a request that the attorney general acceded to. This would later prompt accusations from counsel for the protesters that the court was creating "private criminal law" – protecting the interests of MacMillan Bloedel while denying the alleged contemnors access to trial by jury and other procedural safeguards ordinarily available to people facing serious criminal charges.[14]

A number of factors coalesced in the early 1990s to convince a substantial number of otherwise law-abiding citizens to make a stand at Clayoquot Sound and attract criminal liability for contempt of court by challenging the property rights of MacMillan Bloedel. These factors included unsuccessful attempts to defeat or alter the company's logging plans in the courts, and growing frustration over the "talk-and-log" strategy favoured by government and industry – engaging the public in a dialogue on how forest resources should be managed while at the same time ensuring that logging of old-growth rainforest continued unabated.[15] In 1991, the Sierra Club of Western Canada and the Western Canada Wilderness Committee jointly applied to the BC Supreme Court to have logging and road permits in Vancouver Island's Walbran Valley set aside, arguing that the province's chief forester had improperly extended Fletcher Challenge's licence to TFL 46 without public consultation, and that the logging and road permits issued by the district forester were therefore invalid. The trial judge and BC Court of Appeal dismissed the environmental groups' claims, with Justice Victor Curtis declaring that the chief forester had acted in accordance with the legislation: "The essence of the Petitioners' predicament is not that the law has been broken but rather that they have as yet been unable to convince those duly empowered to set and implement forest policy to accept their views concerning logging in the lower Walbran."[16]

Lack of confidence in the BC judiciary's ability to provide an adequate remedy to environmental concerns was exacerbated in 1993 when the Court of Appeal upheld decisions by an Appeal Board appointed under the *Forest Act* and by the BC Supreme Court, which increased MacMillan Bloedel's Allowable Annual Cut in TFL 44 from 2.42 million cubic metres to 2.68 million cubic metres. MacMillan Bloedel had initiated the appeal after the chief forester established the lower cutting volume. The Sierra Club had intervened in the case against the company's application, arguing that the forestry Appeal Board had applied an incorrect interpretation of the meaning of word "sustained" in the *Forest Act*, resulting in harvesting levels that far exceeded the rate of regeneration of timber in the area.[17]

The Sierra Club's intervention hinged on a narrow question of legal standing, including the status of nonhuman parties in disputes before the courts. This question – whether a natural object such as an old-growth tree has legal standing, and whether a person or organization could initiate legal action to assert rights held by nonhuman species – had been a locus for advocacy and policy development in environmental law circles for decades.[18] Participants in the burgeoning movement to protect Clayoquot Sound subscribed strongly to this conception of how the law must develop. "As values and perceptions change, the law must be recast to reflect new realities," one of the leaders of the protest, Tzeporah Berman, asserted.[19]

The Hot Summer of '93

The stage was set for the unprecedented blockades and legal proceedings of the "hot summer" of 1993. That spring, the BC government announced its Clayoquot Land Use Decision, approving logging by MacMillan Bloedel in TFL 44, which included about two-thirds of the land base in Clayoquot Sound.[20] The environmental activists established a "Peace Camp" near the Kennedy Lake logging road, with logistical muscle provided by Friends of Clayoquot Sound and Greenpeace. On July 5, 1993, following a pre-arranged plan, a dozen protesters, including NDP Member of Parliament Svend Robinson from Burnaby, linked arms across the road at the Kennedy River Bridge, preventing a MacMillan Bloedel truck from proceeding toward the cutblocks. A process server read out Justice Harold Tysoe's order and stuffed paper copies under the arms of each participant in the human chain, asking whether they would abide by the order, to which no one responded in the

FIGURE 15 Arrest in Clayoquot Sound, c. July 1993. More than 860 people were tried for criminal contempt of court for obstructing the logging of old-growth rainforests in Clayoquot Sound, resulting in 626 convictions and sentences of up to $3,000 in fines and sixty days' jail. | Ray Smith, *Times Colonist*

FIGURE 16 Arrest at the Clayoquot blockade, July 30, 1993. | Chuck Stoody, Canadian Press

affirmative. With no RCMP officers present to enforce the court order, the MacMillan Bloedel work crew turned around, under the glare of television cameras and to the applause of hundreds of blockade supporters who lined the road. Beginning the following day, July 6, RCMP officers accompanied the logging crew and arrested any person who violated the order to clear the road.[21]

By the end of July 1993, nearly one hundred people had been arrested for blocking the logging road leading to the Kennedy River Bridge (with more than five hundred alleged to have blocked the road before stepping aside at the request of police). This included Sheila Simpson, the first named defendant in MacMillan Bloedel's civil lawsuit that underpinned the injunction and contempt proceeding, who had two previous convictions for civil contempt of court from logging protests in 1991 and 1992. BC Supreme Court Justice Kenneth Meredith sentenced Simpson to six months in jail for her repeated contempts. The Court of Appeal later deemed this sentence "excessive," longer than any previous sentence imposed for breach of a court order relating to logging operations in the province, and reduced it to four months (with the remaining time to be served via electronic monitoring, followed by two years' probation with community service).[22] The other arrested Clayoquot blockaders were released from RCMP cells on their own recognizance and promise to appear in court, while those who refused to sign the undertaking were held in custody at the Nanaimo Correctional Centre pending trial. On July 16, 1993, a fresh injunction by Chief Justice William Esson replaced the original order of Justice Tysoe, which had been set to expire the following day. Esson retained the terms of the original order and added a clause specifically aimed at curbing the road blockade at the Kennedy River Bridge:

> Any persons attending at or near the Kennedy River Bridge during working hours of the Plaintiff and while vehicles are travelling along the travelled roadway in such area shall situate themselves off that roadway and shall not attend within fifteen feet of that roadway.[23]

Before the end of July, a special assize was scheduled beginning August 30 to try those charged with criminal contempt, as arrests in the vicinity of the Kennedy River Bridge continued on a nearly daily basis. The Peace Camp flourished, attracting an estimated twelve thousand people from across the province and beyond during the summer of 1993, reflecting a strong and diverse foundation established by the Friends of Clayoquot Sound in the preceding years, and an effective, inviting organizational structure grounded in feminist organizing principles.[24] Greenpeace added international reach and a sophisticated public relations approach to the local movement rooted in Clayoquot Sound.

On August 6, Esson, who served as chief justice of the BC Supreme Court (and was therefore responsible for administration of the contempt proceedings against the protesters), met informally with defence counsel, lamenting that another "100 will go and get arrested" next week, and that "the element of deliberation is almost without precedent. Although I agree that it's not violent it is perhaps ritualistic in that manner, but the setting the authority of the court at naught is what lies at the root of it."[25] Esson underestimated the magnitude of the challenge. On August 9, a total of 309 people were arrested for sitting on the logging road near the Peace Camp during a "mass protest" day that attracted 1,000 people to the blockade; a month later, on September 7, another 242 people would be arrested in a single day.[26] Defiance of the court's authority and the perceived threat to the rule of law were at the heart of the judge's objection to the conduct of the environmental protesters – mirroring language used in other instances of social movement challenges to injunctions and private property rights. Esson announced that Justice John Bouck had been named as trial judge, that a pretrial conference would take place on August 18, and that the commencement date for the trial would not be adjusted. On August 26, Justice John Hall dismissed an application from Valerie Langer and Greenpeace Canada to have the injunctions set aside.[27]

The Trials

On August 30, 1993, a special assize opened in Victoria. The additional court sitting was scheduled by the BC Supreme Court's chief justice as the civil disobedience campaign intensified and the number of arrests mounted. This harked back to the "strikers' assizes" of 1913, when arrested Nanaimo coal miners faced a special sitting of the BC Supreme Court during an earlier clash between protesters and corporate property interests. As the Court of Appeal later concluded with respect to the Clayoquot proceeding, lumping the first group of alleged contemnors together into a single trial was justified in light of the heavy burden on court resources. Trying each of the initial forty-four accused individually, with two days allotted for each trial, "would require 88 court days, or 17 weeks," Chief Justice McEachern wrote. Moreover, it was "a matter of historical fact that larger groups of alleged contemnors have been tried together without difficulty in this province even before the advent of videotaped evidence."[28]

At the outset of the first Clayoquot trial, Justice John Bouck rejected an application from defence counsel and a number of the accused to adjourn the proceedings for one month to give them time to prepare their defences, but agreed to a two-day adjournment to give the accused a final opportunity to retain counsel. The trial resumed in earnest on September 1 and unfolded over the next six weeks. The appeal court later acknowledged that "the trial was a most difficult one," and attributed the problems to the accused and their supporters behaving "very badly," making "insulting comments to and about the judge," and introducing "frivolous motions."[29] McEachern elaborated on the dynamic between the largely unrepresented alleged contemnors and trial judge Bouck:

> Some of the Defendants obviously attempted to use the trial as a platform to continue their objection to logging in the Clayoquot area. The circumstances required the judge to attempt to "run a tight ship." If he had not, it is obvious that the trial, which went on far too long, would have gone on much longer.[30]

The trial of the initial forty-four Clayoquot blockaders proceeded at the Victoria Courthouse in September and October. Some of the accused attempted to justify their actions with reference to section 27 of the *Criminal Code,* which allows a person to use as much force as necessary to prevent the commission of an offence, alleging that the logging activities threatened fish-bearing habitat in contravention of section 34 of the *Fisheries Act*. Bouck initially ruled against allowing defence counsel Robert Moore-Stewart to call Mervyn Wilkinson, a professional forester, as an expert witness on the defence of necessity. Following an adjournment and submissions from several of the accused, Bouck relented and allowed Wilkinson to testify and attempt "to show that the actual or proposed logging operations of MacMillan Bloedel Ltd. was so dangerous to the life system of the Clayoquot area" that the accused had no choice but to disobey the court order.[31] During this exchange, the Crown had objected to the admissibility of Wilkinson's evidence on the necessity defence, asserting that the test established by the Supreme Court of Canada in the *Perka* case (described below) had not been satisfied, and that the defence was therefore unavailable to the accused. In response, Moore-Stewart cited case law in *Operation Dismantle* (1985) and *Morgentaler v The Queen* (1975), but Bouck ultimately accepted the Crown's position and ruled that the expert evidence of Wilkinson and others was not admissible to ground necessity defences.[32]

The Court of Appeal later upheld Bouck's ruling that the defence of necessity was unavailable to the accused, agreeing that the test established in *Perka* – serious emergent circumstances that left the accused with no alternative but to disobey the law – was not satisfied. In that earlier case before the Supreme Court of Canada, Justice Brian Dickson had offered a robust (if circumscribed) justification for civil disobedience in certain circumstances: "A liberal and humane criminal law cannot hold people to the strict obedience of laws in emergency situations where normal human instincts, whether of self-preservation or of altruism, overwhelmingly impel disobedience." However, Dickson was clear that such disobedience "must be premised on a right or duty recognized by law," which specifically "excludes conduct attempted to be justified on the ground of an ethical duty internal to the conscience of the accused as well as conduct sought to be justified on the basis of a perceived maximization of social utility resulting from it." Moreover, if "a reasonable legal alternative to disobeying the law [existed], then the decision to disobey becomes a voluntary one."[33] Since none of the accused Clayoquot blockaders had applied to the court to have the injunction set aside (as Langer and Greenpeace Canada later did), they could not claim they had no choice but to disobey the order to prevent the perceived peril from the logging operations.[34] The BC Court of

Appeal went so far as to assert that "the defence of necessity can never be available to avoid a perceived peril that is lawfully authorized," citing the BC Supreme Court decision in *Everywoman's Health Centre Society v Bridges* (1989) and stating that the impugned logging was conducted with valid permits and licences issued by the BC government, and was therefore legally authorized.[35]

In another colourful chapter of the trial, one of the accused, Darrin Mortson, took the stand to make his submissions. He began by declaring that he was legally illiterate and "as much in need of assistance as a person of foreign tongue or a deaf and dumb person," and then promptly proceeded to read the Dr. Seuss children's book *The Lorax* in full, comprising nine pages of court transcript, before leaving the stand. This reflected the "frustration" of the self-represented accused, one lawyer claimed, an explanation with which the appeal court concurred, though it was of no legal consequence.[36]

Perception of an unhealthy relationship between the court and the logging company persisted throughout the trial, particularly when Justice Bouck disallowed questions from the accused relating to activities of MacMillan Bloedel's public relations department. This first occurred during cross-examination of a Crown witness who had introduced newspaper articles to prove the public nature of the contempt. It occurred a second time when defendant Margaret Ormond was cross-examining a MacMillan Bloedel employee and asked what the "MacMillan Bloedel budget is for advertising and how much has been spent for TV and newspaper advertising about the Clayoquot decision?" The Court of Appeal later found that Bouck "rightly stopped" the question in the first instance and similarly "was right" to disallow the question to the company employee.[37]

In the end, Bouck found forty-two of the accused guilty of criminal contempt of court, while two others pleaded guilty before the trial concluded. He imposed sentences of between forty-five and sixty days in jail and fines ranging from $1,000 to $2,000, depending on the number of offences and the conduct of the accused during the trial. He described Andrew Swain, a Victoria teenager who was arrested by sheriffs at his high school for failing to appear in court, as "an insolent young man who has little respect for the institutions that give him the right to peacefully protest," and sentenced him to forty-five days in jail and a $1,500 fine. In his reasons for sentencing, Bouck offered a spirited defence of the rule of law, which he said was integral to the proper functioning of a democracy. He reminded the accused and observers that democracies had failed and that without the rule of law, anarchy and mob rule would prevail.[38] On appeal, the prison sentences against most of the forty-four contemnors were upheld (with Justice Lambert dissenting), though the court suspended the sentence of one contemnor (nineteen-year-old Jennifer Maxwell) and reduced the sentences of two others who had pleaded guilty (including provincial Green Party leader Stuart Parker) from 45 days to 30 days. The court of appeal also set aside the fines against all the contemnors.[39]

Another contemnor, seventeen-year-old Jonathan Pulker, had applied to have his trial transferred to the youth court, as provided for in the federal *Young Offenders Act*, which invested the youth court with "exclusive jurisdiction in respect of every contempt of court" committed by a young person "against any other court otherwise than in the face of that court." However, Justice Bouck denied this application, and tried and sentenced Pulker along with the other accused. The BC Court of Appeal later upheld this ruling on the grounds that superior courts maintained "a core jurisdiction that is beyond the reach of either Parliament or the Legislatures acting other than by way of a constitutional amendment."[40] Concurring with BC Supreme Court Justice B.D. MacDonald's decision in *Wallace*, McEachern found that "the inherent powers of a superior court to use its contempt powers to enforce its orders, and to maintain its authority, was beyond the reach of Parliament."[41] He therefore dismissed this ground of appeal and deemed subsection 47(2) of the *Young Offenders Act* to be unconstitutional to the extent that it intruded on a superior court's authority to try and punish for contempt (a decision with which the Supreme Court of Canada agreed, in a split five-four decision).[42] McEachern opined that

> the essential character of a superior court of law necessarily involves that it should be invested with a power to maintain its authority and to prevent its process being obstructed and abused. Such a power is intrinsic in a superior court; it is its very life-blood, its very essence, its immanent attribute. Without such a power, the court would have form but would lack substance.[43]

Following Bouck's conviction of the initial 44 accused, a succession of BC Supreme Court judges found most of the remaining arrested Clayoquot blockaders guilty of criminal contempt of court in more than a dozen trials extending throughout the autumn and winter of 1993–94. More than 860 people were tried, while charges against several dozen protesters were dropped. Tzeporah Berman, whom the Crown identified as the ringleader of the protests, was acquitted of 857 counts of the *Criminal Code* offence of "aiding and abetting" following a five-day trial.[44] In total, 626 people were convicted of criminal contempt of court and sanctioned with fines of up to $3,000 and jail terms of up to sixty days, the largest incidence until then of mass arrests and convictions arising from social movement protest in Canadian history.[45]

Reaction

In an opinion-editorial piece in the *Globe and Mail,* University of Victoria law professors Hamar Foster and John McLaren argued forcefully that criminal contempt was a legal anachronism in Canada, the "only non-statutory crime known to Canadian law." For contempt committed outside the courtroom, it seemed a stretch to view acts of nonviolent civil disobedience as perilous to social order, particularly when ordinary legal remedies against mischief and other *Criminal Code* offences remained at the disposal of the attorney general and police, who were responsible for enforcing the criminal law. Foster and McLaren argued that "eight hundred prosecutions for criminal contempt" amounted to the unrestrained exercise of the peculiar legal device, threatening the perception of the courts as "impartial arbiters."[46]

The Victoria *Times Colonist,* which sided more often than not with status quo forces rather than insurgent social movements, also condemned the criminal convictions: "To brand as criminal many of our best and most conscientious idealists, can only increase the distance between people of conscience and the state. That would be very bad for our future."[47] In a similar vein, *Vancouver*

FIGURE 17 Protest at the BC legislature during the Clayoquot trials, c. September 1993. | Aldo de Moor

Sun columnist Frances Bula highlighted the irony of how criminal contempt of court proceedings, aimed at engendering respect for the judiciary, often had the opposite effect in the court of public opinion:

> Criminal contempt cases are never much fun for the court system. They usually arise out of the most contentious issues in turbulent times. They become a rallying point for activist groups, to whom the convicting judge becomes, in turn, an anti-union, pro-management toady; a conscienceless person in favor of killing babies; or a cruel represser of people trying save the planet.
>
> As one Canadian law-reform commission noted, the problem with contempt is that it ends up working against itself. "We are therefore faced with a disturbing paradox: contempt was developed mainly to enhance the image of the judicial system but its most publicized forms do just the opposite."[48]

Appeals

"The die seems to have been cast when the trial judge decided to proceed with the trial on September 1, 1993 with many of the Defendants still unrepresented by counsel," Chief Justice McEachern wrote in his appeal reasons in *MacMillan Bloedel v Simpson* (1994).[49] However, he and the two other members of the BC Court of Appeal division, Justices Alan Macfarlane and Josiah Wood, found that Justice Bouck had acted "judicially" and in accordance with "proper principles" of natural justice in refusing to grant the alleged contemnors' application for an adjournment. "[I]t still appears that the Defendants really had no valid defence to the charge that they had committed criminal contempts of the court."[50]

Emphasizing the core legal principle governing injunction and contempt proceedings, the appeal court attributed the drawn-out, unruly trial to the refusal of the accused and their legal counsel to accept the supremacy of the court's authority. As McEachern wrote in his reasons:

> On the theory that an order of a Superior Court must be obeyed until it is set aside, it was not open to these Defendants to question its validity either by their blockades, or by a collateral attack during contempt proceedings. The refusal of the Defendants and some of their counsel to accept this legal truism was one of the reasons why the trial of these matters was so unduly delayed.[51]

The Court of Appeal focused on the contemnors' failure to exhaust available legal remedies – specifically, applying to have the injunction orders set aside – prior to committing the breaches. In the court's judgment, this made the defence of necessity unavailable to the accused. Moreover, McEachern found that the defence of necessity could not operate "to avoid a peril that is lawfully authorized by the law," such as MacMillan Bloedel's right to access stands of Crown timber for lawful harvesting.[52]

The court also rejected the contemnors' argument that denial of trial by jury was unlawful under the Charter, despite section 11 provisions for jury trials for offences where the maximum penalty was imprisonment of five years or more. Citing legal texts by John Fox and by Gordon Borrie and Nigel Lowe on the law of contempt, as well as case law in the labour cases of *Poje* (1953), *Tilco Plastics* (1967), *UFAWU* (1967), and *BCGEU* (1988), the anti-abortion cases of *Everywoman's Health Centre Society v Bridges* (1989) and *Demers* (1992), and an Ontario appeal court decision in *R v Cohn* (1984), the BC Court of Appeal found that judges could deal summarily with contempt proceedings provided the sentence did not exceed five years (the statutory threshold for the right to a jury trial in the *Criminal Code*).[53] McEachern declared confidently that it was "a matter of indisputable record" that prompt judicial action in response to breaches of court orders in "emotional, high-profile disputes" had "preserved the rule of law in this province." Notwithstanding the provisions of the Charter, "the wisdom of history is that the courts must be free to deal directly and decisively with any contempt against its process. So well established is this principle that I would not depart from it."[54]

In one small concession to the defence (which did not alter the result of the appeals), the Court of Appeal found that "it might have been better if the witness had been allowed to say whatever he knew about that question," after Bouck had refused to allow the accused, Robert Maher, to question a Crown witness on whether the Kennedy River Bridge was a "public place" (a question that had legal ramifications in terms of the public, and therefore criminal, nature of the contempt).[55] Similarly, the court conceded that "the trial judge was perhaps not as helpful as a judge on a shorter trial might have been" when several self-represented accused inquired about the lack of availability of the defence of necessity.[56] Still, the court framed these critical comments in a way that ultimately justified Bouck's decisions and prevented the array of procedural irregularities from supporting reversal of the convictions: "The trial judge was attempting to conduct the trial under difficult circumstances and he cannot be expected to stop the proceedings to answer irrelevant questions."[57] The Court of Appeal quoted favourably from a 1970 legal text that stridently defended the court's "inherent jurisdiction" as a core element of the rule of law: the authority of superior courts was an "untouchable core jurisdiction (except by constitutional amendment)."[58]

This line of reasoning on the "inherent jurisdiction" of the courts to decide on matters of contempt was sustained by the Supreme Court of Canada in a narrow five-to-four decision in *MacMillan Bloedel v Simpson* (1995). Canada's highest court agreed to hear the appeal of only one of the Clayoquot blockaders (out of thirty-one who applied), teenager Jonathan Pulker, who claimed that his case should have been tried in youth court rather than in the BC Supreme Court.[59] On the question of whether Parliament possessed the jurisdiction to transfer exclusive jurisdiction over contempt proceedings involving youth from superior courts to youth courts, pursuant to subsection 47(2) of the *Young Offenders Act*, the majority of Supreme Court judges upheld the inherent jurisdiction of the judiciary in contempt proceedings. Removing the jurisdiction of the superior courts "would offend our Constitution," Chief Justice Antonio Lamer declared, expressing the majority view.[60]

A year later, the Supreme Court of Canada considered another appeal arising from the Clayoquot protests, dismissing an application from Greenpeace Canada that challenged the power of the courts to grant injunctions against unnamed members of the public engaged in protests that interfered with private rights. The question rested on whether court orders naming "John" and "Jane Does" were legally valid, or whether the private party initiating the action should be required to name each defendant in the statement of claim. Justice Beverley McLachlin wrote the unanimous decision of the court, commenting on the balancing of rights at the heart of judicial reasoning in response to protests:

> In a society that prizes both the right to express dissent and the maintenance of private rights, a way to reconcile both interests must be found. One of the ways this can be done is through court orders like the one at issue in this case. The task of the courts is to find a way to protect the legitimate exercise of lawful private rights while preserving maximum scope for the lawful exercise of the right of expression and protest.[61]

Reflections on the Legal Wars in the Woods

While the outcome of the Clayoquot trials was widely interpreted as a defeat for the protesters and confirmation of the close relationship between the government, the logging company, and the courts, the social movement mobilization at Clayoquot Sound in 1993 gave impetus to changes in the management of Crown forest lands on Vancouver Island and across British Columbia. Pressure from environmentalists on MacMillan Bloedel's customers in international markets, particularly the lucrative European market, also contributed to improved forest practices and protection of old-growth rainforest (and, ultimately, to MacMillan Bloedel's disappearance after a half-century as British Columbia's predominant forestry firm, when the company was sold to Weyerhaeuser in 1999).[62]

In November 1993, fresh on the heels of the Clayoquot trials and convictions, the BC government established a Scientific Panel for Sustainable Forest Practices in Clayoquot Sound, with a goal "to make forest practices in Clayoquot ... the best in the world."[63] The government also released a draft "Forest Practices Code Discussion Paper" and "Forest Practices Code Rules," inviting comment from the public and stakeholders. It incorporated this feedback into the *Forest Practices Code of British Columbia Act* (1994), prescribing rules including protection of fish-bearing streams and other sensitive ecological areas. The government also initiated consultation on appropriate uses of Crown forest land, building on the earlier CORE (Commission on Resources and Environment) process and culminating in adoption of the Vancouver Island Land Use Plan in 2000. The plan set aside substantial swaths of forest land for conservation purposes and designated "special management zones" where higher standards of forest management would be applied to safeguard biological diversity.[64] Areas of long-standing concern to environmentalists, including the Carmanah and lower Walbran Valleys, were granted protected status.[65] As a government minister later noted, prior to the CORE process, "the forest industry was basically the only tenant of the land. We've established that the land, that is, land use, is a community process."[66]

Within Clayoquot Sound itself, the Nuu-chah-nulth peoples secured an ongoing and central role in management of the area's forest resources (reflecting Indigenous assertions of rights, which I discuss in the next chapter). The BC government announced shortly after the Clayoquot trials that it was entering into treaty talks with the Nuu-chah-nulth, leading to an Interim Measures Agreement that transferred tenure over Crown forest lands from MacMillan Bloedel (and its successor, Weyerhaeuser) to a new company owned by the First Nations (initially as a joint venture with MacMillan Bloedel, and later wholly Indigenous-owned). Iisaak Forest Resources (meaning "respect" and guided by the principle of *Hishuk-ish ts'awalk*, the Nuu-chah-nulth belief in "respecting the limits of what is extracted and the interconnectedness of all things") entered into a memorandum of understanding with several environmental organizations in 1999, signalling a new era in the environmental politics of the sound.[67] In 2016, Iisaak amalgamated with MaMook Natural Resources Ltd., owned by five Nuu-chah-nulth First Nations (Ahousaht, Hesquiaht,

Tla-o-qui-aht, Toquaht, and Ucluelet), which at the time of publication held the harvesting and management rights for TFL 54 and 57, displacing the former non-Indigenous corporate tenure holders.[68] In 2024, the Ahousaht and Tla-o-qui-aht First Nations announced in conjunction with the BC government the establishment of ten new conservancies in Clayoquot Sound to protect old-growth forests, encompassing seventy-six thousand hectares of land.[69]

This tenure reform was not without criticism, however. Political scientist Karena Shaw described the 1994 agreement with the Nuu-chah-nulth as "a classic 'divide-and-conquer' strategy," which "reorganized the strategic terrain" for environmentalists, who could no longer "use the treatment of First Nations as a justification for their own activities, and they would potentially have to confront First Nations if the latter chose to approve logging plans in areas the protesters sought to protect."[70] By entering into the deal with the First Nations and appointing the "Scientific Panel on Clayoquot Sound" to advise on "world-leading practices" in environmentally sustainable forestry, the government had "sought to stitch together the now yawning gap in [its] political authority."[71] Historian Jonathan Clapperton also discussed this dynamic, suggesting that non-Indigenous environmentalists, who had been the driving force behind the 1993 campaign, "arguably ended up being furthest away from the levers of power."[72]

The Clayoquot trials also provoked calls for legal reform, including suggestions that the ambit of judicial discretion in environmental cases be narrowed or removed. "Surely it is time to take this power to make temporary legislation away from judges in cases of public dispute," declared Clayoquot blockader Maurice Gibbons in a volume of essays published shortly after the conclusion of the trials.[73] Tzeporah Berman questioned the economic underpinnings of the rule of law:

> Our society is designed to protect the right to make money before protecting living systems that support us. Standing at the blockades, I discovered that our challenge was to reverse the burden of proof. Why wasn't the burden of proof on corporations – and the governments supporting them – to show that their practices were ecologically and environmentally responsible – especially when they were dealing with public land and public health?[74]

This critique mirrored moves in the United States, where, as Melinda Benson has demonstrated, ostensibly neutral legal procedures are often deployed to the benefit of corporate licence holders and the detriment of ecological interests.[75] Amir Attaran has suggested that administrative law, and specifically a writ of mandamus against the Crown, would provide an effective "third strategy" to respond to civil disobedience and "keep the peace" in the forests, avoiding problems associated with *Criminal Code* charges or civil injunctions and contempt proceedings.[76]

This strategy was supported by BC Supreme Court Justice Mark McEwen in the environmental case *Slocan Forest Products Ltd v John Doe* (2000), which arose from a blockade against logging at Trozzo Creek, near the Slocan Valley in the West Kootenays. The judge found that the provincial government's hands-off policies toward criminal prosecutions in response to environmental road blockades "manifestly fail to appreciate the proper function and limitations of this court's civil processes," raising the spectre of a writ of mandamus against the Crown, provoking the ire of Crown counsel.[77] In granting the injunction to the logging company, however, Justice McEwen discussed the gulf between legitimate legal rights to natural resources invoked by corporate licence holders and "rights" alleged by social movement actors, which had no standing in law and were therefore properly pursued in the political rather than judicial arena:

> The alleged right is, of course, found in the various permits Slocan Forest Products holds, apparently authorizing the activities it is attempting to carry out at Trozzo Creek. As I have said, those who have impeded Slocan have offered no arguable legal right to do what they do. They have set up a competing "right" to clean water, but do not suggest that this right has any legislated or common law status as against the clearly defined rights of Slocan Forest Products. Whether this is as it should be is not a legal question, but a question of social policy. Any change would be the province of legislators, not judges.[78]

Similar reasoning was provided by BC Supreme Court Justice Ian Pitfield later in 2000, in the case of *International Forest Products Ltd et al v Kern et al*, arising from protests against proposed logging of old-growth rainforest in the Upper Elaho Valley north of Vancouver. Justice Pitfield found that the government's failure to enforce the criminal law did not negate the duty of the courts to step in when necessary to uphold the rights of private licence holders facing environmental protests:

> At the end of the day, however, no matter how distasteful the task, the court cannot shirk its responsibility to ensure the rule of law. As affirmed by the Court of Appeal and the Supreme Court of Canada in *MacMillan Bloedel Ltd. v. Simpson,* the court will intervene when conduct which may be criminal in nature

interferes with the exercise of private property rights. It will do so notwithstanding that the public perception may be that the court is favouring the rights of one party to the detriment of another.[79]

Departing from this line of jurisprudence, BC Supreme Court Justice Douglas Thompson issued an unorthodox ruling in September 2021, refusing to extend an injunction for Teal Cedar Products Ltd. after more than eleven hundred people had been arrested protesting old-growth logging at Fairy Creek and Caycuse River in TFL 46 on southern Vancouver Island (surpassing the Clayoquot protests as the largest incidence of civil disobedience leading to arrests in Canadian history).[80] Tensions mounted as the RCMP deployed broad "exclusion zones," checkpoints, "pain compliance techniques," and pepper spray to enforce an injunction issued to Teal Cedar, after more than a year of creative blockading tactics deployed by land defenders who rallied under the umbrella of the "Rainforest Flying Squad." In his reasons for judgment, Justice Thompson found that the public interest in preserving the court's reputation outweighed potential harm to the logging company, concluding that the balance of convenience weighed against extending the injunction. Emphasizing "the strong public interest in keeping the Court away from the front line of this dispute," and "serious and substantial infringement of civil liberties ... in the name of enforcing this Court's order," Thompson chose to "get the Court out from the middle of this dispute, and let the government and police do what they will with the tools at their disposal," endorsing criminal law remedies over the equitable remedy of a court injunction. However, Thompson's decision was stayed by BC Court of Appeal Justice Sunni Stromberg-Stein ten days later, and reversed by a three-judge division of the court in January 2022.[81] The aftershocks of the Fairy Creek protests (including prosecutions of approximately 400 blockaders and tentative steps toward protected area status) are discussed in the Afterword.

To date, proposals to reform the law regarding use of injunctions and contempt proceedings in environmental disputes have not been implemented. While some of the ecological issues that gave rise to the Clayoquot Sound and Fairy Creek protests were resolved, the procedural question of whether injunctions and contempt proceedings are appropriate responses to public protest over environmental issues has not been addressed. There has been no reform in the field of environmental policy equivalent to the *Labour Code* reforms of the 1970s (which substantially reduced courts' jurisdiction to grant injunctions during labour disputes) or the "Bubble Law" of the 1990s (which provided a permanent "legislative injunction" replacing interlocutory court orders against anti-abortion protesters). While controversial, both of these legislative interventions in response to protest appear to have effectively addressed crises of legal legitimacy that arose in response to injunctions and contempt proceedings against striking workers and anti-abortion picketers. In the face of ongoing legal controversy in relation to environmental policy and environmental protest, it appears certain that civil disobedience, judicial interventions, injunctions, arrests, contempt proceedings, and criminal convictions will endure into the future – as will questioning of law's legitimacy by environmentally conscious citizens who find themselves on the receiving end of law's coercive powers for asserting customary claims to natural resources in the face of competing private property claims.

Justice Mary Southin recognized this unresolved "broad political question" in the 2004 BC Court of Appeal decision in *Verchere v Greenpeace Canada:* "To what extent in a free and democratic society may those who perceive social evils for which they have not been able to obtain redress through the normal channels of the political system interfere with the economic lives of others without suffering legal consequences?" The case arose from an anti-logging protest on Roderick Island on the central coast in 1997, and a lawsuit brought by four loggers for the tort of interference with contractual relations, resulting in a damage award against Greenpeace and its lead organizers, including Tzeporah Berman. Writing for the majority of the appellate division, Southin upheld the award of damages but suggested that "sooner or later an answer must come for it is apparent that many citizens have concluded that, unless they adopt strident means, legislators will pay no mind to whatever the perceived ill may be. This appears to be a world in which only squeaky wheels get any grease."[82] Strident challenges to logging on the central coast evolved over time into more collaborative approaches, culminating in the Great Bear Rainforest Agreements of 2006.[83]

Conflict over natural resources, including forest resources, continues to extend into the legal arena. This reflects ongoing controversy over protection of biological diversity in areas that lack legislated protection: in 2003 and again in 2015, and 2025 tensions flared over stands of old-growth rainforest in Vancouver Island's Central Walbran Valley that were left unprotected when the Carmanah-Walbran Provincial Park was created in the 1990s and designated a "special management zone" in the Vancouver Island Land Use Plan (2000), while remaining subject to corporate control in TFL 46.[84] A grandmother named Betty Krawczyk (joined by other protesters) was at the centre of several years of litigation for her role in road blockades against logging in the Walbran and elsewhere – "attempting to get the law enforcement authorities to arrest them for a crime or crimes pursuant to the provisions of the Criminal Code of Canada," BC Supreme Court Justice Bruce Harvey found. "A public trial, perhaps a trial by judge and jury, would then serve as the platform to enable them to proclaim their grievances," which the judge found amounted to criminal contempt of court in convicting Krawczyk. He sentenced her to six months in jail for her repeated contempts.[85] Previously, Krawczyk had been convicted of criminal contempt at Clayoquot Sound, serving a sentence of forty-five days in jail, and was convicted again for two separate breaches in the Elaho Valley in 1999 and 2000, respectively (with the latter breach resulting in three weeks of pretrial custody followed by a six-week jail sentence). For the 1999 Elaho breach (which was tried at a later date, and involved Krawczyk's organization of a group of women to block Interfor's logging activities on three dates in September 1999, in contravention of an injunction), she was sentenced to one year in jail – the stiffest contempt penalty imposed in British Columbia since the jailing of Homer Stevens and Steve Stavenes during the Prince Rupert trawlers' strike of 1967. Krawczyk's appeal against the sentence was allowed by the BC Court of Appeal, which reduced the sentence to the four months in jail she had already served. Justice Ian Donald described this as being "at the top of the range for like cases and I think it is sufficient to meet the goals of a sentence for criminal contempt."[86]

However, Krawczyk continued to engage in direct action to protect the ecology of coastal British Columbia, resulting in further breaches of court orders. In May and June 2006, she was arrested three times and charged with criminal contempt for breaching an injunction enjoining interference with realignment of the Sea to Sky Highway over Eagleridge Bluffs in West Vancouver. BC Supreme Court Justice Brenda Brown sentenced her to ten months in jail for these breaches (which the Court of Appeal upheld).[87] In convicting Krawczyk of these contempts, Justice Brown stated:

> Everyone who breaches a court order faces contempt proceedings, environmental protestor or otherwise. As our courts have stated repeatedly, those who take issue with an order must take appropriate steps to challenge the order, whether by applying to set it aside, or by appeal. One cannot breach now, challenge later. To do so constitutes an impermissible collateral attack ...
>
> There are many in our society who believe passionately that the government response to various issues, be they healthcare, homelessness, or poverty, is wrong. If those with such passionate beliefs were to break court orders to enforce what they believed to be the correct response, our democratic society would fail.[88]

Justice Brown's comments in *R v Krawczyk* (2007), like the approach of Supreme Court and Court of Appeal judges in the trials and appeals of more than eight hundred Clayoquot blockaders, suggested that environmentalists' disregard for the courts' authority posed a fundamental threat to the rule of law, necessitating findings of criminal liability and jail sentences. While the environmentalists asserted ecological claims to Crown forest lands, challenging harvesting rights of companies that held licences to those lands, the injunctions, policing operations, and Crown contempt prosecutions shifted the issue from one of environmental policy to one of public order and the rule of law. Contested conceptions of property – in this case, contested claims to public forest lands asserted by environmentalists and logging companies – and contested conceptions of the appropriate use and organization of space were at the root of protests and legal struggles that erupted in Clayoquot Sound, in the Walbran, Slocan, and Elaho Valleys, and at Fairy Creek.[89]

As we saw in other case studies in this book, these clashes of property claims and resulting legal interventions provoked crises of legal legitimacy, turning otherwise law-abiding citizens into lawbreakers in apparent failures of public policy, while exposing close economic relationships among the provincial government, members of the legal community, and corporate interests. However, as the chapters that follow demonstrate (and as BC Supreme Court Justice Thompson's decision in *Teal Cedar Products Ltd v Rainforest Flying Squad* demonstrated), the willingness of BC judges to intervene forcefully and unilaterally on behalf of private property interests when challenged by social movements appears to be mellowing, with a growing legal recognition of human rights and customary and constitutional claims to property. This suggests a possible shift in the social relations of adjudication and the pattern of property, protest, and the law in British Columbia.

Chapter 5

STANDOFFS, ROADBLOCKS, AND BREAKTHROUGHS FOR INDIGENOUS PROPERTY CLAIMS

IN THE MID-1980S, protest blockades against corporate industrial logging on Crown land at two remote islands off the west coast of British Columbia revealed emerging phenomena in the country's geopolitical and legal landscape: the growing inclination of Indigenous peoples to engage in civil disobedience and embrace tactics of direct action to assert customary claims to property, and a corresponding weakening of the resolve of decision-makers within settler legal institutions to deploy coercive force in defence of colonial property relations. At Wah-nah-jus Hilth-hoo-is (Meares Island) in Clayoquot Sound off Vancouver Island in the autumn of 1984, and at Tllga Kun Gwaayaay (Lyell Island, sometimes also referred to as Athlii Gwaii)[1] in what was then called the Queen Charlotte Islands (now Haida Gwaii) in the autumn of 1985, the creative agency of the Nuu-chah-nulth and Haida peoples thwarted claims of private logging companies to timber resources in their territories.

Both protest movements initially drew a familiar response from members of the settler legal community. Lawyers representing private corporations (in this case, logging companies that held licences and permits to harvest timber on Crown land) applied to the BC Supreme Court for injunctions prohibiting interference with their operations, which were then granted by judges and enforced by RCMP officers, backed by the threat of criminal contempt of court charges and potential imprisonment. These legal actors borrowed and adapted the legal technology of coercion that had been effectively developed and wielded against groups such as trade unionists in earlier decades, demonstrating continuity with earlier social movement challenges to private property rights.

Despite the entrenchment of the *Royal Proclamation of 1763* in section 25 of the *Constitution Act, 1982,* which in conjunction with section 35 provided a foundation for recognition of Indigenous rights, organized Indigenous resistance to uphold these rights still tends to be met with repressive force. The particular circumstances of rights and details of conflict vary, and differences have emerged in the responses of corporations, governments, and the courts. In the cases examined here, which demonstrate shifting attitudes toward Indigenous property claims and an evolving legal response to direct challenges to the settler colonial order, the BC judiciary has displayed a growing unwillingness to unilaterally intervene on behalf of conventional private property interests and against Indigenous interests.

In the Meares Island case, *MacMillan Bloedel Ltd v Mullin,* BC Court of Appeal Justice Peter Seaton adopted a novel interpretation of the established legal test for whether to grant an injunction (which, at the time, was the 1944 BC case *Wheatley v Ellis and Hendrickson*), reversing a lower court decision in finding that the Nuu-chah-nulth claimants (who had countersued the logging company) would suffer irreparable harm if logging were allowed to proceed. Seaton granted an injunction to the Nuu-chah-nulth chiefs that restrained logging by MacMillan Bloedel.[2] The Haida blockade at Lyell Island and subsequent legal proceedings arising from the arrest of more than seventy Indigenous activists (and one Member of Parliament, New Democrat Svend Robinson) exhibited a distinct fact pattern: the Crown's determination to pursue criminal contempt of court charges against the Indigenous land defenders withered in the face of Haida and broader Indigenous and settler-ally opposition. The political crises triggered by the Meares and Lyell standoffs unleashed political pressures that ultimately transformed the approach to land tenure and land management in these territories, initiating a rebalancing of power relations over land and resources in favour of the Nuu-chah-nulth and the Haida.

To be sure, this shifting jurisprudence has been uneven in subsequent decades, as demonstrated by the tense standoff at Ts'Peten (Gustafsen Lake) in 1995 and ongoing reliance on injunctions and other colonial legal tools, for example, in response to the Wet'suwet'en challenge to the Coastal GasLink pipeline and Canada-wide solidarity protests in 2020.[3] However, the Nuu-chah-nulth and Haida cases from the 1980s signalled an important shift in the pattern of state responses to social movement protest in British Columbia generally and to Indigenous protest in particular: an apparent weakening of the resolve of actors within the settler legal order to act unilaterally to buttress private property claims.

This chapter examines Indigenous assertions of customary and constitutional rights through direct action, and corresponding responses by members of the legal community, with particular reference to the Nuu-chah-nulth blockade at Meares Island in 1984 and the Haida blockade at Lyell Island in 1985–86. Indigenous customary laws and practices clashed with property claims of private holders of licences, permits, and titles granted by the settler state, and these clashes were manifested on the land and in legal arenas, and also in cooperation with non-Indigenous social movement allies.[4] The creative assertion of Nuu-chah-nulth and Haida interests through direct action triggered important changes in how settler legal institutions approached Indigenous and colonial property claims, and led to growing unwillingness among members of the settler legal community to deploy coercive powers in response to direct challenges to their authority. This shifting jurisprudence signalled the tentative emergence of a more contingent legal space, one in which property claims were increasingly recognized as concurrent and shared rather than exclusive – thus challenging the prevailing conception of fee simple, *profit-à-prendre,* and other forms of title or interests in property by the settler society.

Conceptualizing Indigenous Challenges to Settler Property Rights

Indigenous and Aboriginal law is perhaps the most dynamic and rapidly evolving area of British Columbian and Canadian law today. In the courts and on the ground, Indigenous peoples and nations have asserted customary and constitutional claims to property, challenging title and licences granted by settler governments and legal institutions and creating a more contingent legal space. In landmark decisions in *Calder* (1973), *Guerin* (1984), *Sparrow* (1990), *Delgamuukw* (1997), *Tsilhqot'in* (2014), and *Cowichan* (2025), the courts have recognized a widening ambit for Indigenous rights, buttressed since the 1980s by interpretations of section 35 of the constitution.[5] On the ground, Indigenous peoples have physically asserted these rights, sometimes through direct action to obstruct corporations from exercising conflicting rights to land and resources. Around the time of the Meares and Lyell standoffs, the council of the Ulkatcho First Nation in the BC interior connected these struggles to the wider global pattern of decolonization: "Since the Second World War, the winds of change have blown through Asia and Africa; Now they are blowing through the Americas and Australia."[6]

To understand Indigenous legal orders and implications for property and other relations in present-day British Columbia and Canada, we can look to a number of recent works.[7] Jisgang Nika Collison, in a collaborative study with the Council of the Haida Nation on the 1985 standoff at Lyell Island, stated: "The boldness was not that of defiance, or blatantly breaking Canadian law. Rather the boldness was upholding Haida laws."[8] Elaborating on this evolving political and legal space, political scientist Warren Magnusson stated in a case study of Clayoquot Sound that "proper recognition of Indigenous peoples is probably impossible within the framework of the state system, as normally conceived ... On any of the familiar principles of property, British Columbia belongs rightfully to the descendants of its original inhabitants ... It sets conceptions of property, as well as sovereignty, in motion."[9] Earlier manifestations of colonial violence – including the phenomenon of "gunboat diplomacy" and remapping of Indigenous territory as colonial space by settler institutions – have cast a long shadow on relations between Indigenous peoples and institutions of the settler society, informing contemporary disputes.[10]

The Nuu-chah-nulth at Meares and the Haida at Lyell asserted that Indigenous laws remained operative, that they had not been superseded or rendered obsolete by the imposition of colonial patterns of land use and property and by the colonial legal system and its coercive apparatus. Over time, the courts have come closer to accepting this viewpoint, resulting in a greater reluctance to issue and enforce injunctions (nevertheless, the colonial law since *Delgamuukw* has recognized Indigenous laws and rights of self-governance [or "self-regulation"] only to the extent that they are consistent with the settler common law, constitution, and statutory law).[11]

There is a strong spatial aspect to Indigenous assertions of rights to land and resources and corresponding state responses. The "scattered geography of colonization" in British Columbia, as legal geographer Nicholas Blomley puts it, has imbued Indigenous peoples with strategic power: resource wealth and transportation corridors pass through Indigenous communities and territories, a relic of the historical disregard for Indigenous interests in the granting of resource licences and construction of infrastructure by colonial authorities. Scattered settler population centres are connected to one another, and to sources of resource wealth as well as external markets, by a relatively sparse transportation network traversing Indigenous territory. This colonial built form now provides a geographical basis for counter-hegemonic challenges to colonial systems of property and law.[12] While lands recognized as Indigenous by settler law represent a small fraction of lands within the traditional territories of these nations (the objection at the heart of many assertions of Indigenous rights), the existing geography of Indigenous-controlled lands and resources proximate to Indigenous communities provides impetus to the phenomenon of road blockades and other forms of direct action against Crown and private property rights.[13] Hamar Foster highlights the contested and grey legal status of highways running through Indigenous communities – and the resulting competing conceptions of the relationship between British Columbia's land tenure system and Indian reserve lands – as well as jurisdictional ambiguity between provincial, federal, and Indigenous powers arising from section 91(24) of the *Constitution Act, 1867*, section 35 of the *Constitution Act, 1982*, and emerging case law.[14]

Insights into the creative assertion of Indigenous interests at Meares and Lyell in the 1980s, and the corresponding corporate and state responses, can be found in case studies by Jisgang Nika Collison and the Council of the Haida Nation and others.[15] We can also look to the testimony of Indigenous elders, activists, and leaders, including Haida leader Guujaaw, who was interviewed for this chapter, and Unist'ot'en spokesperson Howilhkat Freda Huson, who remarked: "My dad used to tell me 'the strongest power you have is to occupy your land.'"[16]

Meares Island and the Assertion of Nuu-chah-nulth Customary Rights

Indigenous resurgence and clashes with colonial legal authority could be discerned at diverse sites in British Columbia in the 1980s, including at Clayoquot Sound on the west coast of Vancouver Island. In the landmark legal decision in the *Mullin* case (*MacMillan Bloedel v Mullin* [1985]), the BC Court of Appeal issued an interlocutory injunction restraining logging operations by licence holder MacMillan Bloedel on Crown land on Wah-nah-jus Hilth-hoo-is (Meares Island), in the territory of the Tla-o-qui-aht and Ahousaht Nuu-chah-nulth people in Clayoquot Sound, pending determination of Aboriginal title.[17] The five-member Court of Appeal panel divided three-to-two in granting Nuu-chah-nulth chiefs Moses Martin and Corbett George the injunction against the logging company. This represented a bold departure from previous legal decisions in which questions of Indigenous rights and title were often ignored or shunted aside as the judiciary sidestepped the unresolved land question and recognized private property rights conferred by the colonial legal system and institutions of the settler state. Writing for the majority, Justice Seaton recognized the symbolic importance of Meares Island as "the front line in the dispute over Indian title. It has also become central to the dispute between the logger and those who favour the preservation of wilderness areas. Meares Island is important to MacMillan Bloedel not because of its trees, but because it is where the line has been drawn. It has become a symbol."[18]

Seaton's willingness to chart a new path in the jurisprudence relating to Indigenous property claims, and to refuse to protect the private interests of the logging corporation, may have reflected his legal career prior to being called to the bench. Many members of the BC judiciary had represented forestry and mining companies while practising with major Vancouver law firms; by contrast, Seaton had been a small-town lawyer working in a general practice in the Okanagan city of Vernon. He was also the youngest person appointed to the BC Supreme Court in over a century, as well as the first graduate of the University of British Columbia law school appointed to a superior court.[19] Seaton can perhaps be viewed as the legal equivalent of an "everyman," detached from the social networks connecting the legal community and resource corporations, and therefore possibly more amenable to views that challenged the interests of corporations holding licences to natural resource wealth.[20]

In November 1984, the elected chief of the Tla-o-qui-aht Nation, Moses Martin, launched a blockade of logging operations on Meares Island, in concert with the environmental organization Friends of Clayoquot Sound. Historian Jonathan Clapperton describes this alliance as occurring within a "contact zone" of Indigenous and non-Indigenous interests.[21] The blockade followed the failure of a process known as the "Meares Island Planning Team," which consisted of two years of talks involving the Tla-o-qui-aht and Ahousaht Nations, the logging company, representatives of provincial departments responsible for forestry, fisheries, tourism, water protection, and archaeological conservation, representatives of the village of Tofino (which drew its drinking

FIGURE 18 Proclamation of the Wah-nah-jus Hilth-hoo-is (Meares Island) Tribal Park at C'isaqis (Heelboom Bay), April 21, 1984. | Friends of Clayoquot Sound

FIGURE 19 Nuu-chah-nulth people and allies rally at the BC legislature with the "Cedar Man," October 20, 1984, calling on the provincial government to respect the Wah-nah-jus Hilth-hoo-is (Meares Island) Tribal Park and revoke logging permits. | *Ha-Shilth-Sa Newspaper*

water from Meares Island), forestry workers in Industrial Woodworkers of America (IWA) Local I-85, and environmental organizations, including the Sierra Club of Western Canada.[22] MacMillan Bloedel walked away from the table after it became clear that the Tla-o-qui-aht and Ahousaht would not tolerate commercial logging on the island, which they claimed as their own in the absence of any treaties. In 1980, the Tla-o-qui-aht and Ahousaht – through the Nuu-chah-nulth Tribal Council – had formally claimed Meares Island and surrounding lands and waters through the federal Comprehensive Land Claims Policy, asserting that the Nuu-chah-nulth people were "the rightful, legal, and sovereign occupants and users"; the Government of Canada had accepted the claim for negotiation.[23] In the century and a half since the imposition of British sovereignty, less than 2 percent of Meares Island had been logged commercially.

In April 1984, the Tla-o-qui-aht had unilaterally proclaimed an *ahoulthlee* (Tribal Park) on Meares, following the earlier example of the Haida at Duu Guusd; Miles Richardson Jr., president of the Council of the Haida Nation, attended the ceremony.[24] The Tla-o-qui-aht Nation's lawyer, Jack Woodward, described the proclamation as a "peaceful, civilized way of observing this sovereignty," suggesting that the legal facts were simple since no treaty had been signed, and noting that land had to be acquired before it could be passed on to others – negating the claim of the Crown and logging company to Meares.[25] Following this assertion of sovereignty, the Tla-o-qui-aht initiated a march to the provincial legislature in October 1984 with a twenty-three-foot carved cedar tree, called "Cedar Man," to ramp up pressure for protection of the island.[26] The village of Tofino formally supported the Nuu-chah-nulth position.

In November 1984, when MacMillan Bloedel proceeded with plans to establish a docking area and log dump at a place called C'isaqis (Heelboom Bay) from which to launch logging operations, the logging company met with opposition. Nuu-chah-nulth and non-Indigenous allies led by Tla-o-qui-aht chief Martin constructed canoes on the foreshore in a visible demonstration of use of the land (which the appeal court would later dismiss as "a sham" designed

FIGURE 20 Bob Martin carves a canoe at C'isaqis (Heelboom Bay) on Meares Island, November 1984. BC Supreme Court Justice Reginald Gibbs granted an injunction to MacMillan Bloedel a week later, restraining the Nuu-chah-nulth and non-Indigenous activists from interfering with logging operations. The following spring, the BC Court of Appeal issued a landmark ruling granting an injunction to Nuu-chah-nulth leaders Moses Martin and Corbett George halting logging operations. | Leigh Hilbert

FIGURE 21 Gathering at C'isaqis (Heelboom Bay), c. November 1984. | Leigh Hilbert

to obstruct MacMillan Bloedel). The protest was hastily mounted on November 21, the day the BC Ministry of Forests approved a cutting permit for 53 percent of the 8,600-hectare island over a thirty-five-year period. In addition to building canoes, the Nuu-chah-nulth and their non-Indigenous allies deployed a flotilla of boats to greet the logging company vessels.[27] Michael Mullin, a Tofino resident and bookseller who had helped found the Friends of Clayoquot Sound in the 1970s (drawing on organizational expertise from civil rights and labour campaigns in Chicago a decade earlier), recalls the actions of Chief Martin during the initial confrontation with the logging company: "Moses stands, and he says, 'And you will respect the native persons in their habitations, their houses and their gardens. You are welcome to come ashore. But you will not do this in our garden. You will cut not trees here.'"[28]

In response to these activities, the logging company applied to the BC Supreme Court for an injunction barring interference with their operations. However, demonstrating the growing legal assertiveness of Indigenous peoples in the wake of constitutional recognition of Aboriginal rights in section 35 of the *Constitution Act, 1982*, Chief Martin and Corbett George, chief of the nearby Ahousaht Nation, applied for their own injunction to permanently restrain MacMillan Bloedel from logging or trespassing on Meares Island. They also

FIGURE 22 Carl Martin and Joe Martin at the cabin at C'isaqis (Heelboom Bay), c. November 1984. | Leigh Hilbert

sought three declarations from the court: (1) affirming Nuu-chah-nulth title to the island; (2) stating that no law of British Columbia had any force or effect in contravention of this title; and (3) stating that the BC government had no authority to issue licences or permits for the harvesting of resources in contravention of this title.[29] The Nuu-chah-nulth chiefs also sought an interlocutory injunction restraining the logging company from undertaking any activities on Meares Island pending consideration of the land claim.

BC Supreme Court Justice Reginald Gibbs considered the logging company's application for interlocutory relief and some procedural matters over two days of hearings in Vancouver in late November 1984. In a preliminary ruling given on December 3, Gibbs attempted to balance the competing assertions of rights – the company's proprietary claim to access and harvest timber from Meares in accordance with its licence from the province, and the Nuu-chah-nulth customary and constitutional claims to the island and its resources. He granted an interlocutory injunction to MacMillan Bloedel, restraining interference with its operations, but limited the company's activities to light survey work, with no construction of docks or roads and no land clearing until the Nuu-chah-nulth application had been heard.[30] This compromise revealed growing (if tentative) recognition of Indigenous customary rights by the judiciary. Two days earlier, the Supreme Court of Canada, in the *Guerin* case (relating to the improper transfer by federal Indian Agents of land belonging to the Musqueam Nation for an elite golf course near Vancouver), recognized Indigenous title as an underlying legal right that preceded the proclamation of British sovereignty, imposing on the Crown a fiduciary duty toward Indigenous peoples where the disposition of land was concerned.[31]

Consideration of the Nuu-chah-nulth application was postponed until the end of January 1985, after the BC government (which had been granted intervenor status) requested time to study another recent court decision from Ontario (the Bear Island case, which found that Crown title to natural resources trumped Indigenous title).[32] In the interim, Justice Gibbs denied an application from MacMillan Bloedel seeking to keep the environmental protesters off Meares Island, amid allegations of "tree spiking" (a form of sabotage that involved driving metal spikes into trees, which could be deadly to fallers and millworkers if their saws hit the spikes). Gibbs said he was "extremely reluctant" to prevent the fifty to sixty people at the Meares Island protest camp from exercising their normal rights to be on Crown land, but he was prepared to do so if necessary to protect the property and rights of others.[33] When the Nuu-chah-nulth application returned to his courtroom, the judge decided in favour of the logging company. In a written decision issued on January 25, he stated that the Indigenous claim had "no prospect of success at trial," that neither party faced irreparable harm to their rights if the injunctions were not granted (both could be compensated with money), and that the Indigenous claimants had "slept on [their] rights."[34]

A spokesperson for the Nuu-chah-nulth, George Watts, responded defiantly to the court's refusal to issue an injunction restraining logging on Meares Island: "We are not going to let MacMillan Bloedel log Meares Island. It is stolen land." Watts described Meares as "the final fight" for Aboriginal title, a fight that would include a legal appeal against Gibbs's ruling as well as direct action: "We are going to go to Meares Island and take it back."[35] Demonstrating disregard for the settler legal order, and a recurring crisis of law's legitimacy when judicial decisions appeared to favour private claims to property over customary claims, Watts declared: "We are going to treat the Canadian justice system with the same respect the Canadian justice system has treated the Canadian Indians."[36] The significance of the issues bound up in the Meares Island case was apparent when several BC Indigenous groups, including the Carrier Sekani Tribal Council, the Gitksan Wet'suwet'en Tribal Council, the Taku River Tlingit First Nation, the Shuswap Tribal Council, and the Union of BC Indian Chiefs, obtained intervenor status in the appeal. Following meetings of the BC section of the Assembly of First Nations, which endorsed the Nuu-chah-nulth position, James Gosnell, president of the Nisga'a Tribal Council, told a news conference: "I don't know what will happen. There could be a bloodbath. But we won't be responsible for it. We will hold the white man responsible."[37]

The Tla-o-qui-aht and Ahousaht chiefs' appeal against Gibbs's decision was based on the unresolved title question, suggesting that the harvesting of trees on Meares Island would result in the irrevocable loss of evidence of long-standing Indigenous occupation and use of the land, evidence that was integral to establishing Nuu-chah-nulth title to the land. As the appeal court would later state, trees on Meares Island held evidence of human use going back to at least 1642, over a century before the first settler set foot on Vancouver Island.

Persuaded by the Nuu-chah-nulth argument, the majority of the BC Court of Appeal division (in a narrow three-to-two decision) reversed Gibbs's ruling denying the Indigenous chiefs' injunction application. The appeal was heard before a division of five judges rather than usual three, reflecting the weight of legal issues at the heart of the case.[38] Writing for the majority, Justice Seaton found that the Tla-o-qui-aht and Ahousaht would be "deprived of valuable ecological rights" if logging were allowed to proceed before the title question had been considered. Seaton rejected the claims of counsel for the logging company and the province that an injunction restraining logging on Meares Island would deal a fatal blow to the forest sector in coastal British Columbia:

> It was strongly pressed on us that an order suspending logging on Meares Island would threaten the whole of the coast, indeed the whole of the Province; that if we made an order here, similar applications would be made for other areas and eventually the forest industry and other industries would be shut down.
>
> I do not believe that to be so. Meares Island has attained a unique importance. I have already said that it has become a symbol for each side in the contest between the forest industry and the Indians. I have also said that to prevent or postpone logging on Meares Island will not have a significant economic impact. When other areas are considered, they will be considered in the light of this decision. They will be seen as an addition to the Meares Island restriction and in consequence, the balance of convenience may be seen to have shifted to favour the industry.
>
> It has also been suggested that a decision favourable to the Indians will cast doubt on the tenure that is the basis for the huge investment that has been and is being made. I am not influenced by the argument. Logging will continue on this coast even if some parts are found to be subject to certain Indian rights. It

> may be that in some areas the Indians will be entitled to share in one way or another, and it may be that in other areas there will be restrictions on the type of logging. There is a problem about tenure that has not been attended to in the past. We are being asked to ignore the problem as others have ignored it. I am not willing to do that.[39]

Justice Alan Macfarlane concurred with Seaton, stating that Indigenous title had been recognized by the courts in the Supreme Court of Canada's *Calder* decision and then in the constitution, that the public anticipated a resolution through negotiation, and that the judicial proceeding was part of a larger process that would "ultimately find its solutions in a reasonable exchange between governments and the Indian nations."[40]

The BC Court of Appeal's March 1985 decision armed the Nuu-chah-nulth people with an injunction restraining logging by MacMillan Bloedel (to protect cultural and ecological rights), while confirming the logging company's injunction against non-Indigenous protesters (to protect "the rights of MacMillan Bloedel to that timber" pending determination of the title question). In deciding in favour of the Tla-o-qui-aht and Ahousaht, Justice Seaton found that the balance of convenience favoured leaving the trees standing rather than permitting the logging company to exercise its harvesting rights. The court's assessment of irreparable harm also favoured the Nuu-chah-nulth position rather than the interests of a corporate entity that sought to generate profit from the forest resources of Meares Island. According to Seaton:

> The proposal is to clear-cut the area. Almost nothing will be left. I cannot think of any native right that could be exercised on lands that have recently been logged. It follows that rights far short of outright ownership might well warrant retaining the area until after a trial.[41]

Justice Macfarlane concurred, noting that "the balance of convenience in this case is not in favour of immediate logging. Justice and convenience are the twin standards to be applied in deciding if an injunction is to be granted ... Justice to the Indian bands in these unusual circumstances means giving a decision on the merits of their claim before destroying the forest involved in that claim." In making this determination, the Court of Appeal recognized the contingency of private property rights conferred by institutions of the settler state in the face of competing assertions of customary and constitutional Indigenous rights – the court's broad discretion to grant or deny the equitable remedy of an injunction based on the specific circumstances in a case – a line of jurisprudence that would expand and evolve in the decades following the Meares Island case.[42]

The Tla-o-qui-aht and Ahousaht victory in the Meares Island case, like the Haida victory in the Lyell Island case, demonstrated that a powerful coalition of forces – a cross-sectional social movement – could be assembled when Indigenous assertions to land and resources were aligned with claims to resources advanced by the settler-based environmental movement. While the Court of Appeal was quick to dismiss the non-Indigenous protesters' appeal against the injunction granted to MacMillan Bloedel, contrasting the company's "restrained and responsible" conduct with "vandalism, threats and physical obstruction" by the environmentalists, the environmental movement was an integral component of the coalition to protect Meares Island, providing material support to the Nuu-chah-nulth chiefs and land defenders during the blockade and legal challenge. William Carroll notes the trend toward "increased collective capacity of Indigenous communities and allies, as they confront various configurations of state and capitalist class power, to resist colonization as an ongoing process while enacting resurgence as a practical form of dis-alienation."[43]

The rebalancing of rights by the BC Court of Appeal in the Meares Island case represented a historic refusal by the courts to enforce Crown licences issued by the settler state, spurring political change.[44] In 1988, the province of British Columbia, which was governed at the time by the conservative Social Credit Party, created a Ministry of Native Affairs as a tentative first step toward engagement with Indigenous title claims. MacMillan Bloedel never resumed logging operations on Meares Island; technically, both injunctions arising from the decision in *MacMillan Bloedel Ltd v Mullin* remain in place. The trial on the Tla-o-qui-aht and Ahousaht land claims extended over 152 days of hearings from the mid-1980s until 1991, when the Crown requested an adjournment to enter into negotiations with the Nuu-chah-nulth.[45] The Tla-o-qui-aht and Ahousaht ultimately acquired a private property interest in the Crown forest lands of Meares Island and Clayoquot Sound, with the transfer of licences to Nuu-chah-nulth–owned Iisaak Forest Resources (now MaMook Natural Resources Ltd.), an interim measure in the wider treaty process.[46]

Drawing the Line at Lyell Island

Members of the Haida Nation at Tllga Kun Gwaayaay (Athlii Gwaii/Lyell Island) in Haida Gwaii also asserted Indigenous property rights and resisted colonial property relations in the mid-1980s. The resulting controversy attracted national and international media attention, and served as a catalyst in transforming the political trajectory of the Haida people, their relations with settler governments, and the management of natural resources in the archipelago of Haida Gwaii. To logging corporations and the BC government, the area was known as the South Moresby Supply Block. To the Haida, the land was a traditional ancestral home, Gwaii Haanas, that bound together cultural practices, spirituality, ecology, and timber and nontimber economic resources. To environmentalists in British Columbia and beyond, it was the "Galapagos of the North," a rare and threatened ecological jewel that sustained some of the greatest biological diversity of flora and fauna on the planet. The legal battle lines for Lyell Island and the broader South Moresby wilderness reflected these competing perspectives.[47]

In the 1970s, members of the Haida Nation began ramping up their claims to Haida Gwaii, which had never been surrendered in treaty. These claims gathered strength in the context of the Supreme Court of Canada's judgment in *Calder* (1973), the growing movement for "red power" and Indigenous rights, and environmental advocacy campaigns by conservation organizations such as Greenpeace, the Sierra Club of Western Canada, and the Western Canada Wilderness Committee.[48] In 1974 a group of Haida established the Council of the Haida Nation, with the intention of organizing Haida citizens into a unified political entity and pursuing "formalization and retention of aboriginal title rather than the surrender of their aboriginal rights forever."[49] That same year, Haida activists and non-Indigenous allies founded the Islands Protection Committee (later incorporated as the Islands Protection Society [IPS]), a forum for "Haida and newcomers [to] join together to seek protection of wilderness areas on Moresby Island."[50] The immediate catalyst for these organizing efforts was the provincial government's decision to issue a permit for logging on pristine Burnaby Island to Rayonier (Canada) Ltd. The Skidegate Band Council and Chief Councillor Kalga Percy Williams opposed that permit, hosting Premier Dave Barrett for a feast at Skidegate and securing a five-year deferral (which shifted Rayonier's focus to Lyell Island).[51] By the mid-1970s, discussions were underway among the Haida, the provincial and federal governments, and conservation organizations to establish a national park reserve to protect the sensitive ecological area in the southern portion of the archipelago that was then known as the "Queen Charlotte Islands." This included the southern portion of vast Moresby Island, as well as Lyell Island, Burnaby Island, and more than one hundred surrounding islands, where scientists had identified thirty-nine endemic plant and animal species existing nowhere else on earth.[52]

In 1978, the Haida challenged the BC minister of forests' pending renewal of Tree Farm Licence 24 in South Moresby to Rayonier (Canada) Ltd., a subsidiary of a US-based corporate conglomerate, on grounds that it infringed on Haida rights and title. The Haida through the IPS demanded public hearings under the *Forest Act*, seeking to highlight the significance of the South Moresby wilderness for Haida cultural survival. In February 1979, Guujaaw (Gary Edenshaw), a Haida carver who had apprenticed with the famous artist Bill Reid and whose family held trapping rights in the area, went to court with Hereditary Chief Gid Kun Nathan Young, trapper Glenn Naylor, and the IPS, seeking an injunction barring Forests Minister Tom Waterland from renewing the licence until public hearings had been held.[53] However, BC Supreme Court Justice George Murray refused to grant the injunction, finding that public hearings were not necessary (since the province was considering renewing an existing licence rather than issuing a new one). Murray also stated that the decision on whether to renew the licence was properly one for the minister, rather than the courts, to decide, and that he was not persuaded to intervene in the interim by granting an injunction.[54] Guujaaw, Young, and the IPS were undeterred. They returned to court in 1981, challenging the minister's renewal of the TFL under the *Judicial Review Procedures Act*, but the BC Supreme Court again refused to intervene. Chief Justice Allan McEachern found that the minister had consulted adequately with the Haida, and he expressed concern that quashing the renewal would set a dangerous precedent.[55] Appeals of these decisions were unsuccessful.[56]

The Haida were unwilling to wait indefinitely for action by the colonial governments, and in 1981 unilaterally proclaimed a Tribal Park at Duu Guusd in the northern portion of the archipelago of Haida Gwaii – the first enactment under a modern, written Haida constitution adopted under the aegis of the Council of the Haida Nation.[57] That year, the Skidegate Band Council sponsored the formation of the Haida Gwaii Watchmen Program, re-establishing a Haida presence at old village sites to manage tourism and protect cultural assets (an alternative structure to the "park wardens" of the settler society).[58] A year earlier, the Haida had filed a comprehensive land claim with the Government of Canada, asserting title to the islands and surrounding waters and demanding that South Moresby and Lyell be preserved as wilderness to protect ecological and cultural values.[59] In 1985, the Haida declared Gwaii Haanas to be a Haida Heritage Site.[60] "We drew a line up north of Lyell," recalled Guujaaw. "It's easy to draw a line. It's harder to hold the line."[61]

According to the Canadian Constitution, the BC government controlled natural resources on Crown lands. The Social Credit government led by

Premier Bill Bennett refused to recognize the Haida declaration of the heritage site and land claim. Instead, it rigorously upheld the Tree Farm Licence issued to Rayonier (and, after 1981, the new Vancouver-based logging corporation Western Forest Products Ltd.) and its contractor, Frank Beban Logging Ltd., under the provisions of the provincial *Forest Act*. Logging had been underway continuously on Lyell Island since 1975, and a portion had been logged earlier in the 1930s and 1940s. Frank Beban Logging maintained a camp at Powrivco Bay valued at $1.5 million, with amenities including a recreation centre and satellite television.[62] The BC government's position, restated many times during the conflict, was that the *British North America Act* did not provide for Indigenous title to land. In its view, the Queen Charlotte Islands properly belonged to the BC Crown, with the government free to license access to resources as it saw fit. The government refused to negotiate with the Haida unless they withdrew their land claim, but, in a concession to the Indigenous and ecological claims to the forest resources, it imposed a moratorium on new logging permits pending a decision by the cabinet on future use of the area.[63] There were also emerging proposals for oil and gas development off the archipelago that raised questions about Indigenous and Crown rights and title.[64]

In the summer of 1985, in the wake of the landmark Meares Island decision, the Haida issued an ultimatum to the BC government: resolve the dispute over Lyell Island or they would intervene directly to stop the logging. "The basic issue is lands and resources and they are Haida lands and resources," said Miles Richardson Jr., president of the Council of the Haida Nation, after meeting with BC's environment minister at Skidegate.[65] In October, with the study on the proposed South Moresby national park reserve still underway, the BC government lifted the moratorium on new logging permits for Lyell Island. It also announced the formation of a wilderness advisory committee to make recommendations on future uses. Approval of three new cutblocks covering eighty-seven hectares of Lyell Island demonstrated the political influence of Western Forest Products and its contractor, Frank Beban Logging, which had recently exhausted its approved harvesting sites on Lyell Island and faced the prospect of laying off eighty workers unless it was granted access to new "fibre." At the time, the unemployment rate in British Columbia stood at 13 percent, the second highest in Canada, a factor behind the government's decisions.[66] The government's approach was a perfect example of the phenomenon that political scientist Jeremy Wilson has described as "talk and log." It also prompted the Haida blockade.[67]

Faced with further despoliation of lands within their heritage site and subject to their land claim, the Haida chose to defy the settler law and take direct action.

They blockaded a road on Lyell Island to stop the harvesting plans of Western Forest Products and Beban Logging. This action represented an assertion of Haida law and a rejection of the settler law, which seemed to the Haida to favour the two companies' commercial interests to the detriment of Haida interests. "We made a decision that the land was going to be protected," Guujaaw recalls.[68]

The Haida launched the road blockade on October 30, 1985. The seine boats *Haida Raider*, *Haida Warrior*, and *Haida Spirit* had sailed from Skidegate loaded with crew and provisions, to a vigorous send-off from the local community, bound for Lyell Island approximately one hundred kilometres south. A landing party disembarked before dawn at Sedgewick Bay, on the southern shore of Lyell, and established a camp. The Haida then moved up to a nearby logging road, refusing to allow workers from the Beban camp, located about ten kilometres away, access to the new cutblocks (which the workers had begun harvesting the previous day). Led by Clarence "Dempsey" Collinson, hereditary chief of the Skidegate clan, the Haida blocked the convoy of loggers when they rounded a curve in the road. "This is Haida land. It has always been our land," Collinson announced. On behalf of the Council of the Haida Nation, Richardson said: "We cannot sit around and wait for all this legal stuff to work itself out. We are staying here."[69] The participation of Collinson and Richardson demonstrated political support for the grassroots action. As company lawyers began compiling evidence and materials for an injunction application, Frank Beban initially struck a conciliatory tone, remaining with his workers at the Powrivco Bay camp: "I don't want to have a confrontation. They are my friends. We're not going to cause violence. We won't log as long as they're stopping us."[70] Two days into the blockade, however, Western Forest Products and Frank Beban Logging filed applications for injunctions, which BC Supreme Court Justice Harry McKay granted a week later.[71]

The injunctions barred the Haida from obstructing the logging road or logging operations on Lyell. During the injunction application hearing in Vancouver, Haida language holder GwaaGanad Diane Brown told the judge, "I don't want my children to inherit stumps," suggesting that unrestrained exploitation of the land threatened the cultural survival of the Haida as a people. Justice McKay expressed sympathy for the Haida position even as he adopted a paternalistic tone: "Mrs. Brown, in my view, the Haida will always be a strong, proud people as long as they keep producing Haida like you." In his reasons for judgment, however, McKay said he had no choice under the law but to grant the injunctions. At the outset of the hearing, he had denied an application from Richardson for a three-month adjournment to allow the Haida to retain and properly instruct legal counsel. "This is a political issue," Richardson told the judge. "It has no place in your courtroom."[72] During the three-day hearing, Richardson represented the Haida defendants, who chose to testify orally rather than give written affidavit evidence. Nineteen Haida addressed the judge, including Hereditary Chief Gid Kun Nathan Young, who testified in Haida aided by a translator, and Kalga Percy Williams, former chief councillor of the Skidegate Band Council, who recounted harvesting food on his family's trapline on Athlii Gwaii every year since his childhood.[73]

Initially, the Haida symbolically complied with the injunctions by allowing two trucks containing Beban and nine of his employees to pass, after a process server read the text of the court orders aloud to Richardson in front of television and police cameras. The process server also attempted to distribute paper copies of the injunctions to the Haida on the road, but most refused to take them. When Beban and his employees attempted to return to the worksite later that day, they were blocked by four elders sitting on the road adjacent to a makeshift

FIGURE 23 RCMP officers read the injunction order to Haida elders Kamee Ethel Jones, Jaadsangkinghliiyas Ada Yovanovich, Gaahlaay Watson Pryce, and Giteewans Adolphus Marks, other Haida citizens, and MP Svend Robinson, Tllga Kun Gwaayaay (Lyell Island), November 16, 1985. | Ann Yow-Dyson

FIGURE 24 Guujaaw drums at the Tllga Kun Gwaayaay (Lyell Island) stand, joined by Hereditary Chief Sgiidagids Clarence "Dempsey" Collinson and other Haida citizens, November 1985. | Mark van Manen, published with permission of *Vancouver Sun*

lean-to in the pouring rain, with several dozen Haida supporters lining the road.[74] The NDP Member of Parliament for Burnaby, activist lawyer Svend Robinson, who served as the party's justice critic, was among those on the Lyell blockade supporting the Haida position.[75] Beban hardened his stance, stating: "I have no respect for any lawbreakers no matter who they are and that's what they are now, is common lawbreakers."[76]

Defiance of the authority of the BC government and colonial courts propelled the Haida dispute into the national and international spotlight. Western Forest Products returned to court, seeking an enforcement order authorizing police to act on Justice McKay's orders, but BC Supreme Court Chief Justice Allan McEachern, who heard the application, told company lawyers that no further order was needed: "Court orders must be obeyed."[77] To this end, twenty-six RCMP officers and several police vehicles were deployed to the remote island to augment the small local force. Demonstrating parallels with state responses to working-class protest earlier in twentieth-century British Columbia, the state deployed coercive force in response to the Haida challenge to state-sanctioned economic interests.[78] At the time, Haida Gwaii had a population of five thousand people, two thousand of whom were Haida. The RCMP detachment was based at Queen Charlotte City (now Daajing Giids), one hundred kilometres to the north of Lyell Island. Two special Haida officers were also deployed to the Lyell Island protest camp.[79]

In total, sixty-five Haida and six other Indigenous and non-Indigenous allies were arrested in the second half of November 1985 for asserting the Haida's customary claim to property in defiance of the court orders. The RCMP superintendent for the area told reporters he had been given a "free hand" by the provincial attorney general to act as he saw fit.[80] On November 16, the police began enforcing Justice McKay's orders. Eighty-year-old Haida elder Gaahlaay Watson Pryce was arrested when he refused to move off the road. Two other Haida elders were arrested that day, sixty-seven-year-old Jaadsangkinghliiyas Ada Yovanovich and sixty-five-year-old Kamee Ethel Jones, who had said earlier, "If they haul us off to jail we'll all go."[81] The elders were treated "gently," according to media reports, and were flown by helicopter to Sandspit, where they were fingerprinted, charged with mischief, and released after promising not to interfere with the logging.[82] Many of those arrested in the days that followed had their faces painted in a traditional Haida style with charcoal and oil, including ten young Haida arrested on November 18 and described as "political prisoners" by a spokesperson from the Haida camp.[83] Svend Robinson, who had returned to Ottawa, declared in Parliament that the arrests contravened the Canadian Constitution, which recognized Aboriginal rights: "If anyone is breaking the law, it's the BC government."[84] The leader of the opposition in the House of Commons, Liberal John Turner (who had visited South Moresby while on vacation the previous summer) alleged that the Haida lands were being "despoiled" and called on Conservative Prime Minister Brian Mulroney to act to protect the "priceless natural treasure."[85]

Seeking to curb the growing civil disobedience movement on Lyell, the logging companies and the BC attorney general applied to the BC Supreme Court in late November 1985 for a declaration converting the charges against seventeen Haida and Robinson from mischief to criminal contempt of court.[86] The case was heard on November 29 before Chief Justice McEachern, at the courthouse in the northern coastal city of Prince Rupert, across Hecate Strait from Lyell and Haida Gwaii. During the hearing, McEachern refused to grant the Anglican Church of Canada intervenor status, stating that "this is no place for the church," and refused to allow the Anglican bishop of northern British Columbia to testify as an expert witness in support of the Haida's spiritual connection to the land. The judge sought to confine the proceedings to the narrow issue of whether the accused had defied the court order and interfered with the logging companies' lawful rights to access the timber.[87]

In his closing remarks on behalf of the Haida, Miles Richardson Jr. said that his people knew in their hearts that Lyell belonged to them, despite the BC government's refusal for a hundred years to acknowledge or negotiate their land claims, and that they were obliged for religious reasons to block the logging and protect the land that sustained their livelihood and culture. Highlighting the clash of legal norms at the root of the blockade and legal proceedings, one of the defendants, Diane Brown, a mother of two, explained her reasons for blocking the road on November 20: "I did it to protect the home of my ancestors. I did it because I felt it was right." McEachern found eleven of the accused guilty of criminal contempt of court but acquitted seven others, stating that he was not convinced beyond a reasonable doubt that they knew they were defying a court order.[88]

This clash of legal authorities was apparent a week later when McEachern and the convicted Haida converged on the Vancouver Courthouse for their sentencing hearing. The judge asked the Haida whether they would promise not to return to Lyell Island for six months. One man, Willard Wilson, the Skidegate band manager (who had been asked by Richardson to continue overseeing administration of the Haida's stand at Lyell Island), agreed to abide by this condition, while insisting "we're not doing anything wrong," and was released without sentence. The nine other Haida refused the judge's request for promises to stay away from the island. "While I respect your courts and your laws, something within me is way more powerful," said Diane Brown. "The need in my soul to protect my land happens to be stronger than your laws." Brown and the others told the judge that they were prepared to do jail time out of allegiance to their customary laws, which obliged them to protect their land and culture. McEachern sentenced the nine Haida to five months in jail but, in a surprise move, suspended their sentences, allowing them to avoid incarceration.[89] "He backed down," Guujaaw suggested in an interview decades later.[90] According to Richardson, McEachern backed down after Richardson asked, in his summation prior to sentencing: "Please explain, before you send my people to jail, how you and British Columbia, through the due process of the law you're upholding, acquired our Title." McEachern left the courtroom and returned about ten minutes later, declaring that he was suspending the sentences and that no one was going to jail.[91] This sentencing decision probably also reflected a practical consideration, which a *Globe and Mail* reporter had articulated prior to the hearing: "There is little doubt the 10 who have been convicted of criminal contempt of court will be considered martyrs in the native community if they go to prison."[92] McEachern also convicted Svend Robinson of criminal contempt and fined him $750.[93]

Guujaaw was among those convicted and sentenced for contempt by Justice McEachern. He reflected on the court proceedings:

> At the time, our people had very little influence over anything. That's what it took to shake it up and change things. It was our fight ... We didn't use lawyers. We represented ourselves. We certainly weren't trying to beat it on technicalities or deny that we did it. We went into court to explain why we felt we had to do it.[94]

Guujaaw described Justice McKay, who had issued the original injunction, as "a pretty decent man," whereas McEachern was "the old tyrant."[95] This was consistent with the attitude of many working-class activists in British Columbia, who had also experienced McEachern's pointed judgments (including the notorious 1983 injunction against court workers that the chief justice pursued all the way to the Supreme Court of Canada).[96]

In the wake of the contempt proceedings, which had been initiated by the logging companies through the civil process, the outstanding criminal charges against the Haida arrested at Lyell Island were quietly disposed of. Mischief charges against sixty-one people were abandoned by Crown prosecutors on the eve of a Provincial Court hearing at Queen Charlotte City in late January 1986. Charges against the eleven remaining accused, including the three elders originally charged with mischief, were converted to criminal contempt of court, but these charges were also dropped after the accused elected to have a trial by judge and jury, and a judge declared at a preliminary hearing in May that he felt there was "little to be gained" by proceeding with the charges.[97]

The Haida struggle on Lyell Island was described in media reports at the time as "an environmental cause celebre that has attracted international attention."[98] This ramped up pressure on the governments of British Columbia and Canada to help broker a solution. International support for the Haida grew on networks established through the Islands Protection Society and South Moresby campaign, networks that extended to globally renowned French explorer and conservationist Jacques Cousteau; several MPs; an array of environmental organizations; the Anglican Church of Canada (which donated $7,000 toward legal and logistical expenses); and American folk singer Pete Seeger and Canadian singer-songwriter Bruce Cockburn, who played benefit concerts to aid the Haida cause.[99] George Erasmus, chief of the Assembly of First Nations, declared that a national alliance of Indigenous and non-Indigenous people was prepared to stand with the Haida. Edwin Newman, a Heiltsuk hereditary chief and president of the Native Brotherhood of British Columbia, described the ruling Social Credit Party as "the enemy of the Indian people" and vowed to "fight every development issue that happens on this coast ... It will never go away until the land claims issue is resolved one way or another."[100] In November 1985, in the midst of the Lyell blockade and wave of arrests, about one hundred people rallied at the provincial legislature in Victoria in solidarity with the Haida land defenders.[101] The following year, a group of Haida and their supporters travelled across Canada in a train they dubbed the "South Moresby Caravan," with elders Ada Yovanovich, Ethel Jones, and Watson Pryce joining for a portion of the journey.[102]

These expressions of support helped focus public attention on the Haida struggle, the unresolved Indigenous land question in British Columbia, and management of natural resources, intensifying political pressure on the provincial and federal governments to act. The BC government faced particular embarrassment when it came to light that members of the cabinet held shares in Western Forest Products and its subsidiaries. One of them, Forests Minister Tom Waterland, was forced to resign from cabinet after ten years in that position.[103] In contrast to the Social Credit government's strident refusal to recognize or negotiate Aboriginal rights, the opposition NDP said it was open to negotiating land claims, a policy the federal government had maintained since it received the Haida claim in 1983.[104] Economic pressure also influenced the BC government's position, as a coalition of Indigenous groups threatened to boycott the Expo 86 world's fair scheduled for Vancouver the following summer, and the influential Business Council of British Columbia said that its members were "tired of always being the bad guys."[105]

Under pressure from an array of social sectors, the BC government reluctantly entered into negotiations with Canada and the Council of the Haida Nation over the future of Lyell Island and the South Moresby wilderness. This decision followed private discussions between Prime Minister Brian Mulroney and Premier Bill Bennett at a first ministers' conference in Halifax. According to one member of Bennett's cabinet, who spoke with this author on condition of anonymity, Bennett called for a cabinet vote on whether or not to negotiate with the Haida. When two-thirds of his ministers voted against, the premier declared emphatically, "The ayes have it," and proceeded to initiate negotiations.[106] RCMP superintendent Bob Currie, responsible for the policing operation at Lyell, said he welcomed government intervention and negotiations "as a way out of the situation we find ourselves in."[107] Attorney General Brian Smith and Haida leader Miles Richardson Jr. met in mid-December 1985, joined by federal Indian Affairs Minister David Crombie, resulting in what the media described as a "temporary truce" (facilitated by a Christmas hiatus in logging operations on Lyell).[108] Early in 1986, the provincial government agreed in principle to the creation of a new national park reserve, while maintaining the hard stance that logging continue on Lyell for at least a decade and that the provincial share of compensation to logging companies for lost harvesting rights be minimal.

During the South Moresby negotiations, the logging operations that had provoked the blockade and arrests were allowed to run their course, reflecting the legal primacy of private property rights over Indigenous rights for the time being. Frank Beban's logging crews returned to Lyell Island in January 1986 after a five-week Christmas break. They were briefly prevented from accessing the cutblocks by five Haida, but the Haida cleared the road at the request of police. The dispute seems to have cooled, perhaps reflecting progress at the negotiating table, perhaps as a result of exhaustion. Beban returned to a more conciliatory tone: "I'm still trying to run this thing as if things are normal. The public have become aware of their [the Haida's] complaint that their land claim has not been addressed. I don't know how much further they have to go to bring it to the government's attention."[109]

In February, as logging in previously approved cutblocks neared completion, the BC government announced that it would not issue new permits until the wilderness advisory committee submitted its recommendations. In July, after the committee recommended that logging continue, the Ministry of Forests approved a fresh permit for a 160-hectare cutblock. This prompted Richardson and eight other Haida to write to the prime minister renouncing their Canadian citizenship.[110] By this time, however, the tide was turning against the industry. As his company faced charges under the federal *Fisheries Act* for "the harmful destruction and alteration" of spawning beds in salmon-bearing Landrick Creek on Lyell Island, Beban reduced the size of his workforce from eighty to fewer than a dozen employees.[111] Though he had earlier claimed that a halt to logging would have devastating consequences for his workers, he now admitted that three-quarters of the displaced loggers had found other work.[112] The Ministry of Forests stopped issuing new permits in the spring of 1987, and in June the last logs from Lyell were loaded into a boom for transport to mills down the coast.[113]

In July 1987, twenty months after the Haida initiated the Lyell blockade, the federal and provincial governments signed a memorandum of understanding that imposed a permanent moratorium on further logging. They also agreed to develop a management plan in concert with the Haida leadership and conservation organizations. The agreement, which was signed at a high-profile ceremony by Prime Minister Brian Mulroney and Premier Bill Vander Zalm, applied not only to Lyell Island but also to the entire southern portion of the archipelago, encompassing 1,470 square kilometres of land and 138 islands. These would be protected as part of the newly created Gwaii Haanas National Park Reserve (originally named the South Moresby Park Reserve).[114] The signing ceremony in Victoria coincided with the homecoming of Bill Reid's canoe *Loo Taas* to Skidegate following a twenty-one-day voyage from Vancouver – after the Haida paddlers had warned they would land at Lyell if the settler governments refused to act.[115]

Miles Richardson Jr. and Guujaaw insisted that the Gwaii Haanas Haida Heritage Site is not a "park," and that the 1987 agreement merely recognized protection that the Haida had introduced several years earlier: "We told them that we did not want a park. We had legislated Gwaii Haanas in 1985 and simply wanted Canada to recognize this and stay out of our way."[116] Frank Beban, who had obtained the injunction against the Haida and whose assets included the $1.5 million camp at Powrivco Bay, claimed that the BC government had "got bulldozed by Eastern political interests."[117] Industry representatives claimed that the creation of the park reserve, which accounted for 70 percent of the land in Western Forest Products' Tree Farm Licence, would result in the permanent loss of nine hundred direct and indirect jobs.[118] Within weeks of the announcement, while supervising the removal of his company's logging equipment from the Lyell Island camp, Beban suffered a fatal heart attack and died at age forty-seven. "He was a man protecting his investment," Haida spokesperson Ernie Collison told a reporter. "We are a people protecting our heritage." He added that Beban was an "honourable man" who "didn't come out making racist comments." Beban's business partner said that uncertainty over the company's operations had taken a toll on the logger.[119] Reflecting the international dimension of the dispute, Beban's death was reported in the pages of the *New York Times*.[120]

Aftershocks: From Ts'Peten to Grace Islet to Unist'ot'en Camp

Other assertions of Indigenous rights to land and resources emerged around this time, with control over timber and petroleum resources often being at the centre of clashes between Indigenous peoples, corporations, and the governments of British Columbia and Canada.[121] Blockades erupted at dozens of sites around the province in the 1980s and 1990s.[122] Tactically, these assertions of Indigenous rights often resembled the actions taken by the Nuu-chah-nulth at Meares Island and the Haida at Lyell Island, in that they deployed what settlers would describe as non-violent civil disobedience – peaceful yet firm action to obstruct access to unceded Indigenous territory (whether by corporate licence holders attempting to extract natural resources, or by members of the public seeking to traverse highways through Indigenous territories). However, one Indigenous protest in the mid-1990s – by the Secwépemc people and their allies at Gustafsen Lake in British Columbia's central interior – moved outside these tactical parameters into the realm of armed conflict, provoking a sharp response from institutions of the settler state.[123] In this respect, the episode bore similarities to the state's response to the standoff at Oka, Quebec, five years earlier.

In the spring of 1995, Secwépemc land defenders, led by elder Wolverine (William Jones Ignace) and joined by Indigenous and non-Indigenous allies, occupied private ranchland at Gustafsen Lake in the BC interior, asserting a right to hold a traditional Sun Dance ceremony at a place they called the Gustafsen Lake Sacred Grounds, or Ts'Peten. The American rancher who had held fee simple title to the land since 1972, Lyle James, had earlier revoked permission to conduct the ceremony at the site, which had taken place each summer for the previous five years. A petition from Secwépemc elder Percy Rosette and medicine man John Stevens to Queen Elizabeth II asserting a legal

FIGURE 25 Secwépemc land defenders led by elder Wolverine (centre) at Ts'Peten, c. August 1995. | Mark van Manen, published with the express permission of *Vancouver Sun*, a division of Postmedia Network Inc.

right to access the site was ignored by the BC government in early 1995, leading to establishment of the protest camp.[124] The dispute escalated over the spring and summer of 1995, with James serving an eviction notice on the camp in June, which the Sun Dancers ignored, asserting an unqualified right to use the land. The defenders proceeded to hold the annual Sun Dance ceremony from July 2 to 12, combining cultural practices from Plains Indigenous nations with elements of Secwépemc culture.[125] The dispute was aggravated by tensions between the Indigenous land defenders at the encampment and elected Secwépemc leaders, who accused the Sun Dancers of mixing religion and politics, and who were themselves dismissed by the Sun Dancers as accomplices of the colonial state. The militant leader Splitting the Sky (a leader of the 1971 Attica prison rebellion and the American Indian Movement who had settled in Canada in the early 1990s after marrying a Cree woman) called for supporters to converge on the site and bring arms.[126] Later in July, an employee of the landowner was shot at but unharmed, presumably by the Secwépemc land defenders, after being sent to retrieve equipment from the ranch. Two provincial forestry workers also claimed to have been fired upon at the site.[127] The tactics and responses of Indigenous peoples, settler-allies, and state institutions to the conflict at Ts'Peten were coloured by the earlier high-profile standoff at Oka in 1990.[128]

As the dispute at Ts'Peten intensified, civil liberties lawyer Cameron Ward called on the provincial government in a *Globe and Mail* commentary to exercise its responsibility for the administration of justice by enforcing the criminal law, rather than requiring private citizens to rely on civil courts and injunctions, which provided few of the procedural protections for defendants in criminal proceedings.[129] NDP attorney general Colin Gabelmann responded that rather than obligate private citizens to enforce the criminal law, the province's current policy allowed police and prosecutors to pursue a "measured response to match the reality of civil disobedience actions, which range from serious criminal incidents to those that can be peacefully resolved at the scene."[130] Gabelmann was replaced by Ujjal Dosanjh as attorney general in the midst of the dispute in August 1995, signalling a hardening of the provincial government's attitude and coinciding with escalation of the conflict.

Two days after Dosanjh's appointment, the Ts'Peten defenders stumbled upon an RCMP emergency response team conducting a surveillance operation in the woods on the perimeter of the site and, believing an attack on the camp was imminent, opened fire. The officers were unharmed, but the incident escalated the dispute into a full-blown armed standoff between the Indigenous land defenders and the settler state. The governments of British Columbia and

Canada responded with a firm hand, deploying a small army of heavily armed RCMP officers, four hundred in total, assisted by Canadian soldiers in an effort known as Operation Wallaby, which included air and ground support with helicopters, surveillance planes, and armoured personnel carriers. Dosanjh articulated the provincial government's hardened position against the Ts'Peten defenders, making it clear that the government would not countenance any armed challenge to the authority of the state, and drawing a line between what the government described as legitimate efforts of recognized Indigenous governments to assert Indigenous rights and title through the treaty process, and lawless challenges to established legal authority by armed sovereigntists. According to the Ts'Peten defenders, the RCMP fired seventy-seven thousand bullets at the Secwépemc lines, including hollow-point bullets banned by the Hague Conventions.[131] The RCMP estimated that its officers fired seven thousand rounds. The operation cost $5.5 million, one of the costliest paramilitary operations in the province until then.[132]

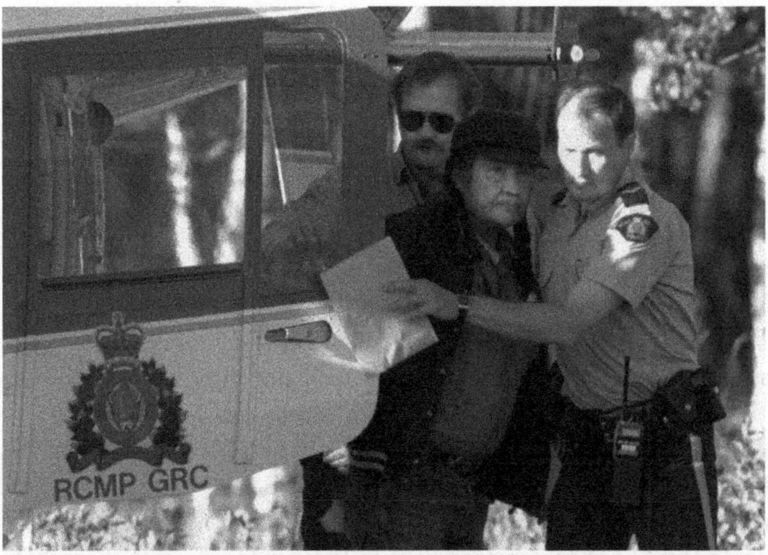

FIGURE 26 Secwépemc elder Wolverine (William Jones Ignace) in RCMP custody following the surrender of the Ts'Peten defenders on September 17, 1995. He served five years in prison for offences that included possession of a weapon for a purpose dangerous to the public peace and using a firearm in committing the assault of police officers. His appeal challenging the jurisdiction of the Provincial Court on unceded Secwépemc territory was dismissed, on the grounds that jurisdiction had existed since the assertion of British sovereignty in 1846. | Chuck Stoody, Canadian Press

Ultimately, the Ts'Peten defenders surrendered peacefully, led by medicine man John Stevens, who had filed the original petition with the Crown eight months earlier, seeking to establish legal access to the ranch to conduct the Sun Dance ceremony. Fourteen Indigenous and four non-Indigenous people were charged with crimes relating to property and possession of firearms. Several were represented by lawyer Bruce Clark. Following a ten-month trial, fifteen were convicted with sentences ranging from six months' to eight years' incarceration. Wolverine served five years in prison for offences that included possession of a weapon for a purpose dangerous to the public peace and using a firearm in committing the assault of police officers. He appealed the conviction on grounds that the Provincial Court lacked jurisdiction on unceded Secwépemc territory. In denying the appeal, the BC Court of Appeal applied the principle of *stare decisis*, finding that the issue of sovereignty had been decided in *Delgamuukw* (1993) and *R v Williams* (1994), with jurisdiction of BC courts established through the assertion of British sovereignty in 1846.[133] There was only one injury relating to gunfire during the Ts'Peten standoff, when a non-Indigenous protester was shot in the arm, allegedly by an RCMP bullet, though police denied this claim. Several RCMP officers claimed to have been shot by automatic gunfire as well, with bulletproof vests preventing any injuries.[134]

* * *

The armed conflict and related state security responses at Gustafson Lake, which bore parallels to other conflicts in the 1990s at Oka and at Ipperwash, Ontario, reflect the escalation of tensions surrounding unresolved Indigenous rights. At the same time, generalizations should recognize complexities, including the particularities of historical experiences and grievances as well as changes in judicial attitudes and differences within the state, between the courts and various levels of government. Compared with the Nuu-chah-nulth standoff at Meares Island and the Haida standoff at Lyell Island, the legal and political outcome of the Secwépemc standoff at Ts'Peten in the summer of 1995 is more opaque. Divisions among the Secwépemc people, particularly the lack of formal support from elected Secwépemc leadership for the challenge to the American rancher's property rights, prevented a more successful assertion of Indigenous rights, limiting the potential support base for the Ts'Peten land defenders within Indigenous communities and the broader settler society.

The "scattered geography of colonization" (as Nicholas Blomley put it) and the unevenness of the colonization process also help explain the different trajectories of Indigenous protests and state responses in modern British Columbia. The Nuu-chah-nulth at Wah-nah-jus Hilth-hoo-is (Meares Island) and the Haida at Tllga Kun Gwaayaay (Lyell Island) benefited from relative geographic isolation, on the northwestern edge of the province, the country, and the continent, which enabled them to enjoy a relatively wider degree of autonomy and relatively greater freedom of action to assert customary property claims. It also meant that state institutions were in a correspondingly weaker position to mount a defence of private property claims.

Much of British Columbia had been radically transformed in the century and a half preceding these conflicts. It had been occupied, remapped, and divided in profound ways, all the while subjected to land surveys, alienation of Indigenous lands into Crown and then fee-simple private lands, and substantial transformation by an onslaught of settler-led development: railways, highways, resource roads, mines, hydroelectric dams, transmission lines, pipelines, ranchlands, farms, towns, and cities. This pattern of colonization had a profound impact on Indigenous peoples, diluting their connections to the land, to one another, and to Indigenous cultural and legal traditions, and thereby depriving them of sources of strength for mounting successful assertions of rights. This pattern of colonization also contributed to dispersion and disunity among Indigenous peoples, encouraged by governance models imposed under the *Indian Act* that disrupted traditional systems of law, governance, and political authority.

By contrast, the colonization process was relatively less advanced in the Nuu-chah-nulth and Haida territories in Clayoquot Sound and Haida Gwaii in the 1980s. Incursions of settler laws, institutions, infrastructure, and industrial activities were more limited in those places in the decades preceding the blockades at Meares and Lyell. While the Nuu-chah-nulth and Haida shared common experiences of land dispossession and cultural genocide by paternalistic state institutions and allied institutions (such as the Indian reserve system and residential school experience), enduring "frontier" characteristics in the old-growth rainforests of Clayoquot Sound and Haida Gwaii had armed them with enduring sources of Indigenous customary law and cultural and political cohesion, which they tapped to mount effective assertions of rights. The formation of the Nuu-chah-nulth Tribal Council and the Council of the Haida Nation in the years preceding these respective land struggles in the 1980s demonstrates this process of political cohesion.

The uneven pattern of colonization also influenced potential support bases in settler society for these assertions of Indigenous rights, an important factor in mobilizing sufficient political pressure to impel settler governments to pursue political solutions. At Meares and Lyell Islands, the Indigenous communities asserting customary rights to the land and resources were buttressed by strong environmental advocacy campaigns. These campaigns were bolstered by the relatively pristine condition of the natural resources of the area, as well as relationships nurtured between Indigenous and non-Indigenous people in preceding years in the vicinity of communities such as Masset, Queen Charlotte City, Tlell, and Tofino. This ecological ethos found formal expression in settler-based advocacy organizations such as the Friends of Clayoquot Sound and the Islands Protection Society in Haida Gwaii, which provided material and political support in the heat of the conflicts. Relations of trust and effective working relationships were established between settlers associated with these groups, and local Indigenous activists and leaders in the nearby Nuu-chah-nulth and Haida communities. These working relationships in turn helped attract support from larger, more financially stable environmental organizations with provincial, national, and international reach, notably Greenpeace, the Sierra Club of Western Canada, and the Western Canada Wilderness Committee, drawing international attention to the ecological values and Indigenous assertions of rights at Meares and Lyell and helping bring sufficient political pressure to bear on settler governments to negotiate political solutions.

* * *

Direct assertions of Indigenous rights since the 1980s coincided with growing, if uneven, legal recognition of Indigenous rights by the BC judiciary, and spurred a renewed commitment to treaty making by sections of the settler and Indigenous communities. In 1990, the government of British Columbia reluctantly agreed to enter into negotiations with Indigenous groups not covered by treaties. In subsequent years, "modern-day" treaties were concluded with the Nisga'a (1999), Tsawwassen (2009), Tla'amin (2016), and five Nuu-chah-nulth communities that are parties to the Maa-nulth Treaty (2011).[135] While these treaties provided recognition, land, compensation, and a wider statutory basis for Indigenous self-government after more than a century of unresolved Indigenous land claims, they also reinforced the supremacy of the settler law of Canada and the subordinate role of Indigenous laws and institutions within the Canadian Constitution. Scholars have offered a robust critique of the ways in which the treaty process translates collective Indigenous rights into private rights, arguing for the pursuit of shared forms of property and rejection of a neoliberal model that seeks to privatize and extinguish Indigenous title.[136]

Growing legal recognition of Indigenous rights and title by the BC judiciary

FIGURE 27 On-the-water protest by W̱SÁNEĆ, Cowichan, and Penelakut Coast Salish peoples and their allies at Grace Islet, challenging construction of a private luxury home on a Coast Salish burial ground, 2014. | Adrian Lam, *Times Colonist*

also translated into growing legal latitude for direct action exercised in pursuit of these rights. This was evident in a case that I became personally involved with in 2014. My involvement in the Grace Islet case did not reflect a decision on my part to pursue "social action research" as part of the methodology for this book; rather, I became a participant in public events that happened to overlap with my topic of research. The dispute involved a rocky outcropping of land known as Grace Islet in Ganges Harbour, off Salt Spring Island in the Salish Sea. The land was owned in fee simple by a businessman named Barry Slawsky, but included approximately two dozen Coast Salish burial cairns recognized by the BC Archaeological Branch, responsible for protection of cultural heritage resources in accordance with the provisions of the *Heritage Conservation Act*, and identified by archaeologists contracted by Slawsky. Hereditary Chief Eric Pelkey of the Tsawout First Nation of the W̱SÁNEĆ Coast Salish peoples claimed that Grace Islet was included among the village sites and fishing grounds recognized in the North Saanich Treaty of 1852 that his ancestors signed with James Douglas.[137] The Cowichan and Penelakut Coast Salish peoples, who had never signed treaties, also claimed Grace Islet as a traditional burial ground and cultural site.

The settler held title to the land but there were overlapping claims of

Indigenous title and customary use. When Slawsky obtained an archaeological alteration permit from the BC government and hired contractors to begin constructing a luxury vacation home, a wave of protest broke out, involving W̱SÁNEĆ, Cowichan, and Penelakut Coast Salish peoples, as well as non-Indigenous allies who objected to the desecration of the heritage site and despoliation of the ecology of the islet. I became involved in the movement to protect Grace Islet and halt the construction process. The protests included rallies in the Ganges townsite, a stone's throw from the islet, as well as on-the-water protests involving flotillas of kayaks, canoes, fishboats, and other watercraft, including vessels from the Penelakut and Cowichan bands. On several occasions, Grace Islet "protectors" landed on the foreshore of the islet, and on one occasion the group entered the construction site, disrupting work.

Slawsky and his lawyer, John Alexander, filed a civil claim and an application for an interlocutory injunction in the BC Supreme Court. However, when the matter went to a hearing in September 2014, BC Supreme Court Justice Douglas Thompson refused to grant the interlocutory injunction. Alexander alleged that it was a case of simple trespass and that the test established in *RJR-MacDonald* had been satisfied, but Thompson was not convinced.[138] Rather than grant an injunction to immediately restrain protest on the islet and surrounding waters, he ordered a one-month recess to allow the Indigenous and other defendants (including me) to further develop their responses. As he ruled in postponing the hearing: "The matter may be as simple as the plaintiff says it is, [or] it may not be that simple."[139] Two weeks later, within hours of receiving responses to the civil claim, in which elected chief Don Tom of the Tsartlip First Nation of the W̱SÁNEĆ Coast Salish peoples, asserted that he was exercising a customary Indigenous right to visit the graves of his ancestors, and I asserted that I was assisting the chief and other Indigenous people in exercising these rights, the private landowner discontinued the civil action and agreed to pay costs.[140]

While we do not know how the matter would have been decided in court, based on Thompson's preliminary ruling in refusing to grant the injunction, we can discern a widening legal ambit for assertions of customary and constitutional Indigenous rights, even when assertion of these Indigenous rights comes into direct conflict with rights of private parties on lands recognized by the settler law as being owned in fee simple. Following discontinuance of the civil action, the BC government intervened to purchase title to Grace Islet from Barry Slawsky (for $5.45 million, which was roughly four times the assessed land value and the owner's sunk costs constructing the building, which was later dismantled). Stewardship of Grace Islet was conferred on a consortium of Coast Salish bands, in partnership with the Nature Conservancy of Canada.[141]

What does the Grace Islet controversy tell us about the historical and legal geography of property and protest? First, that it is fluid, impacted by the political context and the relative strength of the contending parties. It is also impacted by the changing law pertaining to Indigenous rights and title. It is unlikely that the judge would have demonstrated the same reluctance to issue the injunction to the landowner if the Grace Islet protests had been grounded on ecological rather than Indigenous assertions of rights.

* * *

Notwithstanding the wider recognition afforded to assertions of Indigenous customary and constitutional rights to property in recent years, Canadian courts remain more inclined to grant injunctions requested by corporations against Indigenous peoples, and less inclined to grant them to First Nations attempting to enforce Indigenous, environmental, or other rights through legal means. A study from the Yellowhead Institute (2019) based on a review of nearly one hundred cases involving injunctions and Indigenous people found that "76 percent of injunctions filed against First Nations by corporations were granted, while 81 percent of injunctions filed against corporations by First Nations were denied. Perhaps most tellingly, 82 percent of injunctions filed by First Nations against the government were denied."[142] Legal scholar Basil Alexander has noted that "Indigenous demonstrators are often on the receiving end of injunctions."[143]

A recent high-profile case from British Columbia demonstrates the enduring pattern of law's coercive force being deployed disproportionately by colonial authorities to buttress private claims to property in the face of competing Indigenous claims. In December 2018, Coastal GasLink Pipeline Ltd. (CGL), a subsidiary of TransCanada Pipelines, obtained an interim injunction from the BC Supreme Court restraining Wet'suwet'en people in the central interior from obstructing construction of a gas pipeline through their territory.[144] RCMP officers enforced this injunction in January 2019, physically breaking through a barricade and arresting fourteen members of the Gidimt'en clan of the Wet'suwet'en Nation who had established a checkpoint on a service road to prevent access to the area.[145] "They can go anywhere they want, except for on Wet'suwet'en territory," declared Madeek̓, a hereditary chief of the Gidimt'en, prior to the police raid.[146] The dispute was complicated by revenue-sharing agreements signed by *Indian Act* band councils along the proposed pipeline route, even though the hereditary chiefs of the Wet'suwet'en clans unanimously opposed the project.[147] Invoking Wet'suwet'en law, members of the Unist'ot'en clan had established a camp and healing centre on the Widzin Kwah (Morice River) several years earlier, the Unist'ot'en Camp, which served as a focal point for Indigenous and allied opposition. The authority of the Wet'suwet'en hereditary governance system, and the role of hereditary chiefs as the legitimate representatives for collectively held title and rights, had been affirmed by Canadian courts in the landmark ruling in *Delgamuukw* (1997).[148] However, lawyers for the gas company sought to have any affidavits attesting to the hereditary system struck from the record.[149]

Contempt of court charges against the Gidimt'en members arrested in January 2019 were dropped later that year (mirroring the pattern in earlier disputes, where the threat of criminal sanction was lifted after the moment of crisis had passed), but the dispute escalated in 2020 following a successful application from the gas company for an interlocutory injunction to replace the earlier interim injunction.[150] In those proceedings in December 2019, Justice Marguerite Church rejected the assertion of Freda Huson of the Unist'ot'en clan that the checkpoints were legal under Wet'suwet'en law (Huson had contended that the gas company lacked permission from the head of the Dark House clan to enter or pass through the unceded territory). Justice Church chastised Huson and the Wet'suwet'en for their failure to challenge the Crown permits under established legal procedures, characterizing the "self-help" measures pursued by the Wet'suwet'en as an "abuse of process" and "contrary to the rule of law."[151] Huson and the Wet'suwet'en hereditary chiefs responded to Church's interlocutory injunction by issuing an eviction notice to CGL, under authority arising from Wet'suwet'en law, ordering employees of the gas company to leave the territory. Checkpoints were established to enforce the eviction. While CGL temporarily complied, the assertion and enforcement of customary law in defiance of the colonial law prompted a declaration of a provincial emergency by British Columbia's solicitor general, New Democrat Mike Farnworth, and mobilization into Wet'suwet'en territory of scores of RCMP officers from the militarized Community-Industry Response Group (CIRG, which was later rebranded as the Critical Response Unit).[152] In February 2020, the CIRG employed force to break through the Wet'suwet'en checkpoints, arresting twenty-eight Wet'suwet'en land defenders and allies, twenty-two of whom were charged with criminal contempt of court.[153]

The state's response to the Wet'suwet'en assertion of customary rights provoked nationwide protests in Canada in February and March 2020, including blockades and occupations from the provincial legislature in Victoria to the Port of Vancouver, to rail lines in the BC interior, to Montreal, and to many points in between. Freight and passenger rail traffic ground to a halt across most of Canada. Hundreds of cargo ships lay at anchor off the Pacific and Atlantic coasts and in the St. Lawrence Seaway, and goods piled up on the wharves of Vancouver, Prince Rupert, Montreal, and Halifax. Economic disruption arising from the rail blockades was later estimated to have cost $275 million.[154] This pressure brought the governments of Canada and British Columbia to the negotiating table, and led to the signing of a memorandum of understanding with the Wet'suwet'en hereditary chiefs: Wet'suwet'en rights and title would hereafter be recognized. However, the contentious pipeline issue was skirted.[155] The depth and breadth of support for the Wet'suwet'en reflected public sympathy for Indigenous rights, as well as wider debates over climate change and the wisdom of pursuing liquefied natural gas exports and expanded fossil fuel infrastructure.

As in the previous year, charges of criminal contempt of court against twenty-two Wet'suwet'en land defenders were dropped in June 2020 (although several subsequent breaches of the injunction and prosecutions have continued up to the time of publication of this book).[156] Counsel for the alleged contemnors, Martin Peters, noted that "the courts have been very quick to support industry," describing "the ease" with which the injunctions were granted and enforced as "troubling" in light of assertions of unresolved Indigenous rights.[157] A petition for judicial review filed by the Office of the Wet'suwet'en, seeking to quash Environmental Assessment Office approval of the pipeline, was dismissed by the BC Supreme Court in the spring of 2021; later that year, the Environmental Assessment Office issued an enforcement order against CGL for erosion problems along the pipeline route that impacted watercourses and wetlands.[158]

The state's response to Wet'suwet'en assertions of customary rights since 2018 has revealed ongoing deployment of colonial law's coercive violence in aid of private property interests, and the incomplete process of recognition of Indigenous rights within Canadian law. The court's willingness to grant injunctions sought by private industry for use of Crown land, thereby overriding Indigenous claims, appears to confirm the presence of ongoing structural inequities in the settler legal system, notwithstanding apparent advances in recognition of Indigenous rights in cases such as *Tsilhqot'in* (2014) and in British Columbia's and Canada's voluntary recognition of Haida title in 2024.[159] Some scholars have suggested that despite its far-reaching implications, *Tsilhqot'in* continues to legitimize Crown sovereignty, legislative authority, and underlying title, thus maintaining a legal hierarchy where Crown title is treated as legally superior to Indigenous title.[160] Explosive documents emerged in 2019 indicating that the RCMP was prepared to use lethal force against the Wet'suwet'en land defenders to enforce the original injunction – revealing a persistent pattern in the Canadian state's response to Indigenous defiance of colonial law extending back to the Red River Rebellion 150 years earlier.[161] Tens of millions of dollars have been expended since 2019 on RCMP enforcement of CGL's injunctions against the Wet'suwet'en land defenders.[162]

* * *

This chapter has served as a preliminary window into a vital and evolving area of law, examining how Indigenous peoples in late twentieth-century and early twenty-first-century British Columbia challenged colonial property relations, asserting customary claims to land and resources in a manner that provoked coercive legal responses from property owners and institutions of the settler state. Beginning with the assertion of Indigenous rights by Nuu-chah-nulth peoples at Wah-nah-jus Hilth-hoo-is (Meares Island) in Clayoquot Sound in 1984, we observed pronounced linkages between Indigenous peoples and other social movements, and a groundbreaking injunction granted to the Nuu-chah-nulth chiefs by the BC judiciary to restrain the activity of a logging company. Turning to the Haida blockade against logging at Tllga Kun Gwaayaay (Lyell Island) in 1985, we observed how a legal controversy involving seventy-two arrests ultimately had far-reaching political impacts on the Haida people and their relationships with land, resources, and the Canadian state. Moving from injunction law to criminal law, the 1995 standoff at Ts'Peten (Gustafsen Lake) demonstrated the willingness of some Secwépemc peoples and their allies to take up arms to assert customary rights on private ranchland – striking at the root of the Crown's authority to make and enforce law, while attracting much sharper legal penalties with *Criminal Code* convictions and lengthy prison sentences. The brief case study of the stand taken by W̱SÁNEĆ, Cowichan, and Penelakut Coast Salish people and settler-allies to protect the burial ground on Grace Islet in the Salish Sea indicated the potential openness of judges to recognize Indigenous rights capable of intruding on fee-simple title to property (at least at the interlocutory injunction stage). The more recent episode of the Wet'suwet'en struggle against the Coastal GasLink pipeline points to the uneven advance of Indigenous rights within the settler law of Canada.

We turn next to legal responses to property relations and protests in a more urban setting, focusing on the legal politics of homelessness and sheltering in twenty-first century British Columbia.

Chapter 6

THE RIGHT TO SLEEP

Tenting as Protest and the Legal Politics of Shelter in Neoliberal British Columbia

PROPERTY CLAIMS BY public authorities have become more contingent in British Columbia in the opening decades of the twenty-first century, in the face of successful legal assertions of a "right to sleep" and "right to shelter" in public spaces by people who are homeless, buttressed by recognition of the right to life, liberty, and security of the person under section 7 of the *Canadian Charter of Rights and Freedoms*. This is a live and evolving area of law, with recent court rulings conferring a degree of stability on homeless encampments in urban areas, which, at the beginning of the twenty-first century, were often summarily removed through prompt and seemingly straightforward action by property managers, police, and (if necessary) the judiciary. The 2008 BC Supreme Court and 2009 BC Court of Appeal decisions in *Victoria (City) v Adams* represented milestones in the evolving jurisprudence of urban tenting and the right to sleep and right to shelter in British Columbia, recognizing a constitutional right to shelter oneself in a public park in the absence of alternative shelter. This line of legal reasoning reflects growing recognition of constitutional rights of marginalized people. It also highlights entrenchment of a permanent underclass in modern British Columbia, as neoliberal processes of "restraint" have intensified marginalization and displacement of poor people, leading to a situation where courts have felt compelled to recognize specific rights to public spaces such as municipal parks and sidewalks. This could be interpreted as a judicial response to the economic conditions of the neoliberal age, where inequality is increasingly accepted as an inevitable fact rather than attacked through redistributive social programs. However, further evolution of the law in the Victoria Courthouse encampment litigation in *Adamson* (2016) and subsequent decisions provides grounds for cautious optimism, suggesting that growing legal recognition of a customary and constitutional right to shelter may be translating into a positive (if tentative) right to housing in Canadian law.

Contesting the Right to Sleep and Right to Shelter

This final case study examines the legal politics of homelessness, specifically the widening legal ambit for urban tenting and the right to sleep and right to shelter. It explores the ways in which poor peoples' movements and advocates have asserted customary and constitutional rights to public spaces through "tent cities" and similar urban encampments, and how property managers, municipal governments, and members of the legal community have responded to these assertions of rights. This chapter is grounded in evolving case law relating to the right to sleep and right to shelter, as well as theoretical literature on "the right to the city."[1]

Legal scholars Antonio Azuela and Rodrigo Meneses-Reyes define law as a "tool to provide essential order that will regulate the arrangement of things and people on the street."[2] Lynn Staeheli and Don Mitchell argue for the importance of viewing public space as *property*, "a crucial set of relationships that structure the role, function, and nature of public space as space" and open up "new fronts in the ongoing struggles over and interventions in it." They note that "being present in public space – making claims to and becoming visible in the streets, sidewalks, squares, and parks of the city – is a vital, necessary step in making claims *on* the public."[3] Sarah Hamill has examined urban encampment litigation with reference to the concept of "common property."[4] Mark Purcell demonstrates how neoliberal restructuring of the state and society has given rise to specific forms of displacement and marginalization in cities, while simultaneously creating space for new forms of resistance and urban politics.[5] He calls for a renewed approach to the "right to the city" consistent with Henri Lefebvre's original formulation, "to radically rethink the social relations of capitalism, the spatial structure of the city and the assumptions of liberal democracy."[6] In *Poor People's Movements* (1977), Frances Fox Piven and Richard Cloward emphasize the agency of poor people themselves.[7] Similarly, David Harvey suggests that the idea of the right to the city "primarily rises up from the streets, out from the neighborhoods, as a cry for help and sustenance by oppressed peoples in desperate times."[8]

This chapter is also informed by an older, international literature on the social-economic purposes of the law and the ways in which law's violence has been disproportionately directed toward poor people. As noted in the Introduction, Adam Smith wrote in the eighteenth century that "laws and governments may be considered ... as a combination of the rich to oppress the poor, and preserve to themselves the inequality of goods which would otherwise be soon destroyed by the attacks of the poor, who if not hindered by the government would soon reduce the others to an equality with themselves by open violence."[9] Douglas Hay has applied this approach to modern times, suggesting that law's violence is "largely determined by the need to contain the effects, direct and indirect, of substantial social inequality."[10] Hay identifies a close correlation between cyclical economic crises in societies and "peaks in the violence of the gallows," suggesting that more poor people were being subjected to law's violence by the late twentieth century than ever before, reflecting rapid growth in the resources and technology of policing as well as recurring economic crises: "It is highly unlikely that, at any time in the past of English-speaking societies, we have stigmatized such a large proportion of our populations."[11] Hay posits that the inevitable outcome of this skewed deployment of legal power is a crisis of law's legitimacy:

> What does it mean for a society when the experience of law's violence, mainly directed against the poor, occurs at such high rates and at times of greatly increased inequality and sense of powerlessness among the poorest? The longer record suggests that the outcome is a sense of crisis and increased repression. I think that outcome is even more likely where the law's legitimacy is compromised by the fact that unequally distributed violence visibly extends beyond the criminal law.[12]

It remains an open question whether the intensification of violence against the poor, and the corresponding crises of legal legitimacy, has been tempered in the Canadian context by constitutional protections afforded by the *Canadian Charter of Rights and Freedoms* in recent years.

The growing phenomenon of tent cities reflects the confluence of these social forces – a desire for community and security among poor people in the face of enduring systemic and overt legal violence, as well as specific responses to processes of neoliberal restructuring that intensifies marginalization and displacement of poor people while giving rise to new forms of resistance and urban politics.[13] Vancouver activist and writer Harsha Walia described the tent city that took root in Vancouver's Oppenheimer Park in 2014 as "a DIY [do-it-yourself] kind of space. You don't have to stand in a food line – everyone is involved in preparing food. That's a big part of tent cities, and that's what is often missing from the conversation."[14] This sense of solidarity and desire for community and security among marginalized, street-involved people has driven the formation of tent cities in Vancouver, Victoria, and other BC communities since the early 2000s. Tent cities have important parallels with earlier forms of protest in BC legal history, including unemployed organizing in the 1930s and labour struggles throughout the twentieth century – with the common emphasis on conflicting conceptions of property and challenges to economic power and hierarchical class relations. As Mark Zion noted in a recent master's thesis, "tent cities make homeless people more visible by occupying a larger space collectively, disrupting conventional urban maps."[15]

Controversy relating to homelessness, poverty, and marginalization is not confined to British Columbia and Canada. Indeed, varying levels of poverty and economic inequality can be found in every state in the world, in both the Global North and Global South. The intensity of poverty and its visible manifestations depend on a number of factors, including state policies relating to housing, income, taxation, and redistribution; the relative strength of local and national economies; and the functionality of family and other support networks that can contribute to social integration rather than exclusion.[16] In British Columbia, as elsewhere in North America, poverty and visible homelessness have become increasingly acute in recent decades in the context of neoliberal structuring of the state and society.[17] Local responses to destitution can be found in all jurisdictions, demonstrating the international nature of the problem. For example, the Supreme Court of India's decision in the 1980 case of *Ratlam Municipality v Vardhichand* highlighted how a lack of support services left marginalized people to fend for themselves:

> The grievous failure of local authorities to provide the basic amenity of public conveniences drives the miserable slum-dwellers to ease in the streets, on the sly for a time, and openly thereafter, because under Nature's pressure, bashfulness becomes a luxury and dignity a difficult art.[18]

Going further than Canada's courts have been prepared to go, the Supreme Court of India conferred positive rights in that case, recognizing "the social justice component of the rule of law" imparted by the Indian Constitution, as well as common law related to the tort of nuisance. The court ruled that "the

Municipal Council shall, within six months from to-day, construct a sufficient number of public latrines for use by men and women separately [and] provide water supply."[19] This imposed a positive obligation on government to provide a minimum level of services, breaking ground in the terrain of judicial intervention in the executive function of public bodies.

Woodsquat and the Legal Politics of Shelter in Neoliberal British Columbia

In the autumn of 2002, members of Vancouver's street community and housing activists established a squat in and around the abandoned Woodward's department store building on East Hastings Street in Vancouver's Downtown Eastside. Located in the heart of the notorious "poorest postal code in the country," the "Woodsquat" (as the protest camp was called) mushroomed over the course of ten weeks into an eclectic community of nearly two hundred street-involved people and their allies. The Woodward's building had originally been slated for social housing by the previous NDP government, but its future was thrown into doubt when the BC Liberals swept into power in 2001 and cancelled the project as part of a wider ideological assault on social

FIGURE 28 The "Woodsquat" at the boarded-up Woodward's department store in downtown Vancouver, 2002. | Reid

programs and policies associated with an interventionist welfare state. As welfare entitlements were restricted and public sector workers faced job cuts and contract concessions, social movements saw a resurgence, including an eclectic poor peoples' movement. As Piven and Cloward note, "protest tactics which defied political norms were not simply the recourse of troublemakers and fools. For the poor, they were the only recourse."[20]

In the midst of the Woodsquat, the Government of British Columbia, as the owner of the building through a Crown corporation, the Provincial Rental Housing Corporation, initiated civil legal proceedings against the squatters, seeking an injunction ordering them to vacate the building. On September 16, BC Supreme Court Justice Linda Loo granted an *ex parte* interlocutory injunction, leading to the forced removal and arrests of fifty-four people when a hundred police officers reoccupied the building and put an end to the weeklong squat.[21] However, this enforcement action simply moved the protest from the interior of the building to the surrounding public sidewalks, where the protesters dug in, in defiance of the City of Vancouver's *Street and Traffic Bylaw*, establishing a makeshift tent city under the awnings that surrounded the Vancouver landmark. "Tents, mattresses and other objects were placed around the building in contravention of the City's By-law," Court of Appeal Justice Anne Rowles later found.[22] More than two months after the encampment was established on the sidewalks on Hastings, Abbott, and Cordova Streets, and in the midst of a municipal election, the City of Vancouver obtained a subsequent injunction ordering removal of the camp on grounds that it breached the bylaw. Following another week of legal wrangling between lawyers representing the city and the protesters, the city received an enforcement order directing police to disband the camp, which prompted the campers to pack up on their own and vacate the municipal sidewalk, amid promises of social housing from the provincial government and the newly elected left-wing city council.[23]

While no arrests or contempt proceedings arose from the encampment on the sidewalks around the Woodward's building, the squatters (aided by lawyers Cameron Ward and L.J. Tessaro) appealed the injunction issued to the City of Vancouver as well as the original injunction issued to the Provincial Rental Housing Corporation, which provided the legal basis for the police raid and eviction. The provincial government, for its part, appealed a November 2002 ruling awarding $100 in costs to each of thirty-four alleged contemnors who attended a court hearing to learn that contempt charges arising from the original occupation were not being pursued.[24] In 2005, the BC Court of Appeal allowed the two appeals relating to the original injunction, while dismissing the appeal against the injunction awarded to the city.

Arguments presented in *Vancouver (City) v Maurice* (2005) and *Provincial Rental Housing Corporation v Hall* (2005) provide important insights into the legal politics of sheltering and wider questions relating to the exercise of injunctions in response to protest. In their submissions to the appeal court, the housing activists in the Woodsquat litigation took issue with what they described as a pattern of procedural unfairness in injunction proceedings initiated by corporations and governments against social movement actors:

> The appellants argue that since *Everywoman's Health Centre Society (1988) v. Bridges* (1990), 54 B.C.L.R. (2d) 273 (C.A.), it has become almost settled practice in British Columbia for corporations or government entities to attempt to quash political or social protest activities by inviting the courts to grant injunctions and then to exercise the court's powers to punish for contempt. It is the appellants' submission that when the extraordinary remedy of an injunction is sought, the court must ensure that fundamental procedural safeguards are met.[25]

The Court of Appeal dismissed the challenge to the injunction issued to the City of Vancouver, which was confined to narrow technical arguments regarding identification of defendants in the style of cause. The court allowed the appeal against the *ex parte* injunction granted to the Provincial Rental Housing Corporation, with Justice Anne Rowles (on behalf of the three-judge division) stating that the trial judge erred in deciding that the *ex parte* interlocutory injunction posed no risk of harm to the protesters: "An unwarranted or unnecessary stifling of freedom of expression, including the right to dissent, is not something that can be measured monetarily, but 'harm' is not confined to monetary loss." Rowles stated that even if an injunction was urgent (thereby warranting an order without notice to the other side), it ought to have taken the form of "an interim injunction for a short, specified period" rather than an ongoing interlocutory order, thereby placing the burden on the applicant to apply to extend, with proper notice to the defendants.[26]

Notwithstanding growing legal recognition of procedural fairness rights with respect to protests, the BC judiciary continued to respond to injunction applications from managers of public property in predictable ways, citing the court's "narrow discretion" to consider constitutional questions and other factors that would militate against granting interlocutory injunctions. Notably, these public property managers were emboldened with statutory remedies not available to private parties (such as the private entities embroiled in the disputes discussed in the preceding chapters). Unlike strike-bound employers, logging corporations, or nonprofit abortion clinics seeking interlocutory injunctions in equity to restrain protests, municipalities in British Columbia were empowered in the *Vancouver Charter* and *Community Charter* to obtain statutory injunctions to achieve compliance with municipal bylaws, including bylaws governing use of public space.[27] While the test for granting an injunction was the same as when constitutional rights were invoked (*RJR-Macdonald*), the weighing of the public interest at the balance of convenience stage was more circumscribed; courts were less inclined to exercise their discretion by refusing to grant an injunction aimed at enforcing a public right.[28] One line of judicial reasoning suggested that a judge should deny a statutory injunction to a municipality only in "exceptional circumstances."[29]

When street-involved people and their supporters occupied a series of Vancouver parks in 2003 to protest provincial government changes to welfare policy and a shortage of social housing, the judiciary did not hesitate to grant injunctions to the Vancouver Board of Parks and Recreation to remove the camps. The homeless and anti-poverty activists had established a camp at Victory Square on West Hastings Street in July 2003, coinciding with the announcement that Vancouver had been selected to host the 2010 Winter Olympic Games; the campers relocated "Victory Squat" to Thornton Park, near the central railway station, a few weeks later, after war veterans objected to the encampment near the Victory Square cenotaph. In August 2003, as the camp grew to about thirty tents and fifty campers, BC Supreme Court Justice Ian Pitfield granted another injunction to the Parks Board ordering the removal of the Thornton Park camp, suggesting that refusal to do so would be construed as "an open invitation to permit others ... to create tent villages, towns, or cities in other parks in Vancouver" and that "politics, at least as regards the issue of housing for the homeless in Vancouver, is not part of the Parks Board mandate nor is housing an issue with which it should be required to cope." In his decision in *Vancouver Parks Board v Mickelson et al*, Justice Pitfield ruled that the balance of convenience was "not tipped in favour of the defendants by concern for their constitutional rights."[30]

The Victory Squat campers complied with the court ruling, vacating Thornton Park but relocating the Victory Squat to yet another park: Portside (Crab) Park on Vancouver Harbour. Spokesperson Tony Ruzza from the Anti-Poverty Committee explained the political motivation behind the camp:

> This is an open air shelter run by the homeless for the homeless. This makes Victory Squat a political act. This is political protest against the BC Liberals. It is about welfare legislation that has seen more than 70,000 people forced off welfare. It is about a two-year-out-of-five welfare rule that will see more than

> 40,000 more [sic.] thrown off welfare on April 1st. It is about the lack of adequate and affordable housing. What does city council and the parks board think will happen on April 1st?[31]

Two weeks later, BC Supreme Court Justice Ian Meiklem granted another injunction to the Parks Board in the case of *Vancouver Board of Parks v Sterritt*, ordering the campers to vacate Portside Park and declaring that

> the discretion of the court on an application for an interlocutory injunction to compel compliance with a public statute is very limited indeed. Very exceptional circumstances are required to deny an application for a statutorily-enabled injunction, and even if, as Mr. Justice Pitfield held in the Mickelson case, the assertion of a constitutional challenge invokes a different test, one that involves a balance of convenience test, the public interest in enforcement of laws existing and enacted for the public good generally outweighs the interest of individuals who challenge the law on the basis of the constitution or other bases.[32]

In this respect, Justice Meiklem concurred with the reasoning in *British Columbia (Minister of Forests) v Okanagan Indian Band* (2003) that the public interest in seeing the law upheld was not easily outweighed by any prejudice to the defendant.[33] Litigation relating to the Victory Squat demonstrated that recognition of constitutional and customary rights capable of trumping private property rights was a slow and uneven process.

Establishing the Right to Shelter in the Adams *Decision*

The ambit of urban tenting and legal recognition of the right to sleep and right to shelter was expanded in important ways in the 2008 BC Supreme Court and 2009 BC Court of Appeal decisions in *Victoria (City) v Adams*.[34] Those decisions were the culmination of several years of occupations and advocacy by street-involved people in Victoria, British Columbia's capital city – beginning with an encampment at the provincial legislature shortly after Gordon Campbell's Liberal government took office, followed by a cat-and-mouse game between homeless people led by David Arthur Johnston and municipal bylaw officers and police in city parks and provincially owned greenspaces. The controversy culminated in a tent city at a small municipal park called Cridge Park in downtown Victoria in the autumn of 2005.[35] Tensions were exacerbated by proposed provincial legislation, such as the *Trespass to Property Act* (which was subsequently withdrawn) and the *Safe Streets Act* of 2004 (which was adopted by the legislature), aimed at bolstering the powers of private landowners, bylaw officers, and police to displace street-involved people from private and public spaces – augmenting civil remedies in tort and municipal bylaws with quasi-criminal penalties authorized by legislative statute.[36]

Prior to the establishment of the Cridge Park camp, Johnston and other street-involved people had asserted a right to sleep at the nearby St. Ann's Academy grounds, provincially owned land that included the offices of the Ministry of Advanced Education as well as substantial greenspace. Johnston was an unconventional countercultural figure, a self-described "monk" who shunned money, material possessions, and other comforts of modern society.[37] For more than a year beginning in January 2004, he and his associates sought to shelter themselves on a nearly daily basis at the St. Ann's grounds, resulting in trespass notices, repeated arrests, *Criminal Code* allegations of mischief, breach of the peace, and obstruction of justice, and several jail sentences.[38] In September 2005, the Provincial Capital Commission, the Crown corporation responsible for management of the grounds, obtained a civil injunction from BC Supreme Court Justice R.D. Wilson ordering the camp removed.[39]

Johnston and his associates complied with the letter of the court ruling, relocating across the street to the city of Victoria's Cridge Park, establishing a camp that grew over a matter of weeks to encompass about twenty tents and seventy persons. The city applied for and received an interlocutory injunction from Supreme Court Justice Allan Stewart restraining the campers from remaining in the park. By the end of October 2005, police had dismantled the camp.[40] Several years of legal wrangling followed. The city applied for a permanent injunction in the face of ongoing roving tenting by Johnston and others, while counsel for the campers, Victoria lawyers Irene Faulkner and Catherine Boies Parker, sought a court declaration on the constitutional question of whether the city bylaws violated sections 7 and 12 of the Charter, which recognized the right to security of the person and the right not to be subjected to cruel or unusual treatment or punishment. In October 2008, the trial judge, BC Supreme Court Justice Carol Ross, declared that sections of the city's *Parks Regulation Bylaw* and *Streets and Traffic Bylaw* that prohibited overnight sheltering and sleeping in municipal parks and sidewalks violated section 7 of the Charter "in that they deprive homeless people of life, liberty and security of the person in a manner not in accordance with the principles of fundamental justice, and are not saved by s. 1 of the *Charter*." Justice Ross declared that those sections of the bylaws were "of no force and effect insofar ... as they apply to prevent homeless people from erecting temporary shelter."[41]

The city appealed the decision, and the BC attorney general and the Union of BC Municipalities joined the case as intervenors in support of its position, while the BC Civil Liberties Association intervened in support of the campers. In its 2009 decision in *Victoria (City) v Adams,* the Court of Appeal upheld Justice Ross's judgment, declaring: "We find no legal basis to interfere with the trial judge's conclusion ... that the prohibition in the bylaws on the erection of temporary shelter violates the rights of homeless people to life, liberty and security of the person under s. 7, and the violation is not justified under s. 1 of the Charter." The Court of Appeal rejected the city's argument that Ross's decision intruded on the legislative authority of local government to make complex decisions on public policy.[42]

The city responded to the Court of Appeal's decision in *Adams* by amending its *Parks Regulation Bylaw* to permit overnight sheltering by people who were homeless between the hours of 7:00 p.m. and 7:00 a.m. (with some variation for daylight saving time).[43] However, advocates, including the homeless man at the centre of the original litigation, David Arthur Johnston, were not content with the allowance for overnight sheltering. Johnston believed that the right to sleep extended into the daytime hours as well, and proceeded to set up his tent in city parks in defiance of the amended bylaw (an argument the BC Supreme Court and Court of Appeal rejected, finding that the prohibition on daytime sheltering was a reasonable infringement on section 7 rights, and was therefore saved by section 1 of the Charter).[44] Johnston was arrested and convicted on multiple occasions between 2010 and 2013, receiving jail sentences of up to ninety days and embarking on a month-long hunger strike at the Wilkinson Road provincial jail in nearby Saanich.[45] As Mark Zion noted in his master's thesis, Johnston challenged the constitutionality of the civic bylaw's prohibition on daytime sleeping as an affront to his dignity, but failed to satisfy the evidentiary burden to successfully make out this claim in court. "Johnston and others demonstrate that homeless citizens are capable of democratic citizenship that works along an expansive temporal register rooted in the present, but extending 'backward' into more egalitarian predecessors in the past and into a more equal imagined future."[46]

In the wake of the *Adams* decision, the BC courts decided another case relating to the occupation of public space. In *Vancouver (City) v Zhang* (2010), the Court of Appeal struck down sections of a Vancouver municipal bylaw that prohibited the erection of shelters associated with political protest. The case related to a semi-permanent, twenty-four-hour-a-day protest outside the consulate of the Peoples' Republic of China on Granville Street in Vancouver, where members of the Falun Gong sect held vigil to protest human rights violations against their associates in China. In setting aside the impugned sections of the bylaw and a lower court injunction ordering the removal of the shelter, the appeal court allowed that some form of sheltering could be interpreted as ancillary to the section 2 Charter right to freedom of expression. Writing for the appellate division, Justice Carol Huddart found that "the reasonable regulation of commercial and artistic expression cannot justify a by-law that effectively precludes any use of a structure, however minimal, for political expression."[47] However, the courts were later quick to narrow the application of the ruling in *Zhang* to avoid authorizing more wide-scale tent protests. As BC Supreme Court Justice Terence Schultes would declare in the Occupy Victoria case a year later: "A vigil by a single person in a meditation hut next to a sidewalk regulated by a traffic bylaw raises very different concerns than those posed by a significant, ongoing tent encampment in a public square that is regulated by a park use bylaw."[48]

Occupy: Tenting as Political Protest

In September 2011, several hundred protesters occupied Zuccotti Park, a privately owned public square in the heart of Wall Street, New York City's financial district and an epicentre of global finance capital. The Occupy Wall Street encampment, which included daily "peoples' assemblies" of campers and other New York citizens, became a lightning rod for global opposition to the concentration of wealth and power in the hands of an elite "1 percent," inspiring similar occupations and movements by the "99 percent" in approximately one thousand communities around the world, including encampments in British Columbia in Victoria, Vancouver, Nanaimo, Comox, and Nelson.[49]

In Victoria, the Occupy Victoria camp was established in Centennial Square, a municipally owned and operated plaza adjacent to City Hall, on October 15, 2011, an international "day of action" in solidarity with the Wall Street camp and the global movement. Initially, the civic authorities condoned – even supported – the camp and its demands for reform of the global economic system, with Victoria City Council adopting a resolution on October 27 declaring "that the City of Victoria supports the People's Assembly of Victoria in principle and practice" (a decision that coincided with a municipal election campaign and was likely indicative of sitting council members' heightened attentiveness to stakeholder concerns).[50] However, as the camp grew to about seventy tents and the campers' demographic shifted from social justice protesters to street-involved people, opposition among downtown businesses and other interest groups grew. There was also a specific conflicting claim to the municipally owned land in Centennial Square: for a "Christmas tree light-up" and other seasonal events organized by the Downtown Victoria Business Association,

FIGURE 29 Placard at Occupy Victoria protest, c. October 2011. | Tony Sprackett

under a permit issued by the city to promote holiday shopping. In the face of this pressure, and with the municipal election approaching, the City of Victoria reversed its position and applied for an injunction to remove the camp.[51]

On the eve of the November 19 municipal election, the City of Victoria's application against the People's Assembly of Victoria and the Occupy Victoria camp was heard before BC Supreme Court Justice Terence Schultes. The campers were represented by a legal team that included Victoria lawyer Rajinder Sahota, while City Solicitor Tom Zworski represented the city. Despite a formidable defence asserting that the section 2 Charter right to freedom of expression should trump promotional activities that the Downtown Victoria Business Association proposed to conduct in Centennial Square under permit from the city, Justice Schultes granted the injunction on November 18. In his decision in *Victoria (City) v Thompson,* Schultes distinguished "statutorily-based injunctions" from equitable injunctions, suggesting that judges had a very narrow degree of discretion to refuse to grant the former type of relief. Citing the BC Court of Appeal decision in *Vancouver (City) v Maurice* (2005), where Justice Rowles had declared that "the courts will refuse an injunction to restrain the continued breach only in exceptional circumstances," Schultes found that the issues raised by the Occupy Victoria respondents did not amount to "exceptional circumstances."[52] Applying the test from *RJR-MacDonald,* the judge found that "the balance of convenience dictates the petitioner should be free to come to the conclusion that any encampment, wherever and however situated in the square, is not in keeping with the best public use of that space under its delegated legislative powers." He rejected the suggestion that by granting the injunction the court was "validating the [city's] preference for mundane holiday celebrations geared to promoting downtown business over an impassioned fight for global justice." Rather, the court was "upholding the ability of a government to act in exercise of its authority to allocate public space in accordance with a bylaw, whatever its *Charter* deficiencies are found to be at the petition stage." In a concession to the Occupy Victoria protesters, Schultes refused a request from the city for an enforcement order, commending the respondents for "a praiseworthy degree of responsiveness" to the city's concerns and for conducting themselves during the hearing with "a high degree of respect for the law."[53]

However, mirroring earlier injunction proceedings against social movement actors in British Columbia, the City of Victoria did not proceed to a hearing on the merits of its court petition, meaning that the substantive Charter questions alluded to by the judge, and the raison d'être for the Occupy protest movement against inequities in the global distribution of wealth, were never fully aired in the legal arena. The court declined to consider these substantive issues at the injunction hearing, focusing instead on narrower questions relating to municipal authority to regulate use of public space. The Occupy Victoria protesters largely complied with the court's ruling, with fewer than a dozen tents (out of the original seventy) remaining by the November 19 deadline established by Schultes, followed by a final cleanup operation by city crews under police supervision on November 22.[54] With the camp gone, the Downtown Victoria Business Association proceeded unimpeded with its planned seasonal activities; with "normality" restored to the public square, the city no longer had reason to pursue the petition through the court system. The interim relief granted by the BC Supreme Court by way of the interlocutory injunction served a longer-term purpose behind the city's application – displacing the Occupy protesters and restoring "normality" to Centennial Square without the substantive issues of the civil liberties of the protesters or global distribution of wealth and power ever being properly considered in the courtroom.

A similar pattern unfolded in other communities around the province, country, and continent as municipal authorities sought and received orders from courts to remove Occupy encampments and restore normality to public spaces that had been seized by their supporters.[55] In Vancouver, the city received an injunction ordering the removal of the Occupy Vancouver camp that had been established on the grounds of the Vancouver Art Gallery, land leased by the city from the province and therefore subject to the municipal *City Land Regulation Bylaw*, following the high-profile overdose death of a woman at the camp.[56] The judge in that case, BC Supreme Court Associate Chief Justice Anne MacKenzie, suggested that the broader question relating to section 2 freedom of expression rights and other "constitutional arguments are properly examined at the trial of the matter to provide the parties sufficient time to prepare and to allow the attorney general the opportunity to intervene," rather than at the interlocutory injunction application stage.[57] However, as occurred in Victoria, these constitutional questions were never properly considered in a legal arena, since the City of Vancouver did not proceed with a trial, after the raison d'être for the legal action – removal of the camp – was achieved with the granting of the interlocutory injunction. When the Occupy Vancouver campers cheekily responded to the court order by relocating a block away from the Art Gallery to the entrance to the Vancouver Law Courts, Justice MacKenzie issued a subsequent order that the tents be removed within four hours.[58] Occupy Nanaimo, the last encampment in British Columbia associated with the global Occupy movement, was removed on December 9, 2011, after the City of Nanaimo received an injunction from BC Supreme Court Justice Catherine Wedge. The protesters, who had occupied Diana Krall Plaza outside the public library in the city centre for seven weeks, left voluntarily when city officials, armed with the injunction and backed by RCMP officers, ordered them to do so.[59] However, City Councillor Fred Pattje expressed sympathy with the protesters and their cause, declaring: "You can evict a tent, but you can't evict an idea."[60]

Toward Tentative Recognition of Positive Social Rights

As I completed research for this book over the past decade, the jurisprudence relating to urban tenting in British Columbia continued to evolve, particularly in terms of encampments involving people who are homeless, with growing legal recognition of a Charter-protected right to sleep and to shelter oneself in the absence of adequate alternative shelter, arising from the section 7 right to life, liberty, and security of the person. This process has been uneven, however, reflecting specific circumstances in each case as well as latitude in the ways in which individual judges have exercised their discretionary authority when evaluating applications for interlocutory injunctive relief, reflecting the unsettled nature of the conflicting property claims of public authorities and the constitutional rights of campers. A desire for community and security among marginalized, street-involved people in the urban centres of British Columbia underpins the ongoing phenomenon of tent cities – against the backdrop of neoliberal restructuring, which has intensified marginalization and displacement in urban areas, and a devastating opioid crisis that has taken more than eighteen thousand lives since 2016.[61]

In 2014, street-involved people in Vancouver established a large camp at Oppenheimer Park in the Downtown Eastside. The camp existed for three months, from July to October, and included assertions by Indigenous people associated with the camp challenging the city's ownership of the park, in the wake of the Supreme Court of Canada's landmark decision in the *Tsilhqot'in* case. When Vancouver Police delivered an eviction notice to the campers, they responded by serving their own eviction notice on the city, stating that the park was located on unceded Indigenous land. This prompted the traditional speaker for the Musqueam Nation, which claims downtown Vancouver as part of its territory, to visit the camp and state that while the campers were pursuing a "noble cause," it was not appropriate for anyone to use the Musqueam to further their own cause in Musqueam territory; Chief Wayne Sparrow said his nation would pursue its land claim through negotiations with the federal, provincial, and municipal governments. The Squamish and Tsleil-Waututh Nations, which also claim territory in Greater Vancouver, issued their own statements distancing their land claims from the eviction notice issued by the camp. Ed John, representing the BC First Nations Summit, said that Indigenous people were growing impatient: "It's not surprising that First Nations people would get on the land and say, 'This is our land.' Technically, they're right ... but aboriginal title is a collective interest."[62]

In September 2014, the Vancouver Parks Board applied for an injunction to remove the Oppenheimer Park camp, which had grown to nearly two hundred campers. BC Supreme Court Justice Jennifer Duncan initially provided a ten-day adjournment to allow the campers and their counsel additional time to prepare their case, but granted the injunction after the hearing in early October. She conceded that litigation of injunctive relief had evolved to favour "an approach which takes into account Charter issues rather than the consideration of a pure statutory breach," but ruled that the balance of convenience under both the *Thornhill* and *RJR-MacDonald* tests favoured the granting of an interlocutory injunction to the Parks Board.[63] On October 16, 2014, Vancouver Police and Parks Board employees moved in to dismantle the camp; five holdout campers in two tents were arrested for breach of the court order, but no charges were laid, with police saying they had no interest in criminalizing the campers.[64]

Ongoing tensions relating to urban encampments were also manifested in the Fraser Valley of the Lower Mainland, a culturally conservative area often immune from social movement protests. In October 2015, Chief Justice Christopher Hinkson of the BC Supreme Court struck down sections of a bylaw in the city of Abbotsford that prohibited overnight sheltering by people who are homeless. This decision marked the culmination of several years of tensions between municipal officials and street-involved people associated with the BC/Yukon Association of Drug War Survivors and represented by the Vancouver-based Pivot Legal Society (a nonprofit advocacy firm focused on poverty law). The municipal response to homelessness and sheltering in Abbotsford parks had had an ugly edge, reflecting reactionary attitudes in that community and a staunchly conservative mayor and council. In one notorious incident, a municipal parks manager ordered his staff to spread chicken manure in a park where people who were homeless were known to seek shelter. In another incident, parks and bylaw staff slashed tents and used bear spray in a bid to disperse campers.[65] In his decision in *Abbotsford (City) v Shantz*, Chief Justice Hinkson displayed a strong compassionate tone, noting that

> constant movement of the homeless exacerbated their already vulnerable positions, as it inhibited the ability of the service providers who endeavoured to help the City's homeless to actually locate them and provide help. I thus find that the evidence supports a finding that the Impugned Bylaws have had a serious effect on the psychological or physical integrity of the City's homeless.[66]

The *Shantz* decision built on the foundation established in *Adams* in important ways, extending the court's recognition that legal weight should be afforded to the health and well-being of persons who are homeless, and elaborating on how the section 7 right to security of the person specifically translates on the ground into the conditions faced by street-involved people.

This compassionate approach toward the rights of people who are homeless, and nuanced attention to the specific needs of individuals experiencing multiple barriers to housing and health and social challenges, including addictions, was sustained by Chief Justice Hinkson in *British Columbia v Adamson*. In that April 2016 decision, the BC Supreme Court refused an application from the Province of British Columbia for an injunction to displace an encampment consisting of approximately eighty tents and one hundred people on the grounds of the provincial courthouse in downtown Victoria. The case was highly charged with symbolism and immediacy – being heard in a courtroom immediately adjacent to the impugned encampment, which had been entrenched for about five months. Several dozen campers, represented by counsel Catherine Boies Parker and Jasmine MacAdam of the Farris law firm, with financial support provided by the nonprofit Together Against Poverty Society (TAPS), were permitted to directly address the court. Chief Justice Hinkson granted the defendant campers considerable latitude in their verbal submissions, appearing to recognize the multiple and persistent barriers experienced by street-involved people, including mental health and addictions issues. His ruling in *Adamson* sustained the strong element of compassion toward the plight and rights of people who are homeless:

> Ultimately, in determining whether or not to grant an interim injunction at this time, I find that the balance of convenience is overwhelmingly in favour of the defendants, who simply have nowhere to move to, if the injunction were to issue, other than shelters that are incapable of meeting the needs of some of them, or will result in their constant disruption and a perpetuation of a relentless series of daily moves to the streets, doorways, and parks of the City of Victoria.[67]

Adamson went much further than *Adams* in recognizing inadequacies in the emergency shelter system, which often exclude the highest-need individuals, particularly those with addictions issues, and provide inadequate accommodations for couples, people with pets, and other specific demographic groups. In this respect, Hinkson expanded in *Adamson* on his compassionate approach in *Shantz* – suggesting a growing legal recognition of the section 7 right to security of the person that is capable of trumping the assertion of property rights by public institutions – at least at the interlocutory stage, where the balance of convenience is increasingly seen as favouring the rights of people who are homeless to shelter themselves in the absence of adequate alternative shelter. While Hinkson ultimately granted an injunction to the provincial government (when the province applied again three months later), ordering the Victoria Courthouse campers to leave, he suspended its application for more than a month, with the court order "to take effect as soon as new housing created by the Province became available."[68] The provincial government ultimately acquired more than two hundred new units of social housing to meet the conditions established by the chief justice for injunctive relief, purchasing a vacant hotel and a seniors' care home to house the courthouse campers in accordance with a detailed formula established in Hinkson's ruling – breaking new ground in the jurisprudence of tenting and homeless encampments in British Columbia.[69]

The emerging line of jurisprudence in *Adams, Shantz*, and *Adamson* was sustained a year after the Victoria Courthouse encampment litigation, when BC Supreme Court Justice Neena Sharma declined an application from the City of Vancouver for an injunction to disband a homeless camp at a vacant lot on Main Street owned by the city. The parcel, which had been unoccupied for two decades save for a brief homeless encampment a decade earlier, was slated for development for a non-market housing project. In April 2017, homeless people and their allies breached a chain-link fence surrounding the site and established an encampment. The city applied to the BC Supreme Court for an injunction to remove the camp. In a hearing on May 17, counsel for the city pointed to the fact that in previous instances of homeless encampments on municipal land, the city had exercised restraint, suspending action for injunctive relief until such time that the encampment had become unsafe. However, in the case of the Main Street camp, counsel said that the city expedited action to clear the camp because of the pending housing project. Justice Sharma was not convinced of the urgency of the city's application or the avowed risk to funding sources, and accepted arguments by the homeless campers and their

FIGURE 30 Victoria Courthouse encampment, April 2016. Chief Justice Christopher Hinkson of the BC Supreme Court refused to grant an injunction to the provincial government to displace the unhoused people sheltering there, on the grounds that they "simply have nowhere to move to." Three months later, after the province had procured two hundred new units of transitional housing, Hinkson granted an injunction ordering the dismantling of the camp, while suspending its application until the new housing was ready for occupancy. | Darren Stone, *Times Colonist*

advocates that displacing the camp would compromise their safety. Following Chief Justice Hinkson's reasoning in *Adamson,* Sharma found that the City of Vancouver failed to meet the test in *RJR-MacDonald,* with the balance of convenience favouring the homeless persons who were occupying the site rather than the municipality that held title to the land.[70] Describing the ruling as a "very positive development," advocate Maria Wallstam from the Alliance Against Displacement stated: "Part of our argument was that displacing the tent city would jeopardize the Charter right of homeless people to security and liberty, and we won. For now."[71] The trend continued in subsequent years. Other BC Supreme Court judges demonstrated reluctance to issue orders displacing street-involved persons sheltering on municipally owned land in Nanaimo, Maple Ridge, and Prince George, in the absence of alternative indoor housing options.[72]

During the COVID-19 pandemic, as homeless encampments emerged in dozens of BC communities, the provincial government and municipal governments largely abided by the principle that Justice Hinkson had established in the Victoria Courthouse encampment case: that indoor sheltering options should be provided prior to displacement. In Victoria, the Provincial Rental Housing Corporation purchased and leased a half-dozen properties to create transitional and permanent housing for approximately four hundred street-involved people as a preliminary step to enforcement of COVID-era ministerial orders and municipal bylaws disbanding homeless camps in municipal parks and rights-of-way. While the Pivot Legal Society objected to the ministerial orders as "a misuse of the emergency powers" (by pursuing an "enforcement-based decampment plan" under the guise of responding to a health emergency), the provincial government's efforts to secure indoor transitional housing largely deterred legal challenges.[73] In Victoria, dozens of encampments have been disbanded since 2020, with only one formal legal challenge brought on behalf of homeless persons displaced from a camp (arising from amendments to the city's *Parks Regulation Bylaw* in 2024 that further restrained overnight sheltering, with the outcome of that judicial review petition pending at the time of publication).[74]

Conclusion

Do the Victoria Courthouse litigation in *Adamson* and subsequent case law suggest a widening ambit of a positive right to housing in Canada? In the 2008 *Adams* decision, BC Supreme Court Justice Carol Ross did not rule on the question of whether the section 7 Charter right to shelter conferred a positive obligation on government to provide access to housing. Since the defendants in that case had not sought positive benefits – that is, were "not seeking to have the City compelled to provide the homeless with adequate shelter" – Ross ruled that it was "not necessary for the Court to consider whether s. 7 includes a positive right to the provision of shelter."[75] In 2014, the Ontario Court of Appeal, in the case *Tanudjaja v Canada (Attorney General)*, upheld a lower court ruling that found that sections 7 and 15 of the Charter do not impose a positive obligation on the provincial and federal governments to provide a comprehensive housing program. The Superior Court judge ruled that jurisprudence relating to those sections of the Charter had been largely confined to rectifying specific breaches of rights by institutions, rather than imposing broader obligations relating to comprehensive public policy and access to social services. The appellate panel confined its decision to a narrow question of whether the judge had made any errors in law in disallowing the action, and therefore avoided serious consideration of the substantive issue of whether a positive right to housing exists. However, the Court of Appeal conceded that the Supreme Court of Canada had left the door "slightly ajar" in the case of *Gosselin v Quebec (Attorney General)* (2002) on the question of "the extent to which positive obligations may be imposed on government to remedy violations of the Charter."[76]

The line of jurisprudence in *Adamson* (2016), building on the *Adams* (2008 and 2009) and *Shantz* (2015) decisions, suggests that the BC judiciary has recognized a positive (if limited) right to housing at common law, existing where a public authority seeks a court order to prevent people who are homeless from sheltering themselves. Arising from the principle recognized in *Adams* that a blanket prohibition on sheltering by homeless persons infringes their section 7 Charter right in the absence of adequate shelter, the court found in *Adamson* that the balance of convenience in granting an injunction will not be satisfied unless the state can demonstrate that adequate alternative sheltering arrangements exist, with consideration given to the distinct needs and challenges of individuals requiring sheltering, including barriers in the existing housing and sheltering system. This represents an important evolution of Canadian law, moving beyond the traditional "negative liberties" protected in the *Canadian Bill of Rights* (1960) and later the Charter, toward imposing positive obligations on the state to support the social needs of citizens.[77] Whether this line of jurisprudence represents a temporary or limited development, or whether it will become firmly rooted and expand to other social contexts beyond urban homeless encampments, remains to be seen. As Sarah Hamill suggested (with reference to the *Adams* case in British Columbia and Occupy litigation in Ontario), the judiciary continues to adhere to "an understanding of property which assumes private property to be the dominant model," lacking a robust understanding of common property.[78]

Notwithstanding these uncertainties and limitations, my view is that judicial responses to urban tent cities in twenty-first-century British Columbia demonstrate an important shift in the pattern of property, protest, and the law in the province. Courts (or at least a number of judges) appear to be moving beyond overly rigid and narrow conceptions of the rule of law when considering injunction applications from public property managers, to recognize and place proper weight on customary and constitutional claims to public property by poor people. These customary and constitutional claims to public property are increasingly found to outweigh conventional property claims at the interlocutory stage, defeating attempts by property managers to obtain injunctions to displace the homeless campers.

In my opinion, this shift may signal the beginning of a remapping of the legal geography of protest and urban spaces in British Columbia – a relaxing of the judiciary's traditional approach to property, injunctions, and contempt proceedings, and a corresponding diminution of legal technologies traditionally available to conventional property interests to defeat protests involving the control or appropriation of space. To be sure, the case law surrounding tent cities suggests that judges are much more receptive to claims asserted by people who are homeless, invoking section 7 Charter rights to security of the person, than they are to section 2 rights to freedom of expression and assembly asserted by other protest groups, when determining whether the balance of convenience favours the granting of injunctions to public authorities to displace encampments. But even the latter instances of free-speech protests, particularly in the *Zhang* case and to an extent in the Occupy cases, reflect a widening ambit for customary and constitutional claims to property, and a corresponding narrowing of legal recognition of property claims by public entities. This rebalancing of the power and interests of social movement actors and conventional owners and managers of property in the legal arena holds out the promise of sidestepping some of the crises of law's legitimacy that accompanied earlier episodes of protest in British Columbia's legal history – by demonstrating to social movement actors that the law can deliver social, as well as formal, justice.

CONCLUSION

Commenting on the relationship in Canadian law between private rights and public expression, including the right to protest, Justice Beverley McLachlin suggested in the 1996 Supreme Court of Canada decision in the Clayoquot Sound case of *MacMillan Bloedel Ltd v Simpson* that "the task of the courts is to find a way to protect the legitimate exercise of lawful private rights while preserving maximum scope for the lawful exercise of the right of expression and protest."[1]

Throughout British Columbia's legal history, judges and other members of the legal community have struggled to strike an appropriate balance between private and public rights when confronted with protests – in the face of competing claims to property and competing conceptions of space – between customary and constitutional claims of social movement actors on the one hand, and more conventional private property claims on the other. For much of the past century, legal actors sided disproportionately with private interests, deploying injunctions and other legal remedies to defeat customary claims to property and buttress private claims. This frequently provoked crises of legal legitimacy, where social movement actors who found themselves on the receiving end of law's coercive powers questioned the impartiality of judges and the fairness of adjudicative procedures. These crises exposed divergent understandings of the "legal and social zones of toleration" within which protest occurs, and the contested "power-geometry" of public and private rights to property.[2]

More recently, however, this pattern has become blurred, as some judges and other members of the legal community have demonstrated a greater openness to unconventional property claims, striving for a more meaningful balance. This shift has been influenced by the evolution of Indigenous and Aboriginal law, recognition of constitutional rights and human rights enshrined in the *Canadian Charter of Rights and Freedoms*, and assertions of other forms of customary rights. Changes in the composition of the legal profession and judiciary, reflecting changing societal attitudes and representation of more diverse social, cultural, and ideological constituencies, may also be contributing to this shift. The emerging jurisprudence suggests a growing contingency in legal recognition of private property rights when challenged by social movement actors, and a greater openness by legal actors to recognize customary property claims – revealing the emergence of an increasingly liminal legal space in adjudication of disputes between private property interests and social movements over the control and use of space. While this shift has been uneven, inconsistent, and limited in its application, it demonstrates an evolution of the pattern of property, social movements, and the law in British Columbia.

Discerning the Pattern of Property, Social Movements, and the Law

The legal technology deployed in response to social movement challenges to property interests in British Columbia developed primarily in the labour context – for example, in response to picket lines by striking workers barring access to workplaces in order to wield collective bargaining power and advance collective rights to the fruits of production. In the early twentieth century, legal responses to labour protests often relied on the criminal law and proscriptions against rioting, unlawful assemblies, and conspiracies in restraint of trade, informed by residual elements of the common law of master and servant. It was these kinds of charges that accompanied the arrests and imprisonment of two hundred striking coal miners during the "Vancouver Island War" of 1912–14, after the strikers blockaded the entrance to pitheads, attacked company property, and interfered with movement of replacement workers into and out of the mines, prompting deployment of soldiers in "Aid to the Civil Power" to occupy the island coalfields and enforce martial law.

Later in the twentieth century, particularly in the decades following the Second World War, the legal technology shifted from the *Criminal Code* to the equitable remedy of civil injunctions and contempt of court proceedings. It was in this labour context that the modern law of injunctions and contempt became largely settled in British Columbia. The indiscriminate granting of injunctions against striking workers – with more than two hundred injunctions granted by judges in *ex parte* proceedings in the 1950s and 1960s (without unions having knowledge or representation at the hearings) – contributed toward a widely held perception in labour circles that the judiciary was biased in favour of industry and against workers, provoking demands for reform. In the 1970s, this pressure bore fruit with legislative action when the New Democratic Party government of Dave Barrett responded to working-class demands by introducing far-reaching amendments to the province's labour laws that transferred most jurisdiction to grant injunctions during labour disputes away from the courts and to a reformed Labour Relations Board. The changing legal responses to labour protests demonstrated the contested nature of space, and how property owners and social movement actors appealed to an array of legal actors to buttress their own conceptions of the proper organization, use, and control of space and property.

Moving toward the end of the twentieth century, the locus of legal clashes between social movement actors and property interests shifted again, toward Indigenous blockades, at Wah-nah-jus Hilth-hoo-is (Meares Island) in Clayoquot Sound, at Tllga Kun Gwaayaay (Athlii Gwaii/Lyell Island) in Haida Gwaii, and at Ts'Peten (Gustafsen Lake) in the BC interior. These clashes highlighted assertions of Indigenous rights to land and resources, representing a fundamental challenge to private property interests recognized by colonial legal institutions. The protests triggered a range of legal responses – from injunctions and contempt charges on Lyell Island, to *Criminal Code* convictions against the armed sovereigntists at Ts'Peten, to legislative action in the form of treaty making and other measures to give effect to assertions of Indigenous rights – as demonstrated in British Columbia's and Canada's voluntary recognition of Haida title in 2025. Importantly, the decision of Justice Peter Seaton and two fellow judges of the BC Court of Appeal to grant an injunction to the Nuu-chah-nulth chiefs restraining logging operations by MacMillan Bloedel Ltd. in the Meares Island case (1985), on the basis that Crown land in the company's Tree Farm Licence was "subject to certain Indian rights," demonstrated an important shift in the legal landscape governing protests in the province – from steadfast adherence to private property rights narrowly conceived toward an appreciation of the legitimacy of customary and constitutional claims to property by Indigenous peoples and social movement actors.[3]

My approach to customary rights and recognition of competing property claims in this book draws from E.P. Thompson's interpretive lens in *Whigs and Hunters* (1975) and *Customs in Commons* (1991): it is less a question of popular forces arrayed *against* the law, but rather a question of whose conception of the law, and whose claims to rights, property, and space, will prevail in deliberations of members of the legal community and state actors.[4] Or, as

David Harvey suggested in *Rebel Cities* (2012): "We inevitably have to confront the question of whose rights are being identified ... The definition of the right is itself an object of struggle."[5]

This process of recognition of customary and constitutional claims to property and public space, and the corresponding narrowing of the legal ambit of conventional private property claims, has been uneven and inconsistent.[6] This was apparent as the environmental movement emerged as a major locus of clashes with property interests and authority in the closing decades of twentieth-century British Columbia. Repression rather than recognition remained the dominant pattern. While the courts had granted the injunction to the Nuu-chah-nulth chiefs to restrain logging on Meares Island in 1985, protests over logging of old-growth rainforest elsewhere in Clayoquot Sound on Vancouver Island resulted in the arrests of 900 people in the early 1990s on charges of criminal contempt of court for defying injunctions granted to MacMillan Bloedel – the largest act of civil disobedience resulting in arrests to that point in Canadian history. In the Clayoquot trials, the courts imposed stiff penalties against 626 people convicted of criminal contempt for challenging the property interests of the logging company, which held a licence to extract timber from the Crown forest lands. Ecological claims to the forest resources by non-Indigenous people were less likely to attract legal recognition by the courts than Indigenous claims to those resources asserted by the chiefs of the Tla-o-qui-aht and Ahousaht Nations in the Meares Island case.

Environmental road blockades in the twenty-first century, including the major clash at Fairy Creek on Vancouver Island in 2020–21, displayed the familiar pattern of repression rather than recognition from members of the legal community – until BC Supreme Court Justice Douglas Thompson boldly refused to extend a court injunction in September 2021, after more than 1,100 people had been arrested (a decision later reversed by the BC Court of Appeal).[7] Noting "serious and substantial infringement of civil liberties ... in the name of enforcing this Court's order," Thompson chose to "get the Court out from the middle of this dispute, and let the government and police do what they will with the tools at their disposal," favouring criminal law remedies over equitable injunctive relief. He stated that the public interest in preserving the court's reputation outweighed potential harm to the logging company – seeking to avert a crisis of legitimacy arising from further enforcement of the court order.[8] Justice Thompson's subsequent decision in February 2023 to acquit Fairy Creek protester Ryan Henderson based on a strict interpretation of the notice requirements for criminal contempt was consistent with this changing jurisprudence. It demonstrated the shift away from a narrow approach to the law of injunctions and contempt, grounded in a singular focus on private property interests, toward a broader and less orthodox appreciation of the rule of law in protest cases. Henderson's acquittal triggered the collapse of the Crown's cases against half of the approximately 350 blockaders facing prosecution, when the Supreme Court of Canada refused to hear a Crown appeal.

The question of whether public order should be maintained by injunctions or by the ordinary operation of the *Criminal Code* had been raised a generation earlier, by BC Court of Appeal Justice Mary Southin, in response to picketing by an atypical social movement – the conservative "right-to-life" movement, which challenged women's access to abortion services in the wake of the Supreme Court of Canada's 1988 decision striking down Canada's anti-abortion law.[9] While the anti-abortion picketers initially succeeded in asserting a Charter-protected right to freedom of expression and assembly in the vicinity of abortion clinics, defeating attempts by abortion providers to restrain picketing, the reluctance of the judiciary to protect access to abortion services prompted intervention by the cabinet and Legislative Assembly of British Columbia, in the form of the *Access to Abortion Services Act* of 1995. Notwithstanding constitutional challenges to the validity of this legislation, the courts ultimately upheld the "Bubble Law" as a reasonable incursion on freedom of expression to safeguard the conflicting Charter right of women to security of the person and sovereignty over their bodies. Despite the diverse socio-political contexts, these episodes demonstrate legal interventions to curb social movement claims to public space. More recently, further statutory restrictions on protest have been imposed around education and health facilities in response to protests over government policies concerning the COVID-19 pandemic and transgender inclusion.[10]

Against the backdrop of enduring judicial support for conventional property claims, an emerging pattern of jurisprudence can be discerned. In some cases, the courts have demonstrated a growing inclination to recognize customary and constitutional claims to property and public space, and a growing reluctance to hastily authorize law's coercive powers in aid to property interests challenged by social movement actors. This is particularly notable in the emerging jurisprudence on "the right to sleep" – the phenomenon of urban tent cities and poor people's movements appropriating public spaces in British Columbia's towns and cities to challenge public policy and assert a constitutional "right to shelter," attracting injunctions and other legal responses. The line of jurisprudence established in the *Adams, Shantz,* and *Adamson* cases suggests that the courts are increasingly unwilling to recognize property interests asserted by governments to unilaterally regulate public spaces when these regulations are found to unreasonably infringe the Charter-protected right of street-involved people to life, liberty, and security of the person.[11]

Illustrating this emerging pattern in clear terms, a homeless encampment was permitted to operate on the grounds of the provincial courthouse in Victoria for nine months in 2015 and 2016 despite strident opposition from the landowner, the BC government. The dispute revealed the way in which recognition of legally protected Charter rights can translate into the provision of positive social rights (which have hitherto been rarely recognized in Canadian law): the Victoria Courthouse encampment litigation provided sufficient legal leverage to the homeless campers to compel the provincial government to procure several hundred units of social housing to meet the threshold established by the chief justice of the BC Supreme Court for the granting of an injunction. This pattern was repeated during the COVID-19 pandemic: the BC government responded to tent cities in the provincial capital by acquiring and converting a half-dozen motels into "transitional housing," disbanding homeless encampments in a manner capable of withstanding potential Charter challenges. As the foregoing discussion makes clear, the legal technology of coercion in British Columbia has been deployed in diverse social contexts, demonstrating continuity and adaptation over time.

The law of property and the equitable remedy of the injunction and subsequent contempt of court proceedings have figured prominently in this book. So too have the politics of the judiciary and other legal institutions, and debates over law's legitimacy and the relative fairness of the courts, judges, police, and parliaments when adjudicating disputes between property interests and social movement actors. My research was originally grounded in the role of judges in the adjudicative process, but expanded to focus more broadly on "the legal community," recognizing that judges are often not the motive force in legal actions against protesters. Indeed, legal counsel for property owners are usually the driving force in injunction proceedings, initiating the civil claim and invoking familiar and time-tested legal remedies to protect their clients' interests and curb social movement challenges. As we have seen, this legal community has extended at times beyond lawyers and judges to include parliament as a legal institution as well as the military as a mechanism for enforcing legal authority. So this study not only maps the geography of protest but also the geography of the British Columbia legal community and how it has changed over time – illuminating the contested social relations of adjudication.

Theoretically, this book has engaged a diverse, interdisciplinary literature, including the fields of critical geography and legal geography pioneered by Doreen Massey and Nicholas Blomley as well as works on regulation of public space and the "right to the city." This body of scholarship views space and the law as contested and demarcated by class interests, with antecedents in the critical historiographic tradition of Edward Thompson and others. The spatial lens also locates this book in the field of "spatial history" – exploring connections and linkages between space and time, and ways in which the use, regulation, and control of space have been contested and conceptualized historically. Decolonization studies and postcolonial theory also informed my approach to competing property claims, particularly as it relates to overlapping authority between customary Indigenous law and settler colonial law.

Reforming Legal Responses to Protest

In 1937, then labour lawyer (and future chief justice of Canada) Bora Laskin provided a summary of some of the principal criticisms of the law of injunctions at the time:

> The complaints that have been levied against the injunction, particularly of the interlocutory type, may be shortly summarised: (1) They are granted upon affidavit evidence; there is no examination and cross-examination of witnesses or the careful sifting of facts, but the judge, sitting without a jury, is asked to choose between conflicting documentary statements, in which both sides strain the truth, to say the least; (2) They are prepared by the complainant's counsel and accepted by the court with very little ceremony; (3) They prejudge the issues involved in a dispute by acting as strikebreakers; (4) They are couched in broad language and in such far-reaching terms that they implant a fear in men more potent than does the criminal law; (5) They endow the owner of a business or of property with a militant power, little short of sovereignty; (6) They place the judiciary, so far as the labourer is concerned, in the ranks of the employers; (7) They arouse a resentment and antagonism that often leads to active violence where there was none before; (8) They circumscribe union activity far beyond the needs of the particular case; (9) They generally issue ex parte, and quite perfunctorily, on a false analogy to cases involving real property, in which, on occasion, prompt action may well be necessary.[12]

Many of these grievances remain as relevant today as they were when Laskin provided this commentary in the 1930s. In the intervening period, criticism of injunctions has not been confined to labour circles. As noted in Chapter 2, Vancouver lawyer (and future BC Supreme Court and Court of Appeal justice) Mary Southin, who had run for public office under the Progressive Conservative banner, discussed the functioning of injunctions in a 1970 article in *The Advocate:*

> *Ex parte* injunctions or injunctions on such short notice that they are in reality *ex parte* injunctions are still being granted. If somebody is served at midnight to be in Court at 10.00 a.m. the next morning what real opportunity has his Counsel to prepare? Short notice where there is evidence of violence or apprehended violence or damage to property is one thing; short notice where the employer simply says he is losing money, even a lot of money, is another.
>
> It should not be overlooked that when an injunction is granted on no notice or notice so short as to be derisory the men do not think they had a fair hearing and that reinforces their feelings of being victims of judicial bias ...
>
> Nor in my view should any *ex parte* injunction or injunction on short notice be granted with liberty to apply to set aside. All *ex parte* injunctions and if counsel requests, those granted on short notice should be to a day certain with liberty to the Plaintiff to move to continue. That puts the burden where it belongs: on the Plaintiff to show upon a full hearing that it is entitled to what it seeks.[13]

While much of the jurisdiction to grant injunctions during labour disputes was transferred from the courts to the Labour Relations Board in the 1970s, reflecting successful political lobbying by the labour movement, similar institutional reforms and "pressure-release valves" with respect to Indigenous and environmental protests have not occurred. Demands for reform to procedures governing the use of injunctions are not confined to Canada. US magistrate Morton Denlaw suggested in a 2003 essay that a uniform standard for the application of injunctions is "long overdue," creating much greater certainty for judges, courts, and parties to disputes.[14]

Turning to the law of contempt, which frequently intersects with the law of injunctions, the Law Reform Commission of Canada waded into the controversy surrounding the common-law offence of criminal contempt of court in a report in the 1970s. Citing "the potential loss in public respect for the judicial system," the commission advised the Crown to pursue charges only where the infraction was "deliberate, open, public and an evident challenge to the judicial system or an obstruction of justice. All other cases should be dealt with as civil contempt under the rules of practice of the courts or the rules of civil procedure."[15] As the only remaining common-law crime in Canadian law (preserved pursuant to section 9 of the *Criminal Code*) contempt prosecutions lack the procedural safeguards and structural transparency that attach to other criminal offences.

The law is also evolving as it pertains to permissible defences available to people accused of contempt of court for protests that interfere with property rights. In March 2018, a US District Court judge in Massachusetts found that thirteen protesters charged with obstructing construction of a gas pipeline (including the daughter of former US vice president Al Gore) were not responsible, after the accused raised the defence of necessity in relation to climate change.[16] While the defence of necessity has been rejected in several court cases involving social movement protest in British Columbia, including cases of anti-abortion picketers in the 1980s, anti-logging environmentalists in the 1990s, and climate change protesters in the 2020s, Judge Mary Ann Driscoll of West Roxbury District Court was persuaded by the anti-pipeline protesters' arguments. Her decision was celebrated by environmentalists in British Columbia engaged in the fight against the Trans Mountain pipeline expansion.[17] Whether this decision of a lower court in the United States on a misdemeanour charge represents a legal blip, or whether the defence of necessity will gain legal strength in British Columbia and other jurisdictions in the face of intensifying climate and ecological crises, remains to be seen.[18]

* * *

What is the future trajectory of the pattern of property, social movements, and the law in British Columbia? One is left to speculate on whether the ambit of customary and constitutional rights tentatively recognized by the courts and other legal actors will widen and become settled over time, or whether recognition of "the commons" in some recent injunction decisions is merely a limited and temporary aberration, with supremacy of private rights prevailing and remaining firmly rooted. It is my strong hope that the social relations of adjudication are changing and that the emerging pattern will widen and prevail – that the liminal legal space afforded to customary and constitutional rights is becoming a "new norm," and that members of the legal community will place increasing weight on nonconventional assertions of rights when evaluating and adjudicating competing claims to property, power, and public space.

AFTERWORD

As I was researching and writing this book, three major protest movements emerged at the confluence of Indigenous, ecological, and private property claims to use of Crown land in British Columbia: the controversies over (1) the Trans Mountain pipeline, (2) the Coastal GasLink pipeline, and (3) the old-growth rainforests near Fairy Creek on Vancouver Island. As these controversies wound their way through the settler legal system, I obtained a licence to practice law as a barrister and solicitor in British Columbia in 2022. I was subsequently retained as defence counsel by approximately eighty of the Trans Mountain and Fairy Creek land defenders, representing them in proceedings before the BC Supreme Court, BC Court of Appeal, and Supreme Court of Canada.

All three movements involved assertions of customary claims to space and property in the form of blockades, encampments, and occupations, while the corporations that held licences and permits to use the Crown land initiated civil claims in BC Supreme Court and obtained injunctions prohibiting inference with their operations. Large-scale policing operations ensued to enforce the court orders, spearheaded by a new paramilitary unit of the RCMP with a mandate to "address the resource development industry and public order activities": the Community-Industry Response Group (C-IRG, since branded as the Critical Response Unit, or CRU).[1] According to a briefing from RCMP commissioner Brenda Lucki to Canada's minister of public safety, Ralph Goodale, in May 2018, creation of the C-IRG and the wider RCMP response to protests were influenced by several factors, including 472 "major resource projects" anticipated for the next decade and "organized consolidation of environmental groups and individuals," "involvement of professional activists from foreign organizations," "integration and sharing of tactics with other protest groups," "rapid adaption to police tactics and exploitation of gaps," and "use of secure social media and other communications channels to plan actions."[2]

Enforcement of the Trans Mountain, Coastal GasLink and Fairy Creek injunctions have resulted in numerous arrests and subsequent contempt proceedings since 2014: approximately four hundred arrests in the Trans Mountain dispute, more than seventy-five arrests in the Coastal GasLink dispute, and nearly twelve hundred arrests at Fairy Creek. Policing methods in response to all three movements, and judicial intervention in the form of the injunctions and contempt proceedings, occasioned crises of legal legitimacy, with the land defenders and their allies accusing police, prosecutors, and judges of intervening unfairly on behalf of the companies. The Coastal GasLink controversy – and C-IRG enforcement operations in Wet'suwet'en territory in central British Columbia – triggered sympathy blockades in early 2020 that paralyzed rail lines and ports across Canada and triggered a protracted encampment (and one-day blockade) at the BC legislature.

The Trans Mountain conflict arose from permits issued by the National Energy Board of Canada (NEB, now the Canada Energy Regulator) to the petroleum transmission company Kinder Morgan (now the Government of Canada–owned Trans Mountain Pipeline ULC) to replace and double the capacity of the Trans Mountain Pipeline to expand shipment of crude oil and other products from the Alberta tar sands, through British Columbia, to Burrard Inlet for export to overseas markets and domestic use.

In 2014, the City of Burnaby challenged a preliminary NEB regulatory decision authorizing site investigation work on municipal land in the vicinity of Burnaby Mountain. The city sought a statutory injunction pursuant to section 274 of the *Community Charter* to prevent Trans Mountain employees from carrying out work in Burnaby in contravention of municipal bylaws. In its petition to the court, the city asserted a legal right to be consulted before the energy company began site investigation on its land. BC Supreme Court Justice B.J. Brown denied the city's application, recognizing the exclusive jurisdiction of the federal government, acting through the NEB, to govern activities relating to interprovincial energy infrastructure. The judge further stated that the harm Burnaby alleged it would suffer if an injunction were not granted – loss of trees and an inability to enforce its own bylaws – did not satisfy the threshold for irreparable harm.[3]

Figure 31 Rueben George, Amy George, Grand Chief Stewart Phillip, and Chief Na'Moks lead a march of Indigenous and non-Indigenous people opposed to the Trans Mountain Pipeline Expansion Project, Burnaby, November 27, 2014. | Mychaylo Prystupa

Figure 32 RCMP officers arrest a person for breaching a court order prohibiting interference with construction of the Trans Mountain Pipeline Expansion Project, Burnaby, November 2014. | Jonathan Hayward, Canadian Press

As in previous protest movements, citizens responded to the perceived failure of formal legal remedies by obstructing mobility, establishing a blockade on Burnaby Mountain to challenge the pipeline project. Kinder Morgan responded by obtaining an injunction barring interference with its operations, asserting a private property right to use the municipal land arising from its federal permit.[4] The RCMP responded by enforcing Kinder Morgan's injunction, arresting more than one hundred people, including Grand Chief Stewart Phillip of the Union of British Columbia Indian Chiefs (UBCIC) and elders and members from the Tsleil-Waututh Nation, in whose unceded territory the oil terminal is located.[5] Many of those arrested were charged with civil contempt of court. Within a week of the arrests, however, Justice Austin Cullen directed counsel for the pipeline company to vacate the contempt charges after it came to light that Kinder Morgan had based its injunction application on inaccurate geographic information, with GPS coordinates designating an area that was completely outside the protest and drilling site. "Contempt, of course, must be strictly proven to a criminal standard of proof, that is, proof beyond a reasonable doubt, whether it is proceeded with civilly or criminally," Justice Cullen noted.[6] Though grounded in this legal technicality, the decision was celebrated as a victory by opponents of Trans Mountain, as Kinder Morgan proceeded to dismantle its infrastructure and abandon the test site.

In November 2016, however, the Government of Canada gave conditional approval to the pipeline project, and in an extraordinary move in May 2018, it announced that it was purchasing the pipeline from Kinder Morgan for $4.5 billion after the company said the risks were too great to proceed in the face of opposition from Indigenous peoples, environmentalists, and the Government of British Columbia.[7] The company had embarked on preliminary construction activities along the pipeline route and in the vicinity of the Burrard Inlet terminal, provoking a fresh round of civil disobedience by Indigenous and non-Indigenous people, a renewed injunction, and more than two hundred arrests (including Green Party leader and Member of Parliament Elizabeth May).[8] A total of 196 of the accused were convicted of criminal contempt of court, including a half-dozen contemnors who received jail sentences of between fourteen and twenty-eights days (sentences that were upheld by the BC Court of Appeal). May, a licensed lawyer, was fined $1,500 rather than $500 requested by the Crown, with Justice Kenneth Affleck, who had issued the original injunction, finding that "her punishment for criminal contempt must be greater than that of persons who do not hold positions of authority and influence."[9]

In yet another legal turn, the Federal Court of Appeal quashed the federal government's approval of the pipeline in August 2018, finding in favour of

Indigenous groups who asserted they had been inadequately consulted. This prompted a second round of public consultations, culminating in the Government of Canada's decision to once again approve the pipeline in June 2019.[10] The UBCIC lambasted the decision as "a lackadaisical and irresponsible approach to combatting climate change and recognizing the human rights of Indigenous people."[11] In contrast, former Bank of Canada governor David Dodge warned that people would die in the ensuing protests but that the project must proceed.[12] The Federal Court of Appeal upheld the Government of Canada's fresh approval of the pipeline, and the Supreme Court of Canada affirmed this decision by refusing to hear an appeal from the Squamish Nation, the Tsleil-Waututh Nation, and the Coldwater Indian Band.[13]

Further protests, arrests, and contempt prosecutions ensued. Nine people were arrested in October 2020 in connection with a "sacred fire" near Kamloops in Secwépemc territory as the company prepared to drill under the Snek'w7étkwe (Thompson River), resulting in eight convictions and sentences ranging from twenty-eight to thirty-two days in jail (several appeals are ongoing at the time of publication).[14] A number of arrests also occurred throughout 2020 and 2021 in connection with encampments and blockades near a Coast Salish *kwekwecnewtxw* (watch house) on Burnaby Mountain and "tree-sit" protests along the Barnet River in Burnaby. Sentences escalated for these later contempts, reaching ninety days in jail for Anishinaabe land defender Stacy Gallagher after he was convicted of a second breach of the Trans Mountain injunction (a decision upheld by the BC Court of Appeal in 2024).[15]

The escalating sentences appear to have had a deterrent effect on the Trans Mountain direct action movement. Obstructive protests largely tapered off after 2021, at the same time that the Government of Canada ramped up efforts to complete the project, clearing a fifty-metre-wide corridor from the Alberta border to Burrard Inlet adjacent to the existing pipeline. By May 2024, the new twinned pipeline was substantially completed, commencing commercial operations with an expanded capacity of 300,000 to 890,000 barrels per day – even as unprecedented wildfires erupted across British Columbia in the context of the intensifying climate crisis.[16] Canada ultimately spent more than $34 billion purchasing and constructing the pipeline.

With respect to controversy surrounding construction of the Coastal GasLink pipeline from the gas fields of northeastern British Columbia to the North Coast at Kitimat, continuity rather than change was also the dominant pattern when Wet'suwet'en peoples and their allies challenged licences issued by the BC government beginning in 2019. As noted in Chapter 5, the pipeline company, a subsidiary of Royal Dutch Shell, secured consent from *Indian Act* band councils along the proposed pipeline route, but the Wet'suwet'en land defenders invoked the authority of the hereditary governance system and occupied several sites along the Widzin Kwah (Morice River), resulting in injunctions and successive incursions by the RCMP's C-IRG, dozens of arrests, contempt charges and convictions, and Canada-wide solidarity protests.

Divergent approaches of political leadership within Indigenous communities – specifically, between the colonially recognized *Indian Act* band councils and more traditional structures – surfaced again in 2020–21 in the dispute over logging of old-growth rainforests in the vicinity of Fairy Creek and the Caycuse River on southern Vancouver Island. The band council of the Pacheedaht First Nation entered into a revenue-sharing agreement with the BC government, pledging to support "provincially authorized forest activities" in exchange for $277,000 of annual revenue.[17] In contrast, Pacheedaht band members, including elder Bill Jones, elected councillor Roxy Jones, former elected chief councillor Arliss Jones, and a young man named Victor Peter, who was in line to become a hereditary chief, opposed the old-growth logging. They received support from an eclectic, decentralized movement involving several thousand Indigenous and non-Indigenous people, who rallied under the banner of the "Rainforest Flying Squad" and over time established a dozen encampments and blockades in Tree Farm Licence 46.[18] The land defenders established the

FIGURE 33 Pacheedaht hereditary leader Victor Peter and elder Bill Jones challenge an RCMP checkpoint near Fairy Creek on southern Vancouver Island, during enforcement of an injunction order granted to Teal Cedar Products Ltd. to facilitate logging of old-growth rainforests, 2021. | Norman Galimski, *Times Colonist*

FIGURE 34 A "tree-sit" high above the police lines near Fairy Creek on southern Vancouver Island, May 2021. | Mike Graeme

first camps – Ridge Camp and Waterfall Camp – in August 2020 to prevent licence holder Teal Cedar Products Ltd. from accessing approved cutblocks in the headwaters of Fairy Creek, the last unlogged watershed outside the park system on southern Vancouver Island, consisting of a thousand hectares of old-growth rainforest. In the months that followed, other camps and blockades sprouted to protect remnant stands of old-growth forest in a far-flung area extending north to the Caycuse River in the territory of the Ditidaht Nuu-chah-nulth people.

In April 2021, eight months after the blockades began, Teal Cedar obtained an injunction from BC Supreme Court Justice Frits Verhoeven restraining interference with its operations in TFL 46 and establishing an "injunction zone" seventy thousand hectares in size.[19] The C-IRG began enforcing the injunction in May, relying on a rotation of more than four hundred officers drawn from detachments across western Canada. The police began by dismantling the "Caycuse Camp," carrying out several dozen arrests and complex extractions of land defenders from "hard blocks" dug into the logging roads and tree-sits suspended high in the canopy of the old-growth Douglas-fir, western red-cedar, and western hemlock trees; they were followed immediately by Teal Cedar's contracted logging crews, who began felling the approved cutblocks. The C-IRG then turned its attention to the many camps and blockades in the vicinity of Fairy Creek, embarking on six months of enforcement operations that resulted in nearly twelve hundred arrests and ultimately provided access to a single cutblock in the vicinity of the "Heli Camp" just east of Fairy Creek. Shortly after enforcement commenced at Fairy Creek, Pacheedaht chief councillor Jeff Jones called on the non-Indigenous protesters to leave the territory, signing a joint declaration with the neighbouring Ditidaht and Huu-ay-aht bands that endorsed deferral of logging in select old-growth stands while asserting "our governance and stewardship, our sacred principles, and our right to economically benefit from our resources."[20] Meanwhile, Bill Jones and Victor Peter continued to support the non-Indigenous protesters, renewing an invitation to join them in protecting the old-growth rainforests in Pacheedaht territory.[21]

In July 2021, as the number of arrests mounted and the blockades continued, Justice Douglas Thompson (who was based in Nanaimo and had been appointed as the "case management judge" for the Fairy Creek civil proceedings) granted an application from a consortium of independent journalists to vary the terms of the injunction to provide greater protection for freedom of the press, finding that "police actions have seriously and substantially impacted important liberties within the injunction area" and were unlawful.[22] He also granted an application from Teal Cedar to invite the BC Prosecution Service to assume responsibility for conducting the contempt prosecutions, elevating the charges from civil to criminal contempt.[23]

In September (as discussed in Chapter 4), amid evidence of ongoing and widespread civil liberties breaches by the C-IRG, Thompson refused an application from Teal Cedar to extend the injunction for another year (a decision reversed by the BC Court of Appeal).[24] Ultimately, the Crown would approve contempt charges against 336 of the arrestees (and an additional *Criminal Code* mischief charge during the brief hiatus when the injunction was not in place).[25] Of these, approximately half pleaded guilty and received sentences of fines, community service, and (for the most dangerous breaches, involving "tripods," "cantilevers," and other devices that Justice Thompson characterized as being particularly dangerous to the protesters and police) jail sentences of up to seven days.[26] About a dozen of the alleged contemnors pleaded not guilty and went to trial; most of them were convicted amid clear evidence of obstructive conduct. Approximately four were acquitted, including Ryan Henderson, whose acquittal on the narrow technical issue of deficiencies in the "script" the C-IRG read out to blockaders resulted in the collapse of most of the Crown's remaining prosecutions after the Supreme Court of Canada refused to hear a Crown appeal against the acquittal.[27] One land defender, Kwakwaka'wakw land guardian Rainbow Eyes (Angela Davidson) was convicted of seven counts of criminal contempt by Chief Justice Hinkson following a three-week trial, receiving a sentence of sixty days in jail followed by twelve months' probation with seventy-five hours of community service (a sentence later reduced on appeal).[28]

In December 2024, the BC NDP government signalled a commitment to permanently protect the Fairy Creek watershed. This followed on the heels of several "temporary deferrals" that had been agreed to with the Pacheedaht First Nation, beginning during the height of the controversy in June 2021, and reflected the terms of a confidence and supply agreement the government entered into with the BC Green Party's two-member legislative caucus following the October 2024 provincial election.[29]

These recent controversies over oil and gas pipelines and old-growth logging reveal the complexity of social movements and their relationship with Indigenous communities. Critics on opposite sides of these disputes variously allege that Indigenous voices are being exploited by industry, government, and environmental protesters to advance their divergent objectives. According to the social movement critique, government and industry are cynically taking advantage of economically vulnerable Indigenous communities, offering a

FIGURE 35 Pacheedaht elder Bill Jones raises his fists at the Fairy Creek blockades, surrounded by supporters from the Rainforest Flying Squad, pledging to protect the remnant old-growth forests of southern Vancouver Island, May 2021. | Jen Osborne, Canadian Press

small share of revenue to legitimize projects that would otherwise lack social licence. Meanwhile, lobbyists for the natural resources sector accuse environmentalists of perpetuating colonialism by denying Indigenous communities opportunities to finally benefit from resource development within their territories and achieve economic prosperity. Divergent Indigenous perspectives raise fundamental ethical and strategic questions for non-Indigenous environmentalists, while also exposing the gulf in governance between Canada's colonial *Indian Act* band council system and traditional and hereditary forms of authority. These dynamics are likely to remain a central component of social movement challenges to natural resource development in British Columbia for the foreseeable future.

As noted in the Preface, I am not a neutral observer to any of these recent disputes, being philosophically aligned with the ecological viewpoint that favours leaving fossil fuel resources in the ground and leaving old-growth rainforests standing, while being professionally bound to advance the interests of my clients, the land defenders. With respect to the Trans Mountain pipeline, I made submissions to the National Energy Board in my capacity as an elected city of Victoria councillor, suggesting that approval of the pipeline was not in the public interest, and I later represented a number of contemnors at the sentencing and appeal stages. In relation to the Coastal Gaslink controversy, I attended demonstrations in support of Indigenous youth occupying the steps of the provincial legislature in February 2020 to protest C-IRG enforcement of the injunction against Wet'suwet'en land defenders. Regarding the Fairy Creek old-growth blockades, I represented seventy-one alleged contemnors in proceedings in the BC Supreme Court, BC Court of Appeal, and Supreme Court of Canada, including Ryan Henderson and Rainbow Eyes, and earlier acted as a legal assistant gathering evidence of C-IRG overreach, attracting sharp criticism from the elected chief councillor of the Pacheedaht First Nation.[30]

While I am not neutral, I have endeavoured to examine these recent disputes, as well as the other case studies in this book, in an intellectually honest and scholarly, rigorous manner. I have strived to appreciate and fairly convey the distinct interests and perspectives at the heart of each clash between customary and conventional property claims, tracing the pattern of property, social movements, and the law historically and into the future.

APPENDIX 1
Chronology of Key Events

1901 – The LeRoi Mining Company sues the Western Federation of Miners local at Rossland for damages for financial losses suffered during a strike.

1902 – The Legislative Assembly of British Columbia adopts the *Trade-Unions Act, 1902,* indemnifying unions from civil liability in tort for damages incurred by employers during labour disputes, while rejecting a provision that would have removed the jurisdiction of courts to issue injunctions restraining picketing.

1907 – The Parliament of Canada approves the *Industrial Disputes Investigation Act, 1907,* providing a framework for the investigation and conciliation of labour disputes, legislation that would prove to be of limited utility in the years that followed.

1912 September 16 – Coal miners in the newly formed District 28 of the United Mine Workers of America (UMWA) in Cumberland declare a "holiday" to protest the firing of a union-appointed gas inspector under the provisions of the BC *Coal Mines Regulation Act, 1911,* initiating the Vancouver Island miners' strike of 1912–14.

1913 August – Striking coal miners respond to the use of replacement workers by attacking company property in Ladysmith, South Wellington, and Extension, including the homes of mine managers and replacement workers, and by barricading replacement workers in the pits, prompting the BC government to invoke Military Aid to the Civil Power, with one thousand soldiers deployed in the strike zone and more than eight hundred arrests.

1913 OCTOBER – County Court Judge Frederic Howay convicts 38 miners of rioting for their role in the disturbances in Ladysmith, and acquits only one, imposing sentences of between three months' and two years' imprisonment with hard labour (the maximum sentence for rioting in the *Criminal Code*). In contrast, only 12 of 127 miners who are tried before juries in New Westminster in subsequent months are convicted on criminal charges for their conduct during the strike.

1914 JANUARY 20 – Coal miner Joseph Mairs of Ladysmith dies of complications arising from a bowel infection while he was incarcerated at Oakalla prison in Burnaby, serving a jail sentence for the *Criminal Code* offence of rioting in relation to the miners' strike.

1914 AUGUST – The UMWA calls off the Vancouver Island miners' strike following the outbreak of the First World War and as strikers begin returning to work in the mines.

1937 – Labour lawyer (and future chief justice of Canada) Bora Laskin notes in a scholarly article how injunctions "place the judiciary, so far as the labourer is concerned, in the ranks of the employers."

1952 AUGUST – Striking loggers belonging to the International Woodworkers of America (IWA), led by Tony Poje from the union local in the town of Duncan, picket a wharf in Nanaimo, preventing lumber from being loaded onto the MS *Vedby*. Poje is charged and convicted of criminal contempt of court for publicly defying an injunction against secondary picketing, and sentenced to three months' imprisonment and a $3,000 fine, decisions upheld by the Supreme Court of Canada in a landmark case shaping the law of injunctions and contempt in relation to protest.

1959 – George North, editor of *The Fisherman*, newspaper of the militant United Fishermen and Allied Workers' Union (UFAWU), is jailed for thirty days at Oakalla prison for criminal contempt of court, for publishing an editorial lambasting "the closeness of the companies and the courts" during a labour dispute over construction of the Second Narrows Bridge over Burrard Inlet.

1966 – Thirty labour activists, including the secretary-treasurer of the Vancouver Labour Council, are convicted of criminal contempt of court and sentenced to up to six months in jail for mass picketing in protest against the firing of 257 workers during a tense strike at the Lenkurt Electric Company plant in Burnaby. The convictions and sentences fuel a provincial and national campaign by labour organizations against the use of injunctions in labour disputes.

1967–68 – The president and secretary of the United Fishermen and Allied Workers' Union, Steve Stavenes and Homer Stevens, are jailed for nine months at the Mount Thurston prison camp near Chilliwack and other institutions for criminal contempt of court, for refusing to send a telegram to union members ordering them to handle "hot fish" during a strike of Prince Rupert trawlers, in defiance of a court injunction. The union is fined $25,000 for its role in the contempt.

1970 – Women associated with the Vancouver Women's Caucus embark on the "Abortion Caravan" to Ottawa, demanding repeal of Canada's restrictive abortion law, mobilizing support across the country, and culminating in protests at the prime minister's residence and in the gallery of the House of Commons.

1973 – The New Democratic Party government led by Dave Barrett enacts the *Labour Code of British Columbia Act, 1973*, which includes among its provisions a clause transferring most power to grant injunctions during labour disputes out of the hands of judges and into the hands of a reformed Labour Relations Board.

1976 – The *Criminal Code* provision restricting abortions is thrown into doubt when the newly elected Parti Québécois government of Quebec announces that it is abandoning the prosecution of Dr. Henry Morgentaler and several other medical practitioners, declaring that the law is "inapplicable" in Quebec because of the refusal of juries to convict, and demanding that the federal government reform the law.

1981 – The Council of the Haida Nation unilaterally proclaims a Tribal Park in Duu Guusd in Haida Gwaii (and, in 1985, in the South Moresby/Gwaii Haanas wilderness), unwilling to wait for action by the colonial governments. In 1983, the Haida submit a formal land claim to the Government of Canada, calling for conservation of Gwaii Haanas as wilderness to protect ecological and cultural values.

1982 – The *Constitution Act, 1982* is adopted by the Parliaments of Canada and the United Kingdom and by nine of ten provinces, recognizing Aboriginal rights under section 35 as well as in the *Canadian Charter of Rights of Freedoms* under sections 1 to 34, provisions with far-reaching implications for legal recognition of customary and constitutional claims to property and space in subsequent years.

1984 April – The Tla-o-qui-aht First Nation, one of the Nuu-chah-nulth Nations, follows the earlier example of the Haida, unilaterally proclaiming an *ahoulthlee* (Tribal Park) on Wah-nah-jus Hilth-hoo-is (Meares Island) in Clayoquot Sound off Vancouver Island, in a bid to prevent industrial logging, following the breakdown of a process known as the Meares Island Planning Team.

1984 November – The chief of the Tla-o-qui-aht First Nation, Moses Martin, in concert with settler-allies in the conservation organization Friends of Clayoquot Sound, establishes a blockade to prevent the landing of logging equipment at C'isaqis (Heelboom Bay) on Wah-nah-jus Hilth-hoo-is (Meares Island), preventing logging of old-growth rainforest by licence holder MacMillan Bloedel Ltd.

1985 March – The BC Court of Appeal grants an injunction to the chiefs of the Tla-o-qui-aht and Ahousaht First Nations, prohibiting logging on Meares Island in Clayoquot Sound by logging company MacMillan Bloedel – a landmark decision that recognizes Indigenous rights capable of usurping property rights of private licence holders on Crown land. The injunction remains in place.

1985 November – Sixty-five members of the Haida Nation and six supporters are arrested for blocking a logging road on Tllga Kun Gwaayaay (Athlii Gwaii/Lyell Island) in Haida Gwaii, obstructing operations of Frank Beban Logging Ltd. and Western Forest Products Ltd. in defiance of court injunctions. Ten Haida, along with MP Svend Robinson, are convicted of criminal contempt of court. The Haida receive suspended sentences of six months' jail, while Robinson is fined $750. Charges against the other arrested Haida are eventually dropped.

1987 July 11 – The governments of British Columbia and Canada announce that they have entered into an agreement with the Council of the Haida Nation to establish the Gwaii Haanas National Park Reserve at the location of the existing Haida Heritage Site, protecting one-third of the island archipelago, including Lyall Island, from logging and other industrial activities, while recognizing rights of the Haida Nation to natural resources of the area.

1988 JANUARY 28 – The Supreme Court of Canada strikes down restrictions on abortion services in section 251 of the *Criminal Code,* which required authorization by a doctors' committee, as an infringement of a woman's right to security of the person as guaranteed under section 7 of the Charter. Parliament adopts no alternative statutory language to replace the impugned section, so abortion remains unregulated in the criminal law of Canada.

1988 NOVEMBER – The Everywoman's Health Centre opens on East 44th Avenue in Vancouver, providing access to newly decriminalized abortion services, while prompting frequent protests by anti-abortion activists aligned with Christian organizations and the Operation Rescue campaign. In subsequent years, stand-alone abortion clinics and hospital units are established in dozens of communities across British Columbia.

1989 FEBRUARY 7 – One hundred five anti-abortion activists associated with Operation Rescue are arrested for picketing and obstructing access to the Everywoman's Health Centre, in defiance of a court injunction. One hundred two are subsequently convicted of criminal contempt of court and sentenced to three months' jail, which the judge suspends provided the protesters refrain from obstructing access to the abortion clinic for a period of twelve months.

1989 JULY 4 – Paul Jackson, an anti-abortion protester affiliated with Operation Rescue, locks himself to a cement block at the doors of the Everywoman's Health Centre in Vancouver, and is arrested along with four others. Convicted of criminal contempt of court, he is sentenced to six months in jail and a $1,500 fine (with four months of the sentence and the fine suspended on the condition that he keep the peace and stay away from the clinic for two years), in what Justice John Bouck describes as "an escalation of the ordinary sit-in procedure."

1990 – BC Court of Appeal Justice Mary Southin upholds the injunction, convictions, and sentences against the Operation Rescue protesters who picketed the Everywoman's Health Centre, while noting "the grave question of whether public order should be maintained by the granting of an injunction."

1993 JULY–SEPTEMBER – Approximately twelve thousand people converge on a remote logging road near Kennedy Lake in Clayoquot Sound on Vancouver Island, to protest cutting permits granted by the BC government to MacMillan Bloedel for the logging of old-growth rainforest. More than nine hundred are arrested for defying court injunctions against blocking the logging road.

1993–94 – The BC Supreme Court convicts 626 environmental protesters for criminal contempt of court for defying court injunctions granted to MacMillan Bloedel, which holds licences to harvest timber on Crown land in Clayoquot Sound, the largest incidence of convictions arising from civil disobedience until then in Canadian history. Eight hundred sixty people are tried for criminal contempt in more than a dozen trials. The convicted protesters are sentenced to fines of up to $3,000 and imprisonment of up to sixty days.

1995 June – The Legislative Assembly of British Columbia responds to violence against abortion providers and legal ambiguity surrounding anti-abortion picketing by adopting the *Access to Abortion Services Act, 1995*, establishing "bubble zones" around abortion clinics and the offices and homes of abortion providers where protest is prohibited. Following a decade of litigation, the legislation is upheld as a constitutional, reasonable infringement on freedom of expression.

1995 July – Members of the Secwépemc Nation conduct a traditional Sun Dance ceremony on lands at Ts'Peten (Gustafsen Lake), in defiance of a demand by the landowner, an American rancher, that they vacate the property. The dispute escalates into an armed standoff between the Ts'Peten defenders and heavily armed RCMP officers, the largest paramilitary operation on Canadian soil in recent history. Ultimately, the Ts'Peten defenders surrender to police and the dispute ends without bloodshed; fifteen are convicted of *Criminal Code* offences and sentenced to between six months' and eight years' imprisonment.

2002 – A homeless squat in the closed Woodward's department store in downtown Vancouver spirals into a two-month occupation of the sidewalks surrounding the building, highlighting the plight of the urban homeless, the growing movement for housing rights, and the use of injunctions to displace urban tent cities.

2006 – Grandmother Betty Krawczyk is arrested, convicted, and sentenced to ten months in jail for criminal contempt of court, for defying an injunction against obstructing realignment of the Sea to Sky Highway over Eagleridge Bluffs in West Vancouver (a sentence upheld by the BC Court of Appeal, and the stiffest in BC legal history since the UFAWU controversy in 1967–

68). Krawczyk had several prior convictions for criminal contempt at Clayoquot Sound and in Vancouver Island's Central Walbran Valley.

2009 – In the landmark *Adams* decision, BC Supreme Court Justice Carol Ross strikes down provisions of the city of Victoria's *Parks Regulation Bylaw* as unconstitutional, finding that the prohibition on overnight sheltering within municipal parks violates homeless persons' right under section 7 of the Charter to life, liberty, and security of the person, by preventing them from sheltering themselves in the absence of adequate alternative shelter. This decision is upheld by the BC Court of Appeal a year later, forcing the city to amend its bylaw to permit overnight sheltering in parks.

2014 September – BC Supreme Court Justice Douglas Thompson postpones consideration of an application from a landowner for an injunction barring Coast Salish Indigenous peoples and settler-allies from interfering with construction of a luxury home on a burial ground at Grace Islet off Salt Spring Island. Two weeks later, the landowner abandons the injunction application and discontinues the civil action against the elected Indigenous chiefs and settlers. The provincial government purchases the disputed property from the landowner and initiates the dismantling of the luxury home, entrusting stewardship to a conservation organization and a committee of Coast Salish bands.

2014 November–December – More than one hundred people are arrested on Burnaby Mountain for contempt of court for defying a court injunction against interfering with exploratory work by oil company Kinder Morgan for the Trans Mountain Pipeline Expansion Project. The judge refuses to convict, in light of technical defects in the company's injunction application, which the environmentalists herald as a victory.

2016 April – Chief Justice Christopher Hinkson of the BC Supreme Court refuses to grant an injunction to the provincial government to evict approximately one hundred homeless people camping on the Victoria Courthouse grounds, finding that the balance of convenience is "overwhelmingly" in favour of the defendant campers, who "simply have nowhere to move to."

2016 July – Upon receiving a subsequent application from the province, Chief Justice Hinkson grants an injunction to the BC government ordering the Victoria Courthouse campers to leave, but suspends its effect until such time as "new housing created by the Province became available," recognizing a tentative positive right to housing as a condition of issuing an injunction to a public body in some circumstances. Two hundred new units of social housing are acquired by the province to meet this condition.

2018 May – The Government of Canada purchases the Trans Mountain pipeline from Kinder Morgan, stating that the risk is too high for the proposed expansion project to proceed under private ownership due to opposition from Indigenous peoples, environmentalists, and the BC government. More than 200 people had been arrested for defying a fresh injunction in the months preceding the purchase, 196 of whom were convicted of criminal contempt of court.

2018 August – The Federal Court of Appeal quashes the Government of Canada's approval of the Trans Mountain Pipeline Expansion Project, on grounds that the government had failed to adequately consult Indigenous communities. This prompts a new round of consultation and a second federal decision to approve the project, which was upheld by the Federal Court of Appeal. The Supreme Court of Canada refuses an application from several Indigenous groups for leave to appeal, exhausting the possibility of halting the project through the courts. In subsequent years, further arrests and contempt convictions occur in Coast Salish and Secwépemc territory.

2018 December – BC Supreme Court Justice Marguerite Church grants the first of several injunctions to Coastal GasLink Pipeline Ltd., restraining protests by Wet'suwet'en land defenders opposed to construction of a gas pipeline through their territory. RCMP officers enforce the injunction in January 2019 and again in 2020 and 2021, dismantling Wet'suwet'en checkpoints along the Widzin Kwah (Morice River), resulting in more than seventy-five arrests, contempt of court charges, and solidarity protests across Canada.

2021 April – BC Supreme Court Justice Fritz Verhoeven grants an injunction to Teal Cedar Products Ltd., prohibiting interference with old-growth logging operations in the vicinity of Fairy Creek and the Caycuse River on southern Vancouver Island. Nearly 1,200 people are arrested during RCMP enforcement operations in subsequent months, the largest incidence of mass arrests arising from a court order in Canadian history. In September 2021, BC Supreme Court Justice Douglas Thompson refuses to extend the injunction, choosing to "get the Court out from the middle of this dispute," a decision later reversed by the BC Court of Appeal. In February 2022, Justice Thompson acquits Fairy Creek land defender Ryan Henderson based on a strict reading of the notice requirement for criminal contempt, finding that the script the RCMP read out to protesters at Fairy Creek was insufficient. This results in the collapse of Crown prosecutions of approximately 175 out of 336 persons prosecuted for contempt. Most of the others plead guilty or are convicted after trial, receiving sentences ranging from fines of $500 to fifty-one days in jail.

2025 FEBRUARY – BC Supreme Court Justice Michael Tammen finds that the RCMP's Community-Industry Response Group (later rebranded as the Critical Response Unit) breached the section 7 Charter rights of Wet'suwet'en land defenders in making discriminatory comments regarding their red face paint following arrests on the Morice Forest Service Road in November 2021. Tammen imposed reduced sentences on account of the breach.

Source: Compiled by the author.

APPENDIX 2
Case Summaries

R v Guthrie et al (1913), BC County Court, unreported decision made at Nanaimo, October 23, 1913

Also: *R v Angelo,* [1914] 19 BCR 261 (BCCA)

This criminal case arose from unrest in Ladysmith, Nanaimo, and other coal-mining communities during the Vancouver Island miners' strike of 1912–14 (the "Vancouver Island war"). In August 1913, authorities responded to reports of arson and armed clashes between strikers and strikebreakers by invoking Military Aid to the Civil Power under the *Militia Act,* deploying a thousand militiamen and two hundred special police constables by train and steamer to occupy the island coalfields. Approximately 800 miners were detained by the soldiers and police, 213 of whom were held without bail and remanded to custody in Victoria awaiting trial on charges relating to rioting. In the first set of trials in October 1913, 38 Ladysmith miners entered early guilty pleas (rather than proceeding to trial before a jury of their peers), anticipating more lenient, potentially suspended sentences. However, County Court Judge Frederic Howay imposed the stiffest penalties available for the *Criminal Code* offence of rioting, sentencing 5 individuals identified as leaders to two years in jail with hard labour – including the president and vice president of the Ladysmith miners' union local, Sam Guthrie and Joseph Taylor (who also served as vice president of the BC Federation of Labour). Twenty-three other miners identified as joining but not leading the rioting were sentenced to a year in jail and fined $100, including former Ladysmith alderman William Auld and twenty-one-year-old Joseph Mairs (who died of tuberculosis in Oakalla prison three months later). A final 11 miners, who were part of the crowd but were found not to have played a prominent role in the rioting, were sentenced to three months in jail and fined $50. The severity of Howay's sentencing shocked the convicted miners and their families. In contrast, only 12 of 127 miners who were tried before juries in New Westminster in subsequent months were convicted of criminal charges for their conduct during the strike.

Poje v Attorney General for British Columbia, [1953] 1 SCR 516

Also: *Canadian Transport Co (UK) Ltd v Alsbury*, [1952] 6 WWR (NS) 473 (BCSC)
Canadian Transport (UK) Limited v Alsbury, [1953] 1 DLR 385 (BCCA)

This leading Canadian case in the law of contempt of court established the distinction between civil and criminal contempt, as "a public depreciation of the authority of the court tending to bring the administration of justice into scorn." The case also affirmed the principle that when a superior court exercised its inherent jurisdiction at common law to punish persons disobeying its orders for contempt, no rules applied. The case arose during a strike of loggers on Vancouver Island in 1952 who launched a secondary picket at the Nanaimo wharves that prevented the loading of a ship, the MS *Vedby*, owned by a third party. The vessel owner sought and received an *ex parte* injunction against union vice president Tony Poje and other strikers, enjoining them from "watching and besetting" the ship and preventing or interfering with loading or access, which they defied. While the strike was quickly settled and the vessel owner applied to the court to discontinue the civil action, dissolve the injunction, and withdraw a motion for contempt, BC Supreme Court Chief Justice Wendell Farris proceeded by way of his own motion (*ex mero motu*) to punish Poje for "reprehensive conduct" as "ringleader" of "a particularly brazen and contumacious contempt." Farris convicted Poje of criminal contempt and sentenced him to three months in jail and a $3,000 fine (or an additional nine months in jail in default of payment). Fourteen other picketers, who offered complete apologies to the court, received lesser sentences of $300 fines or one month in jail. The BC Court of Appeal and the Supreme Court of Canada upheld this ruling, finding that "the large numbers of men involved and the public nature of the defiance of the order" rendered the conduct criminal contempt of court. In a strong dissenting opinion, however, BC Court of Appeal Justice Cornelius O'Halloran found that Poje and the other picketers were improperly charged and tried, and that the injunction itself should never have been issued *ex parte*, emphasizing the importance of "upholding of civil rights, viz., the legal right to picket."

R v North (1959), BC Supreme Court, unreported decision made at Vancouver, July 14, 1959

Also: *Dominion Bridge v International Association of Bridge, Structural and Ornamental Ironworkers Local 97* (1959), 20 DKR 2d 621 (BCCA)

In 1959, the Dominion Bridge Company sought and received an injunction from BC Supreme Court Justice Alex Manson ordering striking ironworkers employed in construction of the Second Narrow Bridge over Burrard Inlet to return to work. This prompted labour journalist George North to publish an editorial in *The Fisherman* newspaper titled "Injunctions Won't Build Bridges or Catch Fish," lamenting "the closeness of the companies and the courts." Justice Manson responded by taking notice of the editorial in open court and appointed J.A. Clark to act as prosecutor of a criminal contempt charge against North. Another judge, Norman Whitaker, heard the case in July 1959. After rejecting procedural arguments from North's lawyer, Harry Rankin, Whitaker dispensed with submissions from the prosecution and found North guilty of criminal contempt. In his reasons for judgment, Whitaker stated that "the effect of the article is to undermine public confidence in the courts," describing North's conduct as "a particularly flagrant contempt of court." He sentenced North to thirty days in jail and fined his employer, the Fisherman's Publishing Society, $3,000. North's appeal against the conviction was unsuccessful and he served his jail sentence in Burnaby's Oakalla prison before being released to a hero's welcome.

R v United Fishermen and Allied Workers' Union, Stavenes and two others (1967), [1968] 1 CCC 199 (BCSC)

Also: *R v United Fishermen and Allied Workers' Union et al* (1967), 63 DLR (2d) 356 (BCCA)

Also: *R v United Fishermen and Allied Workers' Union et al* (1967), [1968] 2 CCC 257 (BCCA)
United Fishermen & Allied Workers' Union et al v The Queen, [1968] SCR 255

This case is notable for the stiffest sentences imposed on social movement actors for contempt of court in British Columbia's legal history. During a 1967 strike of Prince Rupert trawlers, BC Supreme Court Justice Kirke Smith granted several injunctions sought by vessel owners, ordering members of the United Fishermen and Allied Workers' Union to handle "hot fish" to prevent them from spoiling. One of the injunctions ordered the union's officers to send a telegram to members directing them to unload the vessels. Rather than comply, the union officials conducted a referendum, asking members whether they should abide by the court order and send the telegram. Inflamed, BC Supreme Court Justice Thomas Dohm took notice in open court of the UFAWU leaders' apparent defiance, ordering them to show cause why they should not be found in contempt, and inviting the attorney general to assume conduct of the prosecution. Dohm subsequently found union president Steve Stavenes, secretary Homer Stevens, and business agent Jack Nichol guilty of criminal contempt, for "a planned flouting of the Court's authority" that exceeded anything he had seen in reported cases of contempt going back to 1740. The officers' decision to conduct the referendum represented "a most serious interference," "calculated to deprive this Court of the power of administering justice." In sentencing, Dohm noted that none of the officers had apologized to the court or the public, and that sentences imposed in Canada to date had not had a deterrent effect. He sentenced Stavenes, Stevens, and Nichol to twelve months in jail and fined the union $25,000. While Nichol was acquitted on appeal, due to a lack of evidence implicating him in the contempt, the Court of Appeal concurred with Dohm that Stavenes's and Stevens's conduct was "calculated and intended to ridicule the Court and its process, to lower the authority and prestige of the Court, and to bring it into scorn and disrespect," describing their offence as "a gross contempt." The Supreme Court of Canada refused to hear an appeal against the convictions and sentences, finding that the grounds of appeal had already been rejected by the Court of Appeal, and that it was settled law that the Supreme Court of Canada lacked competence to consider appeals of sentences in criminal matters. Stavenes and Stevens served nine months at the Mount Thurston prison camp and other institutions before being released in September 1968 with remission of the final three months of the sentences.

R v Morgentaler, [1988] 1 SCR 30

In this landmark ruling, the Supreme Court of Canada struck down section 251 of the *Criminal Code*, which imposed restrictions on access to abortion, finding that the impugned provisions were unconstitutional for violating women's right to security of the person as guaranteed under section 7 of the Charter. The court acquitted Dr. Henry Morgentaler of convictions for performing abortions without approval of a hospital committee, as mandated in the statute. In the wake of the ruling, Parliament debated revised provisions governing abortions, but no law was enacted, leaving the *Criminal Code* silent on abortions. (The House of Commons had approved an amendment prohibiting abortions unless a doctor considered the pregnancy to be a threat to a woman's "physical, mental, or psychological health," but the Senate defeated the amendment on a tied vote.) The *Morgentaler* decision and parliamentary gridlock cleared a legal path for the establishment of stand-alone abortion clinics in Vancouver and other communities, as well as improved access to abortion services in hospitals in most provinces. The opening of the Everywoman's Health Centre in East Vancouver inaugurated a new era in the legal politics of abortion in British Columbia, with anti-abortion protesters turning to picketing to impede access to the health service, and women's rights advocates turning to the courts for protection. This was followed by injunctions, arrests, contempt convictions, jail sentences, and ultimately legislative action in the form of the *Access to Abortion Services Act, 1995*.

Everywoman's Health Centre Society v Bridges, 1990 CanLII 5409 (BCCA)

Also: *R v Bridges*, 1989 CanLII 2921 (BCSC)
R v Bridges, 1989 CanLII 5321 (BCSC)
Everywoman's Health Centre Soc (1988) v Bridges, 1989 CanLII 2793 (BCSC)
Everywoman's Health Centre Society v Bridges, 1990 CanLII 1574 (BCSC)
R v Bridges, 1990 CanLII 5419 (BCCA)
Everywoman's Health Centre Society v Bridges, 1991 CanLII 5715 (BCCA)
Everywoman's Health Centre Society (1988) v Bridges, 1993 CanLII 1276 (BCSC)
Everywoman's Health Centre Society (1988) v Watson, 1994 CanLII 1467 (BCCA)

Also: *R v Lewis,* 1996 CanLII 17950 (BC PC)
R v Lewis, 1996 CanLII 3559 (BCSC)

In the wake of the *Morgentaler* decision in 1988, which struck down *Criminal Code* restrictions on access to abortion services, feminists in Vancouver opened the Everywoman's Health Centre. The abortion clinic immediately became a target for opponents of abortion affiliated with churches and an American initiative called Operation Rescue, with the anti-abortionists launching persistent, large-scale picketing, blockades, and "sidewalk counselling" aimed at preventing women from accessing the health service. In January 1989, the clinic obtained an interlocutory injunction from BC Supreme Court Justice Lloyd McKenzie enjoining interference with its operations. In the weeks and months that followed, more than 150 picketers were arrested for breaching the court order and charged with contempt; 42 refused to sign undertakings agreeing to stay away from the clinic and remained in custody. The Crown, represented by Joseph Arvay, assumed conduct of the contempt prosecutions. Following a hearing in March 1989, Justice Josiah Wood convicted 102 people of criminal contempt. He rejected the defence of necessity, on grounds that the alleged harm the contemnors sought to prevent – the killing of unborn children – was not a recognized offence in the *Criminal Code,* and since natural human instincts did not impel all reasonable people to defy the law as the contemnors had done (applying the *Perka* test, which limited the defence to wrongful acts committed under a pressure "which no one could withstand").

In sentencing, Wood noted that none of the accused had sought leave to appeal the injunction, abandoning "any resort to legal process," and that none had admitted they had erred nor provided assurances they would not err again. He described their conduct as "a classic example of organized lawlessness," "large scale, deliberate defiance of an order of the court," which threatened the rule of law: "None who seek to enjoy its benefits can be permitted the occasional anarchical holiday from its mandate." As mitigating factors, Wood described the contemnors as "decent and law-abiding people," "motivated by a genuine belief in the righteousness of [their] cause," but noted that the court applied the law as determined by Parliament and previous court decisions, rather than "the law of God, irrespective of whose interpretation of that law is offered for consideration." He suggested the contemnors had been "led astray by questionable leadership," but was unable to identify the leaders beyond a reasonable doubt, and therefore sentenced all the contemnors as "followers" to three months in jail, which he suspended on the condition that they keep the peace for twelve months. A number of contemnors reattended at the clinic, breaching the terms of their probation and serving jail time. Protests persisted. In July 1989, a man locked himself to a cement block at the doors of the clinic and was sentenced to six months in jail and fined $1,500 (with four months of the jail sentence and the fine suspended on the condition that he keep the peace and stay away from the clinic for two years), in what Justice John Bouck described as "an escalation of the ordinary sit-in procedure." The injunction and contempt convictions were upheld by the BC Court of Appeal, though Justice Mary Southin acknowledged "the grave question of whether public order should be maintained by the granting of an injunction, which often leads thereafter to an application to commit for contempt or should be maintained by the Attorney-General insisting that the police who are under his control do their duty by enforcing the relevant provisions of the Criminal Code." The dispute surrounding anti-abortion picketing and violence against abortion providers spurred enactment of the *Access to Abortion Services Act* in 1995. This "permanent legislative injunction" established "bubble zones" around abortion clinics and the homes and offices of abortion providers. The legislation was later mirrored with statutes restricting protests around hospitals and schools in connection with anti-vaccination picketing during the COVID-19 pandemic and, later, protests relating to transgender inclusion policies.

MacMillan Bloedel Ltd v Simpson, [1996] 2 SCR 1048

Also: *MacMillan Bloedel Ltd v Simpson*, 1993 BCSC 530
MacMillan Bloedel Ltd v Simpson, 1993 BCSC 1295
MacMillan Bloedel Ltd v Simpson, 1994 BCSC 1447
MacMillan Bloedel Ltd v Brown, 1994 BCCA 64
MacMillan Bloedel Ltd v Simpson, 1994 BCCA 187
MacMillan Bloedel Ltd v Simpson, [1995] 4 SCR 725

This case involved the largest number of persons charged and convicted of criminal contempt of court in British Columbia and Canadian history (and the largest number of arrests prior to the Fairy Creek dispute in 2021) – "the current high-water mark for persistent disobedience of Court orders," as Chief Justice of British Columbia Allan McEachern described it in upholding sentences of at least forty-five days in jail against three dozen environmental protesters. In the summer of 1993, more than 900 people were arrested in the vicinity of Kennedy Lake in Clayoquot Sound on Vancouver Island, for breaching the terms of several injunctions enjoining interference with the logging operations of MacMillan Bloedel, licence holder to timber resources in the old-growth rainforests of Clayoquot Sound. The environmental organization Friends of Clayoquot Sound had initiated a "Peace Camp" to draw public attention, attracting an estimated 12,000 people to the rainforest that "hot summer." A total of 860 people were charged with criminal contempt of court for blocking the logging road. The first contested trial took place in the autumn of 1993 before Justice John Bouck in Victoria, who convicted 42 persons of criminal contempt and imposed stiff sentences of between forty-five and sixty days in jail and fines ranging from $1,000 to $2,000, depending on the number of breaches and the contemnor's conduct during the trial. The Court of Appeal upheld the convictions and jail sentences while setting aside the fines (with the exception of three contemnors, two of whom had their custodial sentences reduced to thirty days and one who had her custodial sentence suspended). In an appeal against an injunction order that Justice John Hall granted to MacMillan Bloedel on August 26, 1993, the Court of Appeal split two to one, with the majority finding that the BC Supreme Court, as a superior court of inherent jurisdiction, had jurisdiction to make orders binding on non-parties ("Jane" and "John Does") and that use of such power was justified to preserve the respondent's property rights in the face of mass obstruction. Justice Wood dissented, on the ground that court orders were binding only on named parties to an action, and that the proper remedy when mass action threatened to overrun private rights was for the attorney general to enforce the criminal law. The Supreme Court of Canada agreed with the majority in the Court of Appeal decision and upheld the validity of the injunction. Over the course of a dozen trials in 1993 and 1994, 626 people were convicted of criminal contempt of court for interfering with logging in Clayoquot Sound in 1993, and sanctioned with fines of up to $3,000 and jail terms of up to sixty days.

MacMillan Bloedel Ltd v Mullin, 1985 CanLII 154 (BCCA)

Also: *MacMillan Bloedel Ltd v Mullin*, 1985 CanLII 708 (BCSC)
Martin v BC (Govt), 1986 CanLII 956 (BCSC)

In this unorthodox decision, Justice Peter Seaton and two fellow judges of the BC Court of Appeal granted an injunction to the elected chiefs of the Ahousaht Nation and the Tla-o-qui-aht Nation of the Nuu-chah-nulth Nations, restraining logging activities by MacMillan Bloedel on Wah-nah-jus Hilth-hoo-is (Meares Island) in Clayoquot Sound pending determination of a Nuu-chah-nulth land claim. The case followed several years of controversy over the natural resources of the island, which the Nuu-chah-nulth had stewarded for millennia and which was largely untouched by industrial logging. In April 1984, the Tla-o-qui-aht followed the example of the Haida and proclaimed an *ahoulthlee* (Tribal Park) on Meares, but the provincial government refused to recognize this designation and instead issued cutting permits to MacMillan Bloedel, licence holder of the timber resources on the purported Crown land. The Nuu-chah-nulth and their allies in the Friends of Clayoquot Sound responded by establishing a camp along the shore at C'isaqis (Heelboom Bay), preventing the logging company from unloading equipment and workers. On application from MacMillan Bloedel, BC Supreme Court Justice Reginald Gibbs granted an injunction enjoining interference with logging operations, while denying an injunction requested by the Tla-o-qui-aht and Ahousaht chiefs Moses Martin and Corbett George to maintain the status quo and preserve the resources pending the title determination. In the Court of Appeal decision, Seaton and his two fellow judges granted the injunction sought by the Indigenous leaders while maintaining the injunction issued to the logging company. Writing for the majority of the five-judge division (with two judges dissenting), Seaton stated that the balance of convenience favoured granting the injunction to Martin and George, to preserve old-growth trees that provided evidence of centuries of Nuu-cha-nulth occupation and use, pending determination of the land claim. "There is a problem about tenure that has not been attended to in the past. We are being asked to ignore the problem as others have ignored it. I am not willing to do that," Seaton stated. Subsequent applications by MacMillan Bloedel to dissolve the injunction granted to Martin and George were denied. Following several years of litigation involving 152 hearing days, the Crown requested an adjournment in 1991 to enter into negotiations with the Nuu-chah-nulth. The injunction granted to Martin and George and the original injunction granted to the logging company remain in place four decades later. In subsequent years, the Tla-o-qui-aht and Ahousaht ultimately acquired a private property interest in the Crown forest lands of Meares Island and Clayoquot Sound, with the transfer of licences to Nuu-chah-nulth-owned Iisaak and MaMook Natural Resources Ltd., an interim measure in the wider land claims process.

Western Forest Products Ltd v Collinson et al (1985), BC Supreme Court, unreported decision made at Vancouver, November 29, 1985, Registry No. C854987

Also: *Frank Beban Logging Ltd v Collinson et al* (1985), BC Supreme Court, Vancouver Registry No. C8549788

This case arose from a blockade by members of the Haida Nation of logging operations of Western Forest Products Ltd. and its contractor Frank Beban Logging Ltd. on Tllga Kun Gwaayaay (Athlii Gwaii/Lyell Island) in Haida Gwaii in the autumn of 1985. The blockade followed a decade of lobbying efforts by the Haida and their supporters for protection of the Gwaii Haanas (South Moresby) wilderness area and declaration of a Haida Heritage Site. After the BC government approved fresh cutblocks on Lyell Island, the Haida made their stand, transporting equipment, supplies, and community members by fishboat from Skidegate to Sedgewick Bay, where they built a cabin and blocked the logging road. Western Forest Products and Frank Beban Logging sought and received injunctions from BC Supreme Court Justice Harry McKay in early November 1985, leading to RCMP enforcement on Lyell Island and the arrests of sixty-five Haida and six supporters. Ten Haida, as well as MP Svend Robinson, were convicted of criminal contempt of court. The Haida received suspended sentences of six months in jail, while Robinson was fined $750. Charges against the other arrested Haida were eventually dropped. In subsequent years, political pressure generated by the Athlii Gwaii stand and the wider campaign brought about an end to logging in Gwaii Haanas, co-management of the area by the Council of the Haida Nation and Parks Canada, and revitalization of Haida culture, self-government, and natural resource management.

R v Ignace, 1998 CanLII 4485 (BCCA)

Also: *R v Ignace* (1997), BC Supreme Court, unreported decision made at Vancouver, May 20, 1997, Registry No. CA023439
R v Ignace, 1996 CanLII 2474 (BCCA)
R v Ignace, 1997 CanLII 3776 (BCCA)
R v Ignace, 1998 CanLII 4237 (BCCA)
R v Ignace, 1998 CanLII 4485 (BCCA)

Secwépemc elder Wolverine (William Jones Ignace) and seventeen other land defenders were convicted of serious *Criminal Code* offences in the wake of the Ts'Peten (Gustafsen Lake) standoff on private ranchland near 100 Mile House in the summer of 1995. The dispute arose when the American landowner revoked permission to hold a traditional Sun Dance ceremony on the site, which had occurred for a number of years. Wolverine and other Secwépemc and allied land defenders responded by occupying the site, asserting rights to the land. The dispute quickly escalated, with the RCMP deploying four hundred heavily armed officers, supported by helicopters and armoured personnel carriers. Both sides visibly carried arms. In September 1995, Wolverine and the other land defenders surrendered peacefully and were taken into custody. Following a trial before BC Supreme Court Justice Bruce Josephson and a jury in May 1997, Wolverine was convicted of offences including possession of a weapon for a purpose dangerous to the public peace and using a firearm in committing the assault of police officers. He was sentenced to four and a half years' imprisonment. Wolverine's appeal challenging the jurisdiction of the BC Supreme Court to hear the indictment, on grounds that the alleged offences occurred on unceded Secwépemc lands that the Crown had never acquired by treaty, conquest, or purchase, was denied. Applying the principle of *stare decisis*, the BC Court of Appeal held that the issue of sovereignty had been decided in *Delgamuukw v British Columbia*, 1993 CanLII 4516 (BCCA) and *R v Williams*, 1994 CanLII 3301 (BCCA), with the jurisdiction of British Columbia courts to adjudicate matters throughout the province established with the assertion of British sovereignty in 1846: "It is well established that the courts of British Columbia have jurisdiction over aboriginal accused where an offence has allegedly been committed within the Province, regardless of whether or not the territory could be said to be 'beyond the treaty frontier.'" The appeal court cited the Supreme Court of Canada's findings in *Delgamuukw* that "the purpose of s. 35(1) [of the *Constitution Act, 1982*] is to reconcile the prior presence of aboriginal peoples in North America with the assertion of Crown sovereignty," and that "rights to self-government, if they existed, cannot be framed in excessively general terms" (re-stating the finding from *R v Pamajewon*, [1996] 2 SCR 821). Wolverine's claim to immunity from prosecution was therefore dismissed as being "framed in excessively general terms."

Slawsky v Isitt, 2014 BCSC 1917

This case, in which the author was a named respondent, arose from a dispute over construction of a private luxury home on a Coast Salish burial ground at Grace Islet off Salt Spring Island in the Salish Sea. When construction began in the spring of 2014, members of the W̱SÁNEĆ, Cowichan, and Penelakut Coast Salish peoples and their supporters launched protests against desecration of the burial site, including on-the-water protests with kayaks, canoes, and fishboats in the vicinity of the small island. In August 2014, landowner Barry Slawsky applied to the BC Supreme Court for an injunction imposing a fifty-metre buffer around the islet and enjoining interference with construction activities. He named six defendants, including two elected W̱SÁNEĆ chiefs,

Don Tom and Vern Jacks; a member of the Legislative Assembly, Gary Holman; and a municipal councillor, Ben Isitt. Following a hearing on the injunction application, BC Supreme Court Justice Douglas Thompson postponed a decision on whether to grant the injunction sought by the landowner, stating that the case may be more complicated than a simple matter of trespass on lands owned in fee simple. At the hearing, counsel for elected chief Don Tom of the Tsartlip First Nation suggested that he was exercising a customary right to visit the graves of his ancestors. Thompson granted a one-month adjournment to allow counsel for the Indigenous leaders and other respondents to prepare submissions in response to the injunction application. Upon the filing of responses to the notice of civil claim, the landowner discontinued the underlying action and paid costs incurred by the respondents. The islet was subsequently purchased by the BC government and transferred to the Nature Conservancy of Canada, and is now stewarded in partnership with representatives of the W̱SÁNEĆ, Cowichan, and Penelakut peoples. The brief litigation in the Grace Islet case appeared to demonstrate a retreat from the court's willingness to automatically issue injunctions to restrain interference with private rights, and growing recognition of Indigenous and customary claims to property.

Coastal GasLink Pipeline Ltd v Huson, 2018 BCSC 2343

Also: *Coastal GasLink Pipeline Ltd v Huson*, 2019 BCSC 2264
Coastal GasLink Pipeline Ltd v Huson, 2021 BCSC 2734
Coastal GasLink Pipeline Ltd v Huson, 2021 BCSC 2735
Coastal Gaslink Pipeline Ltd v Huson, 2024 BCSC 509
Coastal Gaslink Pipeline Ltd v Huson, 2024 BCSC 1730
Coastal Gaslink Pipeline Ltd v Huson, 2025 BCSC 643
Coastal Gaslink Pipeline Ltd v Huson, 2025 BCSC 2348

In December 2018, the energy company Coastal GasLink Pipeline Ltd. sought and received an injunction from BC Supreme Court Justice Marguerite Church restraining members of the Wet'suwet'en Nation from interfering with construction of a gas pipeline through their territory along the Widzin Kwah (Morice River) near Houston, BC. While the provincial government had signed revenue-sharing agreements with the *Indian Act* band councils along the proposed pipeline route, the hereditary chiefs of the Wet'suwet'en unanimously opposed the project. For several years, members of the Unist'ot'en clan had maintained a permanent presence on the Widzin Kwah, reviving Wet'suwet'en connections to the land and blocking the path of the pipeline. In January 2019 and continuing in subsequent years, members the Gidimt'en clan established checkpoints to prevent agents of the gas company from entering the territory, prompting enforcement action by the RCMP's Community-Industry Response Group (C-IRG) with dozens of arrests and contempt of court charges. In 2020, RCMP enforcement activities provoked Canada-wide protests, which disrupted rail and marine shipping for several weeks and resulted in economic losses of $275 million. In the autumn of 2021, the dispute escalated again when the Wet'suwet'en issued an eviction notice to the gas company, ordering five hundred contractors at a work camp to leave the territory; this prompted renewed RCMP enforcement action, including the arrest of journalists. The prosecution of the contemnors concluded shortly before this book went to print, with BC Supreme Court Justice Michael Tammen declining to impose jail sentences against *Sleydo* Molly Wickham, Shaylynn Sampson, and Corey Jocko on account of abuse of process by RCMP officers, who had made "grossly offensive, racist, and dehumanizing" comments in their presence.

Victoria (City) v Adams, 2009 BCCA 563

Also: *Victoria (City) v Adams*, 2008 BCSC 1363

This case recognized a constitutional right of people experiencing homelessness to shelter themselves in municipal parks and greenspaces in the absence of adequate alternative shelter. The case arose from several years of advocacy by street-involved people in Victoria, with a "cat-and-mouse" dynamic of homeless encampments emerging in municipally and provincially owned greenspaces before being displaced by police and bylaw officers, who were often armed with court injunctions. However, in 2008, when the City of Victoria applied for a permanent injunction to restrain sheltering in municipal parks and rights-of-way, BC Supreme Court Justice Carol Ross refused to grant the order, declaring that sections of the city of Victoria's *Parks Regulation Bylaw* and *Streets and Traffic Bylaw* that prohibited overnight sheltering and sleeping in municipal parks and sidewalks violated section 7 of the *Canadian Charter of Rights and Freedoms* "in that they deprive homeless people of life, liberty and security of the person in a manner not in accordance with the principles of fundamental justice, and are not saved by s. 1 of the Charter." Justice Ross declared that those sections of the bylaws were "of no force and effect insofar ... as they apply to prevent homeless people from erecting temporary shelter."

The BC Court of Appeal upheld Ross's ruling. As a result, the City of Victoria amended its bylaws to permit overnight sheltering by unhoused individuals. Similar bylaw provisions were subsequently adopted in a number of other BC municipalities to meet the constitutional requirements established in the *Adams* case.

Abbotsford (City) v Shantz, 2015 BCSC 1909

Also: *Abbotsford (City) v Shantz*, 2013 BCSC 2612
BC/Yukon Association of Drug War Survivors v Abbotsford (City), 2014 BCSC 1817
Abbotsford (City) v Shantz, 2014 BCSC 2385
Abbotsford (City) v Shantz, 2015 BCSC 1909
British Columbia/Yukon Association of Drug War Survivors v Abbotsford (City), 2015 BCCA 142

In October 2015, Chief Justice Christopher Hinkson of the BC Supreme Court struck down sections of municipal bylaws in Abbotsford that prohibited overnight sheltering by people who were homeless. This decision marked the culmination of several years of tensions between municipal officials and street-involved people associated with the BC/Yukon Association of Drug War Survivors and represented by the Vancouver-based Pivot Legal Society. The municipal response to homelessness and sheltering in Abbotsford parks had an ugly edge. In one notorious incident, a municipal parks manager ordered his staff to spread chicken manure in a park where people who were homeless were known to shelter. In another incident, parks and bylaw staff slashed tents and used bear spray to disperse campers. In his decision in the *Shantz* case, Chief Justice Hinkson displayed a strong compassionate tone, noting that "constant movement of the homeless exacerbated their already vulnerable positions, as it inhibited the ability of the service providers who endeavoured to help the City's homeless to actually locate them and provide help. I thus find that the evidence supports a finding that the Impugned Bylaws have had a serious effect on the psychological or physical integrity of the City's homeless." Hinkson declared that sections 14 and 15 of Abbotsford's *Consolidated Parks Bylaw* and subsection 2.7(d) of its *Good Neighbour Bylaw*, to the extent that they applied to the city's homeless and prohibited sleeping or being in a city park overnight or erecting a temporary shelter without permits, violated section 7 of the Charter, were of no force or effect, and were not saved by section 1 of the

Charter. The *Shantz* decision built on the foundation established in *Adams* – extending the courts' recognition that legal weight should be accorded to the health and well-being of persons who are homeless, and elaborating on how the section 7 Charter right to security of the person translates on the ground into conditions faced by street-involved people.

British Columbia v Adamson, 2016 BCSC 584

Also: *British Columbia v Adamson*, 2016 BCSC 1245
British Columbia v Adamson, 2017 BCSC 168

This decision of Chief Justice Hinkson of the BC Supreme Court built on the earlier *Adams* and *Shantz* decisions, establishing a higher threshold for the granting of statutory injunctions when public bodies sought to displace homeless persons sheltering on public land. Responding to an application from the BC government in the spring of 2016 to displace more than a hundred persons sheltering on the grounds of the Victoria Courthouse, Hinkson initially refused to grant an injunction, finding that the occupants of the courthouse encampment "simply have nowhere to move to, if the injunction were to issue," and that the balance of convenience therefore "overwhelmingly" weighed in their favour. Three months later, after the provincial government had acquired more than two hundred units of new transitional housing, Hinkson granted an injunction ordering the dismantling of the courthouse camp. The ruling included a detailed formula for registration of unhoused persons seeking indoor housing, balancing privacy concerns of persons living on the margins of society with a mechanism for the orderly dismantling of the camp. The *Adamson* decision introduced a de facto requirement that a public body seeking an injunction to displace a homeless encampment must demonstrate an adequate supply of alternative sheltering options if it hopes to succeed at the balance of convenience stage of the test for the granting of an injunction. This precedent was later followed in sheltering cases involving the City of Nanaimo and City of Prince George, as well as in the provincial government's response to sheltering during the COVID-19 pandemic.

Trans Mountain Pipeline ULC v Mivasair, 2019 BCCA 156

Also: *Trans Mountain Pipeline ULC v Mivasair*, 2018 BCSC 947
Trans Mountain Pipeline ULC v Mivasair, 2018 BCSC 1890

Also: *Trans Mountain Pipeline ULC v Mivasair*, 2020 BCSC 1512
Trans Mountain Pipeline ULC v Mivasair, 2021 BCCA 109
Trans Mountain Pipeline ULC v Mivasair, 2021 BCCA 243
R v Leyden, 2021 BCCA 367
Trans Mountain Pipeline ULC v Mivasair, 2023 BCCA 299
R v Dick, 2024 BCCA 272
R v Cavanaugh, 2025 BCCA 252

This case arose from protests against the Trans Mountain Pipeline Expansion Project in Coast Salish and Secwépemc territory and an injunction awarded to the pipeline company in March 2018 enjoining interference with its operations (replacing an earlier injunction that had resulted in more than 100 arrests in 2014). The RCMP commenced enforcement of the fresh injunction, and in the months that followed, more than 200 people were arrested, 196 of whom were convicted of criminal contempt. Justice Kenneth Affleck dismissed the defence of necessity at the outset of the contempt trials, stating that the evidence failed to demonstrate "an imminent and immediate risk that could be met only with illegal conduct," and that the defence of necessity lacked an air of reality. Initial fines against convicted contemnors increased to custodial jail sentences of between fourteen and ninety days in prison (the latter sentence being imposed on a convicted contemnor who had been sentenced to twenty-eight days in jail on the initial charge and then breached the injunction a second time). Appeals brought by 4 contemnors sentenced early in the proceedings to fourteen days in jail were upheld, with the Court of Appeal finding that general deterrence was an important principle in sentencing. MP Elizabeth May, a lawyer, was convicted of criminal contempt of court for breaching the injunction and fined $1,500, with Justice Affleck finding that she "exploited her role as a member of parliament and as a party leader to encourage others to defy the injunction. Her punishment for criminal contempt must be greater than that of persons who do not hold positions of authority and influence." Several dozen more arrests occurred in 2020 and 2021, including in Kamloops and at "tree-sit" protests along the Barnet River in Burnaby and in the vicinity of a Coast Salish *kwekwecnewtxw* (watch house) on Burnaby Mountain, followed by convictions and jail sentences. One convicted land defender, a Métis man named James Leyden, had his conviction set aside, after the BC Court of Appeal found he had relied on an assurance from police that he would not be arrested for performing a "pipe ceremony" near the watch house. Other appeals were ongoing as of this book's publication date.

Teal Cedar Products Ltd v Rainforest Flying Squad, 2021 BCSC 605

Also: *Teal Cedar Products Ltd v Rainforest Flying Squad*, 2021 BCSC 1554
Teal Cedar Products Ltd v Rainforest Flying Squad, 2021 BCSC 1903
Teal Cedar Products Ltd v Rainforest Flying Squad, 2021 BCCA 387
Teal Cedar Products Ltd v Rainforest Flying Squad, 2021 BCSC 2288
Teal Cedar Products Ltd v Rainforest Flying Squad, 2022 BCSC 2045
Teal Cedar Products Ltd v Rainforest Flying Squad re Henderson, 2023 BCSC 201
Teal Cedar Products Ltd v Rainforest Flying Squad, 2023 BCSC 904
His Majesty the King v Emily Henderson also known as Ryan Henderson, 2023 CanLII 72136 (SCC)
Teal Cedar Products Ltd v Davidson, 2024 BCSC 81
Teal Cedar Products Ltd v Davidson, 2024 BCSC 662
R v Nelson, 2024 BCCA 72
R v Davidson, 2025 BCCA 111

This dispute arose from decades of tension over liquidation of the old-growth rainforests of Vancouver Island, amplified by growing public concern over the impacts of climate change. In August 2020, members of a loosely knit network of environmentalists styled the "Rainforest Flying Squad" initiated blockades at several sites in the vicinity of Fairy Creek on southern Vancouver Island, obstructing logging activities of Teal Cedar Products Ltd., the licence holder to the timber resources on Crown land in Tree Farm Licence (TFL) 46. The Rainforest Flying Squad was aligned with some members of the Pacheedaht First Nation, including elder Bill Jones, while the elected chief councillor, Jeff Jones, asked the protesters to leave the territory. In April 2021, Teal Cedar obtained an interlocutory injunction from BC Supreme Court Justice Fritz Verhoeven, enjoining interference with its operations. The RCMP's C-IRG commenced enforcement of the injunction in May 2021, resulting in nearly twelve hundred arrests in the months that followed. After a hearing in September 2021, BC Supreme Court Justice Douglas Thompson refused to extend the injunction, seeking "to get the Court out from the middle of the dispute," citing "unlawful" RCMP conduct and "serious and substantial infringement of civil liberties, including impairment of the freedom of the press to a marked degree," which risked bringing the court into disrepute. (Thompson had earlier varied the injunction on an application from the Canadian Association of Journalists, to provide express protection for the rights of journalists, amid concerns over imposition of broad "exclusion zones" by the RCMP). The BC Court of Appeal stayed and then reversed Thompson's decision, finding that he had improperly weighed the impact of policing operations in the balance-of-convenience analysis, and reinstating the injunction.

In February 2023, Justice Thompson acquitted protester Ryan Henderson based on a strict reading of the notice requirement for contempt, finding that the script the RCMP read out to protesters was inadequate. This resulted in the collapse of Crown prosecutions against approximately 175 protesters (out of approximately 350 who faced charges) when the Supreme Court of Canada refused to hear a Crown appeal. Most of the others pleaded guilty or were convicted after trials, facing sentences ranging from $750 fines to sixty days in jail (reduced on appeal to 51 days), depending on the timing, number, and severity of the breaches. The Fairy Creek dispute resulted in the largest number of arrests arising from breaches of a court order in Canadian history, up to the date of publication.

Source: Compiled by the author.

APPENDIX 3
Canadian Labour Congress Resolution on Injunctions, June 1966

Whereas the judiciary, by its readiness to grant injunctions, aligns itself on the side of employers; and

Whereas such judicial action inevitably leads to a loss of respect for the judiciary, and is bound just as inevitably to lead to defiance of the law;

Be it therefore resolved that the convention instruct the officers of the Congress and the provincial federations of labour, to urge its affiliated unions:

1 to engage in a strong and militant campaign to eliminate the use of the injunction in labour disputes;
2 to challenge injunctions wherever and whenever they are granted;
3 to organize systems of mutual aid for trade unions and members affected by the use of injunctions; and
4 to promote legislative, political and other activities in opposition to the use of injunctions in labour disputes.

– Resolution adopted by Canadian Labour Congress, June 1966

Source: Labour Gazette, June 1966, 283, as cited in John Stanton, *Never Say Die! The Life and Times of John Stanton, a Pioneer Labour Lawyer* (Ottawa: Steel Rail, 1987), app. A, 243.

NOTES

Introduction: The Social Relations of Property, Protest, and the Law

1 "Union Paper Editor Jailed for Contempt," *Vancouver Sun*, July 15, 1959, 9; John Stanton, *Never Say Die! The Life and Times of John Stanton, a Pioneer Labour Lawyer* (Ottawa: Steel Rail, 1987), 129; "Injunctions Won't Build Bridges or Catch Fish," *The Fisherman* (Vancouver), June 26, 1959.

2 Justice Douglas Thompson remarks during the BC Supreme Court hearing in *Teal Cedar Products Ltd v Rainforest Flying Squad*, Nanaimo, BC, September 14, 2021, as transcribed contemporaneously by the author.

3 *Teal Cedar Products Ltd v Rainforest Flying Squad*, 2021 BCSC 1903 [*Teal* (BCSC)].

4 *Slawsky v Isitt*, 2014 BCSC 1917; "Protesters in Grace Islet Dispute Given Month to Prepare Case," *Times Colonist* (Victoria), September 23, 2014.

5 *British Columbia v Adamson*, 2016 BCSC 584.

6 *Teal* (BCSC). The respite provided by Thompson's decision to deny the injunction extension was short-lived. Ten days later, the BC Court of Appeal stayed his order, which had the effect of reinstating an earlier interim injunction, pending consideration of an appeal by Teal Cedar against Thompson's decision not to extend the injunction. See *Teal Cedar Products Ltd v Rainforest Flying Squad*, 2021 BCCA 387; "Fairy Creek Protesters Vow to Carry on Despite New Injunction," *Globe and Mail*, October 11, 2021.

7 *MacMillan Bloedel Ltd v Mullin*, 1985 CanLII 154 (BCCA) (also *MacMillan Bloedel Ltd v Mullin*, 1985 CanLII 708 [BCSC]).

8 *MacMillan Bloedel Ltd v Mullin*, 1985 CanLII 154 (BCCA).

9 Basil Alexander, "Demonstrations and the Law: Patterns of Law's Negative Effects on the Ground and the Practical Implications," *UBC Law Review* 49, 3 (November 2016): 871. See also Basil Alexander, "Exploring a More Independent Freedom of Peaceful Assembly in Canada," *Western Journal of Legal Studies* 8, 1 (March 2018): 1–20.

10 Irina Ceric, "Beyond Contempt: Injunctions, Land Defense, and the Criminalization of Indigenous Resistance," *South Atlantic Quarterly* 119, 2 (April 2020): 355.
11 *Haida Nation v British Columbia (Minister of Forests)*, 2004 SCC 73, para 14, citing John J.L. Hunter, "Advancing Aboriginal Title Claims after *Delgamuukw:* The Role of the Injunction" (paper presented at the Continuing Legal Education Conference on Litigating Aboriginal Title, June 2000).
12 For a discussion of law's legitimacy, see David Dyzenhaus, "The Legitimacy of Legality," *University of Toronto Law Journal* 46, 1 (Winter 1996): 129–80. See also Alan Hyde, "The Concept of Legitimation in the Sociology of Law," *Wisconsin Law Review* 17 (1983): 379–426.
13 Eric Tucker, "'That Indefinite Area of Toleration': Criminal Conspiracy and Trade Unions in Ontario, 1837–77," *Labour/Le Travail* 27 (Spring 1991): 17.
14 See, for example, E.P. Thompson, *Customs in Common: Studies in Traditional Popular Culture* (New York: New Press, 1991).
15 Thompson, *Customs in Common*, 4, 9.
16 Thompson, *Customs in Common*, 151.
17 See Leo Panitch and Donald Swartz, *From Consent to Coercion: The Assault on Trade Union Freedoms*, 3rd ed. (Toronto: Garamond, 2003); also Leo Panitch and Donald Swartz, "Towards Permanent Exceptionalism: Coercion and Consent in Canadian Industrial Relations," *Labour/Le Travail* 13 (Spring 1984): 133–57. For the retrenchment of workers' rights, and reinforcement of employers' private property rights in the United States, see *Cedar Point Nursery v Hassid*, 594 US 139 (2021); "Supreme Court Rules Against Union Recruiting on California Farms," *New York Times*, June 23, 2021.
18 See Dominique Clément, *Canada's Rights Revolution: Social Movements and Social Change, 1937–82* (Vancouver: UBC Press, 2008); Dominique Clément, *Equality Deferred: Sex Discrimination and British Columbia's Human Rights State, 1953–84* (Vancouver: UBC Press, 2014). Also Ross Lambertson, *Repression and Resistance: Canadian Human Rights Activists, 1930–1960* (Toronto: University of Toronto Press, 2004).
19 See Tucker, "'That Indefinite Area of Toleration,'" 15–54.
20 *Poje v Attorney General for British Columbia*, [1953] 1 SCR 516; also *Canadian Transport Co (UK) Ltd v Alsbury*, [1952] 6 WWR (NS) 473 (BCSC); *United Nurses of Alberta v Alberta (Attorney General)*, [1992] 1 SCR 901.
21 Marie Henein, ed., *2018 Martin's Annual Criminal Code – Student Edition* (Toronto: Thomson Reuters, 2017), 44; *Criminal Code*, RSC 1985, c C-46, s 9.
22 *United Nurses of Alberta v Alberta (Attorney General)*.
23 Law Reform Commission of Canada, *Contempt of Court: Offences Against the Administration of Justice, Working Paper 20* (Ottawa: Department of Justice Canada, 1977), 2.
24 *Law and Equity Act*, RSBC 1996, c 253, s 39(1).
25 The previous leading case on the granting of injunctions in British Columbia, *British Columbia (Attorney General) v Wale*, has been largely superseded by *RJR-MacDonald* in most judicial decisions. In *RJR-MacDonald*, the Supreme Court of Canada built on tests established in the British case *American Cyanamid Co (No 1) v Ethicon Ltd* (1975) and the Canadian case *Manitoba (AG) v Metropolitan Stores Ltd* (1987). The Supreme Court found that the first stage of the test, whether there is a serious issue to be tried, "should be determined by a motions judge on the basis of common sense and an extremely limited review of the case on the merits." See *RJR-MacDonald Inc v Canada (Attorney General)*, [1994] 1

SCR 311; *American Cyanamid Co (No 1) v Ethicon Ltd*, 1975 UKHL 1; *Manitoba (AG) v Metropolitan Stores Ltd*, [1987] 1 SCR 110; *British Columbia (Attorney General) v Wale*, [1986] 9 BCLR (2d) 333 (BCCA); *Wale v British Columbia (Attorney General)*, [1991] 1 SCR 62.

26 Doreen Massey, *Space, Place, and Gender* (Minneapolis: University of Minnesota Press, 1994), 264.

27 Nicholas Blomley, *Law, Space, and the Geographies of Power* (New York: Guilford Press, 1994), xi.

28 Nicholas Blomley, "Law, Property, and the Geography of Violence: The Frontier, the Survey, and the Grid," *Annals of the Association of American Geographers* 93, 1 (March 2003): 121. See also Michael Simpson and Philippe Le Billon, "Reconciling Violence: Policing the Politics of Recognition," *Geoforum* 119 (February 2021): 111–21.

29 See Massey, *Space, Place, and Gender*; Doreen Massey, *Spatial Divisions of Labour: Social Structures and the Geography of Production* (New York: Methuen, 1984; 2nd ed., New York: Routledge, 1995); Nicholas Blomley, David Delaney, and Richard T. Ford, eds., *The Legal Geographies Reader: Law, Power, and Space* (Oxford: Blackwell, 2001); Irus Braverman, Nicholas Blomley, and David Delaney, eds., *The Expanding Spaces of Law: A Timely Legal Geography* (Stanford, CA: Stanford University Press, 2014); Mariana Valverde, *Chronotopes of Law: Jurisdiction, Scale and Governance* (London: Routledge, 2015); Peter Adey, *Mobility* (London: Routledge, 2010); Jane Holder and Carolyn Harrison, *Law and Geography* (New York: Oxford University Press, 2003).

30 Henri Lefebvre, "Le Droit à la ville," *L'Homme et la société* 6 (1967): 29–35; Henri Lefebvre, *Le Droit à la ville* (Paris: Anthropos, 1968); Don Mitchell, *The Right to the City: Social Justice and the Fight for Public Space* (New York: Guilford Press, 2003); David Harvey, *Rebel Cities: From the Right to the City to the Urban Revolution* (London: Verso, 2012); Anna Minton, *Ground Control: Fear and Happiness in the Twenty-First-Century City* (London: Penguin, 2009); Mark Purcell, "Excavating Lefebvre: The Right to the City and Its Urban Politics of the Inhabitant," *GeoJournal* 58 (2002): 99–108; David Mead, *The New Law of Peaceful Protest: Rights and Regulation in the Human Rights Act Era* (Oxford: Hart, 2010); Noel Castree et al., *Spaces of Work: Global Capitalism and Geographies of Labour* (London: Sage, 2004); Andrew Herod, *Geographies of Globalization: A Critical Introduction* (Oxford: Wiley-Blackwell, 2009); Andrew Herod, "Workers, Space, and Labor Geography," *International Labor and Working-Class History* 64 (Fall 2003): 112–38; Al Rainnie, Andrew Herod, and Susan McGrath-Champ, "Spatialising Industrial Relations," *Industrial Relations Journal* 38, 2 (2007): 102–11.

31 Lynn A. Staeheli and Don Mitchell, *The Peoples' Property? Power, Politics, and the Public* (New York: Routledge, 2008), xx. See also Don Mitchell and Lynn A. Staeheli, "Permitting Protest: Parsing the Fine Geography of Dissent in America," *International Journal of Urban and Regional Research* 29, 4 (December 2005): 796–813; Adam J. Barker, "(Re-)Ordering the New World: Settler Colonialism, Space, and Identity" (PhD diss., University of Leicester, 2012).

32 Sarah E. Hamill, "Private Rights to Public Property: The Evolution of Common Property in Canada," *McGill Law Journal* 58 (2012): 365–403. See also Sarah E. Hamill, "Private Property Rights and Public Responsibility: Leaving Room for the Homeless," *Windsor Review of Legal and Social Issues* 30 (2011): 91–116.

33 Melinda Harm Benson, "Rules of Engagement: The Spatiality of Judicial Review," in *The*

Expanding Spaces of Law: A Timely Legal Geography, ed. Irus Braverman, Nicholas Blomley, and David Delaney (Stanford, CA: Stanford University Press, 2014), 217.

34 Eric Tucker, "The Constitutional Right to Bargain Collectively: The Ironies of Labour History in the Supreme Court of Canada," *Labour/Le Travail* 61 (Spring 2008): 161. See also Morton J. Horwitz, "The Conservative Tradition in American Legal History," American *Journal of Legal History* 17, 3 (July 1973): 275–94; Donald J. Bourgeois, "The Role of the Historian in the Litigation Process," *Canadian Historical Review* 67, 2 (June 1986): 195–206; John Phillip Reid, "Law and History," *Loyola of Los Angeles Law Review* 27 (November 1993): 193–223.

35 Alfred H. Kelly, "Clio and the Court: An Illicit Love Affair," *Supreme Court Review* 1965 (1965): 119–58.

36 See Mariana Valverde, "Jurisdiction and Scale: Legal 'Technicalities' as Resources for Theory," *Social and Legal Studies* 18 (2009): 139–57.

37 Nicholas Blomley, "Performing Property: Making the World," *Canadian Journal of Law and Jurisprudence* 26, 1 (January 2013): 45; Joseph William Singer, "The Reliance Interest in Property," *Stanford Law Review* 40, 3 (February 1988): 611–751. See also Joseph W. Singer, "The Reliance Interest in Property Revisited," *Harvard Journal of the Legal Left* 7 (2011): 79–82; Brenna Bhandar, "Disassembling Legal Form: Ownership and the Racial Body," in *New Critical Legal Thinking: Law and the Political*, ed. Matthew Stone, Illan Wall, and Costas Douzinas (Abingdon, UK: Birkbeck Law Press, 2012), 112–27.

38 J.M. Neeson, *Commoners: Common Right, Enclosure and Social Change in England, 1700–1820* (Cambridge: Cambridge University Press, 1992); Minoti Chakravarty-Kaul, *Common Lands and Customary Law: Institutional Change in North India over the Past Two Centuries* (Oxford: Oxford University Pres, 1996); Joel Bakan, *The Corporation: The Pathological Pursuit of Profit and Power* (Toronto: Penguin, 2004).

39 Adam Smith, *Lectures on Jurisprudence*, ed. R.L. Meek, D.D. Raphael, and P.G. Stein (Oxford: Clarendon, 1978), 208, as quoted in Douglas Hay, "Time, Inequality, and Law's Violence," in *Law's Violence*, ed. Austin Sarat and Thomas R. Kearns (Ann Arbor: University of Michigan Press, 1993), 173.

40 Karl Marx, "Preface to *A Contribution to the Critique of Political Economy*," in *Preface and Introduction to* A Contribution to the Critique of Political Economy (1859; repr., Beijing: Foreign Language Press, 1976), 3.

41 Karl Marx and Friedrich Engels, *Manifesto of the Communist Party* (1848; repr., London: Verso, 1998), 55.

42 See William J. Chambliss, "The State, the Legal Order, and Social Problems," in *Social Problems, Law, and Society*, ed. Kathryn A. Stout et al. (Oxford: Rowman and Littlefield, 2004), 407.

43 Andrew Vincent, "Marx and Law," *Journal of Law and Society* 20, 4 (Winter 1993): 371–97; see also Terry Eagleton, "Base and Superstructure Revisited," *New Literary History* 31, 2 (Spring 2000): 231–40.

44 E.P. Thompson, *Whigs and Hunters: The Origin of the Black Act* (London: Pantheon, 1975), 259.

45 Thompson, *Whigs and Hunters*, 260. See also Christopher Hill, *The World Turned Upside Down: Radical Ideas During the English Revolution* (London: Maurice Temple Smith, 1972).

46 Thompson, *Whigs and Hunters*, 265–66.

47 Thompson, *Whigs and Hunters*, 263.

48 Thompson, *Whigs and Hunters*, 268.
49 Thompson, *Whigs and Hunters*, 266.
50 For leading works in the industrial pluralist school, see Paul C. Weiler, *Reconcilable Differences: New Directions in Canadian Labour Law* (Toronto: Carswell, 1980); Harry Arthurs, "Landscape and Memory: Labour Law, Legal Pluralism, and Globalization," in *Advancing Theory in Labour Law and Industrial Relations in a Global Context*, ed. T. Wilthagen (Amsterdam: Koninklijke Nederlandse Akademie van Wetenschappen, 1998) 21–34.
51 Tucker, "The Constitutional Right to Bargain Collectively," 166 and 168; Judy Fudge, "Brave New Worlds: Labour, the Courts, and the Canadian Charter of Rights and Freedoms," *Windsor Year Book of Access to Justice* 28, 1 (2010): 39–40; Judy Fudge, "The Supreme Court of Canada and the Right to Bargain Collectively: The Implications of the Health Services and Support Case in Canada and Beyond," *Industrial Law Journal* 37, 1 (March 2008): 25–48; Dianne Pothier, "Twenty Year of Labour Law and the Charter," *Osgoode Hall Law Journal* 40, 3/4 (2002): 369–99; *Health Services and Support – Facilities Subsector Bargaining Assn v British Columbia*, [2007] 2 SCR 391, 2007 SCC 27.
52 See W.N. Hohfeld, *Fundamental Legal Conceptions as Applied in Legal Reasoning* (New Haven, CT: Yale University Press, 1919); Judy Fudge and Eric Tucker, "The Freedom to Strike in Canada: A Brief Legal History," *Canadian Labour and Employment Law Journal* 15 (2009–10): 337–38.
53 See Bryan D. Palmer, "What's Law Got to Do with It? Historical Considerations on Class Struggle, Boundaries of Constraint, and Capitalist Authority," *Osgoode Hall Law Journal* 41, 2/3 (Summer-Fall 2003): 465–89.
54 John V. Orth, *Combination and Conspiracy: A Legal History of Trade Unionism, 1721–1906* (Oxford: Oxford University Press, 1991); Randall S. Echlin, "From Master and Servant to McKinley and Beyond: 200 Years of Employment Law in British Columbia, 1810 to 2010," in *Employment Law Conference, 2010 – Day 1* (Vancouver: Continuing Legal Education Society of British Columbia, 2010), 1–41; Tucker, "'That Indefinite Area of Toleration,'" 15–54.
55 Echlin, "From Master and Servant to McKinley and Beyond," 6; Hamar Foster, "British Columbia: Legal Institutions in the Far West, from Contact to 1871," Manitoba Law Journal 23 (1996): 309–10. See also Hamar Foster, "Mutiny on the Beaver: Law and Authority in the Fur Trade Navy, 1835–1840," *Manitoba Law Journal* 20 (1991): 15–45; William J. Burrill, "Class Conflict and Colonialism: The Coal Miners of Vancouver Island During the Hudson's Bay Company Era, 1848–1862" (MA thesis, University of Victoria, 1987). The role of the Hudson's Bay Company in relation to Indigenous peoples was highlighted in the *Kikkik* case (1958) and has also been examined in diverse scholarly studies, including Dorothy Eber, *Images of Justice: A Legal History of the Northwest Territories as Traced Through the Yellowknife Courthouse Collection of Inuit Sculpture* (Montreal and Kingston: McGill-Queen's University Press, 1997).
56 Echlin, "From Master and Servant to McKinley and Beyond," 7.
57 Dennis G. Molinaro, *An Exceptional Law: Section 98 and the Emergency State, 1919–1936* (Toronto: University of Toronto Press, 2017); Dennis Molinaro, "State Repression and Political Deportation in Canada, 1919–1936" (PhD diss., University of Toronto, 2015), 189–96; Peter MacKinnon, "Conspiracy and Sedition as Canadian Political Crimes," *McGill Law Journal* 23 (1977): 622–43; Judy Fudge and Eric Tucker, *Labour Before the Law: The*

Regulation of Workers' Collective Action in Canada, 1900–1948 (Toronto: Oxford University Press, 2001), 170; Barry Wright, Eric Tucker, and Susan Binnie, eds., *Canadian State Trials, Volume IV: Security, Dissent, and the Limits of Toleration in War and Peace, 1914–1939* (Toronto: University of Toronto Press, 2015).

58 See Joseph M. Weiler and Peter A. Gall, eds., *The Labour Code of British Columbia in the 1980's* (Calgary and Vancouver: Carswell Legal Publishers, 1984); Alan F.J. Arbitise, "'A Worthy, if Unlikely Enterprise': The Labour Relations Board and the Evolution of Labour Policy and Practice in British Columbia, 1973–1980," *BC Studies* 56 (Winter 1982–83): 3–43.

59 See Fudge and Tucker, *Labour Before the Law;* Peter McInnis, *Harnessing Labour Confrontation: Shaping the Postwar Settlement in Canada, 1943–1950* (Toronto: University of Toronto Press, 2002); Bora Laskin, "Labour Law: 1923–47," *Canadian Bar Review* 26 (1948): 286–94; Earl E. Palmer, "The Short, Unhappy Life of the 'Aristocratic' Doctrine," *University of Toronto Law Journal* 13, 2 (1960): 166–89. For an older literature that illuminates judicial intervention in BC labour disputes, see A.W.R. Carrothers, *The Labour Injunction in British Columbia: A Study of the Operation of the Injunction in Labour-Management Disputes in British Columbia, 1946–1955 with Particular Reference to the Law of Picketing* (Toronto and Montreal: CCH Canadian, 1956); Stuart Marshall Jamieson, *Times of Trouble: Labour Unrest and Industrial Conflict in Canada, 1900–1966* (Ottawa: Task Force on Labour Relations, 1968); Stuart Marshall Jamieson, "Regional Factors in Industrial Conflict: The Case of British Columbia," *Canadian Journal of Economics and Political Science* 28, 3 (August 1962): 405–16; Thomas R. Berger, *Injunctions in British Columbia* (Vancouver: British Columbia Federation of Labour, c. 1966). For more recent studies, see Edward George Fisher, "The Effects of Changes in Labour Legislation on Strike Activity in British Columbia, 1945–1975" (PhD diss., University of British Columbia, 1979); E.G. Fisher, "Strike Activity and Wildcat Strikes in British Columbia: 1945–1975," *Relations industrielles/Industrial Relations* 37, 2 (1982): 284–312; Richard Brown. "Picketing: Canadian Courts and the Labour Relations Board of British Columbia," *University of Toronto Law Journal* 31, 2 (Spring 1981): 153–99; James E. Dorsey, "Abandonment of Trade-Union Bargaining Rights and the Labour Code of British Columbia," *UBC Law Review* 11 (1977): 40–80; Weiler and Gall, *The Labour Code of British Columbia in the 1980's;* Harry Glasbeek, "Class War: Ontario Teachers and the Courts," Osgoode *Hall* Law Journal 37, 4 (1999): 805–42. There is also a recent body of literature examining changes in labour policy under Gordon Campbell's Liberal government of the early twenty-first century and struggles of hospital workers and teachers. See David Camfield, "Neoliberalism and Working-Class Resistance in British Columbia: The Hospital Employees' Union Struggle, 2002–2004," *Labour/Le Travail* 57 (Spring 2006): 9–42; Benjamin Isitt and Melissa Moroz, "The Hospital Employees Union Strike and the Privatization of Medicare in British Columbia, Canada," *International Labor and Working-Class History* 71 (Spring 2007): 91–111; David Camfield, "CUPE's Sympathy Strikes in British Columbia, October 2005: Raising the Bar for Solidarity," *Just Labour: A Canadian Journal of Work and Society* 11 (Autumn 2007): 35–42; David Camfield, "Sympathy for the Teacher: Labour Law and Transgressive Workers' Collective Action in British Columbia, 2005," *Capital and Class* 99 (2009): 81–107; Chris Hurl, "The Structure of Betrayal: Trade Union Bureaucracy and Public Sector Struggles in British Columbia," *Studies in Political Economy* 83 (Spring 2009); David Camfield, "Comment: Analyzing the 2004 HEU Strike and Union Bureaucracy,"

Studies in Political Economy 84 (Autumn 2009): 181–90; Sara Slinn, "Structuring Reality So That the Law Will Follow: British Columbia Teachers' Quest for Collective Bargaining Rights," *Labour/Le Travail* 68 (Fall 2011): 35–77.

60 Berger, *Injunctions in British Columbia,* 17.

61 Alain Touraine, *The Voice and the Eye: An Analysis of Social Movements* (Cambridge: Cambridge University Press, 1981); Frances Fox Piven and Richard A. Cloward, *Poor People's Movements: Why They Succeed, How They Fail* (New York: Pantheon, 1977); Frances Fox Piven, "The Social Structuring of Political Protest," *Politics and Society* 6, 3 (September 1976): 297–326; William K. Carroll, "Social Movements and Counter-Hegemony," in *World to Win: Contemporary Social Movements and Counter-Hegemony,* ed. William K. Carroll and Kanchan Sarker (Winnipeg: ARP Books, 2016), 9–60; William K. Carroll and R.S. Ratner, "Social Movements and Counter-Hegemony: Lessons from the Field," *New Proposals: Journal of Marxism and Interdisciplinary Inquiry* 4, 1 (October 2010): 7–22; Stuart Lowe, *Urban Social Movements: The City After Castells* (London: Macmillan, 1986). For an older collection of essays on social movements, see Samuel Clark, J. Paul Grayson, and Linda M. Grayson, eds., *Prophecy and Protest: Social Movements in Twentieth-Century Canada* (Toronto: Gage, 1975).

62 Manuel Castells, *The City and the Grassroots: A Cross-Cultural Theory of Urban Social Movements* (Berkeley and Los Angeles: University of California Press, 1983). My approach also draws on Jürgen Habermas's work on the role of ideology in social movement mobilization. See Kenneth H. Tucker Jr., "Ideology and Social Movements: The Contributions of Habermas," *Sociology Inquiry* 59, 1 (January 1989): 30–47.

63 Piven and Cloward, *Poor People's Movements,* 3–4.

64 Carroll, "Social Movements and Counter-Hegemony," 47; Antonio Gramsci, *Selections from the Prison Notebooks of Antonio Gramsci* (New York: International Publishers, 1971).

65 John Borrows, *Canada's Indigenous Constitution* (Toronto: University of Toronto Press, 2010); Hamar Foster, Heather Raven, and Jeremy Webber, eds., Let Right Be Done: Aboriginal Title, the Calder Case, and the Future of Indigenous Rights (Vancouver: UBC Press, 2007); Taiaiake Alfred, *Peace, Power, Righteousness: An Indigenous Manifesto* (Don Mills, ON: Oxford University Press, 1999); Glen Sean Coulthard, *Red Skin, White Masks: Rejecting the Colonial Politics of Recognition* (Minneapolis: University of Minnesota Press, 2014). See also Aoife Duffy, "Indigenous Peoples' Land Rights: Developing a Sui Generis Approach to Ownership and Restitution," *International Journal on Minority and Group Rights* 15, 4 (November 2008): 505–38; Felix Hoehn, "The Emerging Equality Paradigm in Aboriginal Law" (LLM thesis, University of Saskatchewan, 2011); Alan Hanna, "Making the Round: Aboriginal Title in the Common Law from a Tsilhqot'in Legal Perspective," *Ottawa Law Review* 45, 3 (2015): 365–402; Michael Fabris (Krebs), "Decolonizing Neoliberalism? First Nations Reserves, Private Property Rights, and the Legislation of Indigenous Dispossession in Canada," in *Contested Property Claims: What Disagreement Tells Us About Ownership,* ed. Maja Hojer Bruun et al. (London: Routledge, 2018), 185–204; Tina Loo, *Making Law, Order and Authority in British Columbia, 1821–1871* (Toronto: University of Toronto Press, 1994); R. Cole Harris, *Making Native Space: Colonialism, Resistance, and Reserves in British Columbia* (Vancouver: UBC Press, 2003).

66 Borrows, *Canada's Indigenous Constitution,* 14.

67 Jisgang Nika Collison, ed., *Athlii Gwaii: Upholding the Law at Lyell Island* (Vancouver: Locarno Press, 2018), 139; Nicholas Blomley, "'Shut the Province Down': First Nations

Blockades in British Columbia, 1984–1995," *BC Studies* 111 (Autumn 1996): 5–35; Steven Point, "Understanding Native Activism," *BC Studies* 89 (Spring 1991): 124–29; Shiri Pasternak and Dayna Nadine Scott, "Introduction: Getting Back the Land," *South Atlantic Quarterly* 119, 2 (April 2020): 205–13; Ceric, "Beyond Contempt," 353–69; Tyler McCreary and Jerome Turner, "The Contested Scales of Indigenous and Settler Jurisdiction: Unist'ot'en Struggles with Canadian Pipeline Governance," *Studies in Political Economy* 99, 3 (February 2019): 1–23; Tyler McCreary, "Between the Commodity and the Gift: The Coastal GasLink Pipeline and the Contested Temporalities of Canadian and Witsuwit'en Law," *Journal of Human Rights and the Environment* 11 (December 2020): 122–45; Michael Simpson and Philippe Le Billon, "Reconciling Violence: Policing the Politics of Recognition," *Geoforum* 119 (February 2021): 111–21; Yale D. Belanger and P. Whitney Lackenbauer, *Blockades or Breakthroughs? Aboriginal Peoples Confront the Canadian State* (Montreal and Kingston: McGill-Queen's University Press, 2015). See also Nicholas Blomley, "Law, Property, and the Geography of Violence: The Frontier, the Survey, and the Grid," *Annals of the Association of American Geographers* 93, 1 (March 2003): 121–41.

68 Michael M'Gonigle, "Green Legal Theory: A New Approach to the Concept of Environmental Law," *Okologisches-Wirtschaften* 4 (2008): 34–38; Jeremy Wilson, *Talk and Log: Wilderness Politics in British Columbia* (Vancouver: UBC Press, 1998); Warren Magnusson and Karena Shaw, eds, *A Political Space: Reading the Global Through Clayoquot Sound* (Montreal and Kingston: McGill-Queen's University Press, 2002); Sarah B. Pralle, *Branching Out, Digging In: Environmental Advocacy and Agenda Setting* (Washington, DC: Georgetown University Press, 2006), 35–138; Frank Zelko, "Making Greenpeace: The Development of Direct Action Environmentalism in British Columbia," *BC Studies* 142/143 (Summer/Autumn 2004): 197–239; Lorna Stefanick, "Baby Stumpy and the War in the Woods: Competing Frames of British Columbia Forests." *BC Studies* 130 (2001): 41–68; Debra J. Salazar and Donald K. Alper, "Reconciling Environmentalism and the Left: Perspectives on Democracy and Social Justice in British Columbia's Environmental Movement," *Canadian Journal of Political Science* 35 (September 2002): 527–66; Ronald MacIsaac and Anne Champagne, eds., *Clayoquot Mass Trials: Defending the Rainforest* (Gabriola Island, BC: New Society, 1994); Ronald B. Hatch, ed., *Clayoquot & Dissent* (Vancouver: Ronsdale, 1995); Pierre Walter, "Adult Learning in New Social Movements: Environmental Protest and the Struggle for the Clayoquot Sound Rainforest," *Adult Education Quarterly* 57, 3 (May 2007): 248–63; Michaela Killoran Mann, "'Clearcut' Conflict: Clayoquot Sound Campaign and the Moral Imagination" (MA thesis, Université Saint Paul University, 2013).

69 Christabelle Sethna and Steve Hewitt, "Clandestine Operations: The Vancouver Women's Caucus, the Abortion Caravan, and the RCMP," *Canadian Historical Review* 90, 3 (2009): 463–95; Ann Thomson, *Winning Choice on Abortion: How British Columbia and Canadian Feminists Won the Battles of the 1970s and 1980s* (Vancouver: Trafford, 2005); Frances Wasserlein, "'An Arrow Aimed at the Heart': The Vancouver Women's Caucus and the Abortion Campaign 1969–1971" (MA thesis, Simon Fraser University, 1990); Don Mitchell, "The S.U.V. Model of Citizenship: Floating Bubbles, Buffer Zones, and the Rise of the 'Purely Atomic' Individual," *Political Geography* 24, 1 (January 2005): 77–100.

70 Margaret E. Beare, Nathalie Des Rosiers, and Abigail C. Deshman, eds., *Putting the State on Trial: The Policing of Protest During the G20 Summit* (Vancouver: UBC Press, 2015). See also Toronto Police Service, *G20 Summit, Toronto, Ontario, June 2010: Toronto*

Police Service After-Action Review (Toronto: Toronto Police Service, 2011); Alexander, "Demonstrations and the Law," 895–920.

71 See, for example, Christopher Moore, *The British Columbia Court of Appeal: The First Hundred Years* (Vancouver: UBC Press, 2010); Hamar Foster and John McLaren. "'For the Better Administration of Justice': The Court of Appeal for British Columbia, 1910–2010," *BC Studies* 162 (Summer 2009): 5–24. Philip Girard, *Bora Laskin: Bringing Law to Life* (Toronto: Osgoode Society for Canadian Legal History, 2005); William Kaplan, *Canadian Maverick: The Life of Ivan C. Rand* (Toronto: University of Toronto Press, 2009).

72 Judy Fudge and Eric Tucker, "'Everybody Knows What a Picket Line Means': Picketing Before the British Columbia Court of Appeal," *BC Studies* 162 (Summer 2009): 75.

73 William K. Carroll, *Corporate Power and Canadian Capitalism* (Vancouver: UBC Press, 1986); William K. Carroll, *Corporate Power in a Globalizing World: A Study of Elite Social Organization* (Toronto: Oxford University Press, 2004); William K. Carroll, *The Making of a Transnational Capitalist Class: Corporate Power in the 21st Century* (London: Zed Books, 2010). See also John Scott and Peter J. Carrington, eds., *Sage Handbook of Social Network Analysis* (London: Sage, 2011); David Knoke and James H. Kuklinski, *Network Analysis* (London: Sage, 1982); David Knoke, *Political Networks: The Structural Perspective* (Cambridge: Cambridge University Press, 1990); David Knoke and Song Yang, *Social Network Analysis*, rev. ed. (London: Sage, 2007); Daniel Martin Katz and Derek K. Stafford, "Hustle and Flow: A Social Network Analysis of the American Federal Judiciary," *Ohio State Law Journal* 71, 3 (2010): 457–509; M.H. Zack, "Researching Organizational Systems Using Social Network Analysis," *Proceedings of the 33rd Annual Hawaii International Conference on System Sciences* (2000).

74 Michael E. Tigar and Madeleine R. Levy, *Law and the Rise of Capitalism*, 2nd ed. (1977; repr., New York: Monthly Review Press, 2000).

75 Reinhold Kramer and Tom Mitchell, *When the State Trembled: How A.J. Andrews and the Citizens' Committee Broke the Winnipeg General Strike* (Toronto: University of Toronto Press, 2010).

76 Michel Foucault, "The Subject and Power," *Critical Inquiry* 8 (Summer 1982): 791; see also Mariana Valverde, "Spectres of Foucault in Law and Society Scholarship," *Annual Review of Law and Social Science* 6 (2010): 45–59.

77 Kate Malleson and Peter H. Russell, eds., *Appointing Judges in an Age of Judicial Power: Critical Perspectives from Around the World* (Toronto: University of Toronto Press, 2006).

78 J.A.G. Griffiths, *The Politics of the Judiciary* (London: Fontana, 1977), 213–14. See also Alan Paterson, "The Judges, the House of Lords and Politics," *International Journal of the Legal Profession* 16, 1 (March 2009): 43–48.

79 Griffiths, *The Politics of the Judiciary*, 213.

80 Griffiths, *The Politics of the Judiciary*, 208.

81 Bertha Wilson, "Will Women Judges Really Make a Difference?" *Osgoode Hall Law Journal* 28 (1990): 507–22; Nathan Theodore Nemetz, "Concept of an Independent Judiciary," *UBC Law Review* 20 (1986): 291–92; Marie-Claire Belleau and Rebecca Johnson, "Judging Gender: Difference and Dissent at the Supreme Court of Canada," *International Journal of the Legal Profession* 15, 1–2 (2008): 57–71.

82 Alan C. Cairns, "The Judicial Committee and Its Critics," *Canadian Journal of Political Science* 4, 3 (1971): 301–45; Alan C. Cairns, *Charter versus Federalism: The Dilemmas of Constitutional Reform* (Montreal and Kingston: McGill-Queen's University Press, 1992);

Peter H. Russell, "The Jurisdiction of the Supreme Court of Canada: Present Policies and a Programme for Reform," *Osgoode Hall Law Journal* 6, 1 (1968): 1–38; F.L. Morton, ed., *Law, Politics and the Judicial Process in Canada*, 3rd ed. (Calgary: University of Calgary Press, 2002). See also "Judge Who Issued Court Injunctions to End Rail Blockades Acted for CN Rail as a Lawyer," *APTN News*, February 12, 2013, https://www.aptnnews.ca/national-news/judge-who-issued-court-injunctions-to-end-rail-blockades-acted-for-cn-rail-as-a-lawyer/.

83 Morton, *Law, Politics and the Judicial Process in Canada*, 169.

84 Nemetz, "Concept of an Independent Judiciary," 290.

85 James W. St. G. Walker, *"Race," Rights and the Law in the Supreme Court of Canada: Historical Case Studies* (Waterloo, ON: Wilfrid Laurier University Press, 1997).

86 Orley Ashenfelter, Theodore Eisenberg, and Stewart J. Schwab, "Politics and the Judiciary: The Influence of Judicial Background on Case Outcomes," *Journal of Legal Studies* 24, 2 (June 1995): 281.

87 Duncan Kennedy, *A Critique of Adjudication: Fin de Siècle* (Cambridge, MA: Harvard University Press, 1997). As Kerry Rittich argued in a review of Kennedy's work, "instability and choice are part of the structure of adjudication itself." Kerry Rittich, "Who's Afraid of the *Critique of Adjudication?* Tracing the Discourse of Law in Development," *Cardozo Law Review* 22 (2001): 929–45. See also Steven J. Burton, *Judging in Good Faith* (Cambridge: Cambridge University Press, 1992), 141.

88 See also Gordon L. Clark, "A Question of Integrity: The National Labor Relations Board, Collective Bargaining and the Relocation of Work," *Political Geography Quarterly* 7, 3 (July 1988): 209–27. As Clark concludes in his study of adjudication, bias, and integrity within the US National Labor Relations Board (NLRB): "One must be also cautious of ascribing too much power to agents and institutions. Having identified the bases of one set of decisions, it should not be assumed that these decisions will hold in all subsequent cases. Again, the evidence presented in this paper should be enough to persuade those who imagine adjudication to be final to realize that this is rarely true. There may be instances where a case is exhausted, but the landscape is littered with the results of previous decisions, some consistent with the past, others quite contrary to the latest incarnation. The map of adjudication must be rationalized, if only to convince others of the integrity of the NLRB" (233). 223.

89 Ian Donald, interviewed by Christopher Moore, May 13, 2008, as quoted in Moore, *The British Columbia Court of Appeal*, 196.

90 Foster and McLaren, "'For the Better Administration of Justice,'" 16–17. See also Robert A.J. McDonald, *Making Vancouver: Class, Status and Social Boundaries, 1863–1913* (Vancouver: UBC Press 1996); Ross Lambertson, "The BC Court of Appeal and Civil Liberties," *BC Studies*, 162 (Summer 2009): 101.

91 Harry Rankin, *Rankin's Law: Recollections of a Radical* (Vancouver: November House, 1975), 149.

92 Rankin, *Rankin's Law*, 72.

93 W. Wesley Pue, "Banned from Lawyering: William John Gordon Martin, Communist," *BC Studies* 162 (Summer 2009): 111–36; see also W. Wesley Pue, *Law School: The Story of Legal Education in British Columbia* (Vancouver: Continuing Legal Education Society of British Columbia/Faculty of Law, University of British Columbia, 1995), 240–44.

94 Robert J. Sharpe, *The Lazier Murder: Prince Edward County, 1884* (Toronto: Osgoode Society for Canadian Legal History/University of Toronto Press, 2011), 6.

Chapter 1: Masters, Servants, and Judges During the "Vancouver Island War"

1 J. Kavanagh, *The Vancouver Island Strike* (Vancouver: British Columbia Miners' Liberation League, n.d. [c. 1913]).

2 Desmond Morton, "Aid to the Civil Power: The Canadian Militia in Support of Social Order, 1867–1914," *Canadian Historical Review* 51, 4 (1970): 423–24; Peter Guy Silverman, "A History of the Militia and Defences of British Columbia, 1871–1914" (MA thesis, University of British Columbia, 1956), 160–92. See also Lt.-Col. F.A. Robertson, "The 5th B.C. Regiment, Canadian Garrison Artillery, and Early Defences of the British Columbia Coast" (manuscript, D. Hist., file 954.203 (D1), ch. 20), as cited in Morton, 424; Maj. T.V. Scudamore, "Aid to the Civil Power," *Canadian Defence Quarterly* 9, 2 (January 1932), 253–60; J. Castell Hopkins, *Canadian Annual Review of Public Affairs* (Toronto: Annual Review Publishing Company, 1913): 681–82; L.W. Bentley, "Aid to the Civil Power: Social and Political Aspects, 1904–1924," *Canadian Defence Quarterly* 8, 1 (1978): 47–51; Desmond Morton, "Bayonets in the Streets: The Canadian Experience of Aid of the Civil Power, 1867–1990," *Canadian Defence Quarterly* 20, 5 (1991): 30–34; Judy Torrance, "The Response of Canadian Governments to Violence," *Canadian Journal of Political Science* 10, 3 (1977): 473–96; Martin F. Auger, "On the Brink of Civil War: The Canadian Government and the Suppression of the 1918 Quebec Easter Riots," *Canadian Historical Review* 89, 4 (December 2008): 503–40.

3 Kavanagh, *The Vancouver Island Strike*, 1.

4 Randall S. Echlin, "From Master and Servant to McKinley and Beyond: 200 Years of Employment Law in British Columbia, 1810 to 2010," in *Employment Law Conference, 2010 – Day 1* (Vancouver: Continuing Legal Education Society of British Columbia, 2010), 1–41; Alan Grove and Ross Lambertson, "Pawns of the Powerful: The Politics of Litigation in the Union Colliery Case," *BC Studies* 103 (Fall 1994): 3–31; Eric Tucker, "'That Indefinite Area of Toleration': Criminal Conspiracy and Trade Unions in Ontario, 1837–77," *Labour/Le Travail* 27 (Spring 1991): 15–54; Judy Fudge and Eric Tucker, "'Everybody Knows What a Picket Line Means': Picketing Before the British Columbia Court of Appeal," *BC Studies* 162 (Summer 2009): 53–79; Judy Fudge and Eric Tucker, "Work on Trial: Canadian Labour Law Struggles," in *Work on Trial: Canadian Labour Law Struggles*, ed. Judy Fudge and Eric Tucker (Toronto: Irwin, 2010), 1–12; Douglas Hay and Paul Craven, eds., *Masters, Servants, and Magistrates in Britain and the Empire, 1562–1955* (Chapel Hill and London: University of North Carolina Press, 1994).

5 John V. Orth, *Combination and Conspiracy: A Legal History of Trade Unionism, 1721–1906* (Oxford: Oxford University Press, 1991), 2.

6 Jan Peterson, *Hub City: Nanaimo, 1886–1920* (Victoria: Heritage House, 2003), 206–12; Lynne Bowen, *Boss Whistle: The Coal Miners of Vancouver Island Remember*, rev. ed. (1982; repr., Nanaimo: Rocky Point Books, 2003); John Douglas Belshaw, *Colonization and Community: The Vancouver Island Coalfield and the Making of the British Columbian Working Class* (Montreal and Kingston: McGill-Queen's University Press, 2002); John R. Hinde, *When Coal Was King: Ladysmith and the Coal-Mining Industry of Vancouver Island* (Vancouver: UBC Press, 2004); Roger Stonebanks, *Fighting for Dignity: The Ginger Goodwin Story* (St. John's: Canadian Committee on Labour History, 2004); Susan Mayse, *Ginger: The Life and Death of Albert Goodwin* (Madeira Park, BC: Harbour Publishing,

1990); Alan John Wargo, "The Great Coal Strike: The Vancouver Island Coal Miners' Strike, 1912–1914" (BA essay, University of British Columbia, 1962); Reginald Roy, "The Seaforths and the Strikers: Nanaimo, August 1913," *BC Studies* 43 (Autumn 1979): 81–93; Daniel Schade, "A Militia History of the Occupation of the Vancouver Island Coalfields, August 1913," *BC Studies* 182 (Summer 2014): 11–44; John Norris, "The Vancouver Island Coal Miners, 1912–1914: A Study of an Organizational Strike," *BC Studies* 45 (1980): 56–72; John R. Hinde, "'Stout Ladies and Amazons': Women in the British Columbia Coal Mining Community of Ladysmith, 1912–14," *BC Studies* 114 (1997): 33–57; Kavanagh, *The Vancouver Island Strike;* Paul A. Phillips, *No Power Greater: A Century of Labour in British Columbia* (Vancouver: Boag Foundation, 1967).

7 Hinde, *When Coal Was King*, 204.

8 Grove and Lambertson, "Pawns of the Powerful," 3–31.

9 Grove and Lambertson, "Pawns of the Powerful," 3–31.

10 For the development of Vancouver Island's coal economy, see H.K. Ralston, "Miners and Managers: The Organization of Coal Production on Vancouver Island by the Hudson's Bay Company, 1848–1862," in E. Blanche Norcross, ed., *The Company on the Coast* (Nanaimo: Nanaimo Historical Society, 1983), 42–55; also Adele Perry, *On the Edge of Empire: Gender, Race, and the Making of British Columbia, 1849–1871* (Toronto: University of Toronto Press, 2001).

11 Martin Robin, "British Columbia: The Company Province," in *Canadian Provincial Politics: The Party Systems in the Ten Provinces, Second Edition*, ed. Martin Robin (Scarborough, ON: Prentice-Hall, 1978), 28–60; James Conley, "Frontier Labourers, Crafts in Crisis and the Western Canadian Labour Revolt," *Labour/Le Travail* 23 (Spring 1989): 1–37; Jeremy Mouat, "The Genesis of Western Exceptionalism: British Columbia's Hard Rock Miners, 1895–1903," *Canadian Historical Review* 71, 3 (September 1990): 317–45.

12 Allen Seager, "Socialists and Workers: The Western Canadian Coal Miners, 1900–21," *Labour/Le Travail* 16 (Fall 1985): 23–60; Gerald Friesen, "Yours in Revolt: Regionalism, Socialism, and the Western Canadian Labour Movement," *Labour/Le Travail* 1 (1976): 141–57; Ross Alfred Johnson, "No Compromise – No Political Trading: The Marxian Socialist Tradition in British Columbia" (PhD diss., University of British Columbia, 1975); Ronald Grantham, "Some Aspects of the Socialist Movement in British Columbia" (MA thesis, University of British Columbia, 1942); A. Ross McCormack, *Reformers, Rebels, and Revolutionaries: The Western Canadian Radical Movement, 1899–1919* (Toronto: University of Toronto Press, 1977).

13 Judy Fudge and Eric Tucker, *Labour Before the Law: The Regulation of Workers' Collective Action in Canada, 1900–1948* (Toronto: Oxford University Press, 2001), 302. See also Tucker, "'That Indefinite Area of Toleration,'" 15–54. For a discussion of reasons for the delayed arrival of labour legislation in British Columbia relative to American and other international jurisdictions, see Harold Fabian Underhill, "Labor Legislation in British Columbia" (PhD dissertation, University of California at Berkley, 1936), 266–81.

14 Hay and Craven, *Masters, Servants, and Magistrates*, 1–3.

15 Fudge and Tucker, *Labour Before the Law*, 2. See also Tucker, "'That Indefinite Zone of Toleration,'" 15–54.

16 See Don Macgillivray, "Military Aid to the Civil Power: The Cape Breton Experience in the 1920's," *Acadiensis* 3, 2 (Spring 1974): 45–64; Morton, "Aid to the Civil Power," 407–25; Jeremy Mouat, "The Politics of Coal: A Study of the Wellington Miners' Strike of 1890–91," *BC Studies* 77 (Spring 1988): 3–29.

17 Phillips, *No Power Greater*, 5–9 and 38–39.
18 Editorial, *Western Socialist* (Vancouver), April 24, 1903, 2.
19 Orth, *Combination and Conspiracy*, 153; see also Paul Craven, "Workers' Conspiracies in Toronto, 1854–72," *Labour/Le Travail* 14 (Fall 1984): 49–70; Tucker, "'That Indefinite Area of Toleration,'" 17.
20 As quoted in A.W.R. Carrothers, "Legislative History of the BC Trade-Unions Act: The Rossland Miners Case," *UBC Legal Notes* 2, 4 (March 1956), 340.
21 Carrothers, "Legislative History of the BC Trade-Unions Act," 341.
22 Phillips, *No Power Greater*, 33–34.
23 Phillips, *No Power Greater*, 33.
24 Canada, *Report of the Royal Commission on Industrial Disputes in the Province of British Columbia* (1903), 73–74; Allan D. Orr, "The Western Federation of Miners and the Royal Commission on Industrial Disputes with Special Reference to the Vancouver Island Coal Miners' Strike" (MA thesis, University of British Columbia, 1968); Paul Craven, *"An Impartial Umpire": Industrial Relations and the Canadian State, 1900–1911* (Toronto: University of Toronto Press, 1980), 240–70.
25 Jeremy Webber, "Compelling Compromise: Canada Chooses Conciliation over Arbitration, 1900–1907," *Labour/Le Travail* 28 (Autumn 1991): 15–57; see also Jeremy H.A. Webber, "Standards of Industrial Justice: Ideology and the Reports of Conciliation Boards Under the Industrial Disputes Investigation Act 1907–1925" (LLM thesis, York University, 1988).
26 Webber, "Standards of Industrial Justice," 339–40.
27 Phillips, *No Power Greater*, 47. See also Webber, "Standards of Industrial Justice," 173–88.
28 See the *Criminal Code* (1892), ss 520–24 (Parts 5 [Unlawful Assemblies, Riots, Breaches of the Peace] and 39 [Offences Connected with Trade and Breaches of Contract]).
29 Fudge and Tucker, *Labour Before the Law*, 74.
30 Canadian Collieries mine manager Robert Henderson later claimed that he ordered contractor Richard Coe to dismiss Mottishaw because he had started work underground without Henderson's permission. The union viewed the dismissal as discrimination for Mottishaw's filing of the gas report with the province's inspector of mines. Stonebanks, *Fighting for Dignity*, 41.
31 Kavanagh, *The Vancouver Island Strike*, 1–2; Stonebanks, *Fighting for Dignity*, 31–39.
32 Stonebanks, *Fighting for Dignity*, 31–36 and 51–52; Kavanagh, *The Vancouver Island Strike*, 4 and 14.
33 Kavanagh, *The Vancouver Island Strike*, 2–3.
34 Phillips, *No Power Greater*, 56–58; Kavanagh, *The Vancouver Island Strike*, 5.
35 Kavanagh, *The Vancouver Island Strike*, 3–4.
36 Phillips, *No Power Greater*, 57.
37 Kavanagh, *The Vancouver Island Strike*, 3; Phillips, *No Power Greater*, 57.
38 "Charmer Carried Mine Workers to Union Bay," *Nanaimo Free Press*, July 8, 1913.
39 "Communication," *Nanaimo Free Press*, July 9, 1913.
40 "Farrington and Trades Unionism," *Nanaimo Free Press*, July 11, 1913. See also "Communication," *Nanaimo Free Press*, August 28, 1913.
41 Reprinted in "Should Government Work Our Mines," *Nanaimo Free Press*, July 21, 1913.
42 "Communication," *Nanaimo Free Press*, July 10, 1913; "Mining Notes," *Nanaimo Free*

Press, July 17, 1913. See also "Letters Between UMW of A and Labor Department," *Nanaimo Free Press,* July 12, 1913.

43 "Crothers a Man of the Moment," *Nanaimo Free Press,* July 10, 1913. See also "Mr. Crothers Interviewed on Mining Situation," *Nanaimo Free Press,* July 15, 1913.

44 Kavanagh, *The Vancouver Island Strike,* 6. See also "Mr. F.H. Shepherd, MP, to Meet Minister Crothers," *Nanaimo Free Press,* July 7, 1913.

45 "Mining Notes."

46 "Minister Visits Union Concert," *Nanaimo Free Press,* July 19, 1913.

47 "Premier May Call Round Table Conference to Settle Strike," *Nanaimo Free Press,* July 19, 1913. The *Nanaimo Free Press,* meanwhile, called on the premier to appoint a stand-alone minister of mines, transferring the portfolio from himself to a "thoroughly practical mining man." "Minister of Mines," *Nanaimo Free Press,* July 19, 1913.

48 "Crothers a Man of the Moment."

49 "Mr. Crothers' Visit," *Nanaimo Free Press,* July 19, 1913.

50 Fudge and Tucker, *Labour Before the Law,* 75–76; Canada, *Report of the Royal Commission on Coal Mining Disputes on Vancouver Island* (Ottawa: King's Printer, 1913); "No Discrimination for Joining a Union," *Globe and Mail,* October 7, 1913.

51 "Skirmishes at Cumberland Between Strikers and Others," *Nanaimo Free Press,* July 21, 1913; Kavanagh, *The Vancouver Island Strike,* 6–7; Bowen, *Boss Whistle,* 152–53. For a rigorous defence of Naylor, see a letter from Cumberland mayor Alexander Campbell to the press: "Communication," *Nanaimo Free Press,* September 2, 1913.

52 Kavanagh, *The Vancouver Island Strike,* 8. Four days after the Cumberland clash, reports surfaced of an attempt to blow up the Trent River bridge, ten kilometres outside the town. See Hinde, *When Coal Was King,* 176.

53 Kavanagh, *The Vancouver Island Strike,* 9.

54 Kavanagh, *The Vancouver Island Strike,* 7–8.

55 Hinde, *When Coal Was King,* 179–81.

56 "Further Evidence of Cases Arising Out of Strike Disturbance," *Nanaimo Free Press,* August 28, 1913; Kavanagh, *The Vancouver Island Strike,* 10; Phillips, *No Power Greater,* 58; Harry Gregson, *A History of Victoria 1842–1970* (Victoria: Victoria Observer Publishing Co., 1970), 145.

57 Kavanagh, *The Vancouver Island Strike,* 9–10; Hinde, *When Coal Was King,* 183–85. The following morning, the Extension strikers burned the mine manager's home to the ground, after members of the militia temporarily left the mining camp. Sixteen-year-old William Bowater Jr. was later charged with the arson. See Bowen, *Boss Whistle,* 181; Hinde, *When Coal Was King,* 190.

58 Hinde, *When Coal Was King,* 199.

59 "Incidents Concerning Local Deadlock," *Nanaimo Free Press,* September 2, 1913.

60 Kavanagh, *The Vancouver Island Strike,* 10.

61 "Mobs Beat Police Forces in Nanaimo and Ladysmith," *Globe and Mail,* August 14, 1913; "Found That Bowser Called Out the Troops," *Vancouver Sun,* August 28, 1913; Schade, "A Militia History of the Occupation of the Vancouver Island Coalfields," 16–17; *Militia Act,* SC 1904 c 23, ss 80–87; Silverman, "A History of the Militia and Defences of British Columbia," 160–92.

62 Roy, "The Seaforths and the Strikers," 81–85; Schade, "A Militia History of the Occupation of the Vancouver Island Coalfields," 20–32; Douglas E. Harker, *The Dukes* (Vancouver:

British Columbia Regiment (DCO), 1973), 47. For biographical information on Hall, see J.F. Bosher, *Imperial Vancouver Island: Who Was Who, 1850–1950* (Woodstock, UK: J.F. Bosher in conjunction with Writersworld, 2012), 329–30.

63 See James Wood, *Militia Myths: Ideas of the Canadian Citizen Soldier* (Vancouver: UBC Press, 2010).

64 "John Place Charged," *Nanaimo Free Press,* August 27, 1913, 1; "Decide to Take Speedy Trial," *Daily Colonist* (Victoria), August 30, 1913, 1; Harker, *The Dukes,* 48; Roy, "The Seaforths and the Strikers," 85–86.

65 Kavanagh, *The Vancouver Island Strike,* 11–12.

66 Kavanagh, *The Vancouver Island Strike,* 12.

67 Kavanagh, *The Vancouver Island Strike,* 13.

68 As quoted in Roy, "The Seaforths and the Strikers," 85.

69 Wargo, "The Great Coal Strike," 129–30; Bowen, *Boss Whistle,* 188. For a discussion of rioting in historical context, see E.P. Thompson, *Customs in Common* (New York: New Press, 1991), 224–51; E.P. Thompson, "The Moral Economy of the English Crowd in the Eighteenth Century," *Past and Present* 50 (February 1971): 76–136; also E.P. Thompson, "Time, Work-Discipline, and Industrial Capitalism," *Past and Present* 38 (December 1967): 56–97.

70 "Strikebreakers for Suquash," *Nanaimo Free Press,* August 26, 1913.

71 "Further Evidence of Cases Arising Out of Strike Disturbance," *Nanaimo Free Press,* August 28, 1913; Hinde, *When Coal Was King,* 193.

72 Kavanagh, *The Vancouver Island Strike,* 14. See also Janet Mary Nicol, "'Not to Be Bought, Nor for Sale': The Trials of Joseph Edward Bird," *Labour/Le Travail* 78 (Fall 2016): 225–26.

73 Walter J. Meyer Zu Erpen, "Toward an Understanding of the Municipal Archives of Nineteenth-Century British Columbia: A Case Study of the Archives of the Corporation of the City of Nanaimo" (MA thesis, University of British Columbia, 1985), 71, 223; Peterson, *Hub City,* 80.

74 *Criminal Code,* SC 1892, c 29, ss 78, 79, 80, 81, 82, 520, 521, and 524; see also Desmond Brown, *The Genesis of the Canadian Criminal Code of 1892* (Toronto: University of Toronto Press, 1989). For the specific charges, see Wargo, "The Great Coal Strike," 129–30. Other elements of the criminal law, notably ss 520, 521, and 524 of the *Criminal Code,* proscribing "combinations in restraint of trade," "criminal breach of contract," and "intimidation," had fallen into disuse in response to labour disputes by the time of the Vancouver Island miners' strike. Section 520 of the *Criminal Code* outlined the offence of "combination in restraint of trade," punishable by two years' imprisonment or a fine of between $200 and $4,000, committed by anyone who "conspires, combines, agrees or arranges with any other person ... to unduly prevent, limit, or lessen the manufacture or production of any such article or commodity [which may be a subject of trade or commerce]." Section 521 outlined the offence of "criminal breach of contract," applying to any person who "wilfully breaks any contract made by him" with the effect of endangering human life, causing serious bodily injury, or "exposing valuable property ... to destruction or serious injury." Section 524 outlined the offence of "intimidation" in relation to labour disputes, making it an indictable offence punishable by two years' imprisonment to "use any violence or threat of violence to any person, with a view to hinder him from working or being employed" in pursuit of "any unlawful combination or conspiracy to raise the rate of wages."

75 Kavanagh, *The Vancouver Island Strike*, 13.
76 "Miners Elect for Speedy Trial," *Nanaimo Free Press*, August 30, 1913.
77 "Miners Elect for Speedy Trial."
78 "30 Local Men Committed for Trial; Two of Accused Dismissed," *Nanaimo Free Press*, August 26, 1913; "Strikebreakers for Suquash"; "Evidence Against the Accused Men," *Nanaimo Free Press*, August 27, 1913; "Further Evidence of Cases Arising Out of Strike Disturbance"; "Magistrate Simpson Admonishes Youths," *Nanaimo Free Press*, August 29, 1913; "Miners Elect for Speedy Trial"; "Important Cases Start Tomorrow Morning," *Nanaimo Free Press*, September 2, 1913; "Seven of the Accused Were Released," *Nanaimo Free Press*, September 3, 1913.
79 "Incidents Concerning the Present Situation," *Nanaimo Free Press*, August 30, 1913; Bowen, *Boss Whistle*, 180.
80 "Incidents on the Strike," *Nanaimo Free Press*, September 3, 1913; Lempi Guthrie, as quoted in Bowen, *Boss Whistle*, 182.
81 "Incidents on the Strike."
82 "Passing Notes on the Situation," *Nanaimo Free Press*, September 4, 1913.
83 "Crown Prosecutor's View of the Situation," *Nanaimo Free Press*, September 5, 1913; "Steel Bridges for E & N Railway," *Nanaimo Free Press*, August 27, 1913; Roy, "The Seaforths and the Strikers," 82; Bowen, *Boss Whistle*, 184.
84 Pinkerton reports, September 12, 1913, file 1, box 19, reel B09324, Attorney General Correspondence, GR-0429, BC Archives, as quoted in Hinde, *When Coal Was King*, 201; "Miners' Appeals Heard," *Daily Colonist* (Victoria), November 15, 1913, 2. Conditions in the prison, including food and sanitation, are described in Bowen, *Boss Whistle*, 180–81.
85 "30 Local Men Committed for Trial."
86 "Magistrate Simpson Admonishes Youths."
87 Nicol, "'Not to Be Bought, Nor for Sale,'" 225; "Tools of Coal Barons Fail to Create Dissension Among Bowser's Victims," *BC Federationist*, October 3, 1913; Order in Council 1340, September 19, 1913, BC Legislative Assembly, https://www.bclaws.gov.bc.ca/civix/document/id/oic/arc_oic/1340_1913.
88 Prior to his appointment to the County Court, Howay had served as secretary of the New Westminster School Board from 1891 to 1907. See W. Kaye Lamb, "Introduction: A Bibliography of the Printed Writings of Frederic William Howay," *British Columbia Historical Quarterly* 8, 1 (January 1944): 27–32; Elections British Columbia, *An Electoral History of British Columbia, 1871–1986* (Victoria: Elections British Columbia, 1988), 102; "Judge F.W. Howay," F.W. Howay School, http://www.howay.ca/about-us/who-was-f-w-howay/ (accessed December 18, 2017).
89 "Mr. Taylor Will Represent Crown," *Nanaimo Free Press*, September 5, 1913.
90 "Remarks of Judge Howay Relative to the Sentencing of Ladysmith Strikers," file 174, 7529-16-13, 7529-16-13, GR-1323, BC Archives, as quoted in Hinde, *When Coal Was King*, 194; also *Ladysmith Chronicle*, October 25, 1913, as quoted in Stonebanks, *Fighting for Dignity*, 51. See also "Ladysmith Riot (transcript re riot cases)," 1913, file 30-15, vol. 30, Frederic William Howay fonds, University of British Columbia Rare Books and Special Collections.
91 "Thirty-Nine Sentenced in Nanaimo Court in Coal Strike Riot Cases," *Victoria Daily Times*, October 23, 1913, 1; "Drastic Sentences Passed upon Nanaimo Strikers," *Inland Sentinel* (Kamloops), October 24, 1913, 1 and 4; Hinde, *When Coal Was King*, 191–92.

92 "Editorial," *Nanaimo Free Press,* September 3, 1913, 2; Kavanagh, *The Vancouver Island Strike,* 14.

93 As quoted in Bowen, *Boss Whistle,* 187. See also "Remarks of Judge Howay Relative to the Sentencing of Ladysmith Strikers."

94 Bowen, *Boss Whistle,* 187; "Strike History as Reviewed by the Miners' Solicitors," *BC Federationist,* November 14, 1913, 1.

95 "Report of Operative 29," November 29, 1913, file 75-G-79/2/1 "Correspondence re: Nanaimo Strike, 1913–14," box 2, BC Provincial Police Records, GR-0068, BC Archives (hereafter BC Provincial Police Records); see also Hinde, "'Stout Ladies and Amazons,'" 51. Operative 29, who was never named, was contracted by the Superintendent of the BC Provincial Police from Pinkerton's National Detective Agency in Seattle. The contract for the agent was discontinued at the end of January 1914, with Superintendent Colin Campbell noting that "matters seem to be settling down." See Colin Campbell to P.K. Ahern, December 15, 1913; Campbell to Ahern, January 31, 1914, file 75-G-79/2/1, box 2, BC Provincial Police Records.

96 Bowen, *Boss Whistle,* 188.

97 "Strike History as Reviewed by the Miners' Solicitors," 1.

98 Kavanagh, *The Vancouver Island Strike,* 14 and 16; also Bowen, *Boss Whistle,* 188–89; Hinde, *When Coal Was King,* 192.

99 "Striking Speech by the Premier," *Daily Colonist* (Victoria), January 24, 1914, 2.

100 Kavanagh, *The Vancouver Island Strike,* 14.

101 Bowen, *Boss Whistle,* 188; Hinde, *When Coal Was King,* 192. See also MS-2472, Aulay Morrison fonds, BC Archives.

102 "Miners to Be Tried in New Westminster," *Daily Colonist* (Victoria), November 15, 1913, 10.

103 "United Labor Will Voice Unanimous Protest," *BC Federationist,* November 7, 1913, 1; "Big Mass Meeting Voices Strong Protest," *BC Federationist,* November 14, 1913, 1; "McBride, Bowser and City Members Invited," *BC Federationist,* December 5, 1913, 1; "The B.C. Miners' Liberation League," *BC Federationist,* December 12, 1913, 3; "Around Vancouver," *Vancouver Daily Province,* December 13, 1913, 22; Kavanagh, *The Vancouver Island Strike,* 13–14; Hinde, *When Coal Was King,* 204; Mark Leier, *Rebel Life: The Life and Times of Robert Gosden, Revolutionary, Mystic, Labour Spy,* Revised Edition (Vancouver: New Star Books, 2013), 31; "Minutes," August 12, 1914, box 3.2, Accession no. 80-59, Victoria Labour Council fonds, University of Victoria Archives and Special Collections.

104 "Report of Operative 29," November 29, 1913.

105 Kavanagh, *The Vancouver Island Strike,* 15.

106 "Report of Operative 29," December 3, 1913, file 75-G-79/2/1, box 2, GR-0068, BC Provincial Police Records.

107 "Report of Operative 29," December 3, 1913.

108 Bowen, *Boss Whistle,* 188–89; Kavanagh, *The Vancouver Island Strike,* 15. Two other cases were decided in November 1913. The first was an appeal from UMWA organizer Chris Pattison of a sentence of three months' imprisonment for vagrancy handed down by Magistrate Simpson, with Justice Baker of Nanaimo dismissing the case and releasing Pattison. The second accused, George Pettigrew, who had been held for two months without bail (during which time his wife had given birth to a child) was tried, sentenced to time already served, and released.

109 See *R v Angelo* (1914), 19 BCR 261 (BCCA), 261–76. The *Criminal Code*, s 999, allowed for a disposition from a preliminary hearing to be admitted as evidence at trial where a judge could reasonably infer, based on evidence adduced at the trial, that the witness was absent from Canada.

110 Hinde, *When Coal Was King*, 190.

111 "Incidents Concerning the Present Situation," 30.

112 "Will Be No General Provincial Strike," *Nanaimo Free Press*, September 5, 1913; "Report of Operative 29," January 8, 1914, file 75-G-79/2/1, box 2, GR-0068, BC Provincial Police Records; Phillips, *No Power Greater*, 59–60; "Minutes," January 21, 1914, Victoria Labour Council fonds, University of Victoria Special Collections; Bent Gestur Sivertz, *The Sivertz Family, Book 1: Christian Sivertz* (Parksville, BC: Arrowmaker, 1984), 44; Stonebanks, *Fighting for Dignity*, 52; Bowen, *Boss Whistle*, 189–90.

113 Roy, "The Seaforths and the Strikers," 83.

114 Phillips, *No Power Greater*, 60. Problems also arose for militiamen absent from work on account of serving strike duty, with employers in Victoria and Vancouver – including the Victoria School Board – threatening to dismiss the men. "Under Militia Act," *Nanaimo Free Press*, August 30, 1913; Bowen, *Boss Whistle*, 184.

115 "Ex-Soldier Relates His Experiences re Strike," *BC Federationist*, June 26, 1914, 1.

116 As quoted in Hinde, *When Coal Was King*, 197.

117 "The Labor Trouble in Nanaimo District: An Address Given Before the Brotherhood of Haliburton Street Methodist Church" (n.d., c. 1913), by Rev. John Hedley, H455, NWp 971.7, BC Archives, as quoted in Stonebanks, *Fighting for Dignity*, 51.

118 "Communication," *Nanaimo Free Press*, September 2, 1913.

119 "Report of Operative 29," January 15, 1914, file 75-G-79/2/1, box 2, GR-0068, BC Provincial Police Records.

120 Colin Campbell to P.K. Ahern, January 31, 1914, file 75-G-79/2/1, box 2, GR-0068, BC Provincial Police Records.

121 "Farris Reveals Actual Cause of Vancouver Island Miners' Strike," *BC Federationist*, January 21, 1916, as quoted in Stonebanks, *Fighting for Dignity*, 51.

122 Canada, *Report of Royal Commission on Industrial Relations* (Ottawa: July 1919), 19.

123 See Francis Brooke Gregory, "Commissioner's Report, Vancouver Island Riots, 1913–14," December 21, 1916, in file 111, box 5, Records of the Commission to Inquire into the Vancouver Island Riots, 1913–1914, Accession no. 197905-009, GR-0518, BC Archives; *Riot Claims Settlement Act*, SBC 1919, c 72.

124 "The Culprits Are Known," *BC Federationist*, February 6, 1914; "Death of Youthful Miner at Prison Farm," *BC Federationist*, January 23, 1914; "Ladysmith Prisoner Dies," *Daily Colonist* (Victoria), January 21, 1914; *Vancouver Daily Sun*, January 21, 1914; Ladysmith Chronicle, January 27, 1914; Mark Leier, "Mairs, Joseph," in *Dictionary of Canadian Biography*, vol. 14, University of Toronto / Université Laval, 2003–, https://www.biographi.ca/en/bio/mairs_joseph_14E.html.

125 "Report of Operative 29," January 28, 1914, file 75-G-79/2/1, box 2, GR-0068, BC Provincial Police Records.

126 Hinde, *When Coal Was King*, 192. The last convicted miner to be released was UMWA organizer Joe Angelo of Ohio, who received the harshest sentence – four years – and was promptly deported to the United States upon his release at the end of September 1914. Two other defendants, Mike Adams and William Jackson, were not covered by McBride's

amnesty, and were later tried and imprisoned for dynamiting Alex Mackinnon's Ladysmith home. See Stonebanks, *Fighting for Dignity,* 49 and 54.

127 Bowen, *Boss Whistle,* 189.

128 "U.M.W. of A. Decide to Stop Strike Pay," *Nanaimo Free Press,* July 21, 1914. In 1913, the *Nanaimo Free Press* reported a weekly strike payroll of $16,000, while Crown prosecutor Shoebottom said that the strikers were paid $4 per week. "Strikebreakers for Suquash"; "Crown Prosecutor's View of the Situation."

129 Fudge and Tucker, *Labour Before the Law,* 76; see also Hinde, *When Coal Was King,* 206.

130 As quoted in Stonebanks, *Fighting for Dignity,* 47–48.

131 "Capitalism the Leveller," *Western Clarion* (Vancouver), August 10, 1912, as quoted in Stonebanks, *Fighting for Dignity,* 45.

132 Orth, *Combination and Conspiracy,* 155.

Chapter 2: "The Closeness of the Companies and the Courts"

1 *Labour Gazette,* June 1966, 283, as cited in John Stanton, *Never Say Die! The Life and Times of John Stanton, a Pioneer Labour Lawyer* (Ottawa: Steel Rail, 1987), app. A, 243.

2 Thomas R. Berger, "Report and Recommendations on the Use of Injunctions in Labour Disputes," October 30, 1966, in Thomas R. Berger, *Injunctions in British Columbia* (Vancouver: British Columbia Federation of Labour, c. 1966), 10; Bora *Laskin,* "The Labour Injunction in Canada: A Caveat," *Canadian Bar Review* 15 (1937): 271–74.

3 Elaine Bernard, *The Long Distance Feeling: A History of the Telecommunications Workers Union* (Vancouver: New Star, 1983), 130. The Lenkurt dispute resurfaced nearly two decades later, during the 1984 BC New Democratic Party leadership campaign, when opponents of leadership candidate (and former deputy attorney general) David Vickers circulated a newspaper column from the Victoria *Times Colonist* highlighting Vickers's role as a company lawyer during the 1966 injunction and contempt litigation. See "Vickers Link to Union Battle Called a Smear by Backers," *Globe and Mail,* April 2, 1984.

4 Berger, *Injunctions in British Columbia,* 17.

5 A.W.R Carrothers, *The Labour Injunction in British Columbia: A Study of the Operation of the Injunction in Labour-Management Disputes in British Columbia, 1946–1955 with Particular Reference to the Law of Picketing* (Toronto and Montreal: CCH Canadian, 1956), 194; Berger, *Injunctions in British Columbia,* 17. Between 1946 and 1955, the BC Supreme Court received sixty-nine applications for injunctions relating to labour disputes and granted all but two.

6 *Poje v Attorney General for British Columbia,* [1953] 1 SCR 516; *Canadian Transport (UK) Limited v Alsbury,* [1953] 1 DLR 385 (BCCA).

7 Stanton, *Never Say Die!,* 124–31.

8 *Labour Gazette,* June 1966, 283, as cited in Stanton, *Never Say Die!,* app. A, 243.

9 David W. Raack, "A History of Injunctions in England Before 1700," *Indiana Law Journal* 61, 4 (1986): 539–92. See also Matthew Bacon, *A New Abridgment of the Law: Volume 3,* 5th ed. (London: Strahan, 1798), 648–59.

10 Eric Tucker and Judy Fudge, "Forging Responsible Unions: Metal Workers and the Rise of the Labour Injunction in Canada," *Labour/Le Travail* 37 (Spring 1996): 89 and 98.

11 Tucker and Fudge, "Forging Responsible Unions," 89.

12 John Fox, *The History of Contempt of Court* (London: Professional Books, 1972); Ian Cram,

ed., *Borrie and Lowe: The Law of Contempt*, 4th ed. (London: LexisNexis Butterworths, 2010); *R. v. Almon* (1765), 97 E.R. 94.

13 Philip Girard, *Bora Laskin: Bringing Law to Life* (Toronto: Osgoode Society for Canadian Legal History, 2005), 87–88; Felix Frankfurter and Nathan Greene, *The Labor Injunction* (New York: Macmillan, 1930).

14 Frankfurter and Greene, *The Labor Injunction*. See also Cleon Oliphant Swayze, *Contempt of Court in Labor Injunction Cases* (New York: Columbia University Press, 1935).

15 Laskin, "The Labour Injunction in Canada," 272–74; see also Girard, *Bora Laskin*, 99; *Bassel's Lunch Ltd v Kick et al*, 1936 OR 445.

16 Judy Fudge and Eric Tucker, "'Everybody Knows What a Picket Line Means': Picketing Before the British Columbia Court of Appeal," *BC Studies* 162 (Summer 2009): 55–59.

17 See Judy Fudge and Eric Tucker, *Labour Before the Law: The Regulation of Workers' Collective Action in Canada, 1900–1948* (Toronto: Oxford University Press, 2001), 297; Carrothers, *The Labour Injunction in British Columbia;* Stuart Marshall Jamieson, *Times of Trouble: Labour Unrest and Industrial Conflict in Canada, 1900–1966* (Ottawa: Task Force on Labour Relations, 1968); Stuart Marshall Jamieson, "Regional Factors in Industrial Conflict: The Case of British Columbia," *Canadian Journal of Economics and Political Science* 28, no. 3 (August 1962): 405–16; Berger, *Injunctions in British Columbia*.

18 *Industrial Conciliation and Arbitration Act*, SBC 1937, c 31.

19 *Industrial Conciliation and Arbitration Act Amendment Act*, SBC 1938, c 23. See also Andrew Parnaby, "What's Law Got to Do with It? The IWA and the Politics of State Power in British Columbia, 1935–1939," *Labour/Le Travail* 44 (Fall 1999): 9–46; Stephen Gray, "Woodworkers and Legitimacy: The IWA in Canada, 1937–1957" (PhD diss., Simon Fraser University, 1989), 18–45; George R. Taft, "Socialism in North America: The Case of British Columbia and Washington State, 1900–1960" (PhD diss., Simon Fraser University, 1983), 242–44; Harold Fabian Underhill. "Labor Legislation in British Columbia" (PhD diss., University of California, Berkley, 1936); Paul A. Phillips, *No Power Greater: A Century of Labour in British Columbia* (Vancouver: Boag Foundation, 1967), 103–4, 115–17.

20 *Industrial Conciliation and Arbitration Act Amendment Act*.

21 *The Wartime Labour Relations Regulations* of February 17, 1944, required employers to recognize, and negotiate with, employee committees chosen by workers. It outlined a procedure for union certification and banned company unions. *Wartime Labour Relations Regulations*, PC 1944-1003, *Labour Gazette* 44, 2 (1944): 136–43.

22 Paul Graham Knox, "The Passage of Bill 39: Reform and Repression in British Columbia's Labour Policy" (MA thesis, University of British Columbia, 1974).

23 Fudge and Tucker, *Labour Before the Law*, 296.

24 *Industrial Conciliation and Arbitration Amendment Act*, SBC 1947, c 44; BC Department of Labour, *Annual Report* (1947), 36–38; *Trade Union Act*, SS 1944, c 69; *Labour Relations Act*, SO 1948, c 51; Fudge and Tucker, *Labour Before the Law*, 295–96; Benjamin Isitt, *Militant Minority: British Columbia Workers and the Rise of a New Left, 1948–1972* (Toronto: University of Toronto Press, 2011), 20–23; Charles W. Smith, "The Politics of the Ontario Labour Relations Act: Business, Labour, and Government in the Consolidation of Post-War Industrial Relations, 1949–1961," *Labour/Le Travail* 62 (Fall 2008): 109–51.

25 *Industrial Conciliation and Arbitration Act Amendment Act*, SBC 1948, c 31. Another provision of benefit to employers was contained in s 50, which empowered the Labour Relations

Board to override unions and conduct a "final offer" vote on terms presented by employers.

26 "Strike – The Vancouver Daily Province," July 13, 1946, file "Canadian Seamen's Union – Vancouver, BC," vol. 2285, series A, RCMP Security Service, RG 146, Canadian Security Intelligence Service records (hereafter CSIS records), Library and Archives Canada (hereafter LAC).

27 Fudge and Tucker, *Labour Before the Law,* 296.

28 Fudge and Tucker, *Labour Before the Law,* 296.

29 "Strike – The Vancouver Daily Province."

30 Stanton, *Never Say Die!,* 130. See also John Stanton, *My Past Is Now: Further Memoirs of a Labour Lawyer* (St John's: Canadian Committee on Labour History, 1994).

31 Tucker and Fudge, "Forging Responsible Unions," 117.

32 Joan Sangster, "'We No Longer Respect the Law': The Tilco Strike, Labour Injunctions, and the State," *Labour/Le Travail* 53 (Spring 2004): 49. Injunctions are discussed further on 49, 55–56, 75–77, and 84–85. See also Jeremy Milloy, "'Chrysler Pulled the Trigger': Competing Understandings of Workplace Violence During the 1970s and Radical Legal Practice," *Labour/Le Travail* 74 (Fall 2014): 51–88.

33 *Canadian Transport Co (UK) Ltd v Alsbury,* [1952] 6 WWR (NS) 473 (BCSC); *Canadian Transport (UK) Limited v Alsbury,* [1953] 1 DLR 385 (BCCA); *Poje v Attorney General for British Columbia,* [1953] 1 SCR 516 [*Poje*]; "Poje to Stay in Jail Until Next Thursday," *Vancouver Sun,* September 19, 1952; Grant MacNeil, *The IWA in British Columbia* (Vancouver: IWA Western Canadian Regional Council No. 1, 1971), 45; Carrothers, *The Labour Injunction in British Columbia,* 11–23. For biographical information on Justice Clyne, see "In Memoriam: John Valentine Clyne, 1902–1989," Minutes of the Senate of the University of British Columbia, September 13, 1989, University of British Columbia Archives; J.V. Clyne, *Jack of All Trades: Memories of a Busy Life* (Toronto: McClelland and Stewart, 1992).

34 *Poje; Canadian Transport (UK) Limited v Alsbury.*

35 *Canadian Transport (UK) Limited v Alsbury.*

36 *Canadian Transport (UK) Limited v Alsbury; Poje;* Stanton, *Never Say Die!,* 126.

37 See *MacMillan Bloedel Ltd v Brown,* 1994 BCCA 64; also "65 Told Contempt Could Be Criminal in Injunction Case," *Times Colonist* (Victoria), December 6, 1994.

38 Isitt, *Militant Minority,* 149–50. See also BC Department of Labour, *Annual Report* (1959), 45; *Constitution Act Amendment Act,* SBC 1959, c 17; James Harding, "The New Left in British Columbia," in *The New Left in Canada,* ed. Dimitrios I. Roussopolous (Montreal: Black Rose, c. 1970), 28; Harry Rankin, *Rankin's Law: Recollections of a Radical* (Vancouver: November House, 1975), 137; "New Democratic Party Policy Statement" and "Report and Recommendations on the Use of Injunctions in Labour Disputes," in Berger, *Injunctions in British Columbia,* 7, 13–14; Jamieson, *Times of Trouble,* 386; "Labor Peace Claimed Due to Socred Legislation," *Ubyssey* (Vancouver), September 28, 1961. Bill 43 replaced the *Trade-Unions Act* (1902), which had relieved "unions and their members from liability in damages and to an injunction in respect of certain types of union activity." According to Berger, this made Carrothers's criticisms of the use of injunctions in labour disputes "carry more weight today than in the past." Berger, "Report and Recommendations on the Use of Injunctions in Labour Disputes," in Berger, *Injunctions in British Columbia,* 10; Carrothers, *The Labour Injunction in British Columbia,* xxiv; Charles Lipton, *The Trade Union Movement*

of Canada 1827–1959 (Toronto, NC Press, 1978), 315. Lipton described Bill 43 as "anti-labour legislation which facilitated injunctions against picketing."

39 Stanton, *Never Say Die!*, 124.
40 *Dominion Bridge Co v International Ass'n of Bridge, Structural and Ornamental Iron Workers Local 97* (1959), 20 DLR (2d) 621 (BCCA).
41 "Injunctions Won't Build Bridges or Catch Fish," *The Fisherman* (Vancouver), June 26, 1959.
42 "Injunctions Won't Build Bridges or Catch Fish."
43 "Judge Hints Contempt Action Against Paper," *Vancouver Sun*, July 2, 1959, 46.
44 "Union Paper Editor Jailed for Contempt," *Vancouver Sun*, July 15, 1959, 9; Stanton, *Never Say Die!*, 125.
45 Stanton, *Never Say Die!*, 125–26.
46 As quoted in Stanton, *Never Say Die!*, 127.
47 Carrothers, *The Labour Injunction in British Columbia*, xxiv.
48 "Union Paper Editor Jailed for Contempt," 9.
49 "Union Paper Editor Jailed for Contempt," 9.
50 "Union Paper Editor Jailed for Contempt," 9; Stanton, *Never Say Die!*, 127–29.
51 "Editor on $1,000 Bail," *Vancouver Sun*, July 16, 1959, 10; "SIU Seeks Injunction to Bar Northland Firings," *Victoria Daily Times*, July 16, 1959, 34.
52 "'Privileges Refused Convicted Editor,'" *Vancouver Sun*, October 10, 1959, 6; "Contempt Appeal Set," *The Province* (Vancouver), September 19, 1959, 2.
53 "'Privileges Refused Convicted Editor,'" 6.
54 "'Contempt' Appeal Fails, Editor Jailed," *Vancouver Sun*, October 21, 1959, 2.
55 "Unions Ask Removal of Judge," *Vancouver Sun*, July 22, 1959, 1.
56 "Socreds Get Union Picket Greeting," *Vancouver Sun*, October 30, 1959, 51.
57 "Unions Seeks Release of Convicted Editor," *The Province*, October 31, 1959, 34; "BC Won't Interfere with Editor's Sentence," *The Province*, November 5, 1959, 35.
58 "Fulton Rules Contempt Fine Stands," *Vancouver Sun*, November 19, 1959, 6; "Capsule News," *Nanaimo Daily Free Press*, November 17, 1959, 1; "Fulton to Decide on BC Editor," *Nanaimo Free Press*, November 7, 1959, 1; "Clemency for City Editor Under Study," *Vancouver Sun*, November 7, 1959, 10.
59 "Editor Cheered on Release from Jail," *Vancouver Sun*, November 14, 1959, 21.
60 "Early Bird," *The Province*, November 5, 1959, 10; "Jack Wasserman," *Vancouver Sun*, November 26, 1959, 2; "This Week," *Richmond Review*, December 2, 1959, 1.
61 Stanton, *Never Say Die!*, 129.
62 Ian MacDonald, "Class Conflict and Political Factionalism: A History of Local 213 of the International Brotherhood of Electrical Workers, 1901–1961" (MA thesis, Simon Fraser University, 1986); Jack Scott, *A Communist Life: Jack Scott and the Canadian Workers Movement, 1927–1985*, ed. and intro. Bryan D. Palmer (St. John's: Canadian Committee on Labour History, 1988), 177–80.
63 "Lawyer to Probe BC Dispute," *Globe and Mail*, May 13, 1966.
64 "Lawyer to Probe BC Dispute."
65 "Lawyer to Probe BC Dispute."
66 Berger, *Injunctions in British Columbia*, 16; Rankin, *Rankin's Law*, 150. For greater detail on the Lenkurt strike, see boxes 5, 8, and 30, International Brotherhood of Electrical Workers Local 213 fonds (hereafter IBEW 213 fonds), BC Federation of Labour fonds

(hereafter BCFL fonds), and Ian MacDonald Collection, University of British Columbia Rare Books and Special Collections (hereafter UBCRBSC). See also "Appeal of Jeffrey James Power," November 3, 1966, McMaster Archives and Research Collections (hereafter MARC).

67 *Labour Gazette*, June 1966, 283, as cited in Stanton, *Never Say Die!*, app. A, 243.

68 "Injunctions in Labour Disputes," box 64, BCFL fonds, UBCSC; Berger, *Injunctions in British Columbia.*

69 Berger, *Injunctions in British Columbia.*

70 "Report from Regional Committee of the Delta-New Westminster Region of the Communist Party of Canada," January 22, 1967, file 23-30 "BC provincial series," reel H1592, Communist Party of Canada fonds, LAC. See also "Canadian Workers Demand Canadian Unions," *Progressive Worker* (Vancouver), September 1966, in which the left-nationalist Progressive Worker Movement railed against the complicity of the international union and celebrated the local labour leadership, with IBEW 213 showing "real initiative."

71 Order of Justice Kirke Smith, March 22, 1967, file 344-1 "Prince Rupert Trawlers Strike," box 344, United Fishermen and Allied Workers' Union fonds (hereafter UFAWU fonds), UBCRBSC; *R v United Fishermen and Allied Workers' Union et al* (1967), [1968] 2 CCC 257 (BCCA); George Hewison, interviewed by Benjamin Isitt, Colwood, BC, April 14, 2013; Geoge North, *A Ripple, a Wave: The Story of Union Organization in the B.C. Fishing Industry*, revised and edited by Harold Griffin (Vancouver: Fisherman Publishing Society, 1974), 30–42; Stanton, *Never Say Die!*, 133–48; Rankin, *Rankin's Law*, 122–36. The genesis of the strike was a jurisdictional dispute between the UFAWU and the much smaller Deep Sea Fishermen's Union (DSFU), which was exploited by the Prince Rupert Vessel Owners' Association. In May 1967, the UFAWU called a strike of all Prince Rupert trawlers and shoreworkers to protect its jurisdiction.

72 *R v United Fishermen and Allied Workers' Union et al.*

73 "Notice of Appeal," May 10, 1967, file 344-2 "Prince Rupert Trawlers Strike," box 344, UFAWU fonds, UBCRBSC; *R v United Fishermen and Allied Workers' Union et al.*

74 "Union Fined, Three Executives in Jail," *Brandon Sun*, June 20, 1967; Homer Stevens and Rolf Knight, *Homer Stevens: A Life in Fishing* (Madeira Park, BC: Harbour Publishing, 1992), 157–73.

75 Stanton, *Never Say Die!*, 137; "Dohm Picked to Head Stock Exchange," *Vancouver Sun*, December 23, 1971; "Dohm Forced to Quit as Exchange Head," *Vancouver Sun*, November 9, 1972; "Obituary: Honourable Thomas Anthony 'Tom' Dohm," *Vancouver Sun*, April 8, 2009.

76 *R v United Fishermen and Allied Workers' Union et al;* Stanton, *Never Say Die!*, 137.

77 "Notice of Appeal," May 10, 1967.

78 Stanton, *Never Say Die!*, 138.

79 "Injunction Granted Halibut Boat Owners," *The Province*, May 12, 1967; "Unionists Face Court," *Winnipeg Free Press*, June 8, 1967.

80 *R v United Fishermen and Allied Workers' Union et al;* George Hewison, interviewed by Benjamin Isitt, Colwood, BC, April 14, 2013; North, *A Ripple, a Wave*, 30–42; Stanton, *Never Say Die!*, 133–48; Rankin, *Rankin's Law*, 122–36; Stevens, *Homer Stevens*, 176–83; file 3041 "UFAWU Contempt, first appeal," box 10; files 3055, 3075, 3076, 3138, box 11, John Stanton fonds, UBCRBSC.

81 "W.A. Women Answer 'Marching Mothers,'" *The Fisherman* (Vancouver), June 9, 1967.
82 Officers' Report, January 3, 1967, file 392-18 "GEB – Minutes – Jan 4 – May 30, 1967," box 392, UFAWU Fonds, UBCRBSC.
83 Minutes, May 14, 1967, Joint Meeting of GEB and Committees, file 392-18 "GEB – Minutes – Jan 4 – May 30, 1967," box 392, UFAWU Fonds, UBCRBSC.
84 Minutes, May 14, 1967, Joint Meeting of GEB and Committees.
85 "Union Men Arrested After Court Order," *Ottawa Journal*, June 8, 1967; "Unionists Face Court"; "Halibut Boat Owners on Guard as Five Vessels Are Cut Adrift," *Nanaimo Daily Free Press*, June 10, 1967; "Women Marchers Stay Home at Rupert, Not Shoreworkers," *Nanaimo Daily Free Press*, June 10, 1967; George Hewison, interviewed by Benjamin Isitt, Colwood, BC, April 14, 2013.
86 Minutes, June 8, 1967, file 392-19 "GEB – Minutes – June 8 – Dec 29, 1967," box 392, UFAWU fonds, UBCRBSC.
87 Minutes, June 11, 1967, file 392-19 "GEB – Minutes – June 8 – Dec 29, 1967," box 392, UFAWU fonds, UBCRBSC. Five days after his arrest, on June 12, 1967, Nichol was flown from Prince Rupert to Vancouver under RCMP guard, pending trial on the contempt charges. Unlike the other arrested UFAWU leaders, he was denied bail. "Demonstrators Greet Fishermen's Union Agent," *Nanaimo Daily Free Press*, June 13, 1967; "Halibut Boat Owners on Guard as Five Vessels Are Cut Adrift."
88 *R v United Fishermen and Allied Workers' Union, Stavenes and two others* (1967), [1968] 1 CCC 199 (BCSC); *R v United Fishermen and Allied Workers' Union et al;* "Union Fined, Three Executives in Jail"; "Fishermen's Union Pays $25,000 Contempt Fine," *Nanaimo Daily Free Press*, June 23, 1967; file 377-8 "Various Trial Exhibits – 1965–1968," box 377, UFAWU fonds, UBCRBSC.
89 "UFAWU Levies $10 Head Tax to Pay Bills," *Nanaimo Daily Free Press*, June 24, 1967; "Stevens Moves from Jail to the Lawyers' Table," *Nanaimo Daily Free Press*, June 24, 1967; "Bonner Agrees to Give Unionists Chance for Bail," *Nanaimo Daily Free Press*, June 24, 1967; Stevens, *Homer Stevens*, 169. The UFAWU membership demanded that the union leaders be released on bail pending their appeal, and wired this request to Attorney General Robert Bonner. See Elgin Neish telegram to Robert Bonner, June 22, 1967, file 370-10 "Publicity – injunctions – jail –etc, 1967–1968," box 370, UFAWU fonds, UBCRBSC.
90 Stevens to All Locals and Women's Auxiliaries, September 12, 1967, file 392-19 "GEB – Minutes – June 8 – Dec 29, 1967," box 392, UFAWU fonds, UBCRBSC.
91 *R v United Fishermen and Allied Workers' Union et al;* "Contempt Appeal Before Court," *Nanaimo Daily Free Press*, September 19, 1967; "Court Fight Funds Sought," *Nanaimo Daily Free Press*, November 8, 1967; "Union Officials Mark Time Before Bail Application Heard," *Nanaimo Daily Free Press*, November 23, 1967; "Christmas 'Break' for Pair?" *Brandon Sun*, December 13, 1967; Stevens, *Homer Stevens*, 176–83.
92 Minutes, December 15, 1967, file 392-19 "GEB – Minutes – June 8 – Dec 29, 1967," box 392, UFAWU fonds, UBCRBSC.
93 For a discussion of anti-Communism within BC labour, see Isitt, *Militant Minority*, 44–83; Irving Abella, "Communism and Anti-Communism in the British Columbia Labour Movement, 1940–1948," in *Western Perspectives 1: Papers of the Western Canadian Studies Conference, 1973*, ed. David Jay Bercuson (Toronto and Montreal: Holt, Rinehart and Winston, 1974), 88–100. For a discussion of radical politics in the UFAWU, see John Peter Frecker, "Militant and Radical Unionism in the British Columbia Fishing Industry" (MA thesis, University of British Columbia, 1972).

94 *United Fishermen & Allied Workers' Union et al v The Queen,* [1968] SCR 255.

95 Minutes, December 1, 1967, file 392-19 "GEB – Minutes – June 8 – Dec 29, 1967," box 392, UFAWU fonds, UBCRBSC; "Christmas 'Break' for Pair?"; Stevens, *Homer Stevens,* 176–78.

96 Minutes, December 1, 1967.

97 Minutes, December 1, 1967.

98 Homer [Stevens] to Audrey, January 22, 1968, file 390-10 "Homer and Steve's letters while in prison, Dec 2, 1967 – Jan 1968," box 390, UFAWU fonds, UBCRBSC; various correspondence, box 2 and box 6 "Camp Thurston Prison Camp Series," Homer Stevens fonds, UBCRBSC.

99 Minutes, February 8, 1968, file 393-16 "Vancouver Fisherman's Local – Minutes – 1967–73," box 393, UFAWU fonds, UBCRBSC.

100 Minutes, February 8, 1968.

101 A year earlier, "the jailing of trade union leaders" had been among the list of priority issues that the UFAWU pursued during its annual lobby to the legislature. See Minutes, February 3, 1967, file 392-18 "GEB Minutes – Jan 4 – May 3, 1967," box 392, UFAWU fonds, UBCRBSC; Minutes, March 15, 1968, file 393-16 "Vancouver Fisherman's Local – Minutes – 1967–73," box 393, UFAWU fonds, UBCRBSC.

102 Minutes, June 13, 1968, file 393-16 "Vancouver Fisherman's Local – Minutes – 1967–73," box 393, UFAWU fonds, UBCRBSC; "Jailed Union Officials Apply for Early Release," *The Province,* June 1, 1968, 11.

103 "Union Leader Freed," *The Province,* September 9, 1968, 23; "Union Head Stavenes Released from Prison," *Vancouver Sun,* September 9, 1968, 27.

104 Mary F. Southin, "The Courts and Labour Injunctions," *The Advocate* 28 (1970): 83–84; Christopher Moore, *The British Columbia Court of Appeal: The First Hundred Years* (Vancouver: UBC Press, 2010), 187–88.

105 *Labour Code of British Columbia Act,* SBC 1973 (2d Sess), c 122 (Bill 11, assented to November 7, 1973); *Public Service Labour Relations Act,* SBC 1973, c 144; British Columbia, *Official Report of the Debates of the Legislative Assembly,* October 25, 1973, 951–74; H.W. Arthurs, "'The Dullest Bill': Reflections on the Labour Code of British Columbia," *UBC Law Review* 9 (1974): 280–340; British Columbia Civil Liberties Association (hereafter BCCLA), *New British Columbia Labour Legislation, Civil Liberties Issues* (Vancouver: BCCLA, May 1974), https://bccla.org/resource/new-british-columbia-labour-legislation-civil-liberties-issues/ (accessed January 4, 2026); Alan F.J. Artibise, "'A Worthy, if Unlikely, Enterprise': The Labour Relations Board and the Evolution of Labour Policy and Practice in British Columbia, 1973–1980," *BC Studies* 56 (Winter 1982): 3–43; "BC Labor Minister's Workload," *Cooperative Press Associates* (Ottawa), September 29, 1972, file 436-26, CCF-NDP fonds, LAC; Bruce McLean, A *Union Amongst Government Employees: A History of the B.C. Government Employees Union 1919–1979* (Vancouver: BCGEU, 1979), 122–26; "Labor Law Change 1½–2 Years Away,' *Vancouver Sun,* November 10, 1972. "The BC Mediation Commission Will Officially Die Nov. 20," the *Sun* reported. See also Lorne John Kavic and Gary Brian Nixon, *1200 Days: A Shattered Dream: Dave Barrett and the NDP in BC 1972–75* (Coquitlam, BC: Kaen, 1978), 145–64; Geoff Meggs and Rod Mickleburgh, *The Art of the Impossible: Dave Barrett and the NDP in Power, 1972–1975* (Madeira Park: Harbour Publishing, 2012), 162–64; Dave Barrett, interviewed by Benjamin Isitt, Esquimalt, BC, April 24, 2006.

106 Judy Fudge and Eric Tucker, "'Everybody Knows What a Picket Line Means': Picketing Before the British Columbia Court of Appeal," *BC Studies* 162 (Summer 2009): 68–70. For evidence of the courts' ongoing role, see Janet Mary Nicol, "'Unions Aren't Native': The Muckamuck Restaurant Labour Dispute, Vancouver, BC (1978–1983)," *Labour/Le Travail* 40 (Fall 1997): 247.
107 BCCLA, *New British Columbia Labour Legislation, Civil Liberties Issues.*
108 Arthurs, "'The Dullest Bill,'" 302–7.
109 See Mark Thompson. "Restraint and Labour Relations: The Case of British Columbia," *Canadian Public Policy* 11, 2 (June 1985): 171–79.
110 *BCGEU v British Columbia (Attorney General)*, 1988 SCC 3.
111 *BCGEU v British Columbia (Attorney General).*
112 See *Industrial Relations Reform Act*, SBC 1987, c 24; Jonathan Goldberg-Hiller, "The Boycott of the Law and the Law of Boycott: Law, Labour, and Politics in British Columbia," *Law and Social Inquiry* 21, 2 (April 1996): 313–51.
113 "BC Seeks Injunction as 1-Day Strike Hits Province," *Montreal Gazette*, June 2, 1987; "BC Labour, NDP Are Outraged by Injunction Bid," *Montreal Gazette*, June 3, 1987; "Berger Set to Fight Bid for Injunction," *Vancouver Sun*, June 5, 1987; "Abridged Text of Statement of Claim," *Vancouver Sun*, June 6, 1987.
114 "Strike Down Injunction Bid, Berger Asks Supreme Court," *Vancouver Sun*, June 8, 1987.
115 *AG (BC) v Georgetti*, 1987 BCSC; "Socreds Lose Injunction Bid as BC Court Quashes Writ," *Globe and Mail*, June 11, 1987; "Resign over Writ Defeat, Labour, NDP Tell Smith," *Vancouver Sun*, June 11, 1987; Goldberg-Hiller, "The Boycott of the Law and the Law of Boycott," 329; John Mackie Shields, "British Columbia's New Reality: The Politics of Neo-Conservatism and Defensive Defiance" (PhD diss., University of British Columbia, 1989), 505–9. For a more recent contempt case arising from a labour injunction, as well as a historical discussion of this area of law, see "65 Told Contempt Could Be Criminal in Injunction Case," *Times Colonist* (Victoria), December 6, 1994.
116 Rankin, *Rankin's Law*, 150.
117 *Canadian Transport Co (UK) Ltd v Alsbury*, [1952] 6 WWR (NS) 473 (BCSC).
118 *MacMillan Bloedel Ltd v Brown*, 1994 BCCA 64.

Chapter 3: Breaching the Bubble Law

1 "Abortion Protest Bill Approved," *Vancouver Sun*, June 28, 1995; British Columbia, *Official Report of the Debates of the Legislative Assembly*, June 27, 1995.
2 *Access to Abortion Services Act*, RSBC 1996, c 1.
3 *Access to Abortion Services Act; Offence Act*, RSBC 1996, c 338; British Columbia, *Official Report of the Debates of the Legislative Assembly*, June 26, 1995.
4 Doreen Massey, *Space, Place, and Gender* (Minneapolis: University of Minnesota Press, 1994), 265; also Doreen Massey, "Power-Geometry and a Progressive Sense of Place," in *Mapping the Futures: Local Cultures, Global Change*, ed. Jon Bird, Barry Curtis, Tim Putnam, George Robertson, and Lisa Tickner (London: Routledge, 1993), 59–69. See also Brenna Bhandar, "Disassembling Legal Form: Ownership and the Racial Body," in *New Critical Legal Thinking: Law and the Political*, ed. Matthew Stone, Illan Wall, and Costas Douzinas (Abingdon, UK: Birkbeck Law Press, 2012), 112–27.
5 *R. v. Morgentaler*, [1988] 1 SCR 30.

6 Ann Thomson, *Winning Choice on Abortion: How British Columbia and Canadian Feminists Won the Battles of the 1970s and 1980s* (Vancouver: Trafford, 2005); Frances Wasserlein, "'An Arrow Aimed at the Heart': The Vancouver Women's Caucus and the Abortion Campaign 1969–1971" (MA thesis, Simon Fraser University, 1990); Christabelle Sethna and Steve Hewitt, "Clandestine Operations: The Vancouver Women's Caucus, the Abortion Caravan, and the RCMP," *Canadian Historical Review* 90, 3 (September 2009): 463–96; Rachael Johnstone, *After Morgentaler: The Politics of Abortion in Canada* (Vancouver: UBC Press, 2017); Don Mitchell, "The S.U.V. Model of Citizenship: Floating Bubbles, Buffer Zones, and the Rise of the 'Purely Atomic' Individual," *Political Geography* 24, 1 (January 2005): 77–100.

7 *Criminal Law Amendment Act, 1968–69*, SC 1968–69, c 38.

8 "Abortion Caravan Demands" (n.d., c. 1970), in Abortion Caravan 2020 Coalition, *Then and Now, 1970–2020: Celebrating the 50th Anniversary of the 1970 Abortion Caravan* (Ottawa: Action Canada for Sexual Health and Rights, 2020), 12, https://www.actioncanadashr.org/resources/reports-analysis/2020-05-12-1970-abortion-caravan-celebrating-50-years.

9 Sethna and Hewitt, "Clandestine Operations," 473.

10 See "Abortion, Free and On Demand, Abortion," *Waffle News* (Toronto), May 1970, file 446-18, CCF-NDP fonds, Library and Archives Canada (hereafter LAC); "Abortion Caravan Scrapbook," n.d. [1970], Marge Hollibaugh Women's Movement Collection, F-73, Simon Fraser University Archives; Wasserlein, "'An Arrow Aimed at the Heart.'"

11 Sethna and Hewitt, "Clandestine Operations," 463–96. See also "Abortion, Free and On Demand, Abortion"; "Abortion Caravan Scrapbook"; Wasserlein, "'An Arrow Aimed at the Heart'"; Thomson, *Winning Choice on Abortion*.

12 Judy Rebick, *Ten Thousand Roses: The Making of a Feminist Revolution* (Toronto: Penguin Canada, 2005), 35. See also Accession no. 2004-017, box 2, file 2.30 "Conference – Reproductive Rights and Reproductive Wrongs, Jan. 1994"; Accession no. 2004-017, box 5, file 5.12 "Victoria Coalition for Choice – Minutes and General, 1988–1989," Status of Women Action Group, Victoria Branch fonds, University of Victoria Archives and Special Collections.

13 Wasserlein, "'An Arrow Aimed at the Heart,'" 107–8.

14 "Abortionist Won Against the Odds," *Globe and Mail*, December 11, 1976; "Quebec Halts Trial of Abortion Doctor," *New York Times*, December 12, 1976; *Morgentaler v The Queen*, [1976] 1 SCR 616; Johnstone, *After Morgentaler*, 96–98.

15 "Ready to Start Illegal Abortion Clinics Across Canada, Morgentaler States," *Globe and Mail*, April 26, 1982; "Angry Man Attacks Morgentaler, but Demonstrators Support Clinic," *Globe and Mail*, June 16, 1983.

16 *R v Morgentaler*, [1988] 1 SCR 30. It should be noted that a majority of Supreme Court of Canada justices objected to s 251 of the *Criminal Code* on somewhat narrow procedural grounds. Only one judge – Justice Bertha Wilson – recognized a constitutional right of a woman "to decide for herself whether or not to terminate her pregnancy." Wilson found that s 251 infringed this s 7 right because it "takes the decision away from the woman at all stages of her pregnancy. It is a complete denial of the woman's constitutionally protected right under s. 7, not merely a limitation on it."

17 "BC Appeal Court Upholds Conviction of Anti-Abortionist," *Globe and Mail*, September 4, 1986; "Abortion Foe Loses," *Montreal Gazette*, September 4, 1986.

18 "Abortion Clinic Sending Women to US," *Vancouver Sun*, January 27, 1989.
19 Janet Epp Buckingham, *Fighting over God: A Legal and Political History of Religious Freedom in Canada* (Montreal and Kingston: McGill-Queen's University Press, 2014), 115.
20 *Everywoman's Health Centre Society v Bridges*, 1990 CanLII 5409 (BCCA).
21 *Everywoman's Health Centre Society v Bridges.*
22 *Everywoman's Health Centre Society v Bridges.*
23 "Abortion Clinic Backers Ponder Counter-Protest," *Vancouver Sun*, January 23, 1989. See also "Abortion Frustration," *Vancouver Sun*, January 24, 1989; "Neighbours Seek End to Abortion Protests," *Vancouver Sun*, January 31, 1989; "Police to Determine Abortion Protest Stand," *Vancouver Sun*, January 23, 1989.
24 "Requests for Enforcement Order Ignored," *Vancouver Sun*, January 30, 1989.
25 "A-G Must Police Contempt at Clinic," *Vancouver Sun*, February 10, 1989.
26 "New Abortion Legislation Felt Answer to Protests," *Vancouver Sun*, February 13, 1989.
27 "Rally Marks Court Ruling on Abortion," *Vancouver Sun*, January 30, 1989.
28 "Abortion Protesters Mount Another Blockade at Clinic," *Vancouver Sun*, February 7, 1989.
29 "'Defiant' Protesters Jailed," *Vancouver Sun*, February 8, 1989.
30 "'Defiant' Protesters Jailed"; "Abortion Protesters Head Back to Court," *Vancouver Sun*, February 8, 1989; "Hymns, Prayers Mark Jail Time for Blockaders," *Vancouver Sun*, February 9, 1989.
31 "Inmates Slam Abortion Foes," *Vancouver Sun*, February 14, 1989; "Lakeside Conflict Resolved over Anti-Abortion Prisoners," *Vancouver Sun*, February 15, 1989; "Women Anti-Abortionists Held Apart from Other Prisoners," *Vancouver Sun*, February 25, 1989.
32 "12 Jailed Anti-Abortionists Offered Review for Remorse," *Vancouver Sun*, February 10, 1989. See also "Oakalla Fails to Deter," *Vancouver Sun*, February 20, 1989; "Protesters Get Terms Suspended," *Vancouver Sun*, March 6, 1990.
33 "Defence of Necessity Pushed," *Vancouver Sun*, February 28, 1989.
34 *R v Bridges*, 1989 CanLII 2921 (BCSC), para 17.
35 *R v Bridges*, 1989 CanLII 5321 (BCSC).
36 *R v Bridges*, 1989 CanLII 5321 (BCSC); "Protesters Get Terms Suspended," *Vancouver Sun*, March 6, 1990.
37 "Protesters Jailed for Violation," *Vancouver Sun*, March 7, 1990.
38 "More Abortion Foes Expected to Face Jail Time," *Vancouver Sun*, March 8, 1989; *Everywoman's Health Centre Soc (1988) v Bridges*, 1989 CanLII 2793 (BCSC).
39 "Anti-Abortionists Appeal Convictions," *Vancouver Sun*, March 11, 1989.
40 Karine Richer, *Abortion in Canada: 20 Years After Morgentaler* (Ottawa: Parliamentary Information and Research Service, Library of Parliament, 2008). See also Mollie Dunsmuir, *Abortion: Constitutional and Legal Development* (Ottawa: Parliamentary Information and Research Service, Library of Parliament, 1998). In February 1989, in the midst of the Everywoman's Health Centre protests, BC premier Bill Vander Zalm had called on the Government of Canada to introduce legislation relating to abortion, which he stated would address some of the concerns of people picketing outside the clinic. See "New Abortion Legislation Felt Answer to Protests."
41 "Abortion Clinic Vandalized," *Vancouver Sun*, February 26, 1990, 9; "Blockading Abortion Clinic Leads to Jail," *Vancouver Sun*, May 11, 1990, 13; "Laying Freedom on the Line," *The Province*, May 22, 1990, 25; Abortion Rights Coalition of Canada, *Position Paper #73: Anti-Choice Violence and Harassment* (Vancouver: September 2006), https://www.arcc-cdac.ca/media/position-papers/73-Anti-choice-Violence-Harassment.pdf.

42 "Abortion Protester Questions Authority," *The Province*, October 11, 1990.
43 *R v Demers*, 1992 BCCA 625. See also *R v Cohn* (1985), 13 DLR (4th) 680 (Ont CA).
44 *Everywoman's Health Centre Society v Bridges*. The *Globe and Mail* cited Justice Southin's ruling in providing commentary during the Clayoquot Sound trials in 1993: "Clayoquot: The Danger of Using Injunctions," *Globe and Mail*, November 5, 1993. Southin's remarks also figured prominently in Justice Douglas Thompson's reasons for judgment in *Teal Cedar Products Ltd v Rainforest Flying Squad*, 2021 BCSC 1903. Police enforcement of court orders was also the subject of commentary by Southin in another protest case from the 1980s: *Canada Post Corp v LCUC, Local 12*, [1987] 15 BCLR (2d) 356 (BCSC).
45 *Everywoman's Health Centre Society v Bridges*.
46 "The Shooting of Dr. Romalis," *Globe and Mail*, November 10, 1994. An American, James Charles Kopp, is the lead suspect in Romalis's shooting, as well as several other shootings of abortion providers in Canada and the United States, including one for which he is currently serving a life sentence in a US federal prison. "Fugitive Anti-Abortion Activist Sought for Questioning in Connection with Three Related Shootings in Canada," *The Star-Phoenix* (Saskatoon), May 7, 1999; "US Fugitive Chief Suspect in Canadian Abortion Shootings," *Toronto Star*, June 25, 1999; "Manhunt Ends in France," *Vancouver Sun*, March 30, 2001; "Abortion Sniper Suspect Arrested," *Calgary Herald*, March 30, 2001; "Abortion Doctor's Murderer Gets Life Sentence," *Times Colonist* (Victoria), June 20, 2007; "Abortion Foe Suspected in Shootings Finally to Face Canadian Questions," *Vancouver Sun*, June 20, 2007; "Conviction, but No Reward," *Winnipeg Free Press*, November 28, 2009.
47 "Vancouver Clinic Wants Anti-Protest Orders Enforced," *Ottawa Citizen*, December 31, 1994. See also "Pro-Choicers Demand Laws Against Foes," *Vancouver Province*, April 22, 1993.
48 *R v Watson*, 2006 BCCA 217; *R v Watson*, 2006 BCCA 367; "Abortion Foe Loses Bid to Overturn Conviction," *Vancouver Sun*, April 11, 1996. See also "Abortion Protest Trio Will Remain in Jail," *Vancouver Sun*, April 22, 1993; "Anti-Abortionists Guilty of Contempt," *The Province*, May 5, 1993.
49 "Abortion Militants Rarer in Canada," *Vancouver Sun*, December 31, 1994. In contrast to the calming tone conveyed by the *Vancouver Sun* headline, the *Kingston Whig-Standard* ran the same article under the headline "Is Anti-Abortion Extremism Spreading in Canada?" on December 31, 1994.
50 Buckingham, *Fighting over God*, 115.
51 "Abortion Foes Face Ban," *The Province*, January 2, 1995.
52 "Buffer Zones on Way for Abortion Clinics, MDs," *Vancouver Sun*, May 11, 1995.
53 British Columbia, *Official Report of the Debates of the Legislative Assembly*, June 19, 1995.
54 British Columbia, *Official Report of the Debates of the Legislative Assembly*, June 22, 1995. MacPhail suggested: "There are manuals on protest on this continent, perpetuated by organizations that are anti-choice and that would deny women their right to reproductive health care. Those manuals advocate violence and denigration of women. We're not doing this for some glib, high-profile reason. We're doing it because we need to stop the concerted impediment."
55 "BC Abortion-Protest Limits Will Likely Endure," *Vancouver Sun*, June 21, 1995.
56 British Columbia, *Official Report of the Debates of the Legislative Assembly*, June 27, 1995.
57 British Columbia, *Official Report of the Debates of the Legislative Assembly*, June 22, 1995.
58 *R v Lewis*, 1996 CanLII 17950 (BC PC) at para 53; "Why We Need Maurice Lewis," *Vancouver Sun*, January 27, 1996.

59 "Factum of the Intervenor," Elizabeth Bagshaw Society et al., May 2, 1996, in Crown appeal against acquittal in *R v Lewis,* BCSC file no. CC960120, Vancouver Registry. The *Keegstra* case involved an Alberta high school teacher who was charged with the *Criminal Code* offence of wilfully promoting hatred against an identifiable group by communicating antisemitic statements to his students. The Supreme Court of Canada overturned a decision of the Alberta Court of Queen's Bench, which had found that s 319(2) and s 319(3) were unconstitutional for infringing the freedom of expression and presumption of innocence protections in s 2(b) and s 11 of the Charter. See *R v Keegstra,* [1990] 3 SCR 697.

60 *R v Lewis,* 1996 CanLII 3559 (BCSC) at para 66.

61 "Court Restores Abortion Clinic Buffer-Zone Law," *Times Colonist* (Victoria), October 9, 1996; "Sidewalks Made Safe from Stress Again," *Vancouver Province,* October 15, 1996.

62 *R v Lewis,* 1996 CanLII 3559 (BCSC) at para 150.

63 "Abortion Bubble-Zone Foe Found Dead in Ontario," *The Star-Phoenix* (Saskatoon), September 6, 1997.

64 *R v Demers,* 2003 BCCA 28; "'Bubble Zone' Challenge Dismissed," *Vancouver Province,* September 26, 2003; *R v Demers,* 1999 BCSC 1224; "Abortion-Protest Law Upheld," *Edmonton Journal,* August 6, 1999. See also *Tremblay v Daigle,* [1989] 2 SCR 530; *Winnipeg Child and Family Services v DFG,* [1997] 3 SCR 925.

65 "Second Attempt Made to Kill Vancouver Abortion Doctor," *Edmonton Journal,* July 12, 2000.

66 "Dosanjh Faces Difficulty Finding Common Ground on Abortion," *The Telegraph-Journal* (St. John, NB), July 31, 2004.

67 Mitchell, "The S.U.V. Model of Citizenship," 77–100.

68 "Factum of the Intervenor The Access Coalition," 8 September 2006, in *R v Watson and Spratt,* BCCA file nos. CA29841 and CA29830, http://www.westcoastleaf.org (viewed May 10, 2016); *R v Spratt and Watson,* 2008 BCCA 340 (Factum of Intervenor, Access Coalition), "Factum of the Intervenor, Canadian Religious Freedom Alliance," September 8, 2006, in *R v Watson and Spratt,* BCCA file nos. CA29841 and CA29830, http://www.evangelicalfellowship.ca/ (viewed May 10, 2016).

69 Factum of the Intervenor, Access Coalition.

70 Factum of the Intervenor, Canadian Religious Freedom Alliance. The Alliance consisted of the Catholic Civil Rights League (CCRL), the Evangelical Fellowship of Canada (EFC), and the Christian Legal Fellowship.

71 *R v Spratt and Watson,* 2008 BCCA 340 at para 91; "BC Court Upholds Abortion Bubble-Zone Law," *Globe and Mail,* September 4, 2008.

72 See *R v Demers,* 2003 BCCA 28; *R v Spratt and Watson; R v Spratt,* 2011 BCSC 1747. See also Tom Sandborn, "BC a Base for Abortion Battlers Trying New Tactics," *The Tyee* (Vancouver), January 3, 2013; "B.C. Expands 'Bubble Zone' Around View Royal Clinic Offering Abortions," *Times Colonist* (Victoria), June 2, 2018.

73 For an American study of judicial restraint of freedom of expression in the vicinity of abortion clinics, see Mitchell, "The S.U.V. Model of Citizenship," 77–100.

74 Bill 20, *Access to Services (COVID-19) Act,* 2nd Sess, 42nd Leg, British Columbia, 2021 (assented to November 25, 2021, and repealed effective July 1, 2023, pursuant to a sunset clause at s 7); *Access to Services (COVID-19) Act,* SBC 2021, c 23; British Columbia, "New Act Protects Important Services from Disruption" (news release, November 15, 2021), https://news.gov.bc.ca/releases/2021PREM0071-002169.

75 "Bubble-Zone Protection Coming for Hospitals and Schools, Farnworth Says," *Times Colonist* (Victoria), October 4, 2021.

76 Bill C-3, *An Act to Amend the Criminal Code and the Canada Labour Code,* 1st Sess, 44th Parl, 2021 (assented to December 17, 2021).

77 *Canadian Frontline Nurses v Canada (Attorney General),* 2024 FC 42, para 372; *Canada (Attorney General) v Canadian Civil Liberties Association,* 2026 FCA 6; Canada, *Report of the Public Inquiry into the 2022 Public Order Emergency* (February 17, 2023).

Chapter 4: Legal Wars in the Woods

1 *MacMillan Bloedel Ltd v Brown,* 1994 BCCA 64, para 42.

2 See R. Peter Gillis and Thomas R. Roach, *Lost Initiatives: Canada's Forest Industries, Forest Policy, and Forest Conservation* (New York: Greenwood Press, 1986); Eryk Martin, "When Red Meets Green: Perceptions of Environmental Change in the BC Communist Left, 1937–1978" (MA thesis, University of Victoria, 2008); John Henry Harter, "'When Blue is Green': Towards a History of Workers as Environmentalists in British Columbia and Beyond" (PhD diss., Simon Fraser University, 2019); Katrin MacPhee, "Canadian Working-Class Environmentalism, 1965–1985," *Labour/Le Travail* 74 (Fall 2014): 123–49.

3 Jeremy Wilson, *Talk and Log: Wilderness Politics in British Columbia* (Vancouver: UBC Press, 1998), 48–49; Richard A. Rajala, *Clearcutting the Pacific Rain Forest: Production, Science, and Regulation* (Vancouver: UBC Press, 1999). See also Jeremy Wilson, "Forest Conservation in British Columbia, 1935–85: Reflections on a Barren Political Debate," *BC Studies* 76 (Winter 1987–88): 3–32. See also John-Henry Harter, "Environmental Justice for Whom? Class, New Social Movements, and the Environment: A Case Study of Greenpeace Canada, 1971–2000," *Labour/Le Travail* 54 (Fall 2004): 83–119.

4 Roger Hayter, "'The War in the Woods': Post-Fordist Restructuring, Globalization, and the Contested Remapping of British Columbia's Forest Economy," *Annals of the Association of American Geographers* 93, 3 (September 2003): 706–29. See also Trevor J. Barnes and Roger Hayter, eds., *Troubles in the Rainforest: British Columbia's Forest Economy in Transition; Canadian Western Geographical Series Vol. 33* (Victoria: Western Geographical Press, 1997).

5 Henry John, "A War in the Woods? Environmentalisms, Old Growth Forests, and the Labour Movement on Southern Vancouver Island, 1970–1995" (PhD diss., University of British Columbia, 2023).

6 Michael Mullin, interviewed by Benjamin Isitt, Tofino, BC, May 24, 2013; C.J. Hinke, "Letters from Gaol: The Prison Experience of a Tree Protector," *Journal of Prisoners on Prisons* 2, 2 (Spring 1990): 43–48. See also "Court Clears Way for Tsitika Logging," *Vancouver Sun,* November 2, 1990.

7 "NDP Stake in MB Rattles Industry," *Vancouver Sun,* March 25, 1993, D1. See also "Sale Brings MB Reins Back to BC," *Vancouver Sun,* February 10, 1993. Half of the BC government's 3.8 million shares in MacMillan Bloedel were acquired through a direct share purchase in early 1993, while the other 1.9 million shares were owned through pension funds and other funds administered by the BC government. The BC government's 3.8 million shares amounted to approximately 3.3 percent of the total value of the company.

8 Maurice Gibbons, "The Clayoquot Papers," in *Clayoquot and Dissent*, ed. Ronald B. Hatch (Vancouver: Ronsdale, 1995), 95; "Clayoquot Protesters Fines," *Times Colonist* (Victoria), December 9, 1993.

9 "Policy – Civil Disobedience," as cited in Amir Attaran, "*Mandamus* in the Enforcement of the Criminal Law: Ending the Anti-Protest Injunction Habit – Issues Arising from MacMillan Bloedel v. Simpson," *UBC Law Review* 33, 1 (1999): 182.

10 "Tree Farm Licence #44 Management Plan #5," June 2010, Western Forest Products, https://www2.gov.bc.ca/assets/gov/farming-natural-resources-and-industry/forestry/timber-tenures/tree-farm-licence/management-plans/tfl-44-mngment-plan-5-2010.pdf (accessed January 12, 2026); Forest Planning Canada, "The Current State of Forest Licences in British Columbia" (Victoria, 1990), http://www.bctwa.org/TFL-14.pdf.

11 *MacMillan Bloedel Ltd v Brown*.

12 "Judge Warns Six Anti-Logging Protesters Courts Must Curb Refusal to Abide by Law," *Vancouver Sun*, December 11, 1991; see also *MacMillan Bloedel Ltd v Brown*.

13 See *Commissioner on Resources and Environment Act*, SBC 1992, c 34; Office of the Ombudsman of British Columbia, *Public Report No. 31: Administrative Fairness of the Process Leading to the Clayoquot Sound Land Use Decision* (Victoria: Office of the Ombudsman of British Columbia, 1993), 19–22; Benjamin Cashore et al., eds., *In Search of Sustainability: Forest Policy in British Columbia in the 1990s* (Vancouver: UBC Press, 2000).

14 "MacBlo's 'Private Criminal Law' Will Come Under Fire by Lawyer," *Vancouver Sun*, July 27, 1993.

15 Karena Shaw, "Encountering Clayoquot, Reading the Political," in *A Political Space: Reading the Global through Clayoquot Sound*, ed. Warren Magnusson and Karena Shaw (Montreal and Kingston: McGill-Queen's University Press, 2002), 32.

16 *Sierra Club of Western Canada v British Columbia (Attorney General)*, 1991 CanLII 233 (BCSC) http://www.courts.gov.bc.ca/search_judgments.aspx?alpha=S&court=1; *Sierra Club of Western Canada v British Columbia (Attorney General)*, 1992 CanLII 1470 (BCCA). See also James Davie, "A Bridge to Nowhere: British Columbia's Capitalist Nature and the Carmanah Walbran War in the Woods (1988–1994)" (MA thesis, University of Victoria, 2019) http://www.courts.gov.bc.ca/search_judgments.aspx?alpha=S&court=1.

17 "MacBlo Beats off Challenge to Island Cut," *Times Colonist* (Victoria), December 24, 1993; *Sierra Club of Western Canada v British Columbia (Chief Forester)*, 1995 CanLII 1448 (BCCA) http://www.courts.gov.bc.ca/search_judgments.aspx?alpha=S&court=1.

18 For a discussion of "environmental property rights" and the "legal rights of nature," see Christopher Stone, "Should Trees Have Standing? Toward Legal Rights for Natural Objects," *Southern California Law Review* 45 (1972): 450–501; Christopher Tribe, "Ways Not to Think About Plastic Trees: New Foundations in Environmental Law," *Yale Law Journal* 83, 7 (1974): 1315–45; Christopher P. Rodgers, "Agenda 2000, Land Use, and the Environment: Towards a Theory of 'Environmental' Property Rights?" in *Law and Geography*, ed. Jane Holder and Carolyn Harrison (New York: Oxford University Press, 2003), 239–58.

19 Tzeporah Berman, "Takin' It Back," in Hatch, *Clayoquot and Dissent*, 2. See also Tzeporah Berman, with Mark Leiren-Young, *This Crazy Time: Living Our Environmental Challenge* (Toronto: Alfred A. Knopf Canada, 2011), 60.

20 Gordon Brent Ingram, "Ecology of a Conflict," in Hatch, *Clayoquot and Dissent*, 9–70; Berman, "Takin' It Back," 3; Berman, *This Crazy Time*, 39–40.

21 For the events culminating in the road blockade of the summer of 1993, see Pierre Walter, "Adult Learning in New Social Movements: Environmental Protest and the Struggle for the Clayoquot Sound Rainforest," *Adult Education Quarterly* 57, 3 (May 2007): 248–63. See also *MacMillan Bloedel Ltd v Simpson*, 1993 CanLII 1068 (BCCA).
22 *MacMillan Bloedel Ltd v Simpson*, 1993 CanLII 1068 (BCCA); "Protester Gets 6 Months," *The Province*, July 16, 1993.
23 *MacMillan Bloedel Ltd v Simpson*, 1994 CanLII 1731 (BCCA), para. 50.
24 See Walter, "Adult Learning in New Social Movements," 248–63; Berman, *This Crazy Time*, 31–81.
25 *MacMillan Bloedel Ltd v Simpson*, 1994 CanLII 1731 (BCCA), para. 83.
26 Sarah B. Pralle, *Branching Out, Digging In: Environmental Advocacy and Agenda Setting* (Washington, DC: Georgetown University Press, 2006), 89; Berman, *This Crazy Time*, 64–65.
27 *MacMillan Bloedel Ltd v Simpson*, 1994 CanLII 1731 (BCCA), para. 17.
28 *MacMillan Bloedel Ltd v Simpson*, 1994 CanLII 1731 (BCCA), para. 97.
29 *MacMillan Bloedel Ltd v Simpson*, 1994 CanLII 1731 (BCCA), para. 94.
30 *MacMillan Bloedel Ltd v Simpson*, 1994 CanLII 1731 (BCCA), para. 108.
31 *MacMillan Bloedel Ltd v Krawczyk*, 1994 CanLII 1140 (BCCA), para. 6; *MacMillan Bloedel Ltd v Simpson*, 1994 CanLII 1731 (BCCA), paras. 173–75.
32 *MacMillan Bloedel Ltd v Simpson*, 1994 CanLII 1731 (BCCA), paras. 173–74. See also *Operation Dismantle*, [1985] 1 SCR 441; *Morgentaler v The Queen*, [1976] 1 SCR 616.
33 *Perka v The Queen*, [1984] 2 SCR 232; *MacMillan Bloedel Ltd v Krawczyk*, 1994 CanLII 1140 (BCCA), paras. 5–11.
34 *MacMillan Bloedel Ltd v Krawczyk*, 1994 CanLII 1140 (BCCA), para. 11.
35 *MacMillan Bloedel Ltd v Krawczyk*, 1994 CanLII 1140 (BCCA), para. 12; *R. v. Bridges*, 1989 CanLII 2921 (BCSC).
36 *MacMillan Bloedel Ltd v Simpson*, 1994 CanLII 1731 (BCCA), para. 193.
37 *MacMillan Bloedel Ltd v Simpson*, 1994 CanLII 1731 (BCCA), paras. 159, 65–166.
38 "Reasons for Sentencing," Bouck J., October 6, 1993, *MacMillan Bloedel Ltd v Simpson*, file no. V02011, Victoria Registry, Andrew Swain Papers (in possession of author); *MacMillan Bloedel Ltd v Simpson*, 1993 CanLII 2529 (BCSC) (reasons for sentence); *Macmillan Bloedel Limited v Simpson*, 1993 CanLII 2799 (BCSC) (conviction reasons). See also Andrew Swain, interviewed by Benjamin Isitt, Victoria, April 16, 2013.
39 *MacMillan Bloedel Ltd v Brown*, 1994 CanLII 3254 (BCCA).
40 *MacMillan Bloedel Ltd v Simpson*, 1994 CanLII 1731 (BCCA), para. 117.
41 *MacMillan Bloedel Ltd v Simpson*, 1994 CanLII 1731 (BCCA), para. 116. See also *Reference re Young Offenders Act (PEI)*, [1991] 1 SCR 252; *British Columbia (Attorney General) v. Mount Currie Indian Band*, 1991 CanLII 130 (BCSC) (re: *Wallace*); Sir Jack Jacob, QC, "The Inherent Jurisdiction of the Court," *Current Legal Problems* 23 (1970): 27–28.
42 *MacMillan Bloedel Ltd v Simpson*, 1994 CanLII 1731 (BCCA), para. 125; *MacMillan Bloedel Ltd v Simpson*, [1995] 4 SCR 725, p. 757.
43 *MacMillan Bloedel Ltd v Simpson*, 1994 CanLII 1731 (BCCA), para. 118.
44 Berman, *This Crazy Time*, 59–64, 75–78; *Criminal Code*, RSC 1985, c C-46, s 21 (1).
45 See Clayoquot Resource Centre fonds, AR031, University of Victoria Archives and Special Collections; *MacMillan Bloedel Ltd v Simpson*, 1993 BCSC 1295, 1431, 1432, 1457, 1467, 1582, 1809; 1994 BCSC 30, 354, 384, 416, 427, 604, 808, 1045, 1285; [1995] 4 SCR 725; [1996] 2 SCR 1048; Ronald B. Hatch, "The Clayoquot Show Trials," in Hatch, *Clayoquot and*

Dissent, 105–53; Ronald MacIsaac and Anne Champagne, eds., *Clayoquot Mass Trials: Defending the Rainforest* (Gabriola Island, BC: New Society, 1994); Ronald B. Hatch, "The Clayoquot Protests: Taking Stock One Year Later," in Hatch, *Clayoquot and Dissent,* 199–208. For data on the number of people tried and convicted, see *MacMillan Bloedel Ltd v Simpson,* [1996] 2 SCR 1048, and Hatch, "The Clayoquot Show Trials," 107.

46 "Clayoquot: The Danger of Using Injunctions," *Globe and Mail,* November 5, 1993.

47 Editorial, *Times Colonist* (Victoria), October 20, 1993, as cited in Berman, "Takin' It Back," 1.

48 "Contempt a Problem for Courts," *Vancouver Sun,* October 20, 1993.

49 *MacMillan Bloedel Ltd v Simpson,* 1994 CanLII 1731 (BCCA), para. 195.

50 *MacMillan Bloedel Ltd v Simpson,* 1994 CanLII 1731 (BCCA), para. 196.

51 *MacMillan Bloedel Ltd v Simpson,* 1994 CanLII 1731 (BCCA), para. 13.

52 *MacMillan Bloedel Ltd v Simpson,* 1994 CanLII 1731 (BCCA), para. 46.

53 John Fox, *The History of Contempt of Court* (London: Professional Books, 1972); Ian Cram, ed., *Borrie and Lowe: The Law of Contempt,* 4th ed. (London: LexisNexis Butterworths, 2010); *Poje v Attorney General of British Columbia,* [1953] 1 SCR 516; *Tilco Plastics Ltd v Skurjat,* [1967] 1 CCC 131, 147 (Ont HC); *BCGEU v AG of British Columbia,* [1988] 2 SCR 214; *Regina v. United Fishermen & Allied Workers' Union et al.,* 1967 CanLII 556 (BCCA), leave to appeal refused *United Fishermen & Allied Workers' Union et al. v The Queen,* 1968 CanLII 84 (SCC), [1968] SCR 255); *Everywoman's Health Centre Society* (1988), C886265, dated June 6, 1989, (B.C.S.C.), Unreported; *R. v. Demers,* 1992 CanLII 2192 (BCCA); *R. v. Cohn,* 1984 CanLII 43 (ON CA).

54 *MacMillan Bloedel Ltd v Simpson,* 1994 CanLII 1731 (BCCA), para. 73.

55 *MacMillan Bloedel Ltd v Simpson,* 1994 CanLII 1731 (BCCA), para. 160.

56 *MacMillan Bloedel Ltd v Simpson,* 1994 CanLII 1731 (BCCA), para. 179.

57 *MacMillan Bloedel Ltd v Simpson,* 1994 CanLII 1731 (BCCA), para. 180.

58 See *McEvoy v AG of New Brunswick,* [1983] 1 SCR 704; *Valente v R,* [1985] 2 SCR 673; and *Hickman v MacKeigan,* [1989] 2 SCR 796.

59 "Only One Clayoquot Appeal to Be Heard," *Times Colonist* (Victoria), October 7, 1994.

60 *MacMillan Bloedel Ltd v Simpson,* [1995] 4 SCR 725, 757.

61 *MacMillan Bloedel Ltd v Simpson,* [1996] 2 SCR 1048, para 13.

62 See W.T. Stanbury and Ilan B. Vertinsky, "The Challenge to Canadian Forest Products in Europe: Managing a Complex Environmental Issue" (paper prepared for Canada–British Columbia Partnership Agreement on Forest Resource Development, March 1995), https://canadacommons.ca/artifacts/36554759/the-challenge-to-canadian-forest-products-in-europe/37454148/ (accessed January 28, 2026); Berman, *This Crazy Time,* 57–58, 99–113; M. Smyth, "Logs, Lies and Greenpeace," *Forestry Chronicle* 73, 5 (September/October 1997): 531; Greenpeace, *The Chain of Destruction: From Canada's Ancient Rainforests to the U.S. Market* (Washington, DC: Greenpeace, 1999); "US Firm Says Its Takeover of MacBlo Creates a Global Leader," *Vancouver Sun,* June 22, 1999; "Canadian Icon Gone, MB's Stephens Says," *Vancouver Sun,* June 22, 1999; "US Giant Urged to Honour Environmental Deals," *Vancouver Sun,* June 22, 1999; Canada, Evidence submitted to House of Commons Standing Committee on Natural Resources and Government Operations, May 14, 1999, Vancouver, https://www.ourcommons.ca/DocumentViewer/en/36-1/NRGO/meeting-73/evidence.

63 Clayoquot Sound Scientific Panel, *Sustainable Ecosystem Management in Clayoquot Sound*

(Victoria: Clayoquot Sound Scientific Panel, 1995), 1. See also Clayoquot Sound Scientific Panel, *Report of the Scientific Panel for Sustainable Forest Practices in Clayoquot Sound* (Victoria: Clayoquot Sound Scientific Panel, January 1994).

64 See *Forest Practices Code of British Columbia Act*, SBC 1994, c 41; British Columbia, *Vancouver Island Land Use Plan* (2000).

65 Hatch, "The Clayoquot Protests," 204–5.

66 William K. Carroll and R.S. Ratner, "The NDP Regime in British Columbia: A Post Mortem," in *Challenges and Perils: Social Democracy in Neoliberal Times*, ed. William K. Carroll and R.S. Ratner (Halifax: Fernwood, 2005), 111.

67 Iisaak Forest Resources, *Sustainable Forest Management Plan* (2011), http://www.iisaak.com (accessed April 27, 2016); Karena Shaw, "Encountering Clayoquot, Reading the Political," in *A Political Space: Reading the Global through Clayoquot Sound*, ed. Warren Magnusson and Karena Shaw (Montreal and Kingston: McGill-Queen's University Press, 2002), 54–57; Dimitri Portier, "The Meares Island Case: Nuu-chah-nulth vs. the Logging Industry," *European Review of Native American Studies* 14, 1 (2000): 36–37; Jonathan Clapperton, "Environmental Activism as Anti-Conquest: The Nuu-chah-nulth and Environmentalists in the Contact Zone of Clayoquot Sound," in *Environmental Activism on the Ground: Small Green and Indigenous Organizing*, ed. Jonathan Clapperton and Liza Piper (Calgary: University of Calgary Press, 2018), 194–95; Berman, *This Crazy Time*, 90.

68 MaMook Natural Resources Ltd., "About," n.d., https://mamookresources.ca/about; British Columbia, "Tree Farm Licence 54: Maquinna Tree Farm Licence," June 1, 2022, https://www2.gov.bc.ca/assets/gov/farming-natural-resources-and-industry/forestry/timber-tenures/tree-farm-licence/licences/tfl54_lic_jun_1_2022.pdf; British Columbia, "Tree Farm Licence 57: Clayoquot Tree Farm Licence," October 27, 2019, https://www2.gov.bc.ca/assets/gov/farming-natural-resources-and-industry/forestry/timber-tenures/tree-farm-licence/licences/tfl_57_lic_03_october_27_2019.pdf.

69 British Columbia, "New Clayoquot Sound Conservancies Help Protect B.C.'s Oldest Forests" (news release, June 18, 2024), https://news.gov.bc.ca/releases/2024FOR0028-000958; Dirk Meissner, "Clayoquot Sound's 'War in the Woods' Battlegrounds to be Permanently Protected," *Times Colonist* (Victoria), June 19, 2024.

70 Shaw, "Encountering Clayoquot," 42.

71 Shaw, "Encountering Clayoquot," 43. See also Maryjka Mychajlowycz, *Overview of Logging in Clayoquot Sound: 2000–2009* (Tofino, BC: Friends of Clayoquot Sound, 2009).

72 Clapperton, "Environmental Activism as Anti-Conquest," 200. See also Berman, *This Crazy Time*, 82–90.

73 Maurice Gibbons, "The Clayoquot Papers," in Hatch, *Clayoquot and Dissent*, 98. See also Debra J. Salazar and Donald K. Alper, "Politics, Policy, and the War in the Woods," in *Sustaining the Forests of the Pacific Coast: Forging Truces in the War in the Woods*, ed. Debra J. Salazar and Donald K. Alper (Vancouver: UBC Press, 2001), 3–21; Lorna Stefanick, "Baby Stumpy and the War in the Woods: Competing Frames of British Columbia Forests," *BC Studies* 130 (2001): 41–68; Michaela Killoran Mann, "'Clearcut' Conflict: Clayoquot Sound Campaign and the Moral Imagination" (MA thesis, Université Saint Paul University, 2013).

74 Berman, *This Crazy Time*, 79.

75 Melinda Harm Benson, "Rules of Engagement: The Spatiality of Judicial Review," in *The*

Expanding Spaces of Law: A Timely Legal Geography, ed. Irus Braverman, Nicholas Blomley, and David Delaney (Stanford, CA: Stanford University Press, 2014), 215–38.

76 Amir Attaran, "*Mandamus* in the Enforcement of the Criminal Law: Ending the Anti-Protest Injunction Habit – Issues Arising from MacMillan Bloedel v. Simpson," *UBC Law Review* 33, 1 (1999): 181–97.

77 *Slocan Forest Products Ltd v John Doe*, 2000 BCSC 150.

78 *Slocan Forest Products Ltd v John Doe.*

79 *Interfor v. Kern et al*, 2000 BCSC 1141, para. 60.

80 *Teal Cedar Products Ltd v Rainforest Flying Squad*, 2021 BCSC 1903). For details on arrests arising from the Fairy Creek protests from May to September 2021, see RCMP Lake Cowichan Detachment, "Update #108 on Police Enforcement of Injunction Order in Fairy Creek Watershed" (media release, September 27, 2021), https://bc-cb.rcmp-grc.gc.ca/ (accessed October 2, 2021). The RCMP media release notes: "Since enforcement began, the RCMP have arrested 1101 individuals; 110 of whom were previously arrested with a combined total of 261 times. Of the total arrested, 865 were for breaching the injunction (contempt of court), 203 were for obstruction, 16 were for mischief, 6 were for breaching their release conditions, 6 were for assaulting a police officer, 2 were for failing to comply with a court order, 1 for counselling to resist arrest, 1 for causing a disturbance, and 1 Immigration Act."

81 *Teal Cedar Products Ltd v Rainforest Flying Squad*, 2021 BCSC 1903; *Teal Cedar Products Ltd v Rainforest Flying Squad*, 2021 BCCA 387; *Teal Cedar Products Ltd v Rainforest Flying Squad*, 2022 BCCA 26; "Fairy Creek Protesters Vow to Carry On Despite New Injunction," *Globe and Mail*, October 11, 2021; "Judge Rebukes Mounties' Handling of Fairy Creek Logging Protest," *New York Times*, October 1, 2021; "Canada: Win for Anti-Logging Protesters as Judge Denies Firm's Injunction Bid," *The Guardian*, September 29, 2021, https://www.theguardian.com/environment/2021/sep/29/canada-logging-protests-vancouver-island-judge.

82 *Verchere v Greenpeace Canada*, 2004 BCCA 242; *Verchere et al v Greenpeace Canada et al*, 2003 BCSC 1571; "Anti-Logging Case Proves Expensive," *CBC News*, May 1, 2003, https://www.cbc.ca/news/canada/british-columbia/anti-logging-protest-proves-expensive-1.373565.

83 Justin Page, *Tracking the Great Bear: How Environmentalists Recreated British Columbia's Coastal Rainforest* (Vancouver: UBC Press, 2014); Diane Pinch, *Passion and Persistence: Fifty Years of the Sierra Club of British Columbia* (Madeira Park, BC: Harbour Publishing, 2019), 147–62.

84 James Davie, "A Bridge to Nowhere: British Columbia's Capitalist Nature and the Carmanah Walbran War in the Woods (1988–1994)" (MA thesis, University of Victoria, 2019).

85 *Hayes Forest Services Ltd v Forest Action Network et al*, 2003 BCSC 1444; *Hayes Forest Services Ltd v Forest Action Network*, 2003 BCSC 1569.

86 *Interfor v Paine and Krawczyk*, 2001 BCCA 48, para 23.

87 *R v Krawczyk*, 2007 BCSC 345, aff'd *R v Krawczyk*, 2010 BCCA 542.

88 *R v Krawczyk*, 2007 BCSC 2011, aff'd *R v Krawczyk*, 2009 BCCA 250. See also *Hayes Forest Services Ltd v Krawczyk*, 2006 BCCA 156.

89 For a discussion of "environmental property rights," see Rodgers, "Agenda 2000, Land Use, and the Environment," 239–58. See also Davie, "A Bridge to Nowhere."

Chapter 5: Standoffs, Roadblocks, and Breakthroughs for Indigenous Property Claims

1 The island of Tllga Kun Gwaayaay (Lyell Island) is at times referred to as Athlii Gwaii, after the movement that came together at that location to protect the larger Gwaii Haanas area. I have used the term "Lyell Island" for the remainder of this chapter. For a discussion of the place name, see Jisgang Nika Collison, ed., *Athlii Gwaii: Upholding the Law at Lyell Island* (Vancouver: Locarno Press, 2018), xi.

2 See *MacMillan Bloedel Ltd v Mullin*, 1985 CanLII 154 (BCCA). For the legal test for the granting of an injunction that was in effect in British Columbia in 1985, see *Wheatley v Ellis and Hendrickson*, [1944] 61 BCR 55. For the current legal test in Canada for the granting of an injunction, see *RJR-MacDonald Inc v Canada (AG)*, [1994] 1 SCR 311.

3 Shiri Pasternak and Irina Ceric, "Injunctions Have Only Served to Prove the Point: Canada Is a Smash-and-Grab Country for Industry," *Globe and Mail*, February 28, 2020; Irina Ceric, "Beyond Contempt: Injunctions, Land Defense, and the Criminalization of Indigenous Resistance," *South Atlantic Quarterly* 119, 2 (April 2020): 353–69; Tyler McCreary and Jerome Turner, "The Contested Scales of Indigenous and Settler Jurisdiction: Unist'ot'en Struggles with Canadian Pipeline Governance," *Studies in Political Economy* 99, 3 (February 2019): 1–23; Tyler McCreary, "Between the Commodity and the Gift: The Coastal GasLink Pipeline and the Contested Temporalities of Canadian and Witsuwit'en Law," *Journal of Human Rights and the Environment* 11 (December 2020): 122–45.

4 For a critical examination of the role of settler-allies in Indigenous land struggles, see Katherine L.E. Milley, "The Colonizer and the Colonizer Who Refuses: Cultural Production and Colonial Crisis at Oka, Ipperwash, Burnt Church and Caledonia" (PhD diss., University of Toronto, 2019).

5 The Supreme Court of Canada first recognized the *sui generis* nature of Indigenous rights in Canadian law in the 1984 *Guerin* decision, moving beyond the court's tentative recognition of title in *Calder* (1973). The decision was affirmed and expanded upon in *Sparrow* (1990), which provided a framework for interpreting s 35(1) of the constitution. These cases provided a foundation for further legal advances by Indigenous peoples within settler legal institutions, including the recognition of collective forms of title in *Delgamuukw* (1997) and the landmark *Tsilhqot'in* decision in 2014, which saw the court formally declare Aboriginal title to lands outside a reserve. See *Calder et al v Attorney-General of British Columbia*, [1973] SCR 313; *R v Taylor and Williams* (1981), 34 OR (2d) 360; *Guerin v The Queen*, [1984] 2 SCR 335; *R v Sparrow*, [1990] 1 SCR 1075; *R v Marshall*, [1990] 3 SCR 456; *R v Van der Peet*, [1996] 2 SCR 507; *Delgamuukw v British Columbia*, [1997] 3 SCR 1010; *Tsilhqot'in Nation v British Columbia*, 2014 SCC 44; *Cowichan Tribes v Canada (Attorney General)*, 2025 BCSC 1490. As the Supreme Court of Canada noted in *Sparrow* (1990), citing favourably from the court's previous ruling in *Guerin* (1984), "the *sui generis* nature of Indian title, and the historic powers and responsibility assumed by the Crown constituted the source of such a fiduciary obligation" to Indigenous people. *Guerin* combined with *R v Taylor and Williams* (1981) provided a "general guiding principle" for the interpretation of s 35(1), that "the Government has the responsibility to act in a fiduciary capacity with respect to aboriginal peoples. The relationship between the Government and aboriginals is trust like, rather than adversarial, and contemporary recognition and affirmation of aboriginal rights must be defined in light of this historic relationship." However, as

Andrea Bowker has suggested, this litigation has been a slow and uneven process: Andrea Bowker, "*Sparrow*'s Promise: Aboriginal Rights in the BC Court of Appeal," *University of Toronto Law Review* 53 (Winter 1995): 1–48.

6 "Ulkatcho Band Wants Say in Development," *Williams Lake Tribune*, January 22, 1985, 5.

7 See John Borrows, *Canada's Indigenous Constitution* (Toronto: University of Toronto Press, 2010); John Borrows, "With or Without You: First Nations Law (in Canada)," *McGill Law Journal* 41 (1996): 629–65; John Borrows, "Indigenous Legal Traditions," *Journal of Law and Policy* 19 (2005): 167–223; John Borrows and Leonard I. Rotman. "The *Sui Generis* Nature of Aboriginal Rights: Does It Make a Difference?" *Alberta Law Review* 36, 1 (1997): 9–45; Sarah Morales, "Snuw'uyulh: Fostering an Understanding of the Hul'qumi'num Legal Tradition" (PhD diss., University of Victoria, 2014); Taiaiake Alfred, *Peace, Power, Righteousness: An Indigenous Manifesto* (Don Mills, ON: Oxford University Press, 1999); Don Monet and Skanu'u (Ardythe Wilson), *Colonialism on Trial: Indigenous Land Rights and the Gitksan and Wet'suwet'en Sovereignty Case* (Gabriola Island, BC: New Society, 1992); Glen Sean Coulthard, *Red Skin, White Masks: Rejecting the Colonial Politics of Recognition* (Minneapolis: University of Minnesota Press, 2014); Hamar Foster, Heather Raven, and Jeremy Webber, eds., Let Right Be Done: Aboriginal Title, the Calder Case, and the Future of Indigenous Rights (Vancouver: UBC Press, 2007); Alan Hanna, "Making the Round: Aboriginal Title in the Common Law from a Tsilhqot'in Legal Perspective," *Ottawa Law Review* 45, 3 (2015): 365–402; Tyler McCreary, "Historicizing the Encounter between State, Corporate, and Indigenous Authorities on Gitxsan Lands," *Windsor Yearbook of Access to Justice* 33, 3 (2016): 163–97; Gordon Christie, "Indigeneity and Sovereignty in Canada's Far North: The Arctic and Inuit Sovereignty," *South Atlantic Quarterly* 110, 2 (2011): 329–46.

8 Collison, *Athlii Gwaii*, 139.

9 Warren Magnusson, "Introduction: The Puzzle of Political," in *A Political Space: Reading the Global through Clayoquot Sound*, ed. Warren Magnusson and Karena Shaw (Minneapolis: University of Minnesota Press, 2002), 10. See also Hamar Foster, "British Columbia: Legal Institutions in the Far West, from Contact to 1871," Manitoba Law Journal 23 (1996): 340; Christopher F. Roth, "Without Treaty, Without Conquest: Indigenous Sovereignty in Post-Delgamuukw British Columbia," *Wicazo Sa Review* 17, 2 (Fall 2002): 143.

10 Barry M. Gough, *Gunboat Frontier: British Maritime Authority and Northwest Coast Indians, 1846–90* (Vancouver: UBC Press, 1984); Daniel Clayton, *Islands of Truth: The Imperial Fashioning of Vancouver Island* (Vancouver: UBC Press, 2000); Chris Arnett, *The Terror of the Coast: Land Alienation and Colonial War on Vancouver Island and the Gulf Islands, 1849–1863* (Vancouver: Talonbooks, 1999); R. Cole Harris, *Making Native Space: Colonialism, Resistance, and Reserves in British Columbia* (Vancouver: UBC Press, 2003). See also Nicholas Blomley, "Law, Property, and the Geography of Violence: The Frontier, the Survey, and the Grid," *Annals of the Association of American Geographers* 93, 1 (March 2003): 121–41. The role of law and development of settler legal institutions during this colonial period has also been examined by historian Tina Loo. See Tina Loo, *Making Law, Order and Authority in British Columbia, 1821–1871* (Toronto: University of Toronto Press, 1994).

11 *Delgamuukw v British Columbia*, [1997] 3 SCR 1010, paras 63–65, 133–34; see also *Delgamuukw v British Columbia*, 1993 CanLII 4516 (BCCA).

12 Nicholas Blomley, "'Shut the Province Down': First Nations Blockades in British Columbia,

1984–1995," *BC Studies* 111 (Autumn 1996): 5–35. See also Steven Point, "Understanding Native Activism," *BC Studies* 89 (Spring 1991): 124–29; Nicholas Blomley, *Law, Space, and the Geographies of Power* (New York: Guilford Press, 1994); Blomley, "Law, Property, and the Geography of Violence," 121–41; Shiri Pasternak and Dayna Nadine Scott, "Introduction: Getting Back the Land," *South Atlantic Quarterly* 119, 2 (April 2020): 205–13; Ceric, "Beyond Contempt," 353–69; McCreary and Turner, "The Contested Scales of Indigenous and Settler Jurisdiction," 1–23; McCreary, "Between the Commodity and the Gift," 122–45; Michael Simpson and Philippe Le Billon, "Reconciling Violence: Policing the Politics of Recognition," *Geoforum* 119 (February 2021): 111–21; Yale D. Belanger and P. Whitney Lackenbauer, *Blockades or Breakthroughs? Aboriginal Peoples Confront the Canadian State* (Montreal and Kingston: McGill-Queen's University Press, 2015).

13 For the evolution of the Indian reserves in British Columbia, see Harris, *Making Native Space*.

14 Hamar Foster, "Roadblocks and Legal History, Part I: Do Forgotten Cases Make Good Law?" *The Advocate* 54, 3 (May 1996): 355–56; and Hamar Foster, "Roadblocks and Legal History, Part II: Aboriginal Title and s. 91(24)," *The Advocate* 54, 4 (July 1996): 531–46. In a recent national study of Indigenous protest, Belanger and Lackenbauer suggest that "blockades and occupations are instrumental and symbolic, a means to reshape the spatiality of power and authority." See Belanger and Lackenbauer, *Blockades or Breakthroughs?* 16. Section 91(24) of the *Constitution Act, 1867*, 30 & 31 Vict, c 3 assigns exclusive legislative authority to the Parliament of Canada for all matters relating to "Indians, and Lands reserved for Indians."

15 Collison, *Athlii Gwaii;* Elizabeth May, *Paradise Won: The Struggle for South Moresby* (Toronto: McClelland and Stewart, 1990); Ian Gill, *All That We Say Is Ours: Guujaaw and the Reawakening of the Haida Nation* (Toronto: Douglas and McIntyre, 2009); Louise Takeda, *Islands' Spirit Rising: Reclaiming the Forests of Haida Gwaii* (Vancouver: UBC Press, 2015); Michael Dean, "'What They Are Doing to the Land, They Are Doing to Us': Environmental Politics on Haida Gwaii" (MA thesis, University of British Columbia, 2009); Dimitri Portier, "The Meares Island Case: Nuu-chah-nulth vs. the Logging Industry," *European Review of Native American Studies* 14, 1 (2000): 31–37; Jonathan Clapperton, "Environmental Activism as Anti-Conquest: The Nuu-chah-nulth and Environmentalists in the Contact Zone of Clayoquot Sound," in *Environmental Activism on the Ground: Small Green and Indigenous Organizing*, ed. Jonathan Clapperton and Liza Piper (Calgary: University of Calgary Press, 2018), 181–205. See also Sarah Whatmore's research on Indigenous challenges to property rights in Australia: Sarah Whatmore, "De/Re-Territorializing Possession: The Shifting Spaces of Property Rights," in *Law and Geography*, ed. Jane Holder and Carolyn Harrison (New York: Oxford University Press, 2003), 211–23.

16 Remarks by Freda Huston at a public event at the University of Victoria, August 17, 2015; notes in possession of the author.

17 *MacMillan Bloedel Ltd v Mullin*, 1985 CanLII 154 (BCCA).

18 *MacMillan Bloedel Ltd v Mullin*, 1985 CanLII 154 (BCCA).

19 Christopher Moore, *The British Columbia Court of Appeal: The First Hundred Years* (Vancouver: UBC Press, 2010), 133–34.

20 In contrast to Seaton, the two appeal court judges who dissented from his majority decision – William Alastair Craig and James A. MacDonald – were well-connected members of

Vancouver's legal establishment (though Craig worked in criminal rather than corporate law). The two judges who concurred with Seaton in granting the injunction against the logging company were John Douglas Lambert, another relative outsider (who was born and raised in Scotland and worked as a government lawyer and then in private practice in Vancouver before being appointed directly to the Court of Appeal at the relatively young age of forty-nine), and Alan Macfarlane of Victoria, son of a Supreme Court judge who served as a Liberal Member of the Legislative Assembly prior to being appointed to the bench. See Moore, *The British Columbia Court of Appeal*, 134–36, 178–81.

21 Jonathan Clapperton, "Environmental Activism as Anti-Conquest: The Nuu-chah-nulth and Environmentalists in the Contact Zone of Clayoquot Sound," in *Environmental Activism on the Ground: Small Green and Indigenous Organizing*, ed. Jonathan Clapperton and Liza Piper (Calgary: University of Calgary Press, 2018), 184.

22 See British Columbia, Ministry of Forests, *Meares Island Planning Options: Report of the Meares Island Planning Team* (Victoria, Ministry of Forests, 1983).

23 *MacMillan Bloedel Ltd v Mullin*, 1985 CanLII 154 (BCCA); "Historical Timeline: 1700s to the Present," Union of British Columbia Indian Chiefs, http://www.ubcic.bc.ca/timeline.

24 "Meares Easter Festival," *Ha-Shilth-Sa* (Port Alberni), April 17, 1984, 1; "Clayoquots Declare Meares Island a Tribal Park," *Ha-Shilth-Sa* (Port Alberni), May 31, 1984, 5; "Wave of Clearcuts Meets Unified Opposition on Meares Island 35 Years Ago," *Ha-Shilth-Sa* (Port Alberni), April 22, 2019.

25 "Clayoquots Declare Meares Island a Tribal Park," 5.

26 "Widespread Support for the Preservation of Meares Island," *Ha-Shilth-Sa* (Port Alberni), October 16, 1984, 1.

27 "Community Fights Plans for Logging on BC Island," *Globe and Mail*, November 21, 1984; "Logging Firm Gets Injunction Against Meares Protesters," *Globe and Mail*, December 4, 1984.

28 Michael Mullin, interviewed by Benjamin Isitt, Tofino, BC, May 24, 2014; "Chief Councillor Remembers the First Days of a Long Battle on Meares," *Ha-Shilth-Sa* (Port Alberni), April 25, 2014.

29 *MacMillan Bloedel Ltd v Mullin*, 1985 CanLII 154 (BCCA). See also Portier, "The Meares Island Case," 33–34.

30 "Logging Firm Gets Injunction Against Meares Protesters"; "Judge Won't Ban Activists from Island Logging Site," *Globe and Mail*, December 18, 1984.

31 The Supreme Court of Canada's decision in *Guerin* was released on December 1, 1984. See *Guerin v The Queen*.

32 "Judge Won't Ban Activists from Island Logging Site"; *MacMillan Bloedel Ltd v Mullin*, 1985 CanLII 154 (BCCA); *Attorney-General for Ontario v. Bear Island Foundation et al.; Potts et al. v. Attorney-General for Ontario*, 1984 CanLII 2136 (ON SC); David T. McNab, *No Place for Fairness: Indigenous Land Rights and Policy in the Bear Island Case and Beyond* (Montreal and Kingston: McGill-Queen's University Press, 2009).

33 "Judge Won't Ban Activists from Island Logging Site."

34 "Court Lets MacMillan Bloedel Start Logging on BC Island," *Globe and Mail*, January 26, 1985; "BC Indians Vow to Halt Logging on Island," *Montreal Gazette*, January 28, 1985; *MacMillan Bloedel Ltd v Mullin*, 1985 CanLII 708 (BCSC); *MacMillan Bloedel Ltd v Mullin*, 1985 CanLII 154 (BCCA).

35 "BC Indians Vow to Halt Logging on Island."
36 Portier, "The Meares Island Case," 34.
37 "Meares Logging Could Be Bloody, BC Indian Says," *Globe and Mail*, January 30, 1985; *MacMillan Bloedel Ltd v Mullin*, 1985 CanLII 154 (BCCA).
38 Portier, "The Meares Island Case," 34.
39 *MacMillan Bloedel Ltd v Mullin*, 1985 CanLII 154 (BCCA).
40 *MacMillan Bloedel Ltd v Mullin*, 1985 CanLII 154 (BCCA); *Calder et al v Attorney-General of British Columbia*, 1973 CanLII 4 (SCC), [1973] SCR 313.
41 *MacMillan Bloedel Ltd v Mullin*, 1985 CanLII 154 (BCCA).
42 *MacMillan Bloedel Ltd v Mullin*, 1985 CanLII 154 (BCCA).
43 William K. Carroll, "Social Movements and Counter-Hegemony," in *World to Win Contemporary Social Movements and Counter-Hegemony*, ed. William K. Carroll and Kanchan Sarker (Winnipeg: ARP Books, 2016), 59.
44 See "Appeal Court Prohibits Meares Island Logging," *Globe and Mail*, March 28, 1985; "Battle for Meares Island is Key to Settlement of Claims," *Times Colonist* (Victoria), June 16, 1985, A5; "Injunction Against Logging Still Stands in BC," *Globe and Mail*, August 1, 1985.
45 Portier, "The Meares Island Case," 35–36.
46 Iisaak Forest Resources, *Sustainable Forest Management Plan* (2011), http://www.iisaak.com (accessed April 27, 2016); Karena Shaw, "Encountering Clayoquot, Reading the Political," in *A Political Space: Reading the Global through Clayoquot Sound*, ed. Warren Magnusson and Karena Shaw (Montreal and Kingston: McGill-Queen's University Press, 2002), 54–57; Portier, "The Meares Island Case," 36–37; Clapperton, "Environmental Activism as Anti-Conquest," 194–95.
47 See "Queen Charlotte Timber Supply Area" and "South Moresby Supply Block," n.d. (c. 1985), file 26-7 "Forestry campaign to save Old Growth forests, 1981–1985," vol. 26, R4377, Greenpeace Canada fonds, Library and Archives Canada (LAC).
48 See Scott Rutherford, *Canada's Other Red Scare: Indigenous Protest and Colonial Encounters During the Global Sixties* (Montreal and Kingston: McGill-Queen's University Press, 2020); Frank Zelko, *Make It a Green Peace! The Rise of Countercultural Environmentalism* (Oxford: Oxford University Press, 2013).
49 Minutes of the Council of the Haida Nation, December 7, 1974, as cited in "Council of the Haida Nation," https://www.haidanation.ca/about/chn; Constitution of the Haida Nation, as adopted on October 18, 2023, https://www.haidanation.ca/about/haida-constitution (accessed January 28, 2026). See also *Haada 'Las* (Old Massett), April 1975, https://www.haidanation.ca/haida-laas.
50 "Athlii Gwaii: 25 Years Down the Road," *Haada 'Las* (Old Massett), November 2010, 3, https://www.haidanation.ca/haida-laas; Collison, *Athlii Gwaii*, 87–94; May, *Paradise Won*.
51 Collison, *Athlii Gwaii*, 10–11 and 148–49.
52 "Haida vs. Loggers: A Polite Drama," *Montreal Gazette*, November 27, 1985; "Haidas Vow to Keep Up Struggle Against South Moresby Logging," *Ottawa Citizen*, July 9, 1986; "9 Haida Will Renounce Citizenship to Protest Logging on BC Island," *Montreal Gazette*, July 15, 1986.
53 Guujaaw, interviewed by Benjamin Isitt, Vancouver, BC, May 25, 2015; Collison, *Athlii Gwaii*, 11–12, 150; "Injunction Delayed," *Victoria Daily Times*, February 10, 1979, 13;

"Haidas Threaten Hunting 'War,'" *Victoria Daily Times*, February 22, 1979, 6. See also "Rayonier Letters Under Fire," *Victoria Daily Times*, October 6, 1978, 10; "Rayonier 'Double Talk,'" *Victoria Daily Times*, March 9, 1978, 9; "Petition Seeks Moresby Hearing," *Victoria Daily Times*, January 31, 1979, 7; "Save-Moresby Group Confused Over Chance," *Victoria Daily Times*, February 7, 1979, 12.

54 "Supreme Court Rejects Tree Farm Hearings," *Victoria Daily Times*, March 7, 1979, 1; "Hearing Not Needed," *Alberni Valley Times*, March 7, 1979, 6; "Athlii Gwaii: 25 Years Down the Road," 3.

55 "Moresby Tree-Farm Licence Challenged," *Vancouver Sun*, March 2, 1981, A3; "Queen Charlotte Tree Licence Protested," *The Province*, March 5, 1981, C10; "Logging Challenge Rejected," *Vancouver Sun*, March 30, 1981, D1. See also "Charlottes' Row Pushed to Courts," *Victoria Daily Times*, April 20, 1979, 8; "Waterland to Meet Petitioners," *Victoria Daily Times*, April 21, 1979, 15; "Moresby: An Island Awaiting Its Fate," *Vancouver Sun*, July 19, 1980, H6; "Forest Managers Blasted," *Vancouver Sun*, May 3, 1982, A13. According to one source, an appeal was unsuccessful, with the Supreme Court of Canada refusing to hear an appeal, describing it as a "provincial matter." See "Athlii Gwaii: 25 Years Down the Road," 3.

56 Collison, *Athlii Gwaii*, 12, 150; May, *Paradise Won*, 47.

57 Collison, *Athlii Gwaii*, 15, 151. See also Constitution of the Haida Nation, as adopted on October 18, 2023, Council of the Haida Nation website, https://www.haidanation.ca/about/haida-constitution (viewed January 28, 2026).

58 Collison, *Athlii Gwaii*, 78–81, 131–34.

59 "Haida vs. Loggers"; Collison, *Athlii Gwaii*, 151.

60 "Haidas Want Queen Charlottes Preserved," *Alberni Valley Times*, 19 June 1984, 1; Collison, *Athlii Gwaii*, 152.

61 Guujaaw interview, May 25, 2015. See also "Guujaaw: A Man of His People," *Vancouver Sun*, March 16, 2002; Gill, *All That We Say Is Ours*.

62 "BC Island Logging Jobs Are Lost Forever, Forestry Boss Says," *Toronto Star*, July 8, 1987.

63 "Loggers to Seek Injunction Against Haida," *Globe and Mail*, November 4, 1985.

64 "Logging, Oil Drilling Decisions Loom for 'Canadian Galapagos,'" *Los Angeles Times*, October 27, 1985.

65 Gillian Shaw, "Indians Set Deadline to Stop Tree Cutting," *Vancouver Sun*, August 17, 1985; Collison, *Athlii Gwaii*, 152.

66 "Haida vs. Loggers."

67 See Jeremy Wilson, *Talk and Log: Wilderness Politics in British Columbia* (Vancouver: UBC Press, 1998). See also Wilderness Advisory Committee series, Accession no. 1995-006, 1995-036, Sierra Club fonds, AR117, University of Victoria Archives and Special Collections.

68 Guujaaw interview, May 25, 2015.

69 "We Are Staying Here: Haidas," *Vancouver Sun*, October 31, 1985, A1 and A10; Collison, *Athlii Gwaii*, 30.

70 "BC Haida Block Road," *Globe and Mail*, October 31, 1985.

71 *Western Forest Products Ltd v Collinson et al* (1985), BC Supreme Court, unreported decision made at Vancouver , November 29, 1985, Registry No. C854987, and *Frank Beban Logging Ltd v Collinson et al* (1985), BC Supreme Court, Vancouver Registry No. C8549788; Collison, *Athlii Gwaii*, 144.

72 "Leave Us More Than Stumps, Haida Tell Vancouver Judge Cruickshank," *Globe and Mail*, November 7, 1985; "BC Judge Forbids Haida Indians from Obstructing Island Logging," *Globe and Mail*, November 9, 1985; "Judge Orders Haidas to Let Logging Proceed on BC Island," *Ottawa Citizen*, November 9, 1985; "Lumber Company Seeks Injunctions," *Ottawa Citizen*, November 2, 1985; "Logging Blockade Dispute Delayed as Lawyer Sought," *Globe and Mail*, November 6, 1985; "Logging Companies to Open New Road After BC Court Gives Access to Island," *Globe and Mail*, November 12, 1985. The *Globe and Mail* reported that in granting the injunctions, "the decision was the first in recent months to go against natives in their battles over aboriginal rights." See "BC Judge Forbids Haida Indians from Obstructing Island Logging"; Collison, *Athlii Gwaii*, 154.

73 Collison, *Athlii Gwaii*, 10 and 144.

74 "Haidas Face Action in Blocking Loggers," *Globe and Mail*, November 15, 1985; "Haidas Block Loggers Despite Injunctions," *Montreal Gazette*, November 15, 1985; "Indians Let Loggers Visit Camp," *Globe and Mail*, November 14, 1985.

75 "Indians Let Loggers Visit Camp."

76 "Haidas Form Human Blockade to Prevent Logging on BC Island," *Ottawa Citizen*, November 15, 1985.

77 "Loggers Embroiled in Dispute with Haidas to Return to Work," *Ottawa Citizen*, November 16, 1985. See also "Haidas Block Loggers Despite Injunctions."

78 See Reg Whitaker, Gregory S. Kealey, and Andrew Parnaby, *Secret Service: Political Policing in Canada from the Fenians to Fortress America* (Toronto: University of Toronto Press, 2012).

79 "RCMP Prepare for Haida-Loggers Showdown," *Ottawa Citizen*, November 13, 1985; "RCMP Hopes to Avert Logging Confrontation," *Globe and Mail*, November 13, 1985; "Loggers Embroiled in Dispute with Haidas to Return to Work"; "Haida vs. Loggers"; Collison, *Athlii Gwaii*, 45–50.

80 The legal authority behind the RCMP's decision to enforce the court order was discussed by RCMP Superintendent Robert Currie, who told the media from Prince Rupert that he had been given a "free hand"' to make decisions by the provincial attorney-general's ministry: "'I felt it was our responsibility to enforce the court order. As long as they continue to block the road, we will continue to make arrests." Currie said there was ample room at RCMP facilities in Queen Charlotte City or Sandspit to confine the Haida if the need arose, "but it is not our intention to hold anybody." See "Haida Preparing for Long Struggle," *Globe and Mail*, November 19, 1985.

81 "Haidas Form Human Blockade to Prevent Logging on BC Island"; "10 More Haida Indians Arrested While Blocking Logging on Queen Charlotte Islands," *Ottawa Citizen*, November 19, 1985; "Haida vs. Loggers"; Collison, *Athlii Gwaii*, 43.

82 "Three Haida Elders Are Arrested in Logging Protest on BC Island," *Montreal Gazette*, November 18, 1985.

83 "Haida Preparing for Long Struggle"; "10 More Haida Indians Arrested While Blocking Logging on Queen Charlotte Islands"; "12 More Haida Indians Arrested," *Ottawa Citizen*, November 21, 1985; "28 Haida Are Arrested in BC Logging Protest," *Globe and Mail*, November 26, 1985; "Haida Not Criminals, Judge Tells B.C. Court Cruickshank," *Globe and Mail*, November 29, 1985; "Haida Ready to Resume Anti-Logging Protests," *Montreal Gazette*, January 9, 1986.

84 "Haida vs. Loggers."

85 Canada, *Report of Debates of the Parliament of Canada*, November 18, 1985, 8534–35; "10 More Haida Indians Arrested While Blocking Logging on Queen Charlotte Islands."

86 Collison, *Athlii Gwaii*, 144.

87 "10 Haida Convicted in Logging Case," *Globe and Mail*, November 30, 1985. See also "Struggle Called 'Human Rights Issue'; Churches Back Haida in Forestry Feud," *Globe and Mail*, November 27, 1985.

88 "10 Haida Convicted in Logging Case," *Globe and Mail*, November 30, 1985; "Judge Tells Haidas: Obey or Go to Jail," *Vancouver Sun*, November 30, 1985, 1; "BC Misled over Timber, Official Says," *Globe and Mail*, December 3, 1985.

89 "Angered Judge Gives Suspended Sentences to Haida Protesters," *Globe and Mail*, December 7, 1985; "MP Fined and 9 Haidas Get Suspended Sentences for Contempt of Court," *Ottawa Citizen*, December 7, 1985; "Haidas Vow to Fight On," *Vancouver Sun*, December 7, 1985, 1; Collison, *Athlii Gwaii*, 41, 144.

90 Guujaaw interview, May 25, 2015.

91 Collison, *Athlii Gwaii*, 21, 23, 144, 157–58.

92 "10 Haida Ponder Jail in Logging Protest," *Globe and Mail*, December 2, 1985.

93 "Haidas Vow to Fight On," 1; "Angered Judge Gives Suspended Sentences to Haida Protesters," *Globe and Mail*, December 7, 1985; "Burnaby MP Refuses to Apologize for Taking Part in Haida Blockade," *Globe and Mail*, December 6, 1985; "MP Cited," *Montreal Gazette*, November 25, 1985; "Haida Not Criminals, Judge Tells B.C. Court Cruickshank"; Collison, *Athlii Gwaii*, 144. Robinson told the media that the decision to stand with the Haida on Lyell Island was not an easy one, he being a lawyer and the NDP's justice critic, but that "there is a point where you have to stand up for what you believe." During the sentencing hearing, Robinson would not apologize to the court for defying the injunction, but he agreed not to return to the blockade. See "RCMP Hopes to Avert Logging Confrontation"; Collison, *Athlii Gwaii*, 23 and 144.

94 "Lyell Island: 25 Years Later," *Vancouver Sun*, November 17, 2010.

95 Guujaaw interview, May 25, 2015.

96 *BCGEU v British Columbia (Attorney General)*, [1988] 2 SCR 214.

97 "Crown Stays Last of Charges Against Haida," *Globe and Mail*, May 30, 1986; "Charges Dropped Against 61 Haida," *Ottawa Citizen*, January 30, 1986; "BC Minister a Victim of Battle for Lyell Island," *Toronto Star*, January 21, 1986; "8 Haida Indians Choose Jury Trials," *Vancouver Sun*, February 27, 1986; "Haida Elect Trial by Judge, Jury," *Ottawa Citizen*, February 27, 1986; "Haida Ready to Resume Anti-Logging Protests."

98 "Judge Orders Haidas to Let Logging Proceed on BC Island." See also "Canadian Indians Resist Loggers: Support Grows for Haidas' Fight Against British Columbia," *Washington Post*, December 6, 1985; and Jane O'Hara, "The Battle for an Island Forest," *Maclean's*, December 9, 1985.

99 File 25-20 "Forests – South Moresby Wilderness, 1983–1984," vol. 25, and file 26-1 "Forests – South Moresby Wilderness, 1985–1987," vol. 26, R4377, Greenpeace Canada fonds, LAC; "Haida Nation Pleads for Money as Blockade Expenses Increase," *Globe and Mail*, November 28, 1985; "Cockburn Concert to Aid the Haidas," *Vancouver Sun*, January 3, 1986; "Cockburn's Benefit Concerts Raise $35,000 for Haidas," *Ottawa Citizen*, February 24, 1986; "Haidas Vow to Keep Up Struggle Against South Moresby Logging," *Ottawa Citizen*, July 9, 1986; "Cockburn Helps Haidas," *Ubyssey* (Vancouver), February 25, 1986; Collison, *Athlii Gwaii*, 87–97, 159–60.

100 "Native Group Urges Battle with Socreds," *Vancouver Sun,* November 5, 1985; "Native Brotherhood Promising Big Fight," *Nanaimo Daily Free Press,* November 5, 1985; "Native Loggers Vow to See Land Claims Settled," *Alberni Valley Times,* November 5, 1985, 2.

101 "Haida Promised Aid in Lyell Island Stand," *Globe and Mail,* November 22, 1985; "Haidas Face Action in Blocking Loggers"; Collison, *Athlii Gwaii,* 100–1, 155. See also "Indians in BC Risk Jail Terms to Force Settlement of Their Land Claims," *Ottawa Citizen,* November 21, 1985.

102 "Athlii Gwaii: 25 Years Down the Road," 7; Collison, *Athlii Gwaii,* 20; "Moresby Row Takes to the Road," *Vancouver Sun,* February 27, 1986.

103 Guujaaw interview, May 25, 2015; "BC Minister a Victim of Battle for Lyell Island"; "BC Axes New Permits for Lyell Island Logging," *Globe and Mail,* February 8, 1986; "BC Opposition Leader Sued by Minister," *Financial Post* (Toronto), February 8, 1986. Forests Minister Thomas Waterland resigned from the cabinet in January 1986, after it was revealed that he held a $20,000 investment in a pulp mill wholly owned by Western Forest Products that relied on Lyell Island timber, through an entity called the Western Pulp Partnership. Energy Minister Stephen Rogers, who sat on the BC cabinet's environment and land use committee, held a $100,000 investment in the mill, which he sold in the heat of the controversy, retaining his ministerial portfolio.

104 "Loggers to Seek Injunction Against Haida"; "Haida vs. Loggers"; "Haidas Face Action in Blocking Loggers." British Columbia's Social Credit attorney general Brian Smith reiterated the provincial government's refusal to recognize or negotiate Aboriginal land claims shortly after the Haida had initiated the blockade on Lyell Island. In November 1985, Forests Minister Tom Waterland articulated the same policy: "The British North America Act in our opinion does not provide native Indians with title to land other than that which they have as reserves."

105 "Temporary Truce Calms Haida-BC Dispute," *Toronto Star,* December 19, 1985; "Native Group Urges Battle with Socreds," *Vancouver Sun,* November 5, 1985.

106 Anonymous informant, interview with author, Victoria, BC, January 1, 2018.

107 "BC Sets Terms for Meeting Haida," *Ottawa Citizen,* November 26, 1985; "Haida Nation Pleads for Money as Blockade Expenses Increase."

108 "Temporary Truce Calms Haida-BC Dispute." Smith had earlier offered to meet with Richardson on behalf of the Haida on the condition that the civil disobedience campaign be called off and that the talks not be interpreted as negotiations over Aboriginal title.

109 "Haida Set to Renew Battle over Logging in Wilderness Area," *Toronto Star,* January 20, 1986; "Haida Reopen Lyell Island Camp," *Globe and Mail,* January 9, 1986; Collison, *Athlii Gwaii,* 23, 158–59.

110 "Logging Going Ahead on Queen Charlottes with BC's Approval," *Globe and Mail,* July 10, 1986; "Logging Resuming on BC's Lyell Island," *Toronto Star,* July 10, 1986; "Indians to Drop Citizenship in Protest Against Logging," *Globe and Mail,* July 15, 1986: "9 Haida Will Renounce Citizenship to Protest Logging on BC Island," *Montreal Gazette,* July 15, 1986; "Haidas Vow To Keep Up Struggle Against South Moresby Logging," *Ottawa Citizen,* July 9, 1986; "BC Axes New Permits for Lyell Island Logging"; "Logging OK," *Montreal Gazette,* March 6, 1986; "Moresby Logging Is Called Vandalism," *Globe and Mail,* March 11, 1986; Collison, *Athlii Gwaii,* 23, 75–76, 160. See also Wilderness Advisory Committee series, Accession no. 1995-006, 1995-036, Sierra Club fonds, AR117, University of Victoria Archives and Special Collections.

111 "Logger Slams Idea of Lyell Island Ban," *Vancouver Sun*, February 21, 1987; "Lyell Island Logger Frank Beban Dies of Heart Attack," *Vancouver Sun*, July 27, 1987; "Charges Dropped Against Logging Firms," *Globe and Mail*, August 13, 1986; "Creek Clean-up for Prince Cancelled," *Vancouver Sun*, June 12, 1987; "Stall on Charging Logging Firm Claimed by NDP MP Fulton," *Vancouver Sun;* November 5, 1988; "First Step Complete on Lyell Replanting," *Vancouver Sun*, June 27, 1989.

112 "Laid-Off Loggers Find New Jobs," *Globe and Mail*, April 29, 1986.

113 "Logging Company Faces Moratorium," *Globe and Mail*, March 23, 1987; "Save South Moresby," *Globe and Mail*, March 23, 1987; "Fighting over the Axing of a Paradise," *Toronto Star*, March 20, 1987; "No Easy Answer," *Globe and Mail*, March 21, 1987; "Haida Return to Lyell Island," *Vancouver Sun*, March 30, 1987; "Logger Awaits Permits to Resume Lyell Work," *Vancouver Sun*, June 17, 1987; "BC Island Logging Jobs Are Lost Forever, Forestry Boss Says."

114 "South Moresby Agreement," BC Government press release, July 11, 1987, file 26-2 "Forests – South Moresby Wilderness, 1987–1991," vol. 26, R4377, Greenpeace Canada fonds, LAC; "Haida Delight over Park Tempered with Concerns About Land Claim," *Vancouver Sun*, July 13, 1987; "Indians Welcome Ottawa's Support in Their Fight to Preserve BC Island," *Toronto Star*, March 11, 1986; "Moresby Park Deal Reached," *Vancouver Sun*, July 7, 1987; "Ottawa, BC Make a Deal on National Park for South Moresby," *Montreal Gazette*, July 7, 1987; "BC Loggers Decry Jobs Lost for Park in South Moresby," *Globe and Mail*, July 8, 1987; "All Commons Parties Back Charlottes Park," *Vancouver Sun*, May 14, 1987; "Year-Old Moresby Park Pact Still in Log Jam," *Vancouver Sun*, July 11, 1988; "Deal Reached on Moresby Park," *Ottawa Citizen*, July 12, 1988; Collison, *Athlii Gwaii*, 160–65; May, *Paradise Won*.

115 Collison, *Athlii Gwaii*, 72–73, 76.

116 See Collison, *Athlii Gwaii*, 25, 109–15; Guujaaw interview, May 25, 2015. For a description of the co-management agreement between the Haida and Canada, as well as Guujaaw's strong views on the term "park," see Transcript of Panel No. 11, Vancouver, BC, December 15, 2010, 59–62,Evidence of Public Hearings of the Commission of Inquiry into the Decline of Sockeye Salmon in the Fraser River, https://iaac-aeic.gc.ca/050/documents_staticpost/cearref_21799/83896/Dec_15_2010_-_Commission_of_Inquiry.pdf / (viewed January 28, 2026) (hereafter Cohen Commission Evidence); Collison, *Athlii Gwaii*, 119–28; Molly Clarkson, "Speaking for Sockeye, Speaking for Themselves: First Nations Engagement in the Cohen Commission, 2009–2012" (MA thesis, University of British Columbia, 2016); *Haida Gwaii Reconciliation Act*, SBC 2010, c 17.

117 "BC Island Logging Jobs Are Lost Forever, Forestry Boss Says."

118 "BC Loggers Decry Jobs Lost for Park in South Moresby"; "BC Island Logging Jobs Are Lost Forever, Forestry Boss Says." See also Gordon Hamilton, "Haida-BC Deal 'Bleak' for Coastal Loggers," *Vancouver Sun*, August 22, 2007. In 2006, an analysis of socio-economic conditions on Haida Gwaii prepared for the BC government noted that the non-Indigenous population of the archipelago had declined by 26 percent between 1981 and 2001 (from 4,719 to 3,485 people), while the Indigenous population on the Old Massett and Skidegate reserves had increased by 60 percent over the same period (from 902 to 1,450 people). The report noted that "the largest drop was on Moresby Island, mainly the result of establishing the Gwaii Haanas protected area," with the population of Moresby Island, where Sandspit was located, declining from 1,278 to 460 people between 1981 and 2001. See BC Ministry of Agriculture and Lands, Integrated Land Management Bureau,

Socio-Economic Assessment of Haida Gwaii/Queen Charlotte Islands Land Use Viewpoints: Final Report (Vancouver: Pierce Lefebvre Consulting, 2006), 75.

119 "Lyell Logger Hailed by Haida," *Vancouver Sun*, July 28, 1987; "Lyell Island Logger Frank Beban Dies of Heart Attack"; "Frank Beban Lost Battle to Log Lyell," *Toronto Star*, July 28, 1987. See also "Victoria Pays $480,000 for Laid-Off Loggers," *Vancouver Sun*, October 5, 1987; "Moresby Money Delay Leaves Loggers in Limbo," *Vancouver Sun*, January 22, 1988.

120 "With Logging Banned, the Logger Is Mourned," *New York Times*, August 15, 1987.

121 Significant cases relating to competing claims to forest resources include action by members of the Kwakwaka'wakw Nation to prevent logging at Deer Island off Fort Rupert in 1986, protracted legal proceedings involving the Okanagan Indian Band in the 1990s, and more recently, litigation by the Tsilhqot'in Nation. In 1999, BC Supreme Court Justice Jon Sigurdson granted an injunction to the BC minister of forests restraining several First Nations in the Okanagan region from logging without a valid permit, in contravention of s 143 of the *Forest Practices Code of British Columbia Act*. Sigurdson ruled in *British Columbia (Minister of Forests) v Okanagan Indian Band* that the public interest in seeing the existing law upheld was not easily outweighed by any prejudice to the defendant, even in the face of assertion of s 35 Aboriginal rights: "The just and equitable order in these circumstances is to ensure the governing law is enforced while allowing the respondents' assertions of aboriginal title to be determined as expeditiously as possible. I grant the injunctions on that basis." See *British Columbia (Minister of Forests) v Wilson*, 1999 BCSC 1723; *British Columbia (Minister of Forests) v Derrickson*, 1999 BCSC 1724; *British Columbia (Minister of Forests) v Okanagan Indian Band*, 2000 BCSC 32; *British Columbia (Minister of Forests) v Adams Lake Indian Band*, 2000 BCCA 98; *British Columbia (Minister of Forests) v Adams Lake Indian Band*, 2000 BCCA 315; *British Columbia (Minister of Forests) v Wilson*, 2000 BCSC 1135; *British Columbia (Minister of Forests) v Adams Lake Band*, 2001 BCCA 647; *British Columbia (Minister of Forests) v Okanagan Indian Band*, 2003 SCC 371.

122 Nicholas Blomley, "'Shut the Province Down': First Nations Blockades in British Columbia, 1984–1995," *BC Studies* 111 (Autumn 1996): 5–35. See also "Indians in BC Risk Jail Terms to Force Settlement of Their Land Claims."

123 See Nicholas D. Shrubsole, "The Sun Dance and the Gustafsen Lake Standoff: Healing Through Resistance and the Danger of Dismissing Religion," *International Indigenous Policy Journal* 2, 4 (October 2011): 1–17. See also Nicholas Shrubsole, "Religion, Land and Democracy in Canadian Indigenous-State Relations" (PhD diss., University of Waterloo, 2013); Ben David Mahony, "'Disinformation and Smear': The Use of State Propaganda and Military Force to Suppress Aboriginal Title at the 1995 Gustafsen Lake Standoff" (MA thesis, University of Lethbridge, 2001); Sandra Lambertus, *Wartime Images, Peacetime Wounds: The Media and the Gustafsen Lake Standoff* (Toronto: University of Toronto Press, 2004); Splitting the Sky, *The Autobiography of Splitting the Sky: From Attica to Gustafsen Lake* (Chase, BC: John Pasquale Boncore, 2001), 94.

124 Shrubsole, "The Sun Dance and the Gustafsen Lake Standoff," 1–17. See also Shrubsole, "Religion, Land and Democracy in Canadian Indigenous-State Relations."

125 Shrubsole, "The Sun Dance and the Gustafsen Lake Standoff," 7–10.

126 See Splitting the Sky. *The Autobiography of Splitting the Sky*, 94.

127 Shrubsole, "The Sun Dance and the Gustafsen Lake Standoff," 10.

128 See Mahony, "'Disinformation and Smear'"; Lambertus, *Wartime Images, Peacetime*

Wounds; Martin J. Morris, "Overcoming the Barricades: The Crisis at Oka as a Case Study in Political Communication," *Journal of Canadian Studies* 30 (Summer 1995): 74–90.

129 "Why Don't BC's Police Move Faster to Deal with Roadblocks?" *Globe and Mail,* July 18, 1995.

130 Colin Gabelmann, "British Columbia's Civil Disobedience Policy – A Measured Response" (1995), as cited in *Slocan Forest Products Ltd v John Doe,* 2000 BCSC 150.

131 Wolverine (William Jones Ignace) to Trudeau, December 30, 2015, as quoted in "Minister of Justice Responds to Call for Inquiry into Gustafsen Lake Standoff," *Vancouver Sun,* January 24, 2016.

132 "AG Dosanjh an Outstanding Man of Principle," *Times Colonist* (Victoria), August 31, 1995; Mahony, "'Disinformation and Smear.'" See also "Justice Minister Won't Rule Out Gustafsen Lake Inquiry," *Globe and Mail,* January 23, 2016.

133 *R v Ignace,* 1998 BCCA 54; see also *R v Williams,* 1994 CanLII 3301 (BCCA); *Delgamuukw v British Columbia,* 1993 BCCA 0400; "Gustafsen Lake Standoff: Protesters Renew Calls for an Inquiry," *CBC News,* January 18, 2016. See also Bruce Clark, *Native Liberty, Crown Sovereignty: The Existing Aboriginal Right of Self-Government in Canada* (Montreal and Kingston: McGill-Queen's University Press, 1990); Bruce Clark, *Justice in Paradise* (Montreal and Kingston: McGill-Queen's University Press, 2004).

134 "Blood Spills in Sacred Circle," *Times Colonist* (Victoria), August 31, 1995; Shrubsole, "The Sun Dance and the Gustafsen Lake Standoff," 1, 10.

135 *Nisga'a Final Agreement,* 1999; British Columbia Treaty Commission, "Negotiations Update," https://www.bctreaty.ca/negotiation-update. The Maa-nulth Treaty includes the Huu-ay-aht First Nations, Ka:'yu:'k't'h'/Che:k'tles7et'h' First Nations, Toquaht Nation, Uchucklesaht Tribe, and Yuułuʔiłʔath First Nation.

136 Shiri Pasternak, "How Capitalism Will Save Colonialism: The Privatization of Reserve Lands in Canada," *Antipode* 47, 1 (April 2014): 1–18; Brian Egan, "Towards Shared Ownership: Property, Geography and Treaty Making in British Columbia," *Geografiska Annalser* 95, 1 (March 2013): 33–50.

137 For information on the North Saanich Treaty, see Janice Rose Knighton, "The Oral History of the 1852 North Douglas Treaty: A Treaty for Peace" (MA Community Governance Project Report, University of Victoria, 2004); Nicholas XEMȻOLTW Claxton, "The Douglas Treaty and WSÁNEC Traditional Fisheries: A Model for Saanich Peoples Governance" (MA Community Governance Project Report, University of Victoria, 2003); Nicholas XEMȻOLTW Claxton, "To Fish as Formerly: A Resurgent Journey Back to the Saanich Reef Net" (PhD diss., University of Victoria, 2015); Raymond Frogner, "'Innocent Legal Fictions': Archival Convention and the North Saanich Treaty of 1852," *Archivaria* 70 (Fall 2010): 45–94.

138 *RJR-MacDonald Inc v Canada (Attorney General),* [1994] 1 SCR 311.

139 *Slawsky v Isitt,* 2014 BCSC 1917; "Protesters in Grace Islet Dispute Given Month to Prepare Case," *Times Colonist* (Victoria), September 23, 2014.

140 John Alexander to Farris et al., October 8, 2014; Notice of Discontinuance, October 8, 2014; Responses to Civil Claim and Affidavits filed by Don Tom and Benjamin Isitt, October 2014, in response to *Slawsky v Isitt et al,* Victoria Civil Registry, 2014.

141 British Columbia, "Partnership Formed to Acquire Grace Islet" (news release, January 15, 2015), https://news.gov.bc.ca/releases/2015FLNR0005-000036; "Province Buys Disputed Grace Islet for $5.45 Million," *Times Colonist* (Victoria), February 16, 2015.

142 Shiri Pasternak and Hayden King, *Land Back: A Yellowhead Institute Red Paper* (Toronto: Yellowhead Institute, 2019), 10. See also Pasternak and Scott, "Introduction: Getting Back the Land," 205–13; Ceric, "Beyond Contempt," 353–69; *Behn v Moulton Contracting Ltd*, 2013 SCC 26. In a case in New Brunswick from 2013 (which, while not binding on British Columbia courts, may have a persuasive effect), the Court of Queen's Bench refused to grant an injunction to the Elsipogtog First Nation to halt exploration for shale gas in its territory. The First Nation asserted that the provincial government and SWN Resources Canada had not adequately consulted them as required under s 35 of the *Constitution Act, 1982*. Justice Judy Clandening ruled against the First Nation, finding that the question of whether adequate consultation had occurred should be determined at trial, rather than at the interlocutory injunction stage, denying the application and allowing the company's gas exploration work to proceed. In response, members of the First Nation blockaded a provincial highway, preventing the firm from accessing its exploration site and, in the weeks that followed, mustered through extra-judicial means sufficient political power to force the company's retreat from the province. See "Anti-Fracking Activists Denied Injunction in Canada," *Al Jazeera*, November 18, 2013; "SWN Ending Exploration Work in NB, Will Be Back in 2015: Elsipogtog War Chief Levi," *APTN News*, December 6, 2013.

143 Basil Alexander, "Demonstrations and the Law: Patterns of Law's Negative Effects on the Ground and the Practical Implications," *UBC Law Review* 49, 3 (November 2016): 890.

144 *Coastal GasLink Pipeline Ltd v Huson*, 2018 BCSC 2343.

145 "14 Arrested as RCMP Break Gate at Gidimt'en Camp Checkpoint Set Up to Stop Pipeline Company Access," *CBC News*, January 7, 2019; Pasternak and King, *Land Back*, 29–30.

146 "Hereditary Chiefs in B.C. Stand Opposed to Coastal GasLink Pipeline Despite Injunction," *CBC News*, January 7, 2019.

147 See *Coastal GasLink Pipeline Project: Natural Gas Pipeline Benefits Agreement between British Columbia and the Wet'suwet'en First Nation* (2014), BC Ministry of Indigenous Relations and Reconciliation, https://www2.gov.bc.ca/assets/gov/environment/natural-resource-stewardship/consulting-with-first-nations/agreements/wetsuweten_first_nation_pba_cgl_signed_bcr_-_jan_2015.pdf.

148 *Delgamuukw v British Columbia*, [1997] 3 SCR 1010; Tyler McCreary, "The Burden of Sovereignty: Court Configurations of Indigenous and State Authority in Aboriginal Title Litigation in Canada," *North American Dialogue* 17, 2 (2014): 64–78; McCreary and Turner, "The Contested Scales of Indigenous and Settler Jurisdiction," 1–23; McCreary, "Between the Commodity and the Gift," 122–45; Michael Asch, "The Judicial Conceptualization of Culture After *Delgamuukw* and *Van der Peet*," *Review of Constitutional Studies* 5, 2 (January 2000): 119–37; Briony Penn, "Who Is Really Breaking the Law?" *Focus Magazine* (Victoria), March-April 2020, https://www.focusonvictoria.ca/focus-magazine-march-april-2020/who-is-really-breaking-the-law-r11/; The Delgamuukw Decision: When the 'Invisible People' Won Recognition," *APTN News*, March 10, 2020, https://www.aptnnews.ca/national-news/the-delgamuukw-decision-when-the-invisible-people-won-recognition/.

149 Pasternak and King, *Land Back*, 10.

150 *Coastal GasLink Pipeline Ltd v Huson*, 2019 BCSC 2264; "Contempt Charges Dropped Against 14 Protesters Blocking B.C. Pipeline Project," *CBC News*, April 15, 2019.

151 *Coastal GasLink Pipeline Ltd v Huson*, 2019 BCSC 2264, para 159; "BC Supreme Court Grants Injunction Against Wet'suwet'en Protesters in Pipeline Standoff," *CBC News*,

December 31, 2019; Hina Alum, "BC Supreme Court Grants Natural Gas Pipeline Company Interlocutory Injunction," *Times Colonist* (Victoria), December 31, 2019; Unist'ot'en Camp, "Wet'suwet'en Hereditary Chiefs Reject the BC Supreme Court Decision to Criminalize Wet'suwet'en Law," http://www.unistoten.camp (accessed December 31, 2019).

152 Mike Farnworth (Minister of Public Safety and Solicitor General) to Jennifer Strachan (Deputy Commissioner, RCMP "E" Division), January 27, 2020, letter in possession of author.

153 "No Charges to Be Laid Against 22 Northern B.C. Pipeline Protesters," *Prince George Citizen*, June 8, 2020.

154 *Vancouver Fraser Port Authority v Doe*, 2020 BCSC 244; *British Columbia (Legislative Assembly) v John Doe*, 2020 BCSC 301; *Canadian Pacific Railway Limited v Doe*, 2020 BCSC 388; *Vancouver Fraser Port Authority v Doe*, 2021 BCSC 1109; *Vancouver Fraser Port Authority v Joseph*, 2021 BCSC 1527; Office of the Parliamentary Budget Officer, "Recent Rail Disruptions Will Cost the Economy $275 Million, Says PBO," March 13, 2020, https://www.pbo-dpb.ca/en/publications/RP-1920-032-S--estimate-impacts-february-2020-rail-disruption--estimation-repercussions-perturbations-transport-ferroviaire-fevrier-2020 (accessed September 4, 2020); "Canadian Ports on Two Coasts Congested Due to Rail Blockades," *Globe and Mail*, February 20, 2020; "Rail Blockades Causing Containers to Pile Up at Canadian Ports Social Sharing," *CBC News*, February 21, 2020.

155 "The Delgamuukw Decision"; "Wet'suwet'en Agree to Deal with Government over Rights and Title," *Times Colonist* (Victoria), April 30, 2020.

156 "No Criminal Charges for People Arrested During Injunction Enforcement on Wet'suwet'en Territory," *CBC News*, June 5, 2020; "No Charges to Be Laid Against 22 Northern B.C. Pipeline Protesters"; "Woman Arrested During Wet'suwet'en Pipeline Blockade Found Not Guilty," *CBC News*, November 29, 2023; *Coastal GasLink Pipeline Ltd v Huson*, 2021 BCSC 2734; *Coastal GasLink Pipeline Ltd v Huson*, 2021 BCSC 2735; *Coastal Gaslink Pipeline Ltd v Huson*, 2024 BCSC 509; *Coastal Gaslink Pipeline Ltd v Huson*, 2024 BCSC 1730; *Coastal Gaslink Pipeline Ltd v Huson*, 2025 BCSC 643; Amnesty International, *"Removed from Our Land for Defending It": Criminalization, Intimidation and Harassment of Wet'suwet'en Land Defenders* (London: Amnesty International, 2023). The protest movement within Wet'suwet'en territory and across Canada was abruptly curbed in March 2020 with the outbreak of the COVID-19 pandemic, on the heels of several court injunctions to break the rail blockades as well as the commencement of conciliatory talks between the governments of British Columbia and Canada and the Wet'suwet'en hereditary leadership. While the BC Environmental Assessment Office found in June 2020 that CGL had failed to protect wetland areas, resulting in several stop-work orders, Crown permits remained in place and work on the pipeline continued largely unimpeded. See British Columbia, "Joint Statement on Discussions on Wet'suwet'en Rights and Title" (news release, March 1, 2020), https://news.gov.bc.ca/21667; "Coastal GasLink Pipe Installation Scheduled to Begin in August," *Vanderhoof Omineca Express*, July 17, 2020.

157 Amanda Follett Hosgood, "How Industry Has Weaponized BC's Courts," *The Tyee* (Vancouver), June 23, 2020, https://thetyee.ca/News/2020/06/23/How-Industry-Weaponized-BC-Courts/.

158 *Wet'suwet'en Treaty Office Society v British Columbia (Environmental Assessment Office)*, 2021 BCSC 717; "BC Supreme Court Hears Petition for Judicial Review of Coastal GasLink

Certificate," *Times Colonist* (Victoria), October 1, 2020; Order EN2021-003, November 9, 2021, BC Environmental Assessment Office, https://projects.eao.gov.bc.ca/api/public/document/619437a5131c0f00221bc81d/download/EN2021-003_Coastal_GasLink_2021-11-09_Section_53_Order_ESC.pdf; "Coastal GasLink Failed to Fix Nearly 2 Dozen Environmental Violations Along Pipeline Route, B.C. Officials Say," *CBC News*, December 6, 2021.

159 See Ceric, "Beyond Contempt," 365–67; McCreary and Turner, "The Contested Scales of Indigenous and Settler Jurisdiction," 1–23; McCreary, "Between the Commodity and the Gift," 122–45; *Tsilhqot'in Nation v British Columbia*, 2014 SCC 44; *Gaayhllxid • Gíihlagalgang "Rising Tide" Haida Title Lands Agreement*, April 14, 2024, https://www2.gov.bc.ca/assets/gov/environment/natural-resource-stewardship/consulting-with-first-nations/agreements/final_gaayhllxid_giihlagalgang_rising_tide_haida_title_lands_agreement.pdf; *Chiixuujin Chaaw Kaawgaa "Big Tide (Low Water)" Haida Title Lands Agreement*, December 4, 2024, https://static1.squarespace.com/static/66a42eb6e157224ea438eb79/t/68504393e300427189d16bf0/1750090648836/CHIIXUUJIN-CHAAW-KAAWGAA-BIG-TIDE-LOW-WATER-SIGNED-IN-COUNTERPART-2024-12-04.pdf (accessed January 28, 2026).

160 Louis-Alfredo Garcia, "Tsilhqot'in Nation v British Columbia: Aboriginal Title, Indigenous Resurgence, and the Politics of Recognition" (MA thesis, Carleton University, 2015).

161 Jaskiran Dhillon and Will Parrish, "Canada Police Prepared to Shoot Indigenous Activists, Documents Show," *The Guardian*, December 20, 2019; Trevor Hewitt, "Skeena-Bulkley Valley MP Calling for Independent Review of RCMP Action at Gidimt'en," *Interior News* (Smithers), December 20, 2019; "BC's Newest Political Party Calls for Investigation of RCMP Actions and Halt to Pipeline Construction," *Rossland Telegraph*, December 24, 2019. See also McCreary and Turner, "The Contested Scales of Indigenous and Settler Jurisdiction," 1–23; McCreary, "Between the Commodity and the Gift"; Simpson and Le Billon, "Reconciling Violence," 111–21.

162 "RCMP Spent More Than $13M on Policing Coastal GasLink Conflict on Wet'suwet'en Territory," *CBC News*, October 21, 2020, https://www.cbc.ca/news/indigenous/rcmp-wetsuweten-pipeline-policing-costs-1.5769555.

Chapter 6: The Right to Sleep

1 Henri Lefebvre, *Le Droit à la ville* (Paris: Anthropos, 1968); Lynn A. Staeheli and Don Mitchell, *The Peoples' Property? Power, Politics, and the Public* (New York and London: Routledge, 2008); Don Mitchell, *The Right to the City: Social Justice and the Fight for Public Space* (New York: Guilford, 2003); David Harvey, *Rebel Cities: From the Right to the City to the Urban Revolution* (London and New York: Verso, 2012); Anna Minton, *Ground Control: Fear and Happiness in the Twenty-First-Century City* (London: Penguin, 2009); Don Mitchell and Lynn A. Staeheli, "Permitting Protest: Parsing the Fine Geography of Dissent in America," *International Journal of Urban and Regional Research* 29, 4 (December 2005): 796–813; Mark Purcell, "Excavating Lefebvre: The Right to the City and Its Urban Politics of the Inhabitant," *GeoJournal* 58 (2002): 99–108; Katherine Beckett and Steve Herbert, *Banished: The New Social Control in Urban America* (Oxford: Oxford University Press, 2010); Timothy Cresswell, *The Tramp in America* (London: Reaktion Books, 2001);

Nicholas Blomley, David Delaney, and Richard T. Ford, eds., *The Legal Geographies Reader: Law, Power, and Space* (Oxford: Blackwell, 2001); R.W.J. Boer and J. de Vries, "The Right to the City as a Tool for Urban Social Movements: The Case of Barceloneta" (paper presented to 4th International Conference of the International Forum on Urbanism, Amsterdam, 2009); Rodrigo Meneses-Reyes and José A. Caballero-Juárez, "The Right to Work on the Street: Public Space and Constitutional Rights," *Planning Theory* 13, 4 (November 2014): 370–86.

2 Antonio Azuela and Rodrigo Meneses-Reyes, "The Everyday Formation of the Urban Space: Law and Poverty in Mexico City," in *The Expanding Spaces of Law: A Timely Legal Geography*, ed. Irus Braverman, Nicholas Blomley, and David Delaney (Stanford, CA: Stanford University Press, 2014), 167–89.

3 Staeheli and Mitchell, *The Peoples' Property?* xiv–xxi. See also Mitchell, *The Right to the City;* Don Mitchell, "Anti-Homeless Laws and Public Space: 1. Begging and the First Amendment," *Urban Geography* 19, 1 (1998): 6–11; Don Mitchell, "The S.U.V. Model of Citizenship: Floating Bubbles, Buffer Zones, and the Rise of the 'Purely Atomic' Individual," *Political Geography* 24, 1 (January 2005): 77–100; Timothy Zick, *Speech Out of Doors: Preserving First Amendment Liberties in Public Places* (New York: Cambridge University Press, 2009).

4 Sarah E. Hamill, "Private Rights to Public Property: The Evolution of Common Property in Canada," *McGill Law Journal* 58 (2012): 365–403. See also Sarah E. Hamill, "Private Property Rights and Public Responsibility: Leaving Room for the Homeless," *Windsor Review of Legal and Social Issues* 30 (2011): 91–116.

5 Purcell, "Excavating Lefebvre," 99.

6 Mark Purcell, *Recapturing Democracy: Neoliberalization and the Struggle for Alternative Urban Futures* (New York: Routledge, 2008), 92; also Mark Purcell, "Citizenship and the Right to the Global City: Reimagining the Capital World Order," *International Journal of Urban and Regional Research* 27, 3 (September 2003): 564–90; Mark Purcell, "The Right to the City: The Struggle for Democracy in the Urban Public Realm," *Politics and Policy* 43, 3 (2013): 311–27.

7 Frances Fox Piven and Richard A. Cloward, *Poor People's Movements: Why They Succeed, How They Fail* (New York: Pantheon, 1977).

8 Harvey, *Rebel Cities,* xiii.

9 Adam Smith, *Lectures on Jurisprudence,* ed. R.L. Meek, D.D. Raphael, and P.G. Stein (1763; repr., Oxford: Clarendon, 1978), 208, as quoted in Douglas Hay, "Time, Inequality, and Law's Violence," in *Law's Violence,* ed. Austin Sarat and Thomas R. Kearns (Ann Arbor: University of Michigan Press, 1993), 173.

10 Hay, "Time, Inequality, and Law's Violence," 151.

11 Hay, "Time, Inequality, and Law's Violence," 148 and 172.

12 Hay, "Time, Inequality, and Law's Violence," 172.

13 Purcell, "Excavating Lefebvre," 99.

14 "Do Tent Cities Work?" *The Province,* July 30, 2014.

15 Mark Zion, "What Is a Right to Shelter in the Desert of Post-Democracy? Tracking Homeless Narratives from the Courtroom to Dissensus" (LLM thesis, University of Victoria, 2015), 145. See also John Franklin Koenig, "Spaces of Denial and the Denial of Place: The Architectural Geography of Homelessness in Victoria, BC" (MA thesis, University of Victoria, 2007); Erin Black, "Private Dwelling in Public Space: Edmonton's Tent City" (PhD diss., University of Alberta, 2010).

16 The specific causes of homelessness in the city of Victoria in the 2000s were enumerated by BC Supreme Court Justice Carol Ross in the important *Adams* decision, based on a "homeless count" questionnaire conducted in 2005, and included the following reasons: getting evicted, illegibility for income assistance, other financial problems, addictions, conflict with families, and domestic abuse (cited by one-third of women who were interviewed for the count). See *Victoria (City) v Adams*, 2008 BCSC 1363, para 59.
17 Seth Klein et al., *A Poverty Reduction Strategy for BC* (Vancouver: Canadian Centre for Policy Alternatives, 2008).
18 *Municipal Council, Ratlam v Shri Vardhichand*, AIR 1980 SC 1622, 1980 CriLJ 1075.
19 *Municipal Council, Ratlam v Vardhichand;* James Billingsley, *Claiming Poor Rights: Narratives of Shelter, Space, and Freedom in India and Canada* (Victoria: Centre for Asia-Pacific Initiatives, University of Victoria, 2013).
20 See Piven and Cloward, *Poor People's Movements*, 3.
21 *Provincial Rental Housing Corporation v Hall*, 2005 BCCA 36; "Squatters Settle In," *The Province*, September 18, 2002.
22 *Vancouver (City) v Maurice*, 2005 BCCA 37.
23 *Vancouver (City) v Maurice;* "The Lesson of 'Woodsquat,'" *Vancouver Sun*, October 15, 2002; "'We Feel Safe in That Place,'" *The Province*, November 21, 2002; "Shelter for Squatters on Offer as Woodward's Deadline Arrives," *Vancouver Sun*, November 25, 2002; "Housing Found for Squatters, but Some Refuse to Leave Woodward's," *Times Colonist* (Victoria), November 25, 2002; "20 Squatters Leave as City Seeks Clearout," *Vancouver Sun*, November 27, 2002; "They're Still Squatting at Woodwards," *Vancouver Sun*, November 30, 2002. The injunction was issued to the City of Vancouver under statutory authority in the *Vancouver Charter*, SBC 1953, c 55, ss 334 and 571.
24 Community Services Minister George Abbott described the decision to appeal Justice Janice Dillon's award of costs to the squatters as a matter of principle: "We're not about to reward people for bad behaviour." "Province Appeals Award to Vancouver Squatters," *Times Colonist* (Victoria), April 11, 2003; *Provincial Rental Housing Corporation v Hall.*
25 *Vancouver (City) v Maurice*. See also *Everywoman's Health Centre Society v Bridges*, 1990 CanLII 5409 (BCCA).
26 *Provincial Rental Housing Corporation v. Hall.*
27 *Vancouver Charter*, ss 334 and 571; *Community Charter*, SBC 2003, c 26, s 274(1). In 2006, the BC legislature adopted an amendment to the *Vancouver Charter* simplifying the process by which the City of Vancouver or the Board of Parks and Recreation could obtain an injunction to secure enforcement of a bylaw. The new provision incorporated the process already available to municipalities outside Vancouver, to initiate proceedings by way of petition rather than the more complex "writ of summons" process. See *Community Services Statutes Amendment Act*, SBC 2006, c 3, ss 28 and 30.
28 For discussion of the appropriate test for interlocutory injunctions issued as a statutory rather than equitable remedy, see *Vancouver Parks Board v Mickelson et al*, 2003 BCSC 1271, para. 20; *Vancouver (City) v Maurice*, para 34; *Vancouver Board of Parks and Recreation v Williams et al*, 2014 BCSC 1926, paras 46–60; *British Columbia v Adamson*, 2016 BCSC 584, paras 21–35; *Victoria (City) v Smith*, 2020 BCSC 1173, paras 25 and 26; *Maple Ridge (District) v Thornhill Aggregates Ltd*, 1998 CanLII 6446 (BCCA), paras 7–9; *RJR-MacDonald Inc. v. Canada (Attorney General)*, [1994] 1 SCR 311. See also *Manitoba (AG) v Metropolitan Stores Ltd*, [1987] 1 SCR 110, paras 54–91; *Burnaby (City) v Pocrnic*, 1999 BCCA 652; *Nelson (City) v Kranz*, [1990] 3 MPLR (2d) 258, 24 ACWS (3d) 370 (BCSC);

Capital Regional District v Smith, [1999] 49 MPLR (2d) 159 (BCCA); *Langley (Township) v Wood*, [1999] 173 DLR (4th) 695 (BCCA); *Martin v Chilliwack (City)*, 2003 BCSC 942; Basil Alexander, "Demonstrations and the Law: Patterns of Law's Negative Effects on the Ground and the Practical Implications," *UBC Law Review* 49, 3 (November 2016): 881–82.

29 See *Maple Ridge (District) v Thornhill Aggregates Ltd*, paras 7–9.

30 *Vancouver Parks Board v Mickelson et al.*

31 Vancouver Anti-Poverty Committee, "Victory Squat Press Conference" (news release, August 15, 2003), http://chodarr.org/sites/default/files/chodarr2300.pdf.

32 *Vancouver Board of Parks v Sterritt et al*, 2003 BCSC 1421.

33 *British Columbia (Minister of Forests) v Wilson*, 2000 BCSC 1135; *British Columbia (Minister of Forests) v Jules (Adams Lake Band)*, 2001 BCCA 647; *British Columbia (Minister of Forests) v Okanagan Indian Band*, 2003 SCC 371.

34 *Victoria (City) v Adams*, 2008 BCSC 1363.

35 See Koenig, "Spaces of Denial and the Denial of Place"; Zion, "What Is a Right to Shelter in the Desert of Post-Democracy?"; Billingsley, *Claiming Poor Rights.*

36 Koenig, "Spaces of Denial and the Denial of Place," 164; Bill M-203, *Trespass to Property Act*, 2004; *Safe Streets Act*, SBC 2004, c 75.

37 "Penniless: Why a Victoria Man Has Gone Two Decades Without Money," *Capital Daily* (Victoria), July 14, 2021, https://www.capitaldaily.ca/news/penniless-two-decades-without-money; *R v Johnston*, 2005 BCPC 69, para 4.

38 *R v Johnston*, 2005 BCPC 69; *R v Johnston*, 2005 BCPC 184; *R v Johnston*, 2006 BCSC 1592; David Arthur Johnston, "Journal of the Occupation of St. Ann's Academy, January 2004 to May 2013 (So Far)," http://www.angelfire.com/apes/hatrackman/welcome.htm.

39 *Provincial Capital Commission v Johnston et al*, 2005 BCSC 1397.

40 *Victoria (City) v Adams*; "Cridge Park Campers Pack Up," *Times Colonist* (Victoria), October 29, 2005.

41 *Victoria (City) v Adams*; "Court Strikes Down Victoria Bylaw Against Homeless Camping," *CBC News*, October 14, 2008; "Victoria Bylaws Unconstitutional, Court Told," *Globe and Mail*, June 17, 2008.

42 *Victoria (City) v Adams*, 2009 BCCA 563.

43 City of Victoria, *Parks Regulation Bylaw*, Amendment Bylaw (No. 06) No. 10-021; City of Victoria, *Parks Regulation Bylaw*, No. 07-059.

44 *Johnston v Victoria (City)*, 2010 BCSC 1707; *Johnston v Victoria (City)*, 2011 BCCA 400.

45 "Homeless Advocate's Outburst Halts Hearing," *Times Colonist* (Victoria), October 20, 2011; "Correction Centre Doctors Keep Close Watch on Hunger Strike Prisoner," *Times Colonist* (Victoria), November 17, 2011; "Right-to-Camp Advocate David Arthur Johnston Sentenced to 90 Days," *Times Colonist* (Victoria), January 15, 2013; Johnston, "Journal of the Occupation of St. Ann's Academy."

46 Zion, "What Is a Right to Shelter in the Desert of Post-Democracy?" 155–57.

47 *Vancouver (City) v Zhang*, 2010 BCCA 450.

48 *Victoria (City) v Thompson*, 2011 BCSC 1810.

49 See Stuart Schrader and David Wachsmuth, "Reflections on Occupy Wall Street, the State and Space," *City* 16, 1–2 (February–April 2012): 243–48; Jonathan Massey and Brett Snyder, "Occupying Wall Street: Places and Spaces of Political Action," *Places* (September 2012);

Michael Bueckert, "Solidarity with Whom? Occupy Wall Street and Responsibility to the Other(s)," in *World to Win: Contemporary Social Movements and Counter-Hegemony,* ed. William K. Carroll and Kanchan Sarker (Winnipeg: ARP Books, 2016), 327–41; Jennifer Koshan, "I Fought the Law: Civil Disobedience and the Law in Canada," *ABlawg.ca* (blog), University of Calgary Faculty of Law, February 27, 2012, http://ablawg.ca/wp-content/uploads/2012/02/blog_jk_occupy_feb2012.pdf.

50 Minutes of Victoria City Council Meeting, October 27, 2011.

51 "Occupy Victoria Protesters Given Notice to Vacate Monday," *Toronto Star,* November 6, 2011.

52 *Victoria (City) v Thompson.* See also *Vancouver (City) v Maurice.*

53 *Victoria (City) v Thompson.*

54 "Occupy Victoria Protesters Go Quietly," *CBC News,* November 19, 2011; "Victoria Granted Injunction Against Occupy Camp," *Globe and Mail,* November 18, 2011; "Occupy Victoria Campers Ordered Off Centennial Square," *Victoria News,* November 18, 2011; "Police Clear Occupy Victoria Site," *Times Colonist* (Victoria), November 22, 2011.

55 Alexander, "Demonstrations and the Law," 892–95.

56 "City Wins Injunctions Against Occupy Vancouver," *Globe and Mail,* November 18, 2011.

57 *Vancouver (City) v O'Flynn-Magee et al,* 2011 BCSC 1647. See also MsC 146, Occupy Vancouver Collection, Simon Fraser University Special Collections and Rare Books.

58 *In the Matter of Access to the Courts of Justice,* 2011 BCSC 1815.

59 "Occupy Group Moves On, but Won't Give Up," *Nanaimo News Bulletin,* December 13, 2011; "No Longer Welcome," *Times Colonist* (Victoria), December 13, 2011.

60 "Occupiers Told To Leave Plaza or Face Legal Action," *Nanaimo News Bulletin,* November 29, 2011.

61 Purcell, "Excavating Lefebvre," 99; "Overdose Awareness Day Shines Light on More Than 7,700 B.C. Lives Lost – and What's Still at Stake," *CBC News,* August 31, 2021.

62 "Vancouver's Oppenheimer Park Protest Raises Question of Aboriginal Title to Urban Centres," *CBC News,* July 23, 2014.

63 *Vancouver Board of Parks and Recreation v Williams et al.*; *Maple Ridge (District of) v Thornhill Aggregates Ltd.*, 1998 CanLII 6446 (BCCA).

64 "With Few Options, Homeless Predict Return to Dismantled Tent City," *Globe and Mail,* October 16, 2014; "VPD Won't Recommend Charges Against Oppenheimer Campers," *Vancouver Courier,* October 16, 2014; "Oppenheimer Homeless Camp to Be Evicted After Injunction Granted," *CBC News,* October 8, 2014.

65 "Manure on Homeless Camp Leads to Abbotsford Lawsuit," *CBC News,* November 26, 2013.

66 *Abbotsford (City) v Shantz,* 2015 BCSC 1909.

67 *British Columbia v Adamson,* 2016 BCSC 584.

68 *British Columbia v Adamson,* 2017 BCSC 168; *British Columbia v Adamson,* 2016 BCSC 1245; "BC Government Granted Injunction to Shut Down Victoria Tent City," *CBC News,* July 5, 2016.

69 *British Columbia v Adamson,* 2016 BCSC 1245; *British Columbia v Adamson,* 2017 BCSC 168; British Columbia, Ministry Responsible for Housing, "Province Shuts Down Courthouse Encampment" (news release, August 8, 2016), https://news.gov.bc.ca/releases/2016MNGD0049-001451. As a representative of the Together Against Poverty Society noted in an affidavit in support of the awarding of public interest special costs on

a full indemnity basis to counsel for the defendant campers in the *Adamson* litigation: "Since Farris took on representation of the Encampment residents we have seen direct and indirect investment in social housing totaling an approximate $86 million. We believe this is in large measure attributable to the legal challenge to the Province's injunction application. This funding has translated into 714 units of housing and shelter space targeted specifically to the homeless that were not even being considered in this community 11 months ago. We have three new buildings dedicated to permanent indoor homes. These are Mt. Edwards (38 spaces), Super 8 (51 spaces, not yet operational), and Central Care Home (140 spaces). All of these are a direct response to the Encampment and the litigation around it. We also have two transitional shelters dedicated to helping people make the important move from the street to the indoors. Choices (78 spaces) and My Place (40 spaces), are both also directly attributable to the Encampment and the legal action." See *British Columbia v Adamson*, 2017 BCSC 168.

70 *Vancouver (City) v Wallstam*, 2017 BCSC 937.

71 "Judge Denies City of Vancouver Application for Injunction to Remove Tent City on Main Street," *Vancouver Sun*, May 17, 2017; "BC Supreme Court Quashes Bid to Take Down Homeless Camp," *Vancouver Sun*, May 18, 2017.

72 *Nanaimo (City) v Courtoreille*, 2018 BCSC 1629; *Maple Ridge (City) v Scott*, 2019 BCSC 157; *Prince George (City) v Stewart*, 2021 BCSC 2089; "Court Allows Tent-City Residents in Nanaimo to Stay Until Nov. 30," *Times Colonist* (Victoria), October 19, 2018; "City Demolishes Portion of Court-Protected Homeless Camp in Prince George," *CBC News*, November 17, 2021. For a protest by citizens opposed to the construction of social housing, which resulted in the province applying for an injunction to proceed with the project in the city of Maple Ridge, see British Columbia, "Province, BC Housing Seek Injunction in Order to Build Supportive Housing" (news release, May 15, 2018), https://news.gov.bc.ca/releases/2018MAH0052-000919.

73 "Decampment of Topaz Park and Pandora Avenue Corridor" (email from Anna Cooper and Caitlin Shane [Pivot Legal Society] to Micah Weintraub [BC Ministry of Attorney General], May 14, 2020), https://www.pivotlegal.org/decampment_of_topaz_park_and_pandora_avenue_corridor; "Province Orders Dismantling of Pandora, Topaz Camps; Residents Moving to Hotels," *Times Colonist* (Victoria), April 25, 2020; Ministerial Order No. M128, "Encampment Health and Safety (COVID-19) Order," April 24, 2020, https://www.bclaws.gov.bc.ca/civix/document/id/mo/hmo/m0128_2020; Ministerial Order No. M150, "Encampment Health and Safety (COVID-19) Order No. 2," May 8, 2020, https://www.bclaws.gov.bc.ca/civix/document/id/mo/hmo/m0150_2020; Ministerial Order No. M166, "Encampment Health and Safety (COVID-19) Victoria Enforcement Order," May 20, 2020, https://www.bclaws.gov.bc.ca/civix/document/id/mo/mo/m0166_2020, all enacted pursuant to the *Emergency Program Act*, RSBC 1996, c 111, s 10; British Columbia, "Province, City of Victoria Sign Agreement to End Encampments" (news release, March 22, 2021), https://news.gov.bc.ca/releases/2021AG0022-000521; "B.C. Signs Deal with City of Victoria to End Homeless Camps, Bring People Inside," *CBC News*, March 23, 2021.

74 In addition to the provincial ministerial orders prohibiting sheltering in Topaz Park and the Pandora Avenue greenway during the "first wave" of the COVID-19 pandemic in 2020, the City of Victoria also sought and obtained an injunction restraining sheltering in "environmentally and culturally sensitive areas" within Beacon Hill Park, while permitting

sheltering by unhoused individuals in other areas of Beacon Hill Park and other parks in order to abide by the principles established in the *Adams* decision. See *Victoria (City) v Smith*. For the more recent challenge to amendments to Victoria's *Parks Regulation Bylaw* that prohibited sheltering in a number of parks, see "Lawsuit Aims to Strike Down City of Victoria's Ban on Sheltering in Parks," *Victoria News*, December 23, 2024. In Vancouver, enforcement of Ministerial Order No. M128 prompted migration of an encampment to land adjacent to Crab Park owned by the Vancouver Fraser Port Authority, resulting in an injunction, arrests, and an invitation by BC Supreme Court Chief Justice Hinkson to the BC Crown Prosecution Service to assess whether prosecutions for criminal contempt should be pursued. See *Vancouver Fraser Port Authority v Brett*, 2020 BCSC 876; *Vancouver Fraser Port Authority v Brett*, 2020 BCSC 1368; "Ian Mulgrew: B.C.'s Top Trial Judge Fed Up with Protesters Ignoring Court Orders," *Vancouver Sun*, September 19, 2020.

75 *Victoria (City) v Adams*.

76 See *Tanudjaja v Canada (Attorney General)*, 2014 ONCA 852; *Gosselin v Quebec (Attorney General)*, 2002 SCC 84; also *Chaoulli v Quebec* (Attorney General), 2005 SCC 35.

77 *Canadian Bill of Rights*, S.C. 1960, c. 44.

78 Sarah E. Hamill, "Private Property Rights and Public Responsibility: Leaving Room for the Homeless," *Windsor Review of Legal and Social Issues* 30 (2011): 97. See also Sarah E. Hamill, "Private Rights to Public Property: The Evolution of Common Property in Canada," *McGill Law Journal* 58 (2012): 365.

Conclusion

1 *MacMillan Bloedel Ltd v Simpson*, [1996] 2 SCR 1048, para 13.

2 Eric Tucker, "'That Indefinite Area of Toleration': Criminal Conspiracy and Trade Unions in Ontario, 1837–77," *Labour/Le Travail* 27 (Spring 1991): 17; Doreen Massey, *Space, Place, and Gender* (Minneapolis: University of Minnesota Press, 1994), 265; also Doreen Massey, "Power-Geometry and a Progressive Sense of Place," in *Mapping the Futures: Local Cultures, Global Change*, ed. Jon Bird, Barry Curtis, Tim Putnam, George Robertson, and Lisa Tickner (London: Routledge, 1993), 59–69.

3 *MacMillan Bloedel Ltd v Mullin*, 1985 CanLII 154 (BCCA).

4 E.P. Thompson, *Whigs and Hunters: The Origin of the Black Act* (London: Pantheon, 1975); E.P. Thompson, *Customs in Common* (New York: New Press, 1991).

5 David Harvey, *Rebel Cities: From the Right to the City to the Urban Revolution* (London and New York: Verso, 2012), xv.

6 See Irina Ceric, "Beyond Contempt: Injunctions, Land Defense, and the Criminalization of Indigenous Resistance," *South Atlantic Quarterly* 119, 2 (April 2020): 361.

7 *Teal Cedar Products Ltd v Rainforest Flying Squad*, 2021 BCSC 1903; *Teal Cedar Products Ltd v Rainforest Flying Squad*, 2021 BCCA 387; *Teal Cedar Products Ltd v Rainforest Flying Squad*, 2022 BCCA 26; "Fairy Creek Protesters Vow to Carry On Despite New Injunction," *Globe and Mail*, October 11, 2021.

8 *Teal Cedar Products Ltd v Rainforest Flying Squad*, 2021 BCSC 1903.

9 *Everywoman's Health Centre Society v Bridges*, 1990 CanLII 5409 (BCCA).

10 Bill 20, *Access to Services (COVID-19) Act*, 2nd Sess, 42nd Leg, British Columbia, 2021 (assented to November 25, 2021, and repealed effective July 1, 2023, pursuant to a sunset clause at s 7); *Access to Services (COVID-19) Act*, SBC 2021, c 23; Bill 22, *Safe Access to*

Schools Act, 5th Sess, 42nd Leg, British Columbia, 2024 (assented to May 16, 2024); *Safe Access to Schools Act*, SBC 2024, c 18; Bill C-3, *An Act to Amend the Criminal Code and the Canada Labour Code*, 1st Sess, 44th Parl, 2021 (assented to December 17, 2021); British Columbia, "New Act Protects Important Services from Disruption" (news release, November 15, 2021), https://news.gov.bc.ca/releases/2021PREM0071-002169; "Health and Education Workers Support Idea of 'Bubble Zones' After Anti-Vaccine Protests at Schools, Hospitals," *CBC News*, September 19, 2021; "Bubble-Zone Protection Coming for Hospitals and Schools, Farnworth Says," *Times Colonist* (Victoria), October 4, 2021; "B.C. to Establish Protest-Free Buffer Zones Around K-12 Schools," *Victoria News*, April 10, 2024.

11 *Victoria (City) v. Adams*, 2008 BCSC 1363; *Victoria (City) v. Adams*, 2009 BCCA 563; *British Columbia v. Adamson*, 2016 BCSC 584; *Abbotsford (City) v. Shantz*, 2015 BCSC 1909.

12 Bora Laskin, "The Labour Injunction in Canada: A Caveat," *Canadian Bar Review* 15 (1937): 271–74.

13 Mary F. Southin, "The Courts and Labour Injunctions," *The Advocate* 28 (1970): 83–84.

14 Morton Denlaw, "The Motion for a Preliminary Injunction: Time for a Uniform Federal Standard," *Review of Litigation* 22, 3 (Summer 2003): 495–539.

15 Law Reform Commission of Canada, *Contempt of Court: Offences Against the Administration of Justice*, Working Paper 20 (Ottawa: Department of Justice Canada, 1977), 29.

16 "Anti-Pipeline Campaigners Found Not Guilty by Judge Because 'Protest Against Climate Change Crisis' Was Legal 'Necessity,'" *Independent* (London), March 27, 2018.

17 Kegan Pepper-Smith, "'Climate Necessity' New Defence in Civil Disobedience Cases," *Vancouver Sun*, April 16, 2018.

18 For a recent BC Provincial Court decision where the defence of necessity was found to lack an "air of reality" and therefore have no application to mischief allegations against two climate change protesters, see *R v Breen*, 2024 BCPC 95; "Road Blockers' 'Defence of Necessity' Argument Rejected," *Times Colonist* (Victoria), May 7, 2024.

Afterword

1 RCMP, "Resource Protests: Briefing to Minister," by Commissioner Brenda Lucki, May 3, 2018, Access to Information and Privacy (ATIP) Release A202107679_2023-08-12_06-03-43, 241; RCMP, "Critical Response Unit – British Columbia (CRU-BC)" September 2024, https://rcmp.ca/en/bc/police-services/critical-response-unit-british-columbia.

2 RCMP, "Resource Protests: Briefing to Minister," 237.

3 *Burnaby (City) v Trans Mountain Pipeline ULC*, 2014 BCSC 1820; *Burnaby (City) v Trans Mountain Pipeline ULC*, 2014 BCCA 465; *Burnaby (City) v Trans Mountain Pipeline ULC*, 2015 BCCA 78; *Burnaby (City) v Trans Mountain Pipeline ULC*, 2015 BCSC 2140; *Burnaby (City) v Trans Mountain Pipeline ULC*, 2017 BCCA 132; "Mayor Derek Corrigan Says Burnaby Will Stop Kinder Morgan Pipeline in the Courts," *Vancouver Sun*, November 18, 2014; "National Energy Board Backs Trans Mountain on Burnaby Pipeline Impasse," *The Province*, December 7, 2017.

4 *Trans Mountain Pipeline ULC v Gold*, 2014 BCSC 2133.

5 "RCMP Responds with Respect as Grand Chief Arrested on Burnaby Mountain," *Vancouver Observer*, November 27, 2014.

6 *Trans Mountain Pipeline ULC v Gold*, 2014 BCSC 2403; "Contempt Charges Thrown Out

in Burnaby Mountain Pipeline Protest," *Vancouver Sun*, November 27, 2014; Irina Ceric, "Beyond Contempt: Injunctions, Land Defense, and the Criminalization of Indigenous Resistance," *South Atlantic Quarterly* 119, 2 (April 2020): 356; Basil Alexander, "Demonstrations and the Law: Patterns of Law's Negative Effects on the Ground and the Practical Implications," *UBC Law Review* 49, 3 (November 2016): 924–25.

7 "Ottawa Approves Two Pipelines," *Financial Post* (Toronto), November 29, 2016; "Trudeau Government to Buy Kinder Morgan's Trans Mountain for $4.5-Billion," *Globe and Mail*, May 29, 2018; "Kinder Morgan to Halt Spending on Trans Mountain Pipeline Due to B.C. Opposition," *The Province*, April 8, 2018; Kinder Morgan, "Kinder Morgan Canada Limited Suspends Non-Essential Spending on Trans Mountain Expansion Project" (news release, April 8, 2018), https://www.transmountain.com/news/kinder-morgan-canada-limited-suspends-non-essential-spending-on-trans-mountain-expansion-project (viewed January 28, 2026); "Federal Court Rejects B.C. Government's Appeal Against NEB's Local Bylaw Ruling," *CBC News*, March 25, 2018; "Trans Mountain Decision by Appeal Court Is a 'Victory' for Alberta and Pipelines, Notley Says," *CBC News*, March 26, 2018.

8 See Order Made After Application, March 16, 2018, File No. S-183541, *Trans Mountain Pipeline ULC v Mivasair et al*, Vancouver Registry; *Trans Mountain Pipeline ULC v Mivasair*, 2018 BCSC 874; *Trans Mountain Pipeline ULC v Mivasair*, 2019 BCCA 267; "National Energy Board Backs Trans Mountain on Burnaby Pipeline Impasse"; "Pipeline Protesters Including MPs Elizabeth May, Kennedy Stewart Should Face Criminal Charge: Judge," *CBC News*, April 9, 2018; "Green Party Leader Elizabeth May Pleads Guilty to Contempt over Pipeline Protest," *CBC News*, May 28, 2018; "Burnaby South MP Kennedy Stewart Convicted of Criminal Contempt of Court in Connection with Pipeline Protest," *Georgia Straight* (Vancouver), May 14, 2018; "Protesting Pastors Arrested at Kinder Morgan Facility in Burnaby," *New Westminster Record*, April 20, 2018; "Arrests to Continue as Kinder Morgan Protests Heat Up," *The Tyee* (Vancouver), April 4, 2018; "B.C. Judge Expands Pipeline Injunction as Protesters Use 'Calculated' Defiance," *Times Colonist* (Victoria), June 1, 2018; "Judge Sends Trans Mountain Pipeline Protesters to Jail for the First Time," *Vancouver Sun*, July 31, 2018.

9 Trans Mountain Pipeline ULC v Mivasair, 2019 BCCA 156; *Trans Mountain Pipeline ULC v Mivasair*, 2018 BCSC 947; "Ian Mulgrew: B.C.'s Top Trial Judge Fed Up with Protesters Ignoring Court Orders," *Vancouver Sun*, September 19, 2020.

10 *Tsleil-Waututh Nation et al v Attorney General of Canada et al*, 2018 FCA 153; "Federal Court of Appeal Quashes Construction Approvals for Trans Mountain, Leaving Project in Limbo," *CBC News*, August 30, 2018; "Trudeau Cabinet Approves Trans Mountain Expansion Project," *CBC News*, June 18, 2019.

11 Union of British Columbia Indian Chiefs, "Canada Approves TMX Despite Failing to Achieve Consent" (news release, June 18, 2019), https://www.ubcic.bc.ca/canada_approves_tmx_despite_failing_to_achieve_consent.

12 "People 'Are Going to Die' Protesting Trans-Mountain Pipeline," *Edmonton Journal*, June 13, 2018. See also Michael Simpson and Philippe Le Billon, "Reconciling Violence: Policing the Politics of Recognition," *Geoforum* 119 (February 2021): 111–21.

13 *Coldwater First Nation v Canada (Attorney General)*, 2020 FCA 34; "Supreme Court Dismisses Indigenous Appeal of Trans Mountain Pipeline Approval," *Times Colonist* (Victoria), July 2, 2020.

14 *Trans Mountain Pipeline ULC v Mivasair,* 2022 BCSC 2386; *Trans Mountain Pipeline ULC v Mivasair,* 2022 BCSC 2388; *Trans Mountain Pipeline ULC v Mivasair,* 2023 BCSC 410; *Trans Mountain Pipeline ULC v Mivasair,* 2023 BCSC 412; *Trans Mountain Pipeline ULC v Mivasair,* 2023 BCSC 925; and *R v Dick,* 2024 BCCA 272.

15 *Trans Mountain Pipeline ULC v Mivasair,* 2021 BCSC 369; *R v Leyden,* 2024 BCCA 227.

16 Office of the Parliamentary Budget Officer, "Trans Mountain Pipeline – 2024 Report," November 8, 2024, https://www.pbo-dpb.ca/en/publications/RP-2425-021-S--trans-mountain-pipeline-2024-report--reseau-pipelines-trans-mountain-rapport-2024.

17 Forest and Range Consultation and Revenue Sharing Agreement between the Province of British Columbia and Pacheedaht First Nation, 2021, BC Ministry of Indigenous Relations and Reconciliation, https://www2.gov.bc.ca/assets/gov/environment/natural-resource-stewardship/consulting-with-first-nations/agreements/pacheedaht_signed_february_17_2021_1.pdf. The share of revenue allocated to the Pacheedaht First Nation was set at $277,000 in the first year of the agreement, and then calculated in future years based on an agreed formula.

18 "The Blockaders," *The Tyee* (Vancouver), March 25, 2021, https://thetyee.ca/News/2021/03/25/Fairy-Creek-Blockaders/.

19 Order made by Justice Verhoeven, April 1, 2021, in the case of *Teal Cedar Products Ltd v Rainforest Flying Squad,* 2021 BCSC 605.

20 Hišuk ma cȧwak Declaration, June 7, 2021, https://huuayaht.org/wp-content/uploads/2021/06/declaration-FINAL-signedpdf.pdf; British Columbia, "Old growth Harvesting Deferred in Fairy Creek, Walbran Areas" (news release, June 9, 2021), https://news.gov.bc.ca/releases/2021PREM0038-001122.

21 Bill Jones to author, July 14, 2021, personal correspondence in possession of author.

22 *Teal Cedar Products Ltd v Rainforest Flying Squad,* 2021 BCSC 1554.

23 *Teal Cedar Products Ltd v Rainforest Flying Squad,* 2021 BCSC 1380; "Prosecution Service Considers Criminal Contempt Charges for Fairy Creek Logging Protesters," *Times Colonist* (Victoria), July 19, 2021.

24 *Teal Cedar Products Ltd v Rainforest Flying Squad,* 2021 BCSC 1903; *Teal Cedar Products Ltd v Rainforest Flying Squad,* 2021 BCCA 387; *Teal Cedar Products Ltd v Rainforest Flying Squad,* 2022 BCCA 26.

25 RCMP Sgt. J. Uzelac, "Community Industry Response Group (C-IRG) 2017–2022," March 7, 2022, 20, ATIP Release A-2021-07952, "Records."

26 *Teal Cedar Products Ltd v Rainforest Flying Squad,* 2022 BCSC 659; *Teal Cedar Products Ltd v Rainforest Flying Squad,* 2022 BCSC 2338.

27 *Teal Cedar Products Ltd v Rainforest Flying Squad re Henderson,* 2023 BCSC 201; *His Majesty the King v Emily Henderson also known as Ryan Henderson,* 2023 CanLII 72136 (SCC); "Fairy Creek Protester Acquitted of Criminal Contempt Due to RCMP Failure to Give Proper Notice," *CBC News,* February 9, 2023; "Cases Dropped Against 146 Fairy Creek Protesters over RCMP's Failure to Read Full Injunction at Arrests," *CBC News,* August 10, 2023; "Cases Against 146 Fairy Creek Logging Protesters Are Dropped After High Court Ruling," *Times Colonist* (Victoria), August 10, 2023.

28 *Teal Cedar Products Ltd v Davidson,* 2024 BCSC 81; *Teal Cedar Products Ltd v Davidson,* 2024 BCSC 662; *R v Davidson,* 2025 BCCA 111.

29 "B.C. Suspends Old-Growth Logging in Fairy Creek at Request of Indigenous Communities," *Globe and Mail,* June 9, 2021; British Columbia, "Province Extends Fairy

Creek Old-Growth Deferral" (news release, June 2, 2023), https://news.gov.bc.ca/releases/2023FOR0033-000860; "Agreement in Principle: Term Sheet for Cooperation and Responsible Government Accord, December 12, 2024," BC Green Party, https://bcgreens.ca/wp-content/uploads/2024/12/Agreement-in-Principle.pdf; "B.C. NDP and B.C. Greens Announce Co-operation Agreement," *CBC News,* December 13, 2024; "B.C. Extends Deferral of Logging in Fairy Creek amid Reports of Tree Spiking," *CBC News,* January 29, 2025.

30 Jeff Jones to Capital Regional District Board of Directors, July 8, 2021, letter in possession of author.

BIBLIOGRAPHY

Legislation

British Columbia

Trade-Unions Act, SBC 1902, c 66
Riot Claims Settlement Act, SBC 1919, c 72
Trade-Unions Act Amendment Act, RSBC 1936, c 239
Industrial Conciliation and Arbitration Act, SBC 1937, c 31
Industrial Conciliation and Arbitration Act Amendment Act, SBC 1938, c 23
Industrial Conciliation and Arbitration Act Amendment Act, SBC 1943, c 28
Industrial Conciliation and Arbitration Act Amendment Act, SBC 1947, c 44
Public Schools Act Amendment Act, SBC 1947, c 79
Civil Service Act Amendment Act, SBC 1948, c 5
Industrial Conciliation and Arbitration Act Amendment Act, SBC 1948, c 31
Legal Professions Act Amendment Act, SBC 1948, c 36
Equal Pay Act, SBC 1953, c 6
Vancouver Charter, SBC 1953, c 55
Labour Relations Act, SBC 1954, c 17
Fair Employment Practices Act, SBC 1956, c 16
Constitution Act Amendment Act, SBC 1959, c 17
Trade-Unions Act, SBC 1959, c 90
Labour Relations Act Amendment Act, SBC 1961, c 31
Mediation Commission Act, SBC 1968, c 26
Labour Relations Act Amendment Act, SBC 1970, c 16
Labour Code of British Columbia Act, SBC 1973, c 122
Public Service Labour Relations Act, SBC 1973, c 144
Industrial Relations Act, SBC 1979, c 212
Industrial Relations Reform Act, SBC 1987, c 24

Commissioner on Resources and Environment Act, SBC 1992, c 34
Forest Practices Code of British Columbia Act, SBC 1994, c 41
Access to Abortion Services Act, RSBC 1996, c 1
Emergency Program Act, RSBC 1996, c 111
Labour Relations Code, RSBC 1996, c 244
Law and Equity Act, RSBC 1996, c 253
Offence Act, RSBC 1996, c 338
Supreme Court Act, RSBC 1996, c 443
Nisga'a Final Agreement Act, SBC 1999, c 2
Health and Social Services Delivery Improvement Act, SBC 2002, c 2
Community Charter, SBC 2003, c 26
Health Sector (Facilities Subsector) Collective Agreement Act, SBC 2004 c 19
Safe Streets Act, SBC 2004, c 75
Community Services Statutes Amendment Act, SBC 2006, c 3
Haida Gwaii Reconciliation Act, SBC 2010, c 17
Declaration on the Rights of Indigenous Peoples Act, SBC 2019, c 44
Access to Services (COVID-19) Act, SBC 2021, c 23
Haida Nation Recognition Act, SBC 2023, c 24
Safe Access to Schools Act, SBC 2024, c 18

Canada

Trade Union Act, SC 1872, c 31
Criminal Law Amendment Act, SC 1872, c 31
Criminal Code, SC 1892, c 29
Railway Disputes Act, SC 1903, c 55
Militia Act, SC 1904, c 23
Industrial Disputes Investigation Act, SC 1907, c 20
Wartime Labour Relations Regulations, PC 1944-1003
Maintenance of Railway Operations Act, SC 1950–51, c 1
British Columbia Coast Steamship Service Act, SC 1958, c 7
Railway Operations Continuation Act, SC 1960, c 2
Public Service Staff Relations Act, SC 1966–67, c 72
Criminal Law Amendment Act, SC 1968–69, c 38
West Coast Ports Operations Act, SC 1972, c 23
Maintenance of Railway Operations Act, 1972. SC 1973–74, c 32
West Coast Grain Handling Operations Act, SC 1974–75–76, c 1
West Coast Ports Operations Act, 1975. SC 1974–75–76, c 32
Criminal Code, RSC 1985, c C-46
Fisheries Act, RSC 1985, c F-14
Labour Code, RSC 1985, c L-2
Public Service Staff Relations Act, RSC 1985, c P35
Prince Rupert Grain Handling Operations Act, SC 1988, c 1
British Columbia Grain Handling Operations Act, SC 1991, c 25
West Coast Ports Operations Act, SC 1994, c 1
West Coast Ports Operations Act, SC 1995, c 2
Public Service Modernization Act, SC 2003, c 22

Railway Continuation Act, SC 2007, c 8
United Nations Declaration on the Rights of Indigenous Peoples Act, SC 2021, c 14
Haida Nation Recognition Act, SC 2024, c 29

United Kingdom

Constitution Act, 1867, 30 & 31 Vict, c 3
Constitution Act, 1982, Schedule B to the Canada Act 1982 (UK), 1982, c 11

Ontario

Labour Relations Act, SO 1948, c 51

Saskatchewan

Trade Union Act, SS 1944, c 69

Case Law

Abbotsford (City) v Shantz, 2015 BCSC 1909
American Cyanamid Co (No 1) v Ethicon Ltd, 1975 UKHL 1
Bassel's Lunch Ltd v Kick et al, 1936 OR 445
BCGEU v British Columbia (Attorney General), 1988 SCC 3
British Columbia v Adamson, 2016 BCSC 584
British Columbia v Adamson, 2016 BCSC 1245
British Columbia v Adamson, 2017 BCSC 168
British Columbia (Attorney General) v Wale, [1986] 9 BCLR (2d) 333 (BCCA)
British Columbia (Minister of Forests) v Adams Lake Indian Band, 2000 BCCA 98
British Columbia (Minister of Forests) v Adams Lake Indian Band, 2000 BCCA 315
British Columbia (Minister of Forests) v Jules (Adams Lake Band), 2001 BCCA 647
British Columbia (Minister of Forests) v Okanagan Indian Band, 2000 BCSC 32
British Columbia (Minister of Forests) v Okanagan Indian Band, 2003 SCC 371
British Columbia (Minister of Forests) v Wilson, 1999 BCSC 1723
British Columbia (Minister of Forests) v Wilson, 2000 BCSC 1135
Burnaby (City) v Trans Mountain Pipeline ULC, 2014 BCSC 1820
Burnaby (City) v Trans Mountain Pipeline ULC, 2014 BCCA 465
Burnaby (City) v Trans Mountain Pipeline ULC, 2015 BCSC 2140
Burnaby (City) v Trans Mountain Pipeline ULC, 2015 BCCA 78
Burnaby (City) v Trans Mountain Pipeline ULC, 2017 BCCA 132
Calder et al v Attorney-General of British Columbia, [1973] SCR 313
Canada (Attorney General) v Canadian Civil Liberties Association, 2026 FCA 6
Canada Post Corp v LCUC, Local 12, [1987] 15 BCLR (2d) 356 (BCSC)
Canadian Frontline Nurses v Canada (Attorney General), 2024 FC 42
Canadian Transport Co (UK) Ltd v Alsbury, [1952] 6 WWR (NS) 473 (BCSC)
Canadian Transport (UK) Limited v Alsbury, [1953] 1 DLR 385 (BCCA)
Cedar Point Nursery v Hassid, 594 US 139 (2021)
Chaoulli v Quebec (Attorney General), 2005 SCC 35
Coastal GasLink Pipeline Ltd v Huson, 2018 BCSC 2343

Coastal GasLink Pipeline Ltd v Huson, 2019 BCSC 2264
Coastal GasLink Pipeline Ltd v Huson, 2021 BCSC 2734
Coastal GasLink Pipeline Ltd v Huson, 2021 BCSC 2735
Coastal Gaslink Pipeline Ltd v Huson, 2024 BCSC 509
Coastal Gaslink Pipeline Ltd v Huson, 2024 BCSC 1730
Coastal Gaslink Pipeline Ltd v Huson, 2025 BCSC 643
Delgamuukw v British Columbia, [1997] 3 SCR 1010
Dominion Bridge Co v International Ass'n of Bridge, Structural and Ornamental Iron Workers, Local 97 (1959), 20 DLR (2d) 621 (BCCA)
Everywoman's Health Centre Soc (1988) v Bridges, 1989 CanLII 2793 (BCSC)
Everywoman's Health Centre Society v Bridges, 1990 CanLII 1574 (BCSC)
Everywoman's Health Centre Society v Bridges, 1990 CanLII 5409 (BCCA)
Everywoman's Health Centre Society v Bridges, 1991 CanLII 5715 (BCCA)
Everywoman's Health Centre Society (1988) v Bridges, 1993 CanLII 1276 (BCSC)
Everywoman's Health Centre Society (1988) v Watson, 1994 CanLII 1467 (BCCA)
Gosselin v Quebec (Attorney General), 2002 SCC 84
Greenpeace Canada v MacMillan Bloedel, 1994 CanLII 943 (BCCA)
Guerin v The Queen, [1984] 2 SCR 335
Haida Nation v British Columbia (Minister of Forests), [2004] 3 SCR 511, 2004 SCC 73
Health Services and Support – Facilities Subsector Bargaining Assn v British Columbia, [2007] 2 SCR 391, 2007 SCC 27
His Majesty the King v Emily Henderson also known as Ryan Henderson, 2023 CanLII 72136 (SCC)
In the Matter of Access to the Courts of Justice, 2011 BCSC 1815
MacMillan Bloedel Ltd v Brown, 1994 BCCA 64
MacMillan Bloedel Ltd v Mullin, 1985 CanLII 708 (BCSC)
MacMillan Bloedel Ltd v Mullin, 1985 CanLII 154 (BCCA)
MacMillan Bloedel Ltd v Simpson, 1993 BCSC 530
MacMillan Bloedel Ltd v Simpson, 1993 BCSC 1295
MacMillan Bloedel Ltd v Simpson, 1994 BCSC 30
MacMillan Bloedel Ltd v Simpson, 1994 BCSC 1447
MacMillan Bloedel Ltd v Simpson, 1994 BCCA 187
MacMillan Bloedel Ltd v Simpson, [1995] 4 SCR 725
MacMillan Bloedel Ltd v Simpson, [1996] 2 SCR 1048
Manitoba (AG) v Metropolitan Stores Ltd, [1987] 1 SCR 110
Morgentaler v The Queen, [1976] 1 SCR 616
Ontario (Attorney General) v Bear Island Foundation (1984), 49 OR (2d) 353 (HC)
Provincial Capital Commission v Johnston et al, 2005 BCSC 1397
R v Angelo, [1914] 19 BCR 261 (BCCA)
R v Bridges, 1989 CanLII 2921 (BCSC)
R v Bridges, 1989 CanLII 5321 (BCSC)
R v Bridges, 1990 CanLII 5419 (BCCA)
R v Cohn (1985), 13 DLR (4th) 680 (Ont CA)
R v Cavanaugh, 2025 BCCA 252
R v Davidson, 2025 BCCA 111
R v Demers, 1992 BCCA 625

R v Demers, 1999 BCSC 1224
R v Demers, 2003 BCCA 28
R v Dick, 2024 BCCA 272
R v Ignace, 1996 BCCA 564
R v Ignace, 1996 BCCA 717
R v Ignace, 1998 BCCA 54
R v Ignace, 1998 BCCA 639
R v Johnston, 2005 BCPC 69
R v Johnston, 2005 BCPC 184
R v Johnston, 2006 BCSC 1592
R. v Marshall, [1990] 3 SCR 456
R v Morgentaler, [1988] 1 SCR 30
R v Sparrow, [1990] 1 SCR 1075
R v Spratt, 2011 BCCA 1747
R v Spratt and Watson, 2008 BCCA 340
R v Taylor and Williams (1981) 34 OR (2d) 360
R v Van der Peet, [1996] 2 SCR 507
R v United Fishermen and Allied Workers' Union et al (1967), 63 DLR (2d) 356 (BCCA)
R v United Fishermen and Allied Workers' Union et al (1967), [1968] 2 CCC 257 (BCCA)
R v United Fishermen and Allied Workers' Union, Stavenes and two others (1967), [1968] 1 CCC 199 (BCSC)
RJR-MacDonald Inc v Canada (Attorney General), [1994] 1 SCR 311
RWDSU v Dolphin Delivery Ltd, 1986 SCC 5
Slawsky v Isitt, 2014 BCSC 1917
Tanudjaja v Canada (Attorney General), 2014 ONCA 852
Teal Cedar Products Ltd v Davidson, 2024 BCSC 81
Teal Cedar Products Ltd v Davidson, 2024 BCSC 662
Teal Cedar Products Ltd v Rainforest Flying Squad, 2021 BCSC 605
Teal Cedar Products Ltd v Rainforest Flying Squad, 2021 BCSC 1554
Teal Cedar Products Ltd v Rainforest Flying Squad, 2021 BCSC 1903
Teal Cedar Products Ltd v Rainforest Flying Squad, 2021 BCCA 387
Teal Cedar Products Ltd v Rainforest Flying Squad re Jaques, 2021 BCSC 2288
Teal Cedar Products Ltd v Rainforest Flying Squad re Moore, 2022 BCSC 659
Teal Cedar Products Ltd v Rainforest Flying Squad re Doyle, 2022 BCSC 2338
Teal Cedar Products Ltd v Rainforest Flying Squad, 2022 BCCA 26
Teal Cedar Products Ltd v Rainforest Flying Squad re Henderson, 2023 BCSC 201
Trans Mountain Pipeline ULC v Gold, 2014 BCSC 2133
Tsilhqot'in Nation v British Columbia, 2014 SCC 44
United Fishermen & Allied Workers' Union et al v The Queen, [1968] SCR 255
United Nurses of Alberta v Alberta (Attorney General), [1992] 1 SCR 901
Vancouver Board of Parks v Sterritt et al, 2003 BCSC 1421
Vancouver (City) v Maurice, 2005 BCCA 37
Vancouver (City) v O'Flynn-Magee, 2011 BCSC 1647
Vancouver (City) v Zhang, 2010 BCCA 450
Vancouver Parks Board v Mickelson et al, 2003 BCSC 1271
Verchere v Greenpeace Canada, 2004 BCCA 242

Verchere et al v Greenpeace Canada et al, 2003 BCSC 1571
Victoria (City) v Adams, 2008 BCSC 1363
Victoria (City) v Adams, 2009 BCCA 563
Victoria (City) v Thompson, 2011 BCSC 1810
Wale v British Columbia (Attorney General), [1991] 1 SCR 62

Archival Sources

Library and Archives Canada
Canadian Labour Congress fonds
Canadian Security Intelligence Service records
CCF-NDP fonds
Communist Party of Canada fonds
Department of Labour Fonds, Strikes and Lockouts Files
Greenpeace Canada fonds

British Columbia Archives
Court Records
Department of Attorney General Papers
Department of Labour Papers

Neish Family Collection (Private collection, Victoria)

Simon Fraser University Special Collections and Rare Books
Hawthornthwaite fonds
Marge Hollibaugh Women's Movement Collection
Occupy Vancouver Collection

University of British Columbia Rare Books and Special Collections
British Columbia Federation of Labour fonds
Frederic William Howay fonds
Homer Stevens fonds
Ian MacDonald Collection
Industrial Wood and Allied Workers fonds
International Brotherhood of Electric Workers Local 213 fonds
John Stanton fonds
New Democratic Party of British Columbia fonds
Thomas R. Berger fonds
United Fishermen and Allied Workers' Union fonds

University of Victoria Archives and Special Collections
Clayoquot Resource Centre fonds
Sierra Club fonds
Status of Women Action Group, Victoria Branch fonds
Victoria Labour Council fonds

Interviews

Guujaaw (Gary Edenshaw), interviewed by Benjamin Isitt, Vancouver, BC, May 25, 2015
Hewison, George, interviewed by Benjamin Isitt, Colwood, BC, April 14, 2013
Mullin, Michael, interviewed by Benjamin Isitt, Tofino, BC, May 24, 2013
Swain, Andrew, interviewed by Benjamin Isitt, Victoria, BC, April 16, 2013
Southin, Mary, interviewed by R. Mackey and G. Zilm, Vancouver, BC, November 22, 2012

Government Records

British Columbia. *Official Report of the Debates of the Legislative Assembly*, 1970–present.
British Columbia. *Report of Board of Reference into the British Columbia Civil Service Act*. Victoria: Queen's Printer, 1959.
British Columbia. *Vancouver Island Land Use Plan*, 2000.
British Columbia, Clayoquot Sound Scientific Panel. *Sustainable Ecosystem Management in Clayoquot Sound*. Victoria: Clayoquot Sound Scientific Panel, 1995.
British Columbia, Department of Labour. *Annual Reports*, 1900–present.
British Columbia, Elections British Columbia. *An Electoral History of British Columbia, 1871–1986*. Victoria: Elections British Columbia, 1988.
British Columbia, Ministry of Agriculture and Lands, Integrated Land Management Bureau. *Socio-Economic Assessment of Haida Gwaii/Queen Charlotte Islands Land Use Viewpoints: Final Report*. Vancouver: Pierce Lefebvre Consulting, 2006.
British Columbia, Ministry of Forests. *Meares Island Planning Options: Report of the Meares Island Planning Team*. Victoria: Ministry of Forests, 1983.
Canada. *Canada Gazette* (Ottawa). 1900–present.
Canada, Department of Labour. *Trade Union Law in Canada*. Ottawa: King's Printer, 1935.
Canada. *Labour Gazette* (Ottawa). 1900–present.
Canada, Law Reform Commission of Canada. *Contempt of Court: Offences Against the Administration of Justice, Working Paper 20*. Ottawa: Department of Justice Canada, 1977.
Canada. *Report of Debates of the Parliament of Canada*. 1900–present.
Canada. *Report of the Royal Commission on Coal Mining Disputes on Vancouver Island*. Ottawa: King's Printer, 1913.
Canada. *Report of the Royal Commission on Industrial Disputes in the Province of British Columbia*. Ottawa: King's Printer, 1903.
Canada. *Report of the Royal Commission on Industrial Relations*. Ottawa: King's Printer, 1919.
Canada, Statistics Canada. *Labour Force Historical Review*. 1970–present.

Newspapers

Alberni Valley Times (Port Alberni)
Brandon Sun
BC Federationist (Vancouver)
Calgary Herald
CBC News Online

Civil Liberties Digest (Vancouver)
Daily Colonist (Victoria)
Financial Post (Toronto)
The Fisherman (Vancouver)
Globe and Mail / Globe (Toronto)
Haada 'Las (Old Massett)
Haida Gwaii Observer (Queen Charlotte)
Ha-Shilth-Sa (Port Alberni)
Interior News (Smithers)
Labor Statesman (Vancouver)
Montreal Gazette
Nanaimo Free Press / Nanaimo Daily Free Press
Native Voice (Vancouver)
New York Times
Ottawa Citizen
Pacific Tribune (Vancouver)
Prince George Daily News
Rossland Telegraph
Times Colonist (Victoria)
Toronto Star
Ubyssey (Vancouver)
Vancouver Observer
Vancouver Daily Province / Vancouver Province / The Province
Vancouver Sun
Victoria Daily Times
Victoria News
Western Clarion
Winnipeg Free Press

Books

Abortion Caravan 2020 Coalition. *Then and Now, 1970–2020: Celebrating the 50th Anniversary of the 1970 Abortion Caravan*. Ottawa: Action Canada for Sexual Health and Rights, 2020.

Adey, Peter. *Mobility*. London: Routledge, 2010.

Alfred, Taiaiake. *Peace, Power, Righteousness: An Indigenous Manifesto*. Don Mills, ON: Oxford University Press, 1999.

Arnett, Chris. *The Terror of the Coast: Land Alienation and Colonial War on Vancouver Island and the Gulf Islands, 1849–1863*. Vancouver: Talonbooks, 1999.

Arthurs, H.W. *Collective Bargaining in the Public Sector: Five Models*. Ann Arbor Institute of Labor and Industrial Relations, University of Michigan-Wayne State University, 1971.

–. *Labour Disputes in Essential Industries*. Ottawa: Privy Council Office, 1968.

–. *'Without the Law': Administrative Justice and Legal Pluralism in Nineteenth-Century England*. Toronto: University of Toronto Press, 1985

Arthurs, H.W., D.D. Carter, J. Fudge, H. Glasbeek, G. Trudeau. *Labour Law and Industrial Relations in Canada*. 4th Edition. Markham: Butterworths, 1993.

Bacon, Matthew. *A New Abridgment of the Law: Volume 3*. 5th ed. London: Strahan, 1798.

Bakan, Joel. *The Corporation: The Pathological Pursuit of Profit and Power*. Toronto: Penguin, 2004.

Beare, Margaret E., Nathalie Des Rosiers and Abigail C. Deshman, eds. *Putting the State on Trial: The Policing of Protest During the G20 Summit*. Vancouver: UBC Press, 2015.

Beatty, David M. *Putting the Charter to Work: Designing a Constitutional Labour Code*. Montreal and Kingston: McGill-Queen's University Press, 1987.

Beckett, Katherine, and Steve Herbert. *Banished: The New Social Control in Urban America*. Oxford: Oxford University Press, 2010.

Belanger, Yale D., and P. Whitney Lackenbauer. *Blockades or Breakthroughs? Aboriginal Peoples Confront the Canadian State*. Montreal and Kingston: McGill-Queen's University Press, 2015.

Belshaw, John Douglas. *Colonization and Community: The Vancouver Island Coalfield and the Making of the British Columbian Working Class*. Montreal and Kingston: McGill-Queen's University Press, 2002.

Berger, Thomas R. *Injunctions in British Columbia*. Vancouver: British Columbia Federation of Labour, c. 1966.

Berman, Tzeporah, with Mark Leiren-Young. *This Crazy Time: Living Our Environmental Challenge*. Toronto: Alfred A. Knopf Canada, 2011.

Billingsley, James. *Claiming Poor Rights: Narratives of Shelter, Space, and Freedom in India and Canada*. Victoria: Centre for Asia-Pacific Initiatives, University of Victoria, 2013.

Blomley, Nicholas. *Law, Space, and the Geographies of Power*. New York: Guilford Press, 1994.

Borrows, John. *Canada's Indigenous Constitution*. Toronto: University of Toronto Press, 2010.

Bowen, Lynne. *Boss Whistle: The Coal Miners of Vancouver Island Remember*. Revised ed. Nanaimo: Rocky Point Books, 2003. First published 1982.

Braverman, Irus, Nicholas Blomley, and David Delaney, eds. *The Expanding Spaces of Law: A Timely Legal Geography*. Stanford, CA: Stanford University Press, 2014.

British Columbia Civil Liberties Association. *New British Columbia Labour Legislation, Civil Liberties Issues*. Vancouver: BCCLA, May 1974.

British Columbia Federation of Labour. *Convention Proceedings*, 1956–72.

–. *A Handbook on the Great Conspiracy*. Vancouver. 1965.

Cairns, Alan C. *Charter versus Federalism: The Dilemmas of Constitutional Reform*. Montreal and Kingston: McGill-Queen's University Press, 1992.

Carroll, William K. *Corporate Power and Canadian Capitalism*. Vancouver: UBC Press, 1986.

–. *Corporate Power in a Globalizing World: A Study of Elite Social Organization*. Toronto: Oxford University Press, 2004.

–. *The Making of a Transnational Capitalist Class: Corporate Power in the 21st Century*. London: Zed Books, 2010.

Carroll, William K., and Kanchan Sarker, eds. *A World to Win: Contemporary Social Movements and Counter-Hegemony*. Winnipeg: ARP Books, 2016.

Carrothers, A.W.R. *Collective Bargaining Law in Canada*. Toronto: Butterworths, 1965.

–. *Labour Arbitration in Canada: A Study of the Law and Practice Relating to the Arbitration of Grievance Disputes in Industrial Relations in Common Law Canada*. Toronto: Butterworths, 1961.

Carrothers, A.W.R. *The Labour Injunction in British Columbia: A Study of the Operation of the Injunction in Labour-Management Disputes in British Columbia, 1946–1955 with Particular Reference to the Law of Picketing.* Toronto and Montreal: CCH Canadian, 1956.

Cashore, Benjamin, et al., eds. *In Search of Sustainability: Forest Policy in British Columbia in the 1990s.* Vancouver: UBC Press, 2000.

Castree, Noel, et al. *Spaces of Work: Global Capitalism and Geographies of Labour.* London: Sage, 2004.

Chakravarty-Kaul, Minoti. *Common Lands and Customary Law: Institutional Change in North India over the Past Two Centuries.* Oxford: Oxford University Pres, 1996.

Christie, I.M. *The Liability of Strikers in the Law of Tort.* Kingston, ON: Industrial Relations Centre, Queen's University, 1967.

Clark, Bruce. *Justice in Paradise.* Montreal and Kingston: McGill-Queen's University Press, 2004.

–. *Native Liberty, Crown Sovereignty: The Existing Aboriginal Right of Self-Government in Canada.* Montreal and Kingston: McGill-Queen's University Press, 1990.

Clark, Samuel, J. Paul Grayson, and Linda M. Grayson, eds. *Prophecy and Protest: Social Movements in Twentieth-Century Canada.* Toronto: Gage, 1975.

Clayoquot Sound Scientific Panel. *Report of the Scientific Panel for Sustainable Forest Practices in Clayoquot Sound.* Victoria: Clayoquot Sound Scientific Panel, January 1994.

Clayton, Daniel. *Islands of Truth: The Imperial Fashioning of Vancouver Island.* Vancouver: UBC Press, 2000.

Clément, Dominique. *Canada's Rights Revolution: Social Movements and Social Change, 1937–82.* Vancouver: UBC Press, 2008.

–. *Equality Deferred: Sex Discrimination and British Columbia's Human Rights State, 1953–84.* Vancouver: UBC Press, 2014.

Clyne, J.V. *Jack of All Trades: Memories of a Busy Life.* Toronto: McClelland and Stewart, 1992.

Collison, Jisgang Nika, ed. *Athlii Gwaii: Upholding the Law at Lyell Island.* Vancouver: Locarno Press, 2018.

Corrigan, Philip and Derek Sayer. *The Great Arch: English State Formation as Cultural Revolution.* New York: Basil Blackwell, 1985.

Coulthard, Glen Sean. *Red Skin, White Masks: Rejecting the Colonial Politics of Recognition.* Minneapolis: University of Minnesota Press, 2014.

Cram, Ian, ed. *Borrie and Lowe: The Law of Contempt.* 4th ed. London: LexisNexis Butterworths, 2010.

Craven, Paul. *'An Impartial Umpire': Industrial Relations and the Canadian State, 1900–1911.* Toronto: University of Toronto Press, 1980.

Cresswell, Timothy. *The Tramp in America.* London: Reaktion Books, 2001.

Dworkin, Ronald. *Law's Empire.* Cambridge, Mass.: Belknap, 1986.

Eber, Dorothy. *Images of Justice: A Legal History of the Northwest Territories as Traced Through the Yellowknife Courthouse Collection of Inuit Sculpture.* Montreal and Kingston: McGill-Queen's University Press, 1997.

Foster, Hamar, Heather Raven, and Jeremy Webber, eds. *Let Right Be Done: Aboriginal Title, the* Calder *Case, and the Future of Indigenous Rights.* Vancouver: UBC Press, 2007.

Fox, John. *The History of Contempt of Court.* London: Professional Books, 1972.

Fudge, Judy, and Eric Tucker. *Labour Before the Law: The Regulation of Workers' Collective Action in Canada, 1900–1948*. Toronto: Oxford University Press, 2001.

–, eds. *Work on Trial: Canadian Labour Law Struggles*. Toronto: Irwin, 2010.

Gill, Ian. *All That We Say Is Ours: Guujaaw and the Reawakening of the Haida Nation*. Toronto: Douglas and McIntyre, 2009.

Gillis, R. Peter, and Thomas R. Roach. *Lost Initiatives: Canada's Forest Industries, Forest Policy, and Forest Conservation*. New York: Greenwood Press, 1986.

Girard, Philip. *Bora Laskin: Bringing Law to Life*. Toronto: Osgoode Society for Canadian Legal History, 2005.

Gough, Barry M. *Gunboat Frontier: British Maritime Authority and Northwest Coast Indians, 1846–90*. Vancouver: UBC Press, 1984.

Gregson, Harry. *A History of Victoria 1842–1970*. Victoria: Victoria Observer Publishing Co., 1970.

Griffin, J.A.G. *The Politics of the Judiciary*. London: Fontana, 1977.

Harris, R. Cole. *Making Native Space: Colonialism, Resistance, and Reserves in British Columbia*. Vancouver: UBC Press, 2003.

Hart, H.L.A. *The Concept of Law*. London: Oxford University Press, 1961.

Harvey, David. *Rebel Cities: From the Right to the City to the Urban Revolution*. London: Verso, 2012.

Hatch, Ronald B., ed. *Clayoquot & Dissent*. Vancouver: Ronsdale, 1995.

Hay, Douglas, and Paul Craven, eds. *Masters, Servants, and Magistrates in Britain and the Empire, 1562–1955*. Chapel Hill and London: University of North Carolina Press, 1994.

Henein, Marie, ed. *2018 Martin's Annual Criminal Code – Student Edition*. Toronto: Thomson Reuters, 2017.

Herod, Andrew. *Geographies of Globalization: A Critical Introduction*. Oxford: Wiley-Blackwell, 2009.

Hill, Christopher. *The World Turned Upside Down: Radical Ideas During the English Revolution*. London: Maurice Temple Smith, 1972.

Hinde, John R. *When Coal Was King: Ladysmith and the Coal-Mining Industry of Vancouver Island*. Vancouver: UBC Press, 2004.

Holder, Jane, and Carolyn Harrison. *Law and Geography*. New York: Oxford, 2003.

Hopkins, J. Castell. *Canadian Annual Review of Public Affairs*. Toronto: Annual Review Publishing Company, 1913.

Isitt, Benjamin. *Militant Minority: British Columbia Workers and the Rise of a New Left, 1948–1972*. Toronto: University of Toronto Press, 2011.

Jamieson, Stuart Marshall. *Industrial Relations in Canada*. Toronto: Macmillan, 1973.

Jamieson, Stuart Marshall. *Times of Trouble: Labour Unrest and Industrial Conflict in Canada, 1900–1966*. Ottawa: Task Force on Labour Relations, 1968.

Johnstone, Rachael. *After Morgentaler: The Politics of Abortion in Canada*. Vancouver: UBC Press, 2017.

Knoke, David, and James H. Kuklinski. *Network Analysis*. London: Sage, 1982.

Knoke, David. *Political Networks: The Structural Perspective*. Cambridge: Cambridge University Press, 1990.

Knoke, David, and Song Yang. *Social Network Analysis*. Revised ed. London: Sage, 2007.

Lambertson, Ross. *Repression and Resistance: Canadian Human Rights Activists, 1930–1960*. Toronto: University of Toronto Press, 2004.

Lambertus, Sandra. *Wartime Images, Peacetime Wounds: The Media and the Gustafsen Lake Standoff*. Toronto: University of Toronto Press, 2004.

Leier, Mark. *Rebel Life: The Life and Times of Robert Gosden, Revolutionary, Mystic, Labour Spy*. Revised Edition. Vancouver: New Star Books, 2013.

Lipton, Charles. *The Trade Union Movement of Canada 1827–1959*. Toronto, NC Press, 1978.

Logan, Harold. *State Intervention and Assistance in Collective Bargaining: The Canadian Experience, 1943–1954*. Toronto: University of Toronto Press, 1956.

Loo, Tina. *Making Law, Order and Authority in British Columbia, 1821–1871*. Toronto: University of Toronto Press, 1994.

Lowe, Stuart. *Urban Social Movements: The City After Castells*. London: Macmillan, 1986.

MacIsaac, Ronald, and Anne Champagne, eds. *Clayoquot Mass Trials: Defending the Rainforest*. Gabriola Island, BC: New Society, 1994.

Magnusson, Warren and Karena Shaw, eds. *A Political Space: Reading the Global through Clayoquot Sound*. Montreal and Kingston: McGill-Queen's University Press, 2002.

Marx, Karl, and Friedrich Engels. *Manifesto of the Communist Party*. London: Verso, 1998. Originally published 1848.

Massey, Doreen. *Space, Place, and Gender*. Minneapolis: University of Minnesota Press, 1994.

–. *Spatial Divisions of Labour: Social Structures and the Geography of Production*. New York: Methuen, 1984; 2nd ed., New York: Routledge, 1995.

May, Elizabeth. *Paradise Won: The Struggle for South Moresby*. Toronto: McClelland and Stewart, 1990.

Mayse, Susan. *Ginger: The Life and Death of Albert Goodwin*. Madeira Park, BC: Harbour Publishing, 1990.

McCormack, A. Ross. *Reformers, Rebels, and Revolutionaries: The Western Canadian Radical Movement, 1899–1919*. Toronto: University of Toronto Press, 1977.

McDonald, Robert A.J. *Making Vancouver: Class, Status and Social Boundaries, 1863–1913*. Vancouver: UBC Press 1996.

McInnis, Peter. *Harnessing Labour Confrontation: Shaping the Postwar Settlement in Canada, 1943–1950*. Toronto: University of Toronto Press, 2002.

McLean, Bruce. *A Union Amongst Government Employees: A History of the B.C. Government Employees Union 1919–1979*. Vancouver: BCGEU, 1979.

McNab, David T. *No Place for Fairness: Indigenous Land Rights and Policy in the Bear Island Case and Beyond*. Montreal and Kingston: McGill-Queen's University Press, 2009.

Meggs, Geoff, and Rod Mickleburgh. *The Art of the Impossible: Dave Barrett and the NDP in Power, 1972–1975*. Madeira Park, BC: Harbour Publishing, 2012.

Molinaro, Dennis G. *An Exceptional Law: Section 98 and the Emergency State, 1919–1936*. Toronto: University of Toronto Press, 2017.

Monet, Don and Skanu'u (Ardythe Wilson). *Colonialism on Trial: Indigenous Land Rights and the Gitksan and Wet'suwet'en Sovereignty Case*. Gabriola Island, BC: New Society, 1992.

Moore, Christopher. *The British Columbia Court of Appeal: The First Hundred Years*. Vancouver: UBC Press, 2010.

Morton, F.L., ed. *Law, Politics and the Judicial Process in Canada*. 3rd ed. Calgary: University of Calgary Press, 2002.

Mychajlowycz, Maryjka. *Overview of Logging in Clayoquot Sound: 2000–2009*. Tofino, BC: Friends of Clayoquot Sound, 2009.

Neeson, J.M. *Commoners: Common Right, Enclosure and Social Change in England, 1700–1820*. Cambridge: Cambridge University Press, 1992.

North, George. *A Ripple, a Wave: The Story of Union Organization in the B.C. Fishing Industry*. Revised and edited by Harold Griffin. Vancouver: Fisherman Publishing Society, 1974.

Orth, John V. *Combination and Conspiracy: A Legal History of Trade Unionism, 1721–1906*. Oxford: Oxford University Press, 1991.

Panitch, Leo, and Donald Swartz. *From Consent to Coercion: The Assault on Trade Union Freedoms*. 3rd ed. Toronto: Garamond, 2003.

Pasternak, Shiri, and Hayden King. *Land Back: A Yellowhead Institute Red Paper*. Toronto: Yellowhead Institute, 2019.

Perry. Adele. *On the Edge of Empire: Gender, Race, and the Making of British Columbia, 1849–1871*. Toronto: University of Toronto Press, 2001.

Phillips, Paul A. *No Power Greater: A Century of Labour in British Columbia*. Vancouver: Boag Foundation, 1967.

Pinch, Diane. *Passion and Persistence: Fifty Years of the Sierra Club of British Columbia*. Madeira Park, BC: Harbour Publishing, 2019.

Piven, Frances Fox, and Richard A. Cloward. *Poor People's Movements: Why They Succeed, How They Fail*. New York: Pantheon, 1977.

Pralle, Sarah B. *Branching Out, Digging In: Environmental Advocacy and Agenda Setting*. Washington, DC: Georgetown University Press, 2006.

Pue, W. Wesley. *Law School: The Story of Legal Education in British Columbia*. Vancouver: Continuing Legal Education Society of British Columbia/Faculty of Law, University of British Columbia, 1995.

Rajala, Richard A. *Clearcutting the Pacific Rain Forest: Production, Science, and Regulation*. Vancouver: UBC Press, 1999.

Rankin, Harry. *Rankin's Law: Recollections of a Radical*. Vancouver: November House, 1975.

Rebick, Judy. *Ten Thousand Roses: The Making of a Feminist Revolution*. Toronto: Penguin Canada, 2005.

Robin, Martin. *The Rush for Spoils: The Company Province, 1871–1933*. Toronto: McClelland and Stewart, 1972.

–. *Pillars of Profit: The Company Province, 1934–1972*. Toronto: McClelland and Stewart, 1973.

Rutherford, Scott. *Canada's Other Red Scare: Indigenous Protest and Colonial Encounters During the Global Sixties*. Montreal and Kingston: McGill-Queen's University Press, 2020.

Sayer, Derek. *The Violence of Abstraction: The Analytical Foundations of Historical Materialism*. New York: Basil Blackwell, 1987.

Selekman, Ben M. *Postponing Strikes: A Study of the Industrial Disputes Investigation Act of Canada*. New York: Russell Sage Foundation, 1927.

Splitting the Sky. *The Autobiography of Splitting the Sky: From Attica to Gustafsen Lake*. Chase, BC: John Pasquale Boncore, 2001.

Staeheli, Lynn A., and Don Mitchell. *The Peoples' Property? Power, Politics, and the Public*. New York: Routledge, 2008.

Stanton, John. *My Past Is Now: Further Memoirs of a Labour Lawyer.* St John's: Canadian Committee on Labour History, 1994.

Stanton, John. *Never Say Die! The Life and Times of John Stanton, a Pioneer Labour Lawyer.* Ottawa: Steel Rail, 1987.

Stevens, Homer, and Rolf Knight. *Homer Stevens: A Life in Fishing.* Madeira Park, BC: Harbour Publishing, 1992.

Stonebanks, Roger. *Fighting for Dignity: The Ginger Goodwin Story.* St. John's: Canadian Committee on Labour History, 2004.

Swayze, Cleon Oliphant. *Contempt of Court in Labor Injunction Cases.* New York: Columbia University Press, 1935.

Takeda, Louise. *Islands' Spirit Rising: Reclaiming the Forests of Haida Gwaii.* Vancouver: UBC Press, 2015.

Thomson, Ann. *Winning Choice on Abortion: How British Columbia and Canadian Feminists Won the Battles of the 1970s and 1980s.* Vancouver: Trafford, 2005.

Thompson, E.P. *Customs in Common: Studies in Traditional Popular Culture.* New York: New Press, 1992.

–. *Whigs and Hunters: The Origin of the Black Act.* London: Pantheon, 1975.

Tigar, Michael E., and Madeleine R. Levy. *Law and the Rise of Capitalism.* 2nd ed. New York: Monthly Review Press, 2000. Originally published 1977.

Touraine, Alain. *The Voice and the Eye: An Analysis of Social Movements.* Cambridge: Cambridge University Press, 1981.

Valverde, Mariana. *Chronotopes of Law: Jurisdiction, Scale and Governance.* London: Routledge, 2015.

Walker, James W. St. G. *"Race," Rights and the Law in the Supreme Court of Canada: Historical Case Studies.* Waterloo, ON: Wilfrid Laurier University Press, 1997.

Weiler, Joseph M. and Peter A. Gall, eds. *The Labour Code of British Columbia in the 1980's.* Calgary and Vancouver: Carswell Legal Publishers, 1984.

Weiler, Paul C. *Reconcilable Differences: New Directions in Canadian Labour Law.* Toronto: Carswell, 1980.

Wilson, Jeremy. *Talk and Log: Wilderness Politics in British Columbia.* Vancouver: UBC Press, 1998.

Wood, James. *Militia Myths: Ideas of the Canadian Citizen Soldier.* Vancouver: UBC Press, 2010.

Wright, Barry, Eric Tucker, and Susan Binnie, eds. *Canadian State Trials, Volume IV: Security, Dissent, and the Limits of Toleration in War and Peace, 1914–1939.* Toronto: University of Toronto Press, 2015.

Zelko, Frank. *Make It a Green Peace! The Rise of Countercultural Environmentalism.* Oxford: Oxford University Press, 2013.

Zick, Timothy. *Speech Out of Doors: Preserving First Amendment Liberties in Public Places.* New York: Cambridge University Press, 2009.

Articles

Abella, Irving. "Communism and Anti-Communism in the British Columbia Labour Movement, 1940–1948." In *Western Perspectives 1: Papers of the Western Canadian Studies Conference, 1973,* edited by David Jay Bercuson, 88–100 (Toronto and Montreal: Holt, Rinehart and Winston, 1974).

Abraham, Steven E. "The Impact of the Taft-Hartley Act on the Balance of Power in Industrial Relations." *American Business Law Journal,* 33:3 (Spring 1996): 341–63.

Alexander, Basil. "Demonstrations and the Law: Patterns of Law's Negative Effects on the Ground and the Practical Implications." *UBC Law Review* 49, 3 (November 2016): 869–930.

–. "Exploring a More Independent Freedom of Peaceful Assembly in Canada." *Western Journal of Legal Studies* 8, 1 (March 2018): 1–20.

Arbitise, Alan F.J. "'A Worthy, if Unlikely, Enterprise': The Labour Relations Board and the Evolution of Labour Policy and Practice in British Columbia, 1973–1980." *BC Studies* 56 (Winter 1982): 3–43.

Arthurs, H.W. "'The Dullest Bill': Reflections on the Labour Code of British Columbia." *UBC Law Review* 9 (1974): 280–340.

–. "Landscape and Memory: Labour Law, Legal Pluralism, and Globalization." In *Advancing Theory in Labour Law and Industrial Relations in a Global Context,* edited by T. Wilthagen, 21–34. Amsterdam: Koninklijke Nederlandse Akademie van Wetenschappen, 1998.

Ashenfelter, Orley, Theodore Eisenberg, and Stewart J. Schwab. "Politics and the Judiciary: The Influence of Judicial Background on Case Outcomes." *Journal of Legal Studies* 24, 2 (June 1995): 257–81.

Attaran, Amir. "*Mandamus* in the Enforcement of the Criminal Law: Ending the Anti-Protest Injunction Habit – Issues Arising from MacMillan Bloedel v. Simpson." *UBC Law Review* 33, 1 (1999): 181–97.

Azuela, Antonio, and Rodrigo Meneses-Reyes. "The Everyday Formation of the Urban Space: Law and Poverty in Mexico City." In *The Expanding Spaces of Law: A Timely Legal Geography,* edited by Irus Braverman, Nicholas Blomley, and David Delaney, 167–89. Stanford, CA: Stanford University Press, 2014.

Belleau, Marie-Claire, and Rebecca Johnson. "Judging Gender: Difference and Dissent at the Supreme Court of Canada." *International Journal of the Legal Profession* 15, 1–2 (2008): 57–71.

Benson, Melinda Harm. "Rules of Engagement: The Spatiality of Judicial Review." In *The Expanding Spaces of Law: A Timely Legal Geography,* edited by Irus Braverman, Nicholas Blomley, and David Delaney, 215–38. Stanford, CA: Stanford University Press, 2014.

Bhandar, Brenna. "Disassembling Legal Form: Ownership and the Racial Body." In *New Critical Legal Thinking: Law and the Political,* edited by Matthew Stone, Illan Wall, and Costas Douzinas, 112–27. Abingdon, UK: Birkbeck Law Press, 2012.

Blomley, Nicholas. "Law, Property, and the Geography of Violence: The Frontier, the Survey, and the Grid." *Annals of the Association of American Geographers* 93, 1 (2003): 121–41.

–. "Performing Property: Making the World." *Canadian Journal of Law and Jurisprudence* 26, 1 (January 2013): 23–48.

–. "'Shut the Province Down': First Nations Blockades in British Columbia, 1984–1995." *BC Studies* 111 (Autumn 1996): 5–35.

Boer, R.W.J. and J. de Vries, "The Right to the City as a Tool for Urban Social Movements: The Case of Barceloneta." Paper presented to 4th International Conference of the International Forum on Urbanism, Amsterdam, 2009.

Borrows, John. "Indigenous Legal Traditions." *Journal of Law and Policy* 19 (2005): 167–223.
–. "With or Without You: First Nations Law (in Canada)." *McGill Law Journal* 41 (1996): 629–65.
Borrows, John, and Leonard I. Rotman. "The *Sui Generis* Nature of Aboriginal Rights: Does It Make a Difference?" *Alberta Law Review* 36, 1 (1997): 9–45.
Bourgeois, Donald J. "The Role of the Historian in the Litigation Process." *Canadian Historical Review* 67, 2 (June 1986): 195–206.
Bowker, Andrea. "*Sparrow*'s Promise: Aboriginal Rights in the BC Court of Appeal." *University of Toronto Law Review* 53 (Winter 1995): 1–48.
Brown, Richard. "Picketing: Canadian Courts and the Labour Relations Board of British Columbia." *University of Toronto Law Journal* 31, 2 (Spring 1981): 153–99.
Cairns, Alan C. "The Judicial Committee and Its Critics." *Canadian Journal of Political Science* 4, 3 (September 1971): 301–45.
Carroll, William K. and R.S. Ratner. "The NDP Regime in British Columbia: A Post Mortem." In *Challenges and Perils: Social Democracy in Neoliberal Times,* edited by William K. Carroll and R.S. Ratner, 105–36. Halifax: Fernwood, 2005.
–. "Social Movements and Counter-Hegemony: Lessons from the Field." *New Proposals: Journal of Marxism and Interdisciplinary Inquiry* 4, 1 (October 2010): 7–22.
Camfield, David. "Comment: Analyzing the 2004 HEU Strike and Union Bureaucracy." *Studies in Political Economy* 84 (Autumn 2009): 181–90.
–. "CUPE's Sympathy Strikes in British Columbia, October 2005: Raising the Bar for Solidarity." *Just Labour: A Canadian Journal of Work and Society* 11 (Autumn 2007): 35–42.
–. "Neoliberalism and Working-Class Resistance in British Columbia: The Hospital Employees' Union Struggle, 2002–2004." *Labour/Le Travail* 57 (Spring 2006): 9–42.
–. "Sympathy for the Teacher: Labour Law and Transgressive Workers' Collective Action in British Columbia, 2005." *Capital and Class* 99 (2009): 81–107.
Carrothers, A.W.R. "British Columbia Labour Relations Act Amendment Act, 1961." *University of Toronto Law Journal,* 14, no. 2 (1962): 263–68.
–. "The British Columbia Trade-Unions Act, 1959." *University of Toronto Law Journal,* 13, no. 2 (1960): 278–81.
–. "The Labour Injunction in Canada." *Relations industrielles / Industrial Relations,* 13, no. 1 (1958): 2–27.
–. "Legislative History of the BC Trade-Unions Act: The Rossland Miners Case." *UBC Legal Notes* 2, 4 (March 1956): 339–46.
–. "Recent Developments in the Tort Law of Picketing." *Canadian Bar Review,* 35, no. 9 (November 1957): 1005.
–. "The Right to Picket in British Columbia: A Study in Statute Interpretation." *University of Toronto Law Journal,* 9, no. 2 (1952): 250–87.
Ceric, Irina. "Beyond Contempt: Injunctions, Land Defense, and the Criminalization of Indigenous Resistance." *South Atlantic Quarterly* 119, 2 (April 2020): 353–69.
Chambliss, William J. "The State, the Legal Order, and Social Problems." In *Social Problems, Law, and Society,* edited by Kathryn A. Stout et al., 405–18. Oxford: Rowman and Littlefield, 2004).
Christie, Gordon. "Indigeneity and Sovereignty in Canada's Far North: The Arctic and Inuit Sovereignty." *South Atlantic Quarterly* 110, 2 (2011): 329–46.

Clapperton, Jonathan. "Environmental Activism as Anti-Conquest: The Nuu-chah-nulth and Environmentalists in the Contact Zone of Clayoquot Sound." In *Environmental Activism on the Ground: Small Green and Indigenous Organizing*, edited by Jonathan Clapperton and Liza Piper, 181–205. Calgary: University of Calgary Press, 2018.

Clark, Gordon L. "A Question of Integrity: The National Labor Relations Board, Collective Bargaining and the Relocation of Work." *Political Geography Quarterly* 7, 3 (July 1988): 209–27.

Craven, Paul. "Workers' Conspiracies in Toronto, 1854–72." *Labour/Le Travail* 14 (Fall 1984): 49–70.

Dickinson, G.M., and R.D. Gidney. "History and Advocacy: Some Reflections on the Historian's Role in Litigation." *Canadian Historical Review*, 68:4 (December 1987): 576–85.

Duffy, Aoife. "Indigenous Peoples' Land Rights: Developing a Sui Generis Approach to Ownership and Restitution." *International Journal on Minority and Group Rights* 15, 4 (November 2008): 505–38.

Dyzenhaus, David. "The Legitimacy of Legality." *University of Toronto Law Journal*, 46, no. 1 (Winter 1996): 129–80.

Eagleton, Terry. "Base and Superstructure Revisited." *New Literary History* 31, 2 (Spring 2000): 231–40.

Earl, Jennifer. "Controlling Protest: New Directions for Research on the Social Control of Protest." In *Authority in Contention: Research in Social Movements, Conflicts and Change*, edited by Daniel J. Myers and Daniel M. Cress (Bingley, UK: Emerald, 2004): 55–83.

Echlin, Randall S. "From Master and Servant to McKinley and Beyond: 200 Years of Employment Law in British Columbia, 1810 to 2010." In *Employment Law Conference, 2010 – Day 1*, 1–41. Vancouver: Continuing Legal Education Society of British Columbia, 2010.

Egan, Brian. "Towards Shared Ownership: Property, Geography and Treaty Making in British Columbia." *Geografiska Annaler* 95, 1 (March 2013): 33–50.

Fabris (Krebs), Michael. "Decolonizing Neoliberalism? First Nations Reserves, Private Property Rights, and the Legislation of Indigenous Dispossession in Canada." In *Contested Property Claims: What Disagreement Tells Us About Ownership*, edited by Maja Hojer Bruun et al., 185–204. London: Routledge, 2018.

Finkelman, Jacob. "The Law of Picketing in Canada: I." *University of Toronto Law Journal*, 2:1 (1938): 67–102.

–. "The Law of Picketing In Canada: II." *University of Toronto Law Journal*, 2:2 (1938): 344–60.

Fisher, E.G. "Strike Activity and Wildcat Strikes in British Columbia: 1945–1975." *Relations industrielles/Industrial Relations*, vol. 37, no. 2 (1982): 284–312.

Foster, Hamar. "British Columbia: Legal Institutions in the Far West, from Contact to 1871." *Manitoba Law Journal* 23 (1996): 293–340.

–. "Mutiny on the Beaver: Law and Authority in the Fur Trade Navy, 1835–1840." *Manitoba Law Journal* 20 (1991): 15–45.

–. "Roadblocks and Legal History, Part I: Do Forgotten Cases Make Good Law?" *The Advocate* 54, 3 (May 1996): 355–56.

–. "Roadblocks and Legal History, Part II: Aboriginal Title and s. 91(24)." *The Advocate* 54, 4 (July 1996): 531–46.

Foster, Hamar, and John McLaren. "'For the Better Administration of Justice': The Court of Appeal for British Columbia, 1910–2010." *BC Studies* 162 (Summer 2009): 5–24.
Foucault, Michel. "The Subject and Power." *Critical Inquiry* 8 (Summer 1982): 777–95.
Frogner, Raymond. "'Innocent Legal Fictions': Archival Convention and the North Saanich Treaty of 1852." *Archivaria* 70 (Fall 2010): 45–94.
Fudge, Judy. "Brave New Worlds: Labour, the Courts, and the Canadian Charter of Rights and Freedoms." *Windsor Year Book of Access to Justice* 28, 1 (2010): 39–40.
–. "The Supreme Court of Canada and the Right to Bargain Collectively: The Implications of the Health Services and Support Case in Canada and Beyond." *Industrial Law Journal* 37, 1 (March 2008): 25–48.
Fudge, Judy and Harry Glasbeek. "Civil Disobedience, Civil Liberties and Civil Resistance: Law's Role and Limits." *Osgoode Hall Law Journal,* 41, no. 2 and 3 (2003): 165–73.
Fudge, Judy, and Eric Tucker, "'Everybody Knows What a Picket Line Means': Picketing Before the British Columbia Court of Appeal." *BC Studies* 162 (Summer 2009): 53–79.
–. "The Freedom to Strike in Canada: A Brief Legal History." *Canadian Labour and Employment Law Journal* 15 (2009–10): 333–53.
Glasbeek, Harry. "Class War: Ontario Teachers and the Courts." *Osgoode Hall Law Journal* 37, 4 (1999): 805–42.
Goldberg-Hiller, Jonathan. "The Boycott of the Law and the Law of Boycott: Law, Labour, and Politics in British Columbia." *Law and Social Inquiry* 21, 2 (April 1996): 313–51.
Grove, Alan, and Ross Lambertson. "Pawns of the Powerful: The Politics of Litigation in the Union Colliery Case." *BC Studies* 103 (Fall 1994): 3–31.
Hamill, Sarah E. "Private Property Rights and Public Responsibility: Leaving Room for the Homeless." *Windsor Review of Legal and Social Issues* 30 (2011): 91–116.
–. "Private Rights to Public Property: The Evolution of Common Property in Canada." *McGill Law Journal* 58 (2012): 365–403.
Hanna, Alan. "Making the Round: Aboriginal Title in the Common Law from a Tsilhqot'in Legal Perspective." *Ottawa Law Review* 45, 3 (2015): 365–402.
Harding, James. "The New Left in British Columbia." In *The New Left in Canada,* edited by Dimitrios I. Roussopolous, 17–40. Montreal: Black Rose, c. 1970.
Harter, John-Henry. "Environmental Justice for Whom? Class, New Social Movements, and the Environment: A Case Study of Greenpeace Canada, 1971–2000." *Labour/Le Travail* 54 (Fall 2004): 83–119.
Hatch, Ronald B. "The Clayoquot Protests: Taking Stock One Year Later." In *Clayoquot & Dissent,* edited by Ronald B. Hatch, 199–208 (Vancouver: Ronsdale, 1995).
Hay, Douglas. "Time, Inequality, and Law's Violence." In *Law's Violence,* edited by Austin Sarat and Thomas R. Kearns, 141–73 (Ann Arbor: University of Michigan Press, 1993).
Hayter, Roger. "'The War in the Woods': Post-Fordist Restructuring, Globalization, and the Contested Remapping of British Columbia's Forest Economy." *Annals of the Association of American Geographers* 93, 3 (September 2003): 706–29.
Herod, Andrew. "Workers, Space, and Labor Geography." *International Labor and Working Class History* 64 (Fall 2003): 112–38.
Hinke, C.J. "Letters from Gaol: The Prison Experience of a Tree Protector." *Journal of Prisoners on Prisons* 2, 2 (Spring 1990): 43–48.
Horwitz, Morton J. "The Conservative Tradition in American Legal History." American *Journal of Legal History* 17, 3 (July 1973): 275–94.

Hurl, Chris. "The Structure of Betrayal: Trade Union Bureaucracy and Public Sector Struggles in British Columbia." *Studies in Political Economy* 83 (Spring 2009): 141–61.

Hyde, Alan. "The Concept of Legitimation in the Sociology of Law." *Wisconsin Law Review* 17 (1983): 379–426.

Isitt, Benjamin, and Melissa Moroz. "The Hospital Employees Union Strike and the Privatization of Medicare in British Columbia, Canada." *International Labor and Working-Class History* 71 (Spring 2007): 91–111.

Jamieson, Stuart Marshall. "Regional Factors in Industrial Conflict: The Case of British Columbia." *Canadian Journal of Economics and Political Science* 28, 3 (August 1962): 405–16.

Kelly, Alfred H. "Clio and the Court: An Illicit Love Affair." *Supreme Court Review* 1965 (1965): 119–58.

Koshan, Jennifer. "I Fought the Law: Civil Disobedience and the Law in Canada." ABlawg.ca (blog), University of Calgary Faculty of Law, February 27, 2012, http://ablawg.ca/wp-content/uploads/2012/02/blog_jk_occupy_feb2012.pdf.

Lamb, W. Kaye. "Introduction: A Bibliography of the Printed Writings of Frederic William Howay." *British Columbia Historical Quarterly* 8, 1 (January 1944): 27–32.

Lambertson, Ross. "The BC Court of Appeal and Civil Liberties." *BC Studies*, 162 (Summer 2009): 81–109.

Laskin, Bora. "The Labour Injunction in Canada: A Caveat." *Canadian Bar Review* 15 (1937): 270–83.

–. "Labour Law: 1923–47." *Canadian Bar Review* 26 (1948): 286–94.

–. "Picketing: A Comparison of Certain Canadian and American Doctrines." *Canadian Bar Review*, 15 (1937): 10–19.

Lefebvre, Henri. "Le Droit à la ville." *L'Homme et la société* 6 (1967): 29–35.

Leier, Mark. "Mairs, Joseph." In *Dictionary of Canadian Biography*, vol. 14, University of Toronto / Université Laval, 2003–, https://www.biographi.ca/en/bio/mairs_joseph_14E.html.

Macgillivray, Don. "Military Aid to the Civil Power: The Cape Breton Experience in the 1920's." *Acadiensis* 3, 2 (Spring 1974): 45–64.

MacKinnon, Peter. "Conspiracy and Sedition as Canadian Political Crimes." *McGill Law Journal* 23 (1977): 622–43.

MacPhee, Katrin. "Canadian Working-Class Environmentalism, 1965–1985." *Labour/Le Travail* 74 (Fall 2014): 123–49.

McCreary, Tyler. "Between the Commodity and the Gift: The Coastal GasLink Pipeline and the Contested Temporalities of Canadian and Witsuwit'en Law." *Journal of Human Rights and the Environment* 11 (December 2020): 122–45.

–. "The Burden of Sovereignty: Court Configurations of Indigenous and State Authority in Aboriginal Title Litigation in Canada." *North American Dialogue* 17, 2 (2014): 64–78.

–. "Historicizing the Encounter between State, Corporate, and Indigenous Authorities on Gitxsan Lands." *Windsor Yearbook of Access to Justice* 33, 3 (2016): 163–97.

McCreary, Tyler, and Jerome Turner. "The Contested Scales of Indigenous and Settler Jurisdiction: Unist'ot'en Struggles with Canadian Pipeline Governance." *Studies in Political Economy* 99, 3 (February 2019): 1–23.

M'Gonigle, Michael. "Green Legal Theory: A New Approach to the Concept of Environmental Law." *Okologisches-Wirtschaften* 4 (2008): 34–38.

Massey, Doreen. "Power-Geometry and a Progressive Sense of Place." In *Mapping the Futures: Local Cultures, Global Change,* edited by Jon Bird, Barry Curtis, Tim Putnam, George Robertson, and Lisa Tickner, 59–69. London: Routledge, 1993.

Massey, Jonathan, and Brett Snyder. "Occupying Wall Street: Places and Spaces of Political Action." *Places* (September 2012).

Meneses-Reyes, Rodrigo, and José A. Caballero-Juárez. "The Right to Work on the Street: Public Space and Constitutional Rights." *Planning Theory* 13, 4 (November 2014): 370–86.

Midanik, S. "Problems of Legislation Relating to Collective Bargaining." *Canadian Journal of Economics and Political Science,* 9:3 (August 1943): 348–56.

Milloy, Jeremy. "'Chrysler Pulled The Trigger': Competing Understandings of Workplace Violence During the 1970s and Radical Legal Practice." *Labour/Le Travail* 74 (Fall 2014): 51–88.

Mitchell, Don. "Anti-Homeless Laws and Public Space: 1. Begging and the First Amendment." *Urban Geography* 19, 1 (1998): 6–11.

–. "The S.U.V. Model of Citizenship: Floating Bubbles, Buffer Zones, and the Rise of the 'Purely Atomic' Individual." *Political Geography* 24, 1 (January 2005): 77–100.

Mitchell, Don, and Lynn A. Staeheli. "Permitting Protest: Parsing the Fine Geography of Dissent in America." *International Journal of Urban and Regional Research* 29, 4 (December 2005): 796–813.

Morris, Martin J. "Overcoming the Barricades: The Crisis at Oka as a Case Study in Political Communication." *Journal of Canadian Studies* 30 (Summer 1995): 74–90.

Morton, Desmond. "Aid to the Civil Power: The Canadian Militia in Support of Social Order, 1867–1914." *Canadian Historical Review* 51, 4 (1970): 407–25.

Mouat, Jeremy. "The Genesis of Western Exceptionalism: British Columbia's Hard Rock Miners, 1895–1903." *Canadian Historical Review* 71, 3 (September 1990): 317–45.

–. "The Politics of Coal: A Study of the Wellington Miners' Strike of 1890–91." *BC Studies* 77 (Spring 1988): 3–29.

Nemetz, Nathan Theodore. "Concept of an Independent Judiciary." *UBC Law Review* 20 (1986): 285–96.

Nicol, Janet Mary. "'Not to Be Bought, Nor for Sale': The Trials of Joseph Edward Bird." *Labour/Le Travail* 78 (Fall 2016): 219–36.

–. "'Unions Aren't Native': The Muckamuck Restaurant Labour Dispute, Vancouver, BC (1978–1983)." *Labour/Le Travail* 40 (Fall 1997): 235–51.

Ormsby, Margaret. "T. Dufferin Pattullo and the Little New Deal." *Canadian Historical Review,* 43:4 (December 1962): 277–97.

Palmer, Bryan D. "What's Law Got to Do With It? Historical Considerations on Class Struggle, Boundaries of Constraint, and Capitalist Authority." *Osgoode Hall Law Journal* 41, 2/3 (Summer-Fall 2003): 465–89.

Palmer, Earl E. "The Short, Unhappy Life of the 'Aristocratic' Doctrine." *University of Toronto Law Journal* 13, 2 (1960): 166–89.

Panitch, Leo, and Donald Swartz. "Towards Permanent Exceptionalism: Coercion and Consent in Canadian Industrial Relations." *Labour/Le Travail* 13 (Spring 1984): 133–57.

Parnaby, Andrew. "What's Law Got to Do With It? The IWA and the Politics of State Power in British Columbia, 1935–1939." *Labour/Le Travail* 44 (Fall 1999): 9–46.

Pasternak, Shiri. "How Capitalism Will Save Colonialism: The Privatization of Reserve Lands in Canada." *Antipode* 47, 1 (April 2014): 1–18.

Pasternak, Shiri, and Dayna Nadine Scott. "Introduction: Getting Back the Land." *South Atlantic Quarterly* 119, 2 (April 2020): 205–13.

Point, Steven. "Understanding Native Activism." *BC Studies* 89 (Spring 1991): 124–29.

Portier, Dimitri. "The Meares Island Case: Nuu-chah-nulth vs. the Logging Industry." *European Review of Native American Studies* 14, 1 (2000): 31–37.

Pothier, Dianne. "Twenty Year of Labour Law and the Charter." *Osgoode Hall Law Journal* 40, 3/4 (2002): 369–99.

Pue, W. Wesley. "Banned from Lawyering: William John Gordon Martin, Communist." *BC Studies* 162 (Summer 2009): 111–36.

Purcell, Mark. "Excavating Lefebvre: The Right to the City and Its Urban Politics of the Inhabitant." *GeoJournal* 58 (2002): 99–108.

Piven, Frances Fox. "The Social Structuring of Political Protest." *Politics and Society* 6, 3 (September 1976): 297–326.

Rainnie, Al, Andrew Herod, and Susan McGrath-Champ. "Spatialising Industrial Relations." *Industrial Relations Journal* 38, 2 (2007): 102–11.

Reid, John Phillip. "Law and History." *Loyola of Los Angeles Law Review* 27 (November 1993): 193–223.

Robin, Martin. "British Columbia: The Company Province." In *Canadian Provincial Politics: The Party Systems in the Ten Provinces, Second Edition*, edited by Martin Robin, 28–60. Scarborough, ON: Prentice-Hall, 1978.

Rodgers, Christopher P. "Agenda 2000, Land Use, and the Environment: Towards a Theory of 'Environmental' Property Rights?" In *Law and Geography*, edited by Jane Holder and Carolyn Harrison, 239–58. New York: Oxford University Press, 2003.

Roth, Christopher F. "Without Treaty, Without Conquest: Indigenous Sovereignty in Post-Delgamuukw British Columbia." *Wicazo Sa Review* 17, 2 (Fall 2002): 143–65.

Russell, Peter H. "The Jurisdiction of the Supreme Court of Canada: Present Policies and a Programme for Reform." *Osgoode Hall Law Journal* 6, 1 (1968): 1–38.

Salazar, Debra J., and Donald K. Alper. "Politics, Policy, and the War in the Woods." In *Sustaining the Forests of the Pacific Coast: Forging Truces in the War in the Woods*, edited by Debra J. Salazar and Donald K. Alper, 3–21. Vancouver: UBC Press, 2001.

–. "Reconciling Environmentalism and the Left: Perspectives on Democracy and Social Justice in British Columbia's Environmental Movement." *Canadian Journal of Political Science* 35 (September 2002): 527–66.

Sangster, Joan. "'We No Longer Respect the Law': The Tilco Strike, Labour Injunctions, and the State." *Labour/Le Travail* 53 (Spring 2004): 47–87.

Schade, Daniel. "A Militia History of the Occupation of the Vancouver Island Coalfields, August 1913." *BC Studies* 182 (Summer 2014): 11–44.

Schrader, Stuart and David Wachsmuth., "Reflections on Occupy Wall Street, the State and Space." *City* 16, 1–2 (February–April 2012): 243–48.

Scudamore, Maj. T.V. "Aid to the Civil Power." *Canadian Defence Quarterly* 9, 2 (January 1932): 253–60.

Sethna, Christabelle, and Steve Hewitt. "Clandestine Operations: The Vancouver Women's Caucus, the Abortion Caravan, and the RCMP." *Canadian Historical Review* 90, 3 (September 2009): 463–96.

Sherbanuk, Douglas J. "Actions by and against Trade Unions in Contract and Tort." *University of Toronto Law Journal*, 12:2 (1958): 151–205.

Shrubsole, Nicholas D. "The Sun Dance and the Gustafsen Lake Standoff: Healing Through Resistance and the Danger of Dismissing Religion." *International Indigenous Policy Journal* 2, 4 (October 2011): 1–17.

Simpson, Michael, and Philippe Le Billon. "Reconçiling Violence: Policing the Politics of Recognition." *Geoforum* 119 (February 2021): 111–21.

Singer, Joseph William. "The Reliance Interest in Property." *Stanford Law Review* 40, 3 (February 1988): 611–751.

–. "The Reliance Interest in Property Revisited." *Harvard Journal of the Legal Left* 7 (2011): 79–82.

Slinn, Sara. "Structuring Reality So That the Law Will Follow: British Columbia Teachers' Quest for Collective Bargaining Rights," *Labour/Le Travail* 68 (Fall 2011): 35–77.

Smith, Charles W. "The Politics of the Ontario Labour Relations Act: Business, Labour, and Government in the Consolidation of Post-War Industrial Relations, 1949–1961." *Labour/Le Travail* 62 (Fall 2008): 109–51.

Southin, Mary F. "The Courts and Labour Injunctions." *The Advocate* 28 (1970): 74–84.

Stefanick, Lorna. "Baby Stumpy and the War in the Woods: Competing Frames of British Columbia Forests." *BC Studies* 130 (2001): 41–68.

Stone, Christopher. "Should Trees Have Standing? Toward Legal Rights for Natural Objects." *Southern California Law Review* 45 (1972): 450–501.

Stone, Katherine. "The Post-War Paradigm in American Labor Law." *Yale Law Journal,* 90 (June 1981): 1509–80.

Thompson, E.P. "The Moral Economy of the English Crowd in the Eighteenth Century." *Past and Present* 50 (February 1971): 76–136.

–. "Time, Work-Discipline, and Industrial Capitalism." *Past and Present* 38 (December 1967): 56–97.

Thompson, Mark. "Restraint and Labour Relations: The Case of British Columbia." *Canadian Public Policy* 11, 2 (June 1985): 171–79.

Tribe, Christopher. "Ways Not to Think About Plastic Trees: New Foundations in Environmental Law." *Yale Law Journal* 83, 7 (1974): 1315–45.

Tucker, Eric. "The Constitutional Right to Bargain Collectively: The Ironies of Labour History in the Supreme Court of Canada." *Labour/Le Travail* 61 (Spring 2008): 151–80.

–. "'That Indefinite Zone of Toleration': Criminal Conspiracy and Trade Unions in Ontario, 1837–77." *Labour/Le Travail* 27 (Spring 1991): 15–54.

Tucker, Eric, and Judy Fudge, "Forging Responsible Unions: Metal Workers and the Rise of the Labour Injunction in Canada." *Labour/Le Travail* 37 (Spring 1996): 81–120.

Tucker, Kenneth H., Jr. "Ideology and Social Movements: The Contributions of Habermas." *Sociology Inquiry* 59, 1 (January 1989): 30–47.

Valverde, Mariana. "Jurisdiction and Scale: Legal 'Technicalities' as Resources for Theory." *Social and Legal Studies* 18 (2009): 139–57.

–. "Spectres of Foucault in Law and Society Scholarship." *Annual Review of Law and Social Science* 6 (2010): 45–59.

Vincent, Andrew. "Marx and Law." *Journal of Law and Society* 20, 4 (Winter 1993): 371–97.

Walter, Pierre. "Adult Learning in New Social Movements: Environmental Protest and the Struggle for the Clayoquot Sound Rainforest." *Adult Education Quarterly* 57, 3 (May 2007): 248–63.

Webber, Jeremy. "Compelling Compromise: Canada Chooses Conciliation over Arbitration, 1900–1907." *Labour/Le Travail* 28 (Autumn 1991): 15–57.
–. "The Malaise of Compulsory Conciliation: Strike Prevention in Canada during World War II." *Labour / Le Travail*, 15 (1985): 57–88.
Whatmore, Sarah. "De/Re-Territorializing Possession: The Shifting Spaces of Property Rights." In *Law and Geography*, edited by Jane Holder and Carolyn Harrison, 211–23. New York: Oxford University Press, 2003.
Wilcox, T.R. "Labour Relations-Picketing-Illegal Strike-Injunction." *Canadian Bar Review*, 29 (1951): 531–36.
Williams, C. Brian. "Notes on the Evolution of Compulsory Conciliation in Canada." *Relations Industrielles*, 19 (1964): 292–23.
Wilson, Jeremy. "Forest Conservation in British Columbia, 1935–85: Reflections on a Barren Political Debate." *BC Studies* 76 (Winter 1987–88): 3–32.
Woods, H.D. "Canadian Collective Bargaining and Dispute Settlement Policy: An Appraisal." *Canadian Journal of Economics and Political Science*, 21, no. 4 (November 1955): 447–65.
–. "Difficulties and Opportunities in Canadian Mediation." *Labor Law Journal*, 13, no. 10 (October 1962): 815–24.
Yarmie, Andrew. "The State and Employers' Associations in British Columbia: 1900–1932." *Labour/Le Travail*, 45 (Spring 2000): 53–101.
Zelko, Frank. "Making Greenpeace: The Development of Direct Action Environmentalism in British Columbia." *BC Studies* 142/143 (Summer/Autumn 2004): 197–239.

Theses and Dissertations

Atherton, J.J. "The Department of Labour and Industrial Relations, 1900–1911." Master's thesis, Carleton University, 1972.
Barker, Adam J. "(Re-)Ordering the New World: Settler Colonialism, Space, and Identity." PhD diss., University of Leicester, 2012.
Black, Erin. "Private Dwelling in Public Space: Edmonton's Tent City." PhD diss., University of Alberta, 2010.
Burrill, William J. "Class Conflict and Colonialism: The Coal Miners of Vancouver Island During the Hudson's Bay Company Era, 1848–1862." MA thesis, University of Victoria, 1987.
Claxton, Nicholas XEMŦOLTW. "The Douglas Treaty and WSÁNEC Traditional Fisheries: A Model for Saanich Peoples Governance." MA Community Governance Project Report, University of Victoria, 2003.
–. "To Fish as Formerly: A Resurgent Journey back to the Saanich Reef Net." PhD diss., University of Victoria, 2015.
Davie, James. "A Bridge to Nowhere: British Columbia's Capitalist Nature and the Carmanah Walbran War in the Woods (1988–1994)." MA thesis, University of Victoria, 2019.
Dean, Michael. "'What They Are Doing to the Land, They Are Doing to Us': Environmental Politics on Haida Gwaii." MA thesis, University of British Columbia, 2009.
Disbrow, Jamie. "Exclusion by Due Process – Martin v. Law Society of British Columbia: A Cold War Eclipse of Civil Liberties." Master's thesis, University of Ottawa, 1996.

Fabris, Michael P.C. "Beyond the New Dawes Act: A Critique of the First Nations Property." Master's thesis, University of British Columbia, 2016.

Fisher, Edward George. "The Effects of Changes in Labour Legislation on Strike Activity in British Columbia, 1945–1975." PhD diss., University of British Columbia, 1979.

Frecker, John Peter. "Militant and Radical Unionism in the British Columbia Fishing Industry." MA thesis, University of British Columbia, 1972.

Garcia, Louis-Alfredo. "Tsilhqot'in Nation v British Columbia: Aboriginal Title, Indigenous Resurgence, and the Politics of Recognition." MA thesis, Carleton University, 2015.

Gray, Stephen. "Woodworkers and Legitimacy: The IWA in Canada, 1937–1957." PhD diss., Simon Fraser University, 1989.

Harter, John Henry. "'When Blue is Green': Towards a History of Workers as Environmentalists in British Columbia and Beyond," PhD diss., Simon Fraser University, 2019.

Hoehn, Felix. "The Emerging Equality Paradigm in Aboriginal Law." LLM thesis, University of Saskatchewan, 2011.

John, Henry. "A War in the Woods? Environmentalisms, Old Growth Forests, and the Labour Movement on Southern Vancouver Island, 1970–1995." PhD diss., University of British Columbia, 2023.

Johnstone, Rachael Elizabeth Grace. "The Politics of Abortion in Canada After Morgentaler: Women's Rights as Citizenship Rights." PhD diss., Queen's University, 2012.

Knighton, Janice Rose. "The Oral History of the 1852 North Douglas Treaty: A Treaty for Peace." MA Community Governance Project Report, University of Victoria, 2004.

Knox, Paul Graham. "The Passage of Bill 39: Reform and Repression in British Columbia's Labour Policy." MA thesis, University of British Columbia, 1974.

Koenig, John Franklin. "Spaces of Denial and the Denial of Place: The Architectural Geography of Homelessness in Victoria, BC." MA thesis, University of Victoria, 2007.

Mahony, Ben David. "'Disinformation and Smear': The Use of State Propaganda and Military Force to Suppress Aboriginal Title at the 1995 Gustafsen Lake Standoff." MA thesis, University of Lethbridge, 2001.

Mann, Michaela Killoran. "'Clearcut' Conflict: Clayoquot Sound Campaign and the Moral Imagination." MA thesis, Université Saint Paul University, 2013.

Martin, Eryk. "When Red Meets Green: Perceptions of Environmental Change in the BC Communist Left, 1937–1978." MA thesis, University of Victoria, 2008.

Martin, W. Steward. "A Study of Legislation Designed to Foster Industrial Peace in the Common Law Jurisdictions of Canada." PhD diss., University of Toronto, 1954.

Milley, Katherine L.E. "The Colonizer and the Colonizer Who Refuses: Cultural Production and Colonial Crisis at Oka, Ipperwash, Burnt Church and Caledonia." PhD diss., University of Toronto, 2019.

Molinaro, Dennis. "State Repression and Political Deportation in Canada, 1919–1936." PhD diss., University of Toronto, 2015.

Morales, Sarah. "Snuw'uyulh: Fostering an Understanding of the Hul'qumi'num Legal Tradition." PhD diss., University of Victoria, 2014.

Orr, Allan D. "The Western Federation of Miners and the Royal Commission on Industrial Disputes with Special Reference to the Vancouver Island Coal Miners' Strike." MA thesis, University of British Columbia, 1968.

Safton, Bryce. "Growing Louder: The Environmental Movement in Clayoquot Sound, 1980–93." B.A. Honours thesis, University of Victoria, 2017.
Shields, John Mackie. "British Columbia's New Reality: The Politics of Neo-Conservatism and Defensive Defiance." PhD diss., University of British Columbia, 1989.
Shrubsole, Nicholas. "Religion, Land and Democracy in Canadian Indigenous-State Relations." PhD diss., University of Waterloo, 2013.
Silverman, Peter Guy. "A History of the Militia and Defences of British Columbia, 1871–1914." MA thesis, University of British Columbia, 1956.
Taft, George R. "Socialism in North America: The Case of British Columbia and Washington State, 1900–1960." PhD diss., Simon Fraser University, 1983.
Underhill, Harold Fabian. "Labor Legislation in British Columbia." PhD diss., University of California at Berkeley, 1936.
Wargo, Alan John. "The Great Coal Strike: The Vancouver Island Coal Miners' Strike, 1912–1914." BA essay, University of British Columbia, 1962.
Wasserlein, Frances. "'An Arrow Aimed at the Heart': The Vancouver Women's Caucus and the Abortion Campaign 1969–1971." MA thesis, Simon Fraser University, 1990.
Webber, Jeremy H.A. "Standards of Industrial Justice: Ideology and the Reports of Conciliation Boards Under the Industrial Disputes Investigation Act 1907–1925." LLM thesis, York University, 1988.
Zion, Mark. "What Is a Right to Shelter in the Desert of Post-Democracy? Tracking Homeless Narratives from the Courtroom to Dissensus." LLM thesis, University of Victoria, 2015.

INDEX

Note: "(f)" after a page number indicates a figure.

Printed and bound in Canada by Friesens
Set in Caslon and Fournier by Julie Cochrane

Copyeditor: Frank Chow
Cover designer: George Kirkpatrick
Cover images: *Top:* UFAWU march at BC Legislature,
February 15, 1968; courtesy Fisherman Publishing Society Collection-UBC.
Bottom: Rueben George, Amy George, Grand Chief Stewart Phillip,
and Chief Na'Moks lead a march opposing the Trans Mountain Pipeline
Expansion Project, Burnaby, November 27, 2014; photo by Mychaylo Prystupa.

Authorized Representative: Easy Access System Europe –
Mustamäe tee 50, 10621 Tallinn, Estonia,
gpsr.requests@easproject.com